The MARQUETRY MANUAL

The MARQUETRY MANUAL

William A. Lincoln

Fully Illustrated

LINDEN PUBLISHING INC.
FRESNO, CALIFORNIA

Dedicated to the first marquetarian
whose picture is accepted for exhibition
at the Royal Academy of Art

THE MARQUETRY MANUAL

ISBN: 0-941936-19-8

35798642
First United States Publication September 1990

Manufactured in the United States of America

Originally published by Stobart & Sons London England

Library of Congress Cataloging-in-Publication Data
Lincoln, W. A. (William Alexander)
The marquetry manual / William A. Lincoln.
p. cm.
ISBN 0-941936-19-8 : $19.95
1. Marquetry. I. Title.
TT192.L56 1990 *90-40525*
745.51 -- dc20 *CIP*

LINDEN PUBLISHING
3845 N. Blackstone Fresno, CA 93726 USA

By the same author:

THE ART & PRACTICE OF MARQUETRY

THE COMPLETE MANUAL OF WOOD VENEERING

WORLD WOODS IN COLOUR

Front Cover: *Tawny at the Wheel*
by Peter J. White.
Marquetry Society Rosebowl winner

Contents

Preface

COME WITH me and let me be your guide into the fascinating world of marquetry. If my enthusiasm proves to be infectious, the joys and delights of marquetry will remain with you for the rest of your life.

There is an enthralling profusion of rare and exotic wood veneers from around the world and in the following pages I'll show you how to exploit their beautiful figures, swirling grains, peculiar markings and textures to create colourful pictures and projects.

My own introduction began when I discovered marquetry by accident, only to learn that marquetry was as ancient as the pyramids.

The origins of marquetry are lost in antiquity, but we know from hieroglyphics in the tombs of the Pharoahs, that the Egyptians used bronze adzes and axes to produce their veneers and also imported more exotic species to create inlay work in mosaic art forms to decorate their multi-layered wooden caskets.

Veneer decoration was highly prized during the Graeco–Roman period. The 14th century saw the emergence of the 'cloistered intarsiatori' from the order of Olivetans at Monte Oliveto, who were sent out from Siena to decorate the cathedrals in northern Italy.

Today, marquetry is enjoyed by thousands of people all over the world and pictures are being created of incredibly high standards.

The Marquetry Society, founded in 1952, now has 30 groups in the U.K. and abroad. The Marquetry Society of America was formed in 1972.

This book launches the search for artists to take up the challenge to work in this wonderful medium. I hope it will encourage a new generation of artists to produce works of art of the highest aesthetic value, to be acclaimed and accepted for hanging by the Royal Academy.

Whatever talent you bring to marquetry, it will reward you by giving in return, a lifetime of pleasure.

Acknowledgements

THE CHALLENGING task of compiling this marquetry manual has been accomplished due to the generous response and unstinting help offered to me by many leading marquetarians.

This involved a considerable volume of correspondence around the world and I must therefore begin by apologising to the marquetarians and many friends I cannot mention by name due to lack of space. I wish to thank every one of them whose picture appears in this book, for their kind permission to reproduce their copyright material.

My special thanks are due to Mr and Mrs L. Reed of the Art Veneers Co. Ltd. of Mildenhall, for kind permission to reproduce AVCO copyright designs. Also for providing me with facilities at the factory and at their home, for special photography and for taking the photographs.

To Mr Ben Bedford, Chairman of the Marquetry Society, for arranging permission to reproduce the Society's copyright material to illustrate the book, first published in *'The Marquetarian'*.

To Mrs Pat Austin, Hon. General Secretary of the Marquetry Society for supplying me with the transparencies and making special arrangements for photography at the National Exhibition at Chelmsford. Also for supplying detailed information on the prizewinners.

To Ken Southall the Hon. Distribution and computer liaison officer who kindly supplied me with valuable back numbers of *The Marquetarian* to replace those lost in my travels to Spain.

To Peter J. White, whose Rosebowl winning picture 'Tawny at the Wheel' adorns the front cover, my very sincere thanks for the considerable help given to me which included providing me with a portfolio of all his work; taking more than sixty photographs of pictures made by members of the Bexley group of the Society, and illustrations of various 'hands at work' shots, including the car jack press and sand shading techniques.

To Mr and Mrs B. H. Shellard, for their kind permission to reproduce the marvellous work of the late Richard Shellard, who won the Rosebowl three times. They arranged for his cousin Ross Lee Shellard to take special photographs for the book.

To Charles Good — a former 'Marquetarian of the Decade' winner for supplying a portfolio of his works and details of the Harrow mural.

Fraternal greetings are also extended to members of the Marquetry Society of America, and in particular to the President Gene Weinberger, for his generosity in supplying back numbers of the *Newsletter*, illustrations of prizewinning pictures, details of his own 'sticking' technique and use of templates; research information and contacts which proved of great value.

Special mention and thanks are due to the following friends in America for their invaluable contributions.

To George L. Monks the wildlife artist of San Diego, California for his detailed photographs and information on bleaching technique.

To Silas Kopf, Northampton, Ma, for prints of his highly original approach to 'illusion' marquetry furniture.

To Dr Donald E. Winchell of Lancaster, Ohio, for a series of photographs of his fretsawing rig-up and most detailed constructional details.

To G. Clifton, of Oregon for fretsaw photographs and know-how on how to build a foldaway fretsaw rig-up.

To Willard Bondhus of Minnesota, USA, for his help on fretsaw technique.

To Bill Rondholz of New York, for permission to reproduce his ingenious 'Op-Art' technique. To Gary Wright, professional marquetarian, permission to reproduce his work.

A really special vote of thanks are extended to John Sedgwick of Ontario Canada, for his magnificent contribution which not only included prints of prizewinning pictures, but detailed information of fretsawing and inlaying techniques.

To Professor Pierre Ramond of *l'Ecole Boulle des arts appliques* of Paris — the leading school of marquetry in the world — for transparencies of students' work.

To Emanuela Marassi of Trieste, Italy, for prints of her inspirational marquetry sculpture and from her book *'Il Bosco di Arianna'*.

Also to Poul Middelboe of Sweden, a professional marquetarian for his very useful advice and help.

To Brian J. Davies of Stobart & Son Ltd., for his inestimable help in editing the manuscript.

Finally, and most important of all, to my wife Kathy for her patience and forebearance during the eighteen months the book was in preparation.

The MARQUETRY MANUAL

1
The Grain & Figure of Veneer

THE MOST massive *living* thing on earth is the Californian giant sequoia tree (*Sequoia gigantea*) named General Sherman, which stands 280 feet (85 metres) tall, and has a girth at its widest point of 79.8 feet (24.32 metres),and weighs over 1998 tons (2030 tonnes). However, its timber is of little commercial value.

From the ninety thousand different species of wood known to man, only about 580 species are being utilised – many in their country of origin – and of these, fewer than a hundred are commercially available at any one time wherever you live.

A veneer is a thin slice of wood, its thickness determined by its end use, either constructional (for corestock or plywood) or for decorative purposes.

Our palette of available colours for marquetry is derived from decorative veneers produced to display aesthetic surface appeal, and are cut from both softwoods and hardwoods. It is the combined effect of colour, texture, grain, figure, markings, lustre and working potential for matching, laying and finishing, which affects their value to the marquetarian.

Softwoods and Hardwoods

These are terms universally applied to the two main classes of commercial timber and may be misleading to the layman. Balsa (*Ochroma pyramidale*), one of the softest and lightest woods known, is actually a hardwood; American pitch pine (*Pinus palustris*) is much harder than many hardwoods, but is a softwood.

They are distinguished by a botanical distinction. The 'softwoods' are the *gymnospermae* cone bearing types with evergreen needles or scale-like leaves which we know as conifers, such as pine, spruce, fir, larch, hemlock, cedar and yew. They grow in the cool, temperate zones and mountain regions and supply the bulk of the world's commercial timbers.

The 'hardwoods' group are the *angiospermae* which produce the broad leaved trees with fruits and flowers, which are deciduous (they shed their leaves in the autumn) in the temperate zones and which provide the bulk of decorative woods. For a more detailed botanical description of the way a tree grows and its cell structure etc., and how they are cut into veneers, please refer to *The Complete Manual of Wood Veneering* and *World Woods in Colour* both published by Stobart & Son Ltd.

The marquetarian is primarily concerned with the types of veneer available to him.

Types of Veneer

The surface pattern of the veneer results from two main factors: (a) natural features; the scarcity or frequency of growth rings; the colourtone variations between earlywood and latewood; peculiarities and combinations of grain types; pigments and markings; contortions around knots, butts and burrs; and the tree's reaction to the effects of tension and compression during its life. And (b) the way the log is cut into veneers; (the angle of the knife-cut to the longitudinal axis of the log).

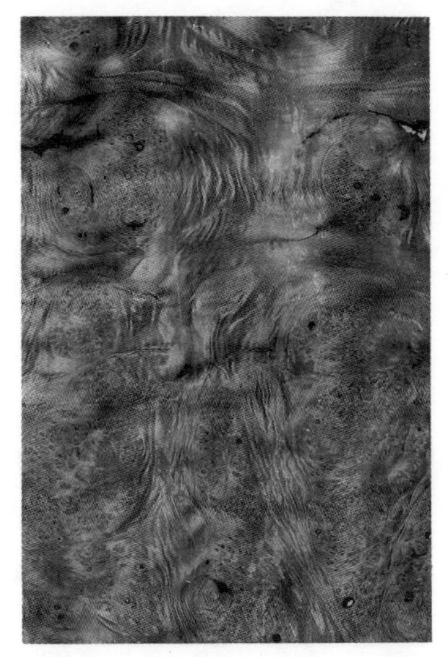

Fig. 1 Maple burry-butt

Fig. 2 American walnut butt

Fig. 3 Thuya burr

Butts or stumpwood

The butt or stump of the tree is the section immediately above ground and nearest to the root base and can yield highly figured fancy butt veneers.

Burry-butts

As burrs (burls) form near the buttress of the tree, some attractive figure is obtained from burry-butts. They possess the advantages of both the swirling butt figure and patches of burr figure. These are less brittle and easier to handle.

Burrs or burls

These are the rounded wart-like growths found on a tree and appear as end-grain, tightly clustered dormant buds, each with a darker pith, which, through stunted growth caused by injury, failed to develop into twigs or branches. Figured burr veneers appear as clusters of tiny knot formations like masses of small eyes, surrounded by swirling contorted lines and pigmented veins and are the most highly valued of all veneers, and the most expensive.

Fig. 4 Walnut burr

Fig. 5 Oak burr

Fig. 6 Elm burr

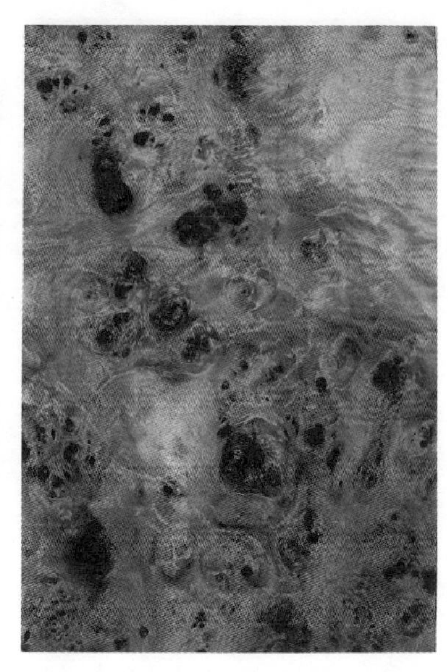

Fig. 7 Poplar burr

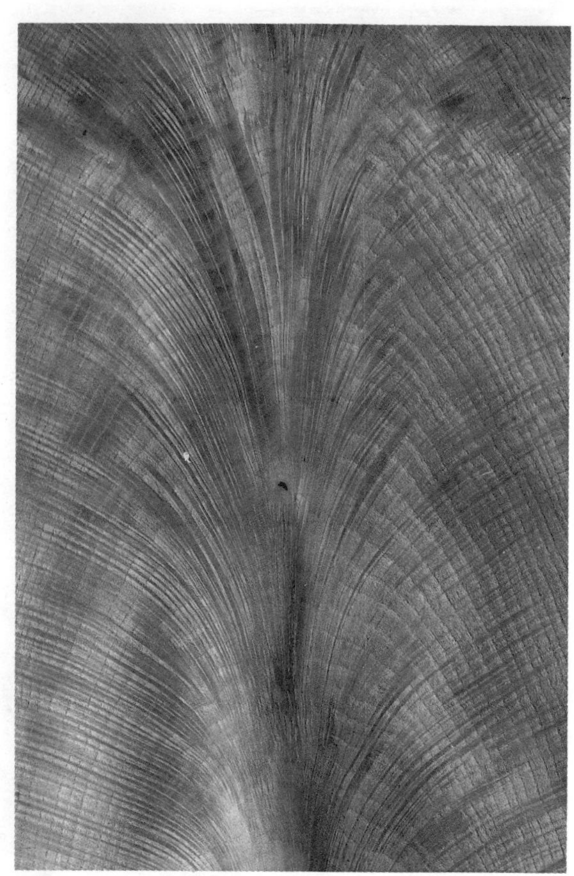

Fig. 8 Ash curl

Curls or crotches

The intersection of a limb or branch with the trunk of the tree produces a veneer 'curl' figure, also known as crotch, crutch, fan or fork.

The wood fibres in the trunk begin to suffer from reaction of either compression or tension caused by the weight of the branch. When cut into veneer, it produces a distinctive 'curl' figure, elliptical in outline with a strong central 'feather-like' plume.

By its nature, the curl veneer tends to buckle in the centre afer drying as it tries to return to its natural shape. In cabinetwork, the curl is usually inverted from the position it occupied in the growing tree.

Texture

The variation in size of the earlywood and latewood cells produces the texture of veneer. Woods known as 'even-textured' are diffuse-porous, with narrow vessels and fine rays, such as sycamore; ring-porous woods with wide vessels and broad rays are 'coarse textured', such as oak. Mahogany is medium textured.

Lustre

The ability of the cells to reflect light is closely associated with texture. Smooth textured woods are likely to be more lustrous than coarse textured woods. However, the potential for a veneer to take a high polish does not equate to its lustre potential.

Odour

The majority of woods lose their characteristic natural odour in processing, but in a few cases the odour may be put to good use, such as camphor and cedar for clothes closet interiors; cigar box cedar for humidifiers. Resinous pines and spicey aromas can be pleasant, but others may be fetid and unpleasant.

False heart

This is a feature caused by natural mineral stains. For example, the black heart in ash or the brown heart in beech. It is not a defect and the veneer is sound and decorative.

Grain

The term 'grain' is often misapplied. 'cross grained' or 'coarse grained' actually refer to the texture of the wood surface. 'silver grain' seen on quartered oak refers to the prominent ray figure; various cuts through a log are often referred to as 'end grain', 'side grain' or 'flat grain', when referring to transverse, (crosscut); tangential (surface cut, parallel with growth rings) and radial (surface cut at right angles to the growth rings).

The grain is the arrangement of wood fibres in relation to the main axis of the tree and there are eight types.

(1) *Straight grain:* The fibres run parallel to the vertical axis of the tree.
(2) *Irregular grain.* The fibres contort around knots, butts and curls.
(3) *Cross grain* The fibres are not parallel to the main axis of the tree.
(4) *Wavy grain:* The fibres form short, undulating waves in regular sequence.
(5) *Curly grain:* The fibres form short undulating waves in irregular sequence.
(6) *Spiral grain:* The fibres form a spiral around the circumference of the tree. giving the tree a twisted appearance. A veneer would have diagonal grain.
(7) *Diagonal grain:* The result of a true flat veneer of spiral grain or a milling defect in straight grained timber may have the same appearance.
(8) *Interlocked grain:* Where the fibre angles have changed from a right- handed

Fig. 9 Olive ash

Fig. 10 Zebrano

Fig. 11 Bird's eye maple

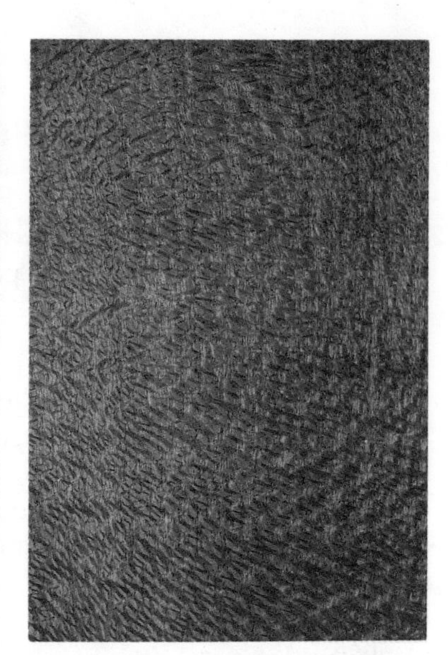

Fig. 12 Australian silky oak

spiral to a left-handed spiral and back again at intervals of a few years.

Figure

Wavy and curly grains provide us with 'fiddleback' figure as in magogany and sycamore, or the 'beeswing' figure of satinwood. Both of these are further enhanced by the effects of light refraction at different viewing angles.

Where wavy and spiral growth combine, a 'block-mottled' figure is obtained as in eucalyptus; a 'roe figure' is produced from a combination of interlocked grain and wavy grain, as found in afrormosia.

Reverse spiral growth produces interlocked grain. It yields an appearance of light and dark striped veneers which alternate when inverted or viewed from a different position – an invaluable feature for veneer matching.

A variation in the natural pigmentation of veneers produces the attractive zebra-like striped markings of zebrano when radially cut. Irregular grain gives us 'blistered' and 'quilted' figures and other combinations offer a wonderful variety of special figure effects such as 'pommelle', 'moiree', plum pudding' 'snail-quilt' etc.

Radially cut veneers, cut parallel with the rays, produce a strong ray figure on the surface such as in 'raindrop' or 'splash' figured oak; the 'lacewood' figure in planetree, and the 'lace' figure in sycamore and Australian silky oak.

Fig. 16 Masur birth

Fig. 13 Castello

Fig. 14 Avodire

Fig. 15 Cherry, flat cut

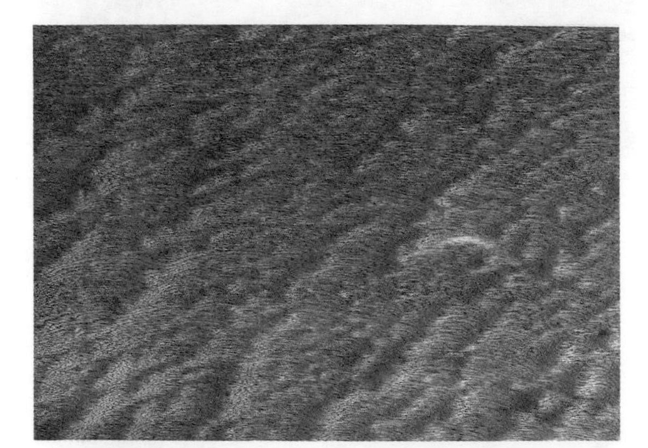

Fig. 17 Pommelle

Fig. 18 Yew

Fig. 19 Macassar ebony

2
How Veneers are Cut

A VENEER log is the straight, cylindrical section of the tree's bole, measured from just above the root-buttress up to the first limb, but where butt figure is required the cut may include part of the buttress.

At the juncture of the trunk with the roots, the wood fibres are distorted due to compression caused by the weight of the tree. They are difficult to machine, but the magnificient highly figured butts of walnut and olive ash are examples of stumpwood.

A mahogany tree might comprise four large logs, each cut into six 'flitches', and yield about 100,000 sq. feet (9,290 sq. metres) of veneer. A flitch can be a half, quarter or sixth of a log, depending on its size.

Generally a tree produces only one veneer log, which divides into two or four flitches and would yield up to about ten thousand sq. feet. A walnut log of two flitches would amount to between 3,000 and 7,000 sq. feet each (278 – 650 sq. metres)

All veneers are cut, bought and sold in flitches. After felling, the logs are usually kept under water (or immersed in special tanks) until required to prevent them from splitting and to protect them from insect attack.

All logs are de-barked and pass through electronic metal detecting machinery to discover the presence of metal fragments which may be buried deep within the tree and grown around. The log is then clamped to a moving carriage and travels on rails to meet a giant bandmill saw.

Fig. 20 A giant log being transported

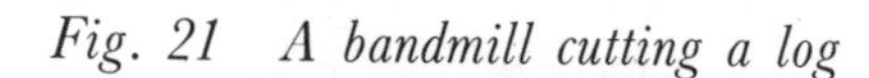

Fig. 21 A bandmill cutting a log

A tangential cut is made from one side of the log known as a 'slab' cut. Sometimes this slab cut is quite large to enable a large log to clear the upper limits of the saw carriage when turned on to the flat base. (This does not apply to logs for rotary peeling, which are dealt with in the round.)

The next cut is the 'opening cut', in which the log is cut into two 'halves' through the heart of the log. Tropical timbers have their heart near the centre of the log which will produce two almost equal halves. But a log from the temperate zones of Europe or the southern hemisphere will have its heart to one side, off-centre because more growth will have occurred on the side that grew facing the sun.

All logs are bought 'in the round'. Not until the log is opened can the log buyer sigh with relief. Whether this log was hauled from distant jungle, rain forest or someone's front garden, uncertainty existed until this vital moment. Now its secrets are laid bare and its value can be determined.

If we look at a cross-section of a tree at its cell structure, we can see evidence of all the hazards and events the tree enjoyed or endured during its life: years of plenty or drought, hunger or maltreatment, plagued by insects or disease, or damaged by fire.

However, it is these external influences which produce the 'freak' configuration so eagerly sought by marquetarians.

Every angle of cut through a tree will provide a different pattern of grain, texture, colour and markings and depends on the way the veneer was cut from the log, (i.e. the angle of the knife-cut to the longitudinal axis of the log). These are known collectively as the 'figure' and this will vary, not only between two trees of the same species, but even in the same log.

It is the physical appearance of the figure of the veneer which largely governs its value. The dimensions, accuracy of cut, evenness of gauge, dryness and other technical factors also affect the price.

Now the specialist veneer cutter can determine how to proceed to extract the best value from the log.

He examines the exposed surfaces for figure, grain, defects, evidence of insect or fungal attack, mineral stains, reaction wood, thunder shakes etc. He marks out any pithy or spongy heartwood, and determines exactly how he wants the log cut into the required number of flitches.

Saw-cut veneers

Until the mid-twentieth century, all veneers were sawcut. First on huge pitsaws by hand-held saws. Later the pitsaws were harnessed to watermills, and then to steam driven saws.

Today, sawing is only used in exceptional cases on woods too long for the slicer or lathe to take; too hard to cut by the knife, such as Gabon ebony; or of such small girth or length, as to make it impracticable or uneconomic for knife cutting.

Sawing is far too wasteful, as each saw kerf destroys the equivalent of five sheets of veneer. By knife cutting we get a yield of 400. sq. feet (37 sq. metres) of matched veneer, instead of the equivalent of only 36 sq. ft. (3 sq. metres) of timber.

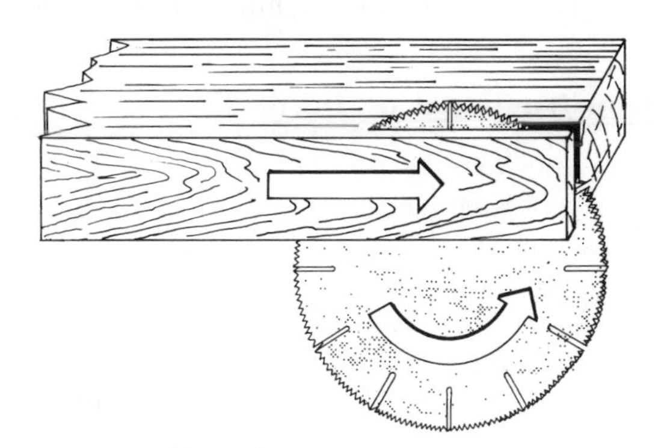

Fig. 22 Sawcutting

Some small diameter trees such as holly, box, tulipwood, ebony, laburnum, lignum vitae, are only available as short 'billets', or small sections.
Oyster veneers for English parquetry – a form of marquetry for furniture – are sawn from the limbs of trees which have a marked contrast between sapwood and heartwood.

Veneer knife cutting methods

For this method of cutting, the flitches (half, quarter, or sixth) of the log are then placed in pre-conditioning vats for steaming or hot water treatment for a controlled period varying from hours to days depending on the species, hardness of the log, size of the flitch and the thickness it is to be cut.
Certain white veneers such as sycamore, horse chestnut and maple, would immediately discolour if subjected to heat, and have to be cut 'cold'.

Even small knots, which would slice easily if softened, are as hard as flint if the log is cut without heat treatment and have to be hacked out with an axe. The resulting hole reduces the yield of veneer from the log, and there is the risk of chipping a knife and halting production. For this reason veneer mills do not like cutting veneers without pre-treatment.

In modern veneer mills the whole process is fully automated and computer controlled.

Constructional or Decorative

Any species may be cut into constructional or decorative veneer depending upon the thickness at which it is cut, the type of cut through the log, and the surface appeal of the figure displayed after cutting.

For example, walnut (*Juglans regia*) may be cut in one thickness but in nine different ways, each producing entirely different visual surface figures. Japanese birch (*Betula maximowicziana*) is sometimes cut into 'scale' thickness of 0.1mm.

Knife cutting methods

There are five methods:
(1) *Rotary cut veneers*
The complete log in the round up to 78 inches (2 metres) in diameter and up to 150 inches (3.8 metres) long, is mounted in the giant lathe and forced against a pressure-bar and rotated against the knife. A continuous sheet of veneer is 'peeled' from the log – rather like unwrapping a roll of paper, as in Fig.23.

The long sheet of veneer is the length of the log and of continuous width. By this method of cutting, the line of cut follows around the path of the growth rings, and the knife travels one veneer thickness, towards the chucks at the centre, with each revolution of the log.

The resulting surface pattern on the veneer leaf shows a large swirly grain. The rotary peeled veneer is passed to an automatic machine where it is clipped to pre-determined widths and the defects clipped out. Rotary cut veneers vary in thickness from 1/100th of an inch (.25mm) up to 3/8 inch (9.5mm) and are used

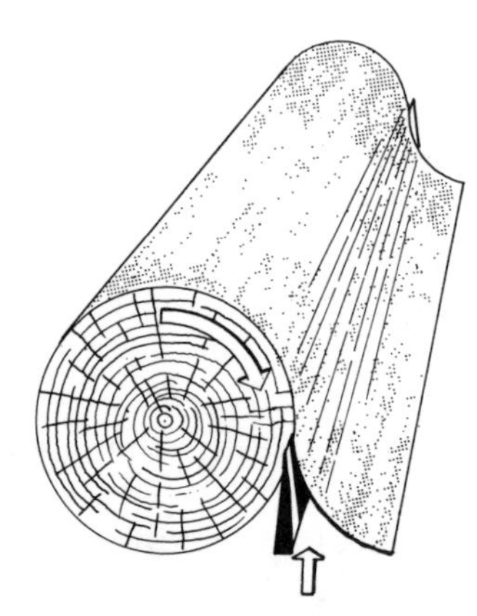

Fig. 23 Rotary cutting

for the plywood, constructional and utility industries. It is also used to produce highly figured decorative veneers suitable for marquetry, where the peculiar type of figure cannot be extracted by any of the other cutting methods. The species most usually cut into decorative veneers by this method are bird's eye maple, Canadian birch, masur birch, kevazingo, obeche, utile, tiama, gaboon, etc.

(2) *Rotary eccentric cutting*

When the log is located off-centre between the chucks of the lathe, the eccentrically mounted log meets the knife for only about a quarter of its revolution, which gradually increases as the diameter of the log reduces.

This enables extra wide veneers to be produced (wider than by flat sliced crown cutting), with a flowery looped heart pattern in the centre. The line of cut does not follow the growth rings but takes an increasingly wider sweep across them as the cutting proceeds, as shown in Fig.24.

(3) *Stay-log rotary cutting*

A slab-cut is taken off one side of the log at the band-mill, to enable the log to be mounted on a stay-log in the lathe. The resulting cut takes a more shallow sweep across the growth rings than by eccentric cutting, but wider veneers than by flat sliced crown cutting, as in Fig. 25.

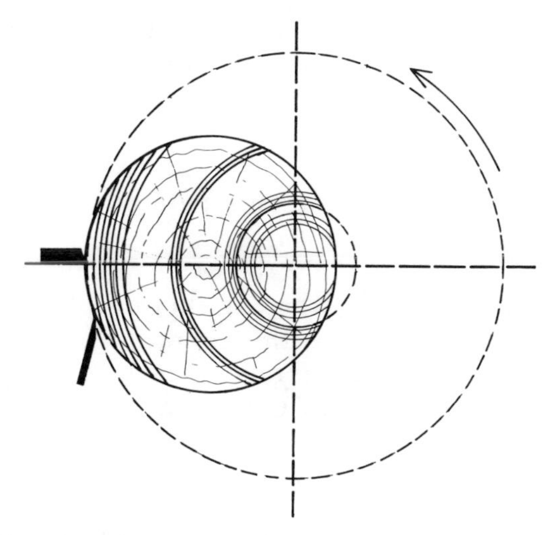

Fig. 24 Rotary eccentric cutting

(4) *Stay-log true half-rounding*

A section up to about half a log is mounted in the stay-log and cutting commences at the sapwood side of the log. This method produces wider veneers than by other flat cut methods as the line of cut takes a longer sweep across the growth rings following a curved direction. It is used in species with prominent rings. See Fig.26.

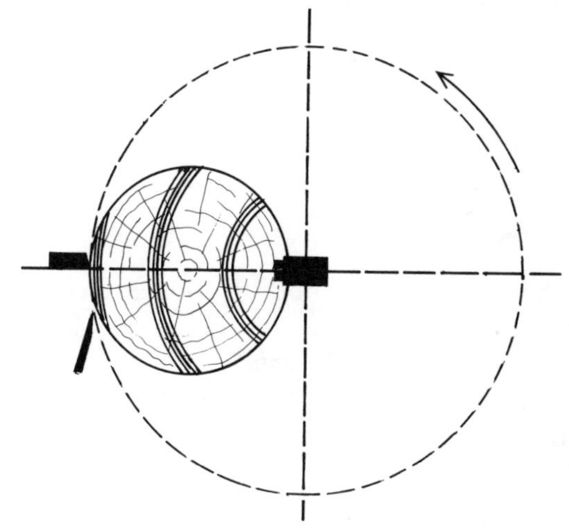

Fig. 25 Stay log rotary cutting

(5) *Stay-log, half-rounding, back cutting*

A flitch, or a section which can be up to about half a log, is mounted on the stay-log at the sappy outer edge, and cutting commences at the heart side. The line of cut takes a sweep at an an even greater angle than true cutting, and is used for cutting fancy butts and stumpwood, and logs containing a 'double-heart' feature such as curls (crotches) are usually back-cut this way, as in Fig.27.

Curl (crotch) veneers are formed at the junction of a branch with the main trunk.

All decorative veneers are kept in precisely the same sequence as they are cut from the flitch, and every flitch kept in the order it was cut from the log. This is essential

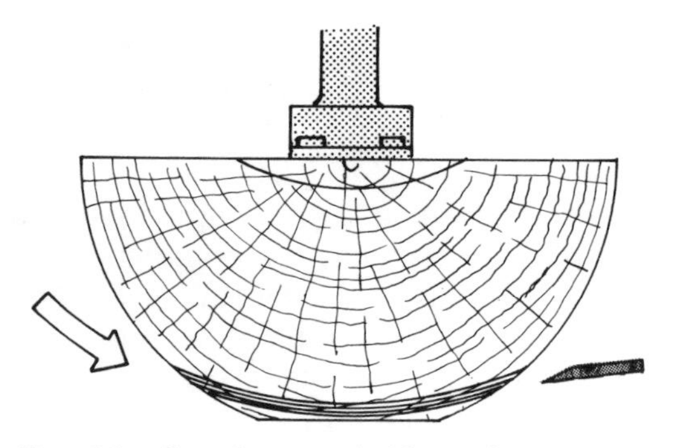

Fig. 26 Stay-log true half-rounding

for decorative veneering, where consecutive matching leaves are opened like a book to form 'mirror matching' patterns.

Sliced veneers

There are four methods of slicing decorative veneers.

(1) *True quartered, radial*

The flitch, mounted horizontally between 'dogs' on the slicer bed, is swept up and down at about 90 strokes per minute against the knife, which moves forward the thickness of the veneer as each is cut. It can cut from 1/120 to 3/32 of an inch (0.2 to 2.38mm) in thickness.

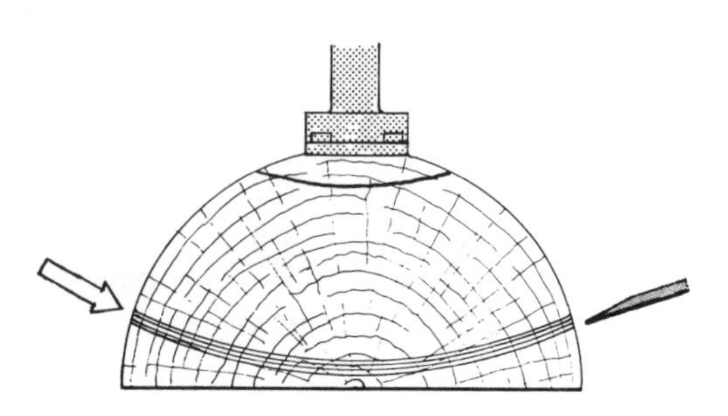

Fig. 27 Stay-log, half rounding, back cutting

Ideally the path of the cut should be parallel to the rays, but as these radiate like the spokes of a wheel, the flitch is cut to try to maximise the number of rays cut approximately at 90 degrees to the growth rings.

From this cut we obtain the beautifully striped veneers such as 'pencil striped sapele', 'splash' and 'raindrop' figured oak, Australian silky oak and the lacewood figure in planetree and 'lace' sycamore.

(2) *Flat quartered, tangential*

The cut is made parallel to the majority of the growth rings and approximately 90 degrees to the rays. This produces a veiny, heart-type figure in the leaf centre with stripey edges.

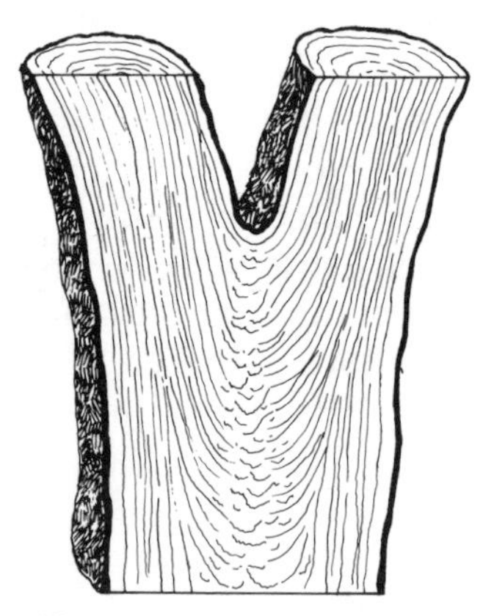

Fig. 28 How curl veneers are formed

Although the actual figure may be superior in *quality* to the full width crown cut veneers, it cannot provide the equivalent *quantity* of continuous sequential figure throughout the log for matching purposes.

It is this continuity of sequence which enables the marquetarian to make elaborate matches without a perceptible shift or pattern jump in the figure pattern.

(3) *Faux quartered, diagonal*

This is a compromise between radial and tangential cutting, where the line of cut runs at 45 degrees to both the rays and the growth rings. This extracts some heart-type figure at one side of the leaf and a rather curved stripey pattern across the leaf, which makes up very well in veneer matches.

(4) *Flat sliced crown*

A half-sawn log is laid on its flat base and fastened by clamps or vacuum, to a horizontal slicer, which although slower than the vertical slicer, can cut far wider flitches. The cutting commences at the crown to extract a very attractive figure which displays sappy edges at both sides of the leaf and a looped, arched pattern in the centre. Wide leaves of ash, elm, mahogany, rosewood, teak, and walnut are cut this way for cabinets, flush doors and architectural panels.

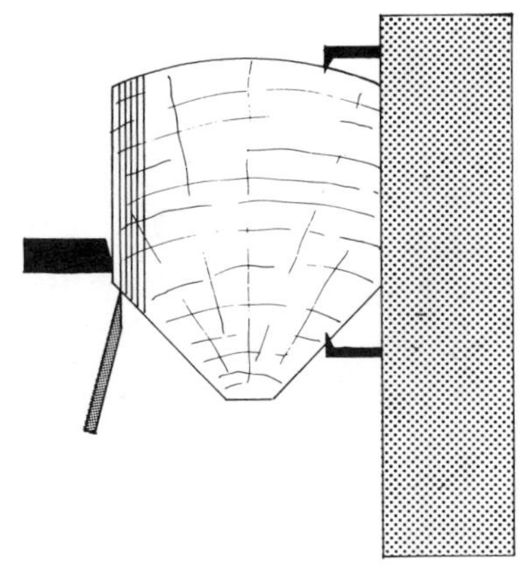

Fig. 29 True quartered, radial cut

As in flat sawn timber, the growth rings should meet the surface of the veneer at an angle of less than 45 degrees. Fig. 33 shows the parts of the tree where the various cuts are usually applied.

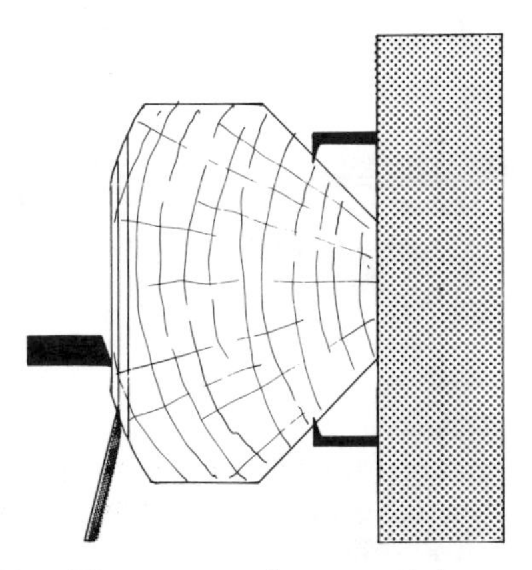

Fig. 30 Flat quartered, tangential

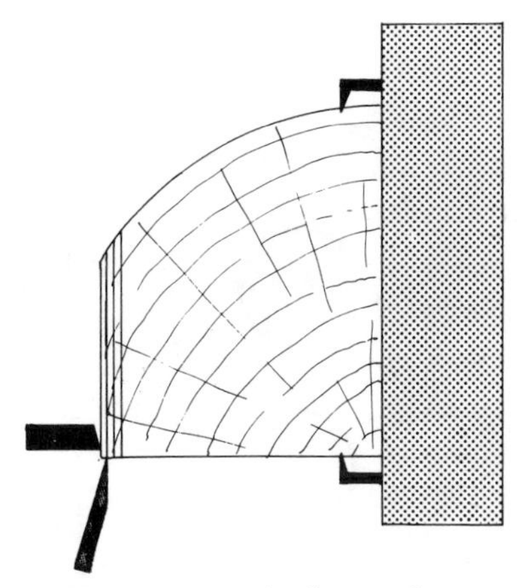

Fig. 31 Faux quartered, diagonal

Next, the 'set' of veneers passes through the mill to the mechanical drier where they are jet air dried to an exact moisture content. Water found in the wood cells is of two types: 'free-water' in the cell cavities and 'absorbed-water' in the cell walls.

The weight of water in a freshly felled 'green' log can amount to more than 100 per cent of its dry weight. When a log has been kept in a mill pond, boiled or steamed, it is completely saturated. It has to be dried

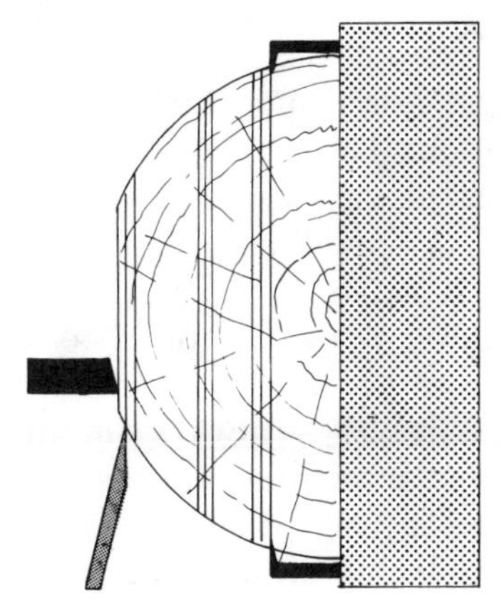

Fig. 32 Flat sliced crown

to the point where it loses all its free water from the cell cavities, but leaving the cell walls intact.

This is known as 'fibre saturation point' beyond which, as the cell walls begin to dry

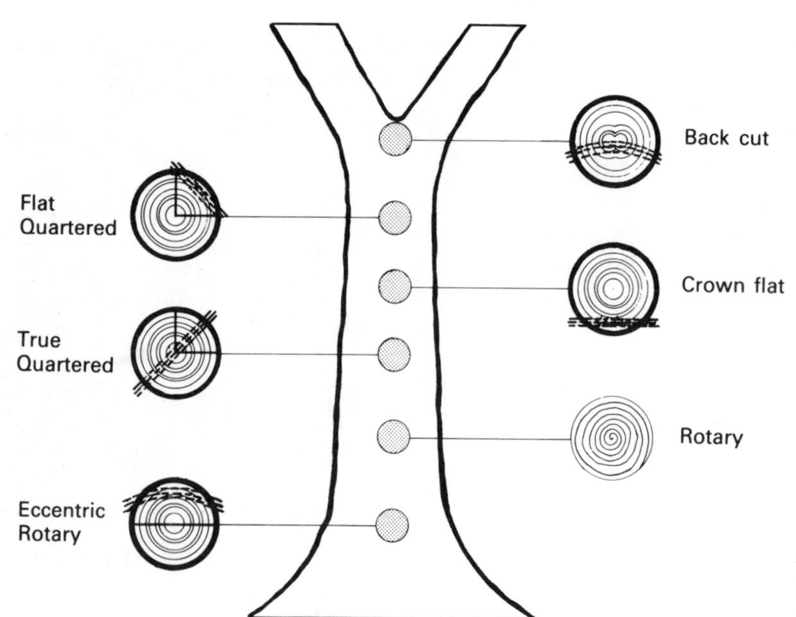

Fig. 33 Different cuts through the tree are shown by the dotted lines

out, shrinkage will take place. As wood is hygroscopic it will absorb or shed its moisture content with changes in atmospheric conditions, therefore the drying process is aimed at reducing the moisture content to bring the veneer into equilibrium with local atmospheric conditions. This is usally about 12½ per cent in the U.K. for all normal domestic purposes, and between 14 and 18 per cent for external use,and varies in different parts of the world.

The flitch is then clipped to width and 'bundled' in leaves of the same width in 24, 28 or 32 leaves – always in multiples of four – for matching purposes. After the complete log, comprising all its flitches, is re-formed in bundles, it is graded.

The grader assesses the structural soundness of the log to see that it is free from natural and milling defects. It is the physical appearance of the veneer that then governs its value: the coloration and figure, markings and texture, quantity, and in particular the length.

Dimensions

Thickness

Decorative veneers produced in Europe are cut into 0.6mm to 0.9mm thickness for 'face' quality. Average thickness 0.7mm or about 1/40th of an inch. Export quality veneers are cut 0.9mm for the U.S.A.

Backing grade veneers, vary from 0.5mm to 0.6mm (downgraded veneers) and are also used for marquetry purposes.

U.S.A. and Australia

Most domestic veneers are cut into 0.9mm which is 1/28th of an inch, and other gauges are imported.

Africa and Asia

Veneers are produced in the required thickness for the intended country of consumption. When exported to Europe 0.7mm and for America 0.9mm.

Length
The length of veneer (when the figure and quality are identical) governs its price. Architectural panel grade veneers are stocked up to 18 feet (5.5 metres) long, minimum 8ft 3in (2.5 metres.) Veneers over 6ft 9in (2.05 metres) are suitable for flushdoors, and below this length for cabinet makers. Fortunately, marquetarians can utilise veneers which are too short for cabinet makers. It does not mean that veneers of short length are of lower quality.

The most precious and highly prized veneers ever produced are much smaller in length, such as burrs (burls) and curls (crotches) and butts (stumpwood). It is also true that 'face' quality top grade veneers below 3 feet (900mm) in length, although too small for most cabinet making, may be far superior to those of architectural length.

Marquetry veneer sizes
Specialist stockists have to guillotine their stocks to standard sizes for reasons of storage, cataloguing and pricing etc.

A range of sizes for collections are available in 4 × 3 inch (100 × 75mm) sizes and 6 × 4 inch (150 × 100mm). Standard stock sizes are 12 × 4 inch (300 × 100mm), and 18 x 6 inch (450 × 150mm).

When the marquetarian requires veneers for special marquetry effects such as low horizon skies, one piece backgrounds for portraiture, etc.) he may have to buy

Fig. 34 Veneer slicing in progress

complete leaves of veneer in full length, to obtain his desired width.

When the marquetarian requires consecutive matching leaves for his border surrounds, or for applied marquetry work on table tops, etc., he will have the same requirements as the cabinet maker. Yet his pictorial marquetry needs are entirely different from those of a cabinet maker. A stained veneer discarded by a cabinet maker may be eagerly sought by the marquetarian.

My advice is, whenever possible, avoid all so called 'job-lot' special offers of offcuts for marquetry. These pieces have been discarded for good reason! Select your marquetry veneers from the stocks of a marquetry specialist and rely upon the integrity of the supplier.

3
The Names of Woods

THESE STANDARD names are the names recommended in the Nomenclature of Commercial Timbers (BS 881 and BS 589; 1974 and subsequent issues) of the British Standards Institution.

Commercial names

Trade names are based upon long established trade custom, and always include the standard name. For example, in the U.K. the name "Scots pine" is used for homegrown timber and "redwood" for the imported species.

Many trade names are invented by merchants seeking to glamorise an indifferent species with a more romantic name. These can be very misleading. For example, "black Italian poplar" is white in colour and grows in the U.K., and there are more than 80 different species called 'ironwood'.

Often, commercial names have become standard names, even though botanically unrelated. 'Queensland walnut' is from the *Lauraceae* family; "African walnut" from the *Meliaceae* family, neither of which are true walnuts from the *Juglandaceae* family.

The importance of standard names is underlined by the wide divergence of commercial names in the English speaking world. For example "Australian silky oak" (*Cardwellia sublimis*) in the U.K. is known as lacewood in America. Lacewood (*Platanus acerifolia*) of the U.K. is called sycamore in America, while sycamore (*Acer pseudoplatanus*) in the U.K. is known as maple in America.

Other names

Many timbers have foreign language names and are known only by that name in the country of origin. Sometimes the wood is named after the locality of growth or even the port of shipment.

For these reasons, specialists around the world have come to rely upon the botanical names for specific identification. It is the universal practise to use the binomial system of latinised names, where the first name is assigned to the genus and the second to a specific epithet to indicate a species of that genus.

The best way to start is to obtain a basic 'bank' of veneers which will cover your early requirements. As you gain experience and wish to extend your range, you can build upon your initial stock.

This list is intended as a guide. You are recommended to refer to *World Woods in Colour*, (Stobart & Son Ltd, London and Macmillan Publishing Company, New York), in which 276 woods are illustrated in full colour, together with their standard, trade, vernacular and other names, and botanical names, cross referenced and indexed in full.

Also, for full details of 250 veneers with usage, details of grain, texture, hardness, supply, price guide and other information, refer to *The Complete Manual of Wood Veneering*, (Stobart & Son Ltd, London and Macmillan Publishing Company, New York).

With these two books as references, you will able to choose veneers which are available from your specialist supplier. As availability will fluctuate, the books will help you select suitable alternatives and substitutes.

ONE HUNDRED POPULAR MARQUETRY VENEERS

Note 1. The asterisk * after the name of a species, (for example ASH, AMERICAN *(H) indicates that the wood may also be treated as harewood in various shades of grey. For further information please refer to Chapter 4 Artificial colour.
Note 2. Hardwoods and softwoods are identified in the text with the letters (H) or (S) after the name.

1. **ABURA** * (H) Tropical West Africa
Mitragyna ciliata
Colour description: pale orange-brown to reddish brown with darker streaks. Cuts easily. Special effects: sunset sky effects, and foreshore sea effects, roofs, shadows, portraiture, animals.

2. **AFARA (LIMBA)** (H) West Africa
Terminalia superba
Colour description: pale yellow-brown to straw with grey-black streaks in heartwood. Special effects: cornfields, thatch, floral subjects, walls, doors, costume and drapery.

3. **'AFRICAN WALNUT'** (H)
Tropical West Africa
Lovoa trichilioides
Colour description: bronze golden-brown, with black lines or streaks. Ribbon striped figure. Easy to cut. Special effects: borders, cross-bandings, mid-distance fields, wooden subjects, thatch, beaches, interiors.

4. **AFRORMOSIA** (H) West Africa
Pericopsis elata
Colour description: orange gold to light brown. Rope striped figure.
Special effects: borders, cross-bandings, mid-distance fields, thatch, beaches, boats, interiors. Watch for blue stain due to tannin.

5. **AFZELIA** (H) West and East Africa
Afzelia spp.
Colour description: straw sap, orange to red-brown heartwood. Special effects: wooden subjects, roofs, mid-distance fields,costume, still-life, portraits.

6. **AGBA** * (H) Tropical West Africa
Gossweilerodendron balsamiferum
Colour description: pinkish-straw to light golden brown. Special effects: sandy beaches, fields, wooden objects, boats, thatch. Avoid gum patches.

7. **ANINGERIA** (H)
West and East Africa
Aningeria spp.
Colour description: cream to tan with pink tinge. Special effects: when mottled used for sky and sea effects, mid-distance fields, foreshores, costume and drapery.

8. **ANTIARIS** * (H)
West, Central and East Africa
Antiaris toxicaria
Colour description: creamy yellow. Special effects: striped material for borders. Ideal for 'window-wasters'. Mineral stained material for sky effects. Shades well.

9. **APPLE** * (H)
Europe, South West Asia, U.S.A
Malus sylvestris
Colour description: pink-biscuit to light red. Special effects: portraiture, floral subjects, costume, sky effects, walls, doors. Sand shades well.

10. **ASH, AMERICAN** *(H) Canada and U.S.A
Fraxinus americana
Colour description: grey-brown, tinged with red. Special effects: sky and sea, water effects, snow scenes. Shades for floral and costume subjects.

11. **ASH, EUROPEAN** * (H) Europe, N.Africa, W.Asia
Fraxinus excelsior
Colour description: cream to pale biscuit. Special effects: sky, water and snow scenes. Sand shades for floral and costume. Also available as Olive ash with dark brown streaks and wild markings, ideal for water effects and rocks etc.

12. **ASH, JAPANESE** * (H) South East Asia
Fraxinus mandschurica
Colour description: straw biscuit to light brown. Special effects: mottled, fiddleback, swirl grains and 'peanut' figure. Sky and sea, snow scenes. Shades well.

13. **ASPEN, CANADIAN** * (H) Canada and U.S.A
Populus tremuloides
Colour description: cream-yellow, often found with pink, orange and golden streaks. Special effects: ideal for sky and sea effects, floral and costume. Sand shades well.

14. **'AUSTRALIAN SILKY OAK'** Queensland, Australia
Cardwellia sublimis
Colour description: red-brown, darkens with age. Special effects: strong silver-ray figure when quartered; mountains, rocks, foregrounds, trees.

15. **AVODIRÉ** (H) Tropical West Africa
Turraeanthus africanus
Colour description: golden yellow. Special effects: quartered veneer has strong mottle, ideal for sky effects, cornfields, costume and floral subjects. Shades well.

16. **AYAN** (H) Tropical West Africa
Distemonanthus benthamianus
Colour description: bright golden yellow to orange. Special effects: strong mottle, ideal for fields, floral, costume, still-life, and sandy beaches.

17. **BASSWOOD** (H) Eastern Canada and U.S.A
Tilia americana
Colour description: creamy-white tinged with pink-tan. Special effects: window-wasters, snow scenes, shades well for floral, costume and drapery, portraiture.

18. **BEECH** * (H) Europe. West Asia
Fagus sylvatica
Colour description: creamy pink. Often steamed to red-brown. Special effects: flecked ray figure suitable for mountains, rocks, and stonework. Note: BEECH, AMERICAN *Fagus grandifolia* and BEECH, JAPANESE *Fagus crenata* are both used for similar purposes.

19. **BERLINIA** (H) Tropical West Africa
Berlinia spp.
Colour description: pink-red to red-brown with darker purple-brown veins or streaks. Commercial name 'Rose Zebrano'. Special effects: wooden subjects in sunset scenes, fences, boats. Flat-cut material used for sky and sea.

20. **BIRCH, EUROPEAN** * (H) Europe, Scandinavia
Betula pendula and spp;
Colour description: cream-white to biscuit. Special effects: 'flame' 'curly' and 'ice' figure suitable for sky, water, snow scenes, floral, costumes. Note: MASUR BIRCH: creamy white with dark brown pith flecks and wild swirls suitable for rocks, roads, walls, shingle, foreshores.

21. **BIRCH, YELLOW** * (H)
Canada and U.S.A
Betula alleghaniensis
Colour description: salmon-pink to red-brown. Special effects: mottled and veined figure for sky and water, floral subjects,landscape. Shades well. Note: BIRCH,PAPER *Betula papyifera* and BIRCH, JAPANESE *Betula maximowicziana* are both used for similar purposes.

22. **BLACKBUTT** (H) Australia
Eucalyptus pilularis
Colour description: pale tan-brown tinged with pink. Special effects: block-mottled figure for fields, stonework, walls, rocks, mountains, foreshores.
Note: BOX, WHITE TOPPED *Eucalyptus quadrangulata* is used for similar purposes.

23. **BLACKWOOD, AUSTRALIAN** (H) Australia
Acacia melanoxylon
Colour description: red-brown with chocolate brown ring figure. Mottled or fiddle-back. Special effects: animals, birds, wooden subjects, foregrounds, portraiture, boats.

24. **BUBINGA** (H)
Cameroon,Gabon,Zaire
Guibourtia demeusei & spp;
Colour description: red-brown with light red to purple veining. When rotary cut, has a wild, swirling veined figure and called KEVASINGO. Special effects: roofs, mountains, foregrounds, boat sails, shadows.

25. **CEDAR OF LEBANON** (S)
Middle East.
Cedrus libani
Colour description: creamy-pink to biscuit. Growth rings show as veins. Special effects: crown cut for skys, wooden subjects, walls, still life. Shades well.

26. **CHERRY, AMERICAN** (H)
Canada and U.S.A
Prunus serotina
Colour description: rich red to reddish-brown. Special effects: sunset or sunrise sky and water effects, mid-distance fields, foregrounds, stonework.

27. **CHERRY EUROPEAN** (H)
Europe, Scandinavia, N.Africa
Prunus avium
Colour description: pale pink-brown, with veins and lace ray figure on quartered surfaces. Special effects: sky, water, stonework, roads, paths, mid-distance fields.
Note: CHERRY, JAPANESE *Prunus japonica* is used for similar purposes.

28. **CHESTNUT, HORSE** * (H)
Europe
Aesculus hippocastanum
Colour description: creamy-white. Special effects: one of the whitest woods. Window-waster, snow scenes, floral, skys, portraits, highlights. Sand shades well and takes harewood treatment. Borders and backgrounds.

29. **CHESTNUT, SWEET** (H)
Europe, Asia Minor
Castanea sativa
Colour description: biscuit to light tan. Special effects: borders, wooden subjects, boats, interiors, sea and landscapes, fields. Resembles oak.

30. **COURBARIL** (H)
Central & South America. W.Indies
Hymenaea courbaril
Colour description: orange-red to brown with russet and dark brown wild markings. Special effects: night sky and seas, foregrounds, trees, hills, roads, shadows, boats.

31. **DOUGLAS FIR** (S)
Canada and U.S.A. Australasia
Pseudotsuga menziesii
Colour description: pale pink to fawn with red-brown prominent ring figure as veins or stripes. Special effects: borders, cross-bands, fences, wood subjects.

32. **EBONY, MACASSAR** (H)
Celebes Islands
Diospyros celebica
Colour description: dark brown to black, with streaks of beige, grey-brown or pale-brown. Special effects: crossbandings, inlays; shadows, trees, interiors, mountains, foregrounds, land and seascapes, portraits,animals, still-life. Note: EBONY, AFRICAN *Diospyrus crassiflora*, used for similar purposes.

33. **ELM, AMERICAN WHITE** * (H)
Canada and U.S.A
Ulmus americana
Colour description: medium reddish-brown. Special effects: fields, foregrounds, shorelines, interiors, backgrounds for portraits, wooden subjects.
Note: ELM, ROCK* *Ulmus thomasii* (Canada and USA) used for same purposes.

34. **ELM, DUTCH and ENGLISH** * (H)
Europe and U.K
Ulmus hollandica & U. procera
Colour description: biscuit to light red-brown, with prominent ring figure, or lace figure. Special effects: foregrounds, wooden subjects, landscapes, trees, boats,fences, interiors. Suitable for borders.
Note: ELM, SMOOTH LEAVED* *Ulmus carpinifolia* (Europe) used for the same purposes.

35. **FREIJO** (H) Brazil
Cordia goeldiana
Colour description: Golden to dark brown with pronounced ray figure on quartered surfaces. Special effects: rocks, stonework, gravel, shingle, foreshores, sea effects, walls, landscapes.

36. **GABOON** (H)
Equatorial Guinea, Gabon and Congo
Aucoumea klaineana
Colour description: light pinkish-brown. Special effects: lustrous mottle, suitable for sky and water, floral, costume, portraits. Shades well.

37. **GEDU NOHOR** (H)
West, Central and E. Africa
Entandrophragma angolense
Colour description: plain, dull light to deep red brown. Special effects: used for borders and backing. Also for roofs, sails, shadows, boats, animal and bird subjects, and for portraiture backgrounds.

38. **GONCALO ALVES** (H) Brazil
Astronium fraxinifolium & A. graveolens
Colour description : red-brown with darker brown streaks and spots. Special effects: night sky and water effects, foregrounds,trees, boats, animals, interiors.

39. **GUAREA** (H) Tropical West Africa
Guarea cedrata & G.thompsonii
Colour description: pink-brown mahogany. Special effects: foregrounds, portraits, shadows, floral, costume.

40. **GUM, AMERICAN RED** (H)U.S.A
Liquidambar styraciflua
Colour description: pale brown to red-brown with dark brown marbled streaks. Special effects: sunset skies and water reflections, landscape and seascapes, interiors.

41. **HORNBEAM** * (H) Europe, Asia Minor
Carpinus betulus
Colour description: cream-biscuit, grey streaks, ray figure. Special effects: wooden subjects, walls, doors, interiors, snow scenes, floral subjects. Shades well.

42. **IDIGBO** (H) West Africa
Terminalia ivorensis
Colour description: pale yellow-brown. Special effects: ideal for floral subjects, sand shades well. Also for sandy foreshores, cornfields, costumes.

43. **IMBUYIA** (H) Brazil
Phoebe porosa
Colour description: yellow-olive to chocolate-brown with variegated streaks and stripes, often mottled.
Special effects: fields and foregrounds in landscape, roofs, animals, portraits, boats and interiors.

44. **'INDIAN ALMONDWOOD'** (H) India
Terminalia catappa
Colour description: pinkish-yellow with brown-red variegated streaks and stripes. Special effects: wide leaves ideal for sunset, sunrise skies, reflected water effect. Landscape, seascape, floral and costume.

45. **'INDIAN LAUREL'** (H) Indian continent
Terminalia alata & Spp:
Colour description: light to chocolate brown with irregular dark brown streaks or lines. Special effects: dark foregrounds, trees, night water effects, rocks, wooden piers, interiors, portraiture.

46. **IROKO** (H) West and East Africa
Chlorophora excelsa
Colour description: golden orange-light brown. May have calcium specks in grain with discoloured wood around them. Special effects: fields, sandy foreshores, takes sand shading well for floral and costume subjects.

47. **JARRAH** (H) Australia
Eucalyptus marginata
Colour description: rich, dark, brown-red often with dark boat-shaped flecks caused by the fungus *Fistulina hepatica* Special effects: landscape and seascape foregrounds, interiors, boats and sails, roofs, trees.

48. **KINGWOOD** (H) South America
Dalbergia cearensis
Colour description: violet background with variegated streaks of dark violet, violet-brown and black. Special effects: borders and crossbandings, inlay bandings,interior scenes, trees, boat planking, piers.

49. **LARCH, EUROPEAN** (S) Alpine Europe and W.Russia
Larix decidua
Colour description: golden pink-brown to reddish-brown. Special effects: wide crown veneer suitable for sky or water, fences, roads, shades for floral and costume.

50. **LAUAN, WHITE** (H) Philippines
Shorea contorta
Colour description: cream to grey with pink tinge. Special effects: window-wasters, background for still-life or portraits. Shades for floral and costume.

51. **LATI** (H) Tropical West Africa
Amphimas pterocarpoides
Colour description: orange, with distinct orange-brown growth ring figure. Special effects: sky and water effects, sea-shore, landscape, costume and drapery.

52. **LIME** (H) Europe
Tilia vulgaris & T. europaea
Colour description: cream-yellow to yellow-fawn. Special effects: crown cut for sky effects; sand shades for floral and costume subjects, cornfields.

53. **MAGNOLIA** (H) U.S.A
Magnolia grandiflora & spp.
Colour description: greenish-beige with dark purple streaks, with fine pale parenchyma lines. Special effects: selected parts for grass, foliage, leaves, floral subjects, distant hills, still-life, shadows.

54. **MAHOGANY, AFRICAN** (H) Tropical Africa
Khaya ivorensis & spp;
Colour description: medium red-brown. Special effects: borders, backing, landscapes, seascapes, portrait, interiors, still-life.

55. **MAHOGANY, AMERICAN** (H) Central & South America
Swietenia macrophylla
Colour description: pale orange-brown to dark red-brown. Special effects: animal subjects, foregrounds, trees, houses, interiors, sails, boats and still-life.

56. **MAKORÉ** (H) West Africa
Tieghemella heckelii & spp:
Colour description: blood-red to red-brown, some with 'moiré' silk figure. Sometimes has blue stain. Special effects: roofs, bushes, distant foliage, costume and drapery, interiors, shadows, boats and sails, still-life.

57. **MANSONIA** (H) West Africa
Mansonia altissima
Colour description: grey-mauve sap to purple-blue heart with dark bands and streaks. Special effects: light mansonia ideal for sandy foreshores; dark mansonia for distant hills, mountains, trees, boats, shadows, portraits.

58. **MAPLE, EUROPEAN** * (H) Europe, Asia Minor, Russia
Acer campestre
Colour description: cream-white, weathers to light-tan. Special effects: treated as harewood, veins remain tan coloured. Sky and sea effects, water, sand shades for floral subjects, costume and drapery, still-life.

59. **MAPLE, ROCK** * (H) Canada, Eastern U.S.A
Acer saccharum & A.nigrum
Colour description: cream-white with pink tinge. Fine brown lines. Rotary cut to produce Bird's eye maple. Special effects: sliced for sky effects, sand shades well for floral and costume. Treated as harewood for sea and water. Bird's eye maple for roads, paths, rocks. Borders and backing veneers.
Note: MAPLE,SOFT * Acer spp (Canada and USA) used for similar purposes.

60. **'MARACAIBO BOXWOOD'** * (H) West Indies, S.America
Gossypiospermum praecox
Colour description: lemon-yellow. Special effects: inlay lines and bandings, fillet borders.. Sand shades for floral, costume and drapery subjects. Highlights.
Note: BOXWOOD, EUROPEAN * *Buxus sempervirens* is used for similar purposes.

61. **MERANTI, DARK RED; SERAYA, DARK RED; LAUAN, RED.**(H) Malaysia, Sarawak, Indonesia, Philippines.
Shorea spp
Colour description: medium to dark red-brown. Special effects: borders, backing, foregrounds, trees, interiors, boats and sails. (Note: meranti, seraya, and lauan also available in light red, white and yellow).

62. **MENGKULANG** (H)
Malaysia, S.E Asia
Heritiera javanica & spp:
Colour description: medium to dark red-brown with red flecked ray figure when quartered. Special effects: sunset seas, fields, roads, trees, rocks, interiors.

63. **MUNINGA** (H)
Central and South Africa
Pterocarpus angolensis
Colour description: golden to chocolate brown, dark red streaks. Special effects: fields, hills, trees, animal subjects, interiors, fences, walls, portraits, boats, rocks.

64. **NIANGON** (H) West Africa
Tarrietia utilis & T.densiflora
Colour description: reddish-brown with ray figure on quartered surfaces. Special effects: mid-distance fields, foregrounds, roofs, sunset water, interiors, animals.

65. **NYATOH** (H) Malaya and S.E.Asia
Palaquium maingayi & spp:
Colour description: red-brown wih darker streaks and moiré watersilk figure. Special effects: roofs, bushes, distant foliage, costume and drapery, floral subjects, interiors, shadows, boats and sails, still-life.

66. **OAK, EUROPEAN** (H)
Europe, Asia Minor, N.Africa
Quercus petraea & Q.robur:
Colour description: light tan to biscuit with silver ray figure on quartered surfaces. Special effects: borders, crossbands, backs, wooden subjects, interiors, walls, fields, shingle foreshores, stonework, boats, doors.
Note (1): BROWN OAK useful for animals, land and seascapes and BOG OAK used for trees, shadows, rocks, wooden subjects, interiors.
Note (2): OAK,AMERICAN RED ; OAK, AMERICAN WHITE (USA and Canada) and OAK, JAPANESE *Quercus spp*; are all used for similar purposes.

67. **OBECHE** * (H)
Tropical West Africa
Triplochiton scleroxylon
Colour description: cream to pale yellow. Special effects: sand shades for floral and costume subjects, cornfields, doors, walls. With scattered blue mineral stain is ideal for sky and sea effects.

68. **OLIVE, EAST AFRICAN** (H)
East Africa
Olea hochstetteri & O.welwitschii
Colour description: orange-brown with irregular marbled streaks of grey, brown and black. Special effects: sky and sea effects, foreshores, middle distance fields, roads, paths, and perspective scenes.

69. **OPEPE** (H) West Africa
Nauclea diderrichii
Colour description: orange-brown with copper lustre and roll figure. Special effects: sunset hills, animals, landscape, portraits, wooden subjects and interiors.

70. **PADAUK, ANDAMAN** (H)
Andaman Islands
Pterocarpus dalbergiodes
Colour description: crimson to brick red, with red-brown streaks. Special effects: sunset foregrounds, floral subjects, costume, roofs, sails, still-life.
Note: PADAUK, AFRICAN (Central and West Africa.) (*Pterocarpus soyauxii* & *P.osun*) :(blood red, to purple brown with red streaks) and PADAUK, BURMA (*Pterocarpus macrocarpus*) (brick-red to orange red-brown) are used for similar special effects.

71. **PALDAO** (H) Philippines
Dracontomelum dao
Colour description: orange-brown background with irregular dark brown to black streaks. Special effects: foregrounds,tree trunks, animals, fields, hills, rocks. Note: 'NEW GUINEA WALNUT'
(*D.mangiferum*) is similar and used for same purposes.

72. **'PARANA PINE'** (S) Brazil, Paraguay, Argentina
Araucaria angustifolia
Colour description: straw-biscuit, sometimes streaked with red. Special effects: sky or sea effects. Sand shades well for sea-shores or floral and costumery.
Note: Pine, Japanese Red; Pine, American Pitch; Pine, Ponderosa; Pine, Radiata; Pine, Siberian Yellow; Pine, Western White; and Pine Yellow (*Pinus spp*); are all used for similar purposes.

73. **PEAR** * (H) Europe and W.Asia
Pyrus communis
Colour description: pink to pink-brown, with mottle on quartered surfaces. Special effects: portraiture, sand shaded for floral and costume subjects, pastel walls.

74. **PEROBA, ROSA** (H) Brazil
Aspidosperma peroba
Colour description: pink to rose red, with variegated yellow, orange or purple streaks. Special effects: sunset and sunrise skies; floral, costume and drapery; portraiture, shadows, interiors.Sand shades well.

75. **PEROBA,WHITE** (H) Brazil
Paratecoma peroba
Colour description: light golden-brown with variegated streaks of yellow, green or red streaks or stripes. Special effects: shades well for floral subjects, costume and drapery, sandy beaches, fields, thatch.

76. **PLANE, EUROPEAN** * (H) Europe
Platanus hybrida
Colour description: light red-brown with conspicuous broad ray flecked figure on quartered surfaces, sold as LACEWOOD. Special effects: roads, paths, rocks, shingle, stonework.

77. **POPLAR** * (H) Europe
Populus spp;
Colour description: creamy-white to grey. Special effects: window-wasters. Sky effects, and snow scenes. Sand shades well for floral and costume subjects. Takes harewood treatment for sea and water effects.

78. **PRIMA VERA** (H) Central America
Tabebuia donnell-smithii
Colour description: yellow-rose pink with red,orange and golden-brown streaks. Special effects: excellent sky effects and reflected water, sandy beaches, seascape foregrounds. Shades for floral and costume subjects.

79. **PURPLEHEART** (H) Central and South America
Peltogyne pubescens & spp:
Colour description: purple to violet-brown. Special effects: distant hills, heather; floral, costume and drapery. Roofs, walls, shadows, sails, interiors.

80. **'QUEENSLAND MAPLE'** (H) Australia, Papua New Guinea
Flindersia brayleyana & spp:
Colour description: flesh-pink to pale brown, lustrous with moiré, mottle, fiddleback figure. Special effects: mid-distance fields roofs, mountains, rocks, sails, costume, drapery, floral subjects, interiors, boats.

81. **'QUEENSLAND WALNUT'** (H) Australia
Endiandra palmerstonii
Colour description: medium brown streaked with pink, grey, greenish black stripes on quartered surfaces. Special effects: border mounts, backing veneers, tree trunks, fields, foregrounds, hills, interior scenes, costume.

82. **ROSEWOOD, BRAZILIAN** (H) Brazil
Dalbergia nigra
Colour description: chocolate to violet brown streaked with gold-red to black. Special effects: night skies and seas, foregrounds, roads, mountains, fields, trees. Note: ROSEWOOD, HONDURAS (*Dalbergia stevensonii*) has similar uses.

83. **ROSEWOOD, INDIAN** (H) Southern India. Java
Dalbergia latifolia
Colour description: rose-red to purple-brown with purple-black growth ring lines. Special effects: quartered material for borders, crossbandings and backs. Mountains, dark foregrounds, trees, interiors, costumes.

84. **SAPELE** (H) West and East Africa
Entandrophragma cylindricum
Colour description: medium red-brown. With 'ribbon' or 'pencil-striped' figure on quartered surfaces. Special effects: border mounts, crossbandings, boats, sails, trees, roofs, wooden subjects, interiors, parquetry. Note: POMELLE is a highly mottled, quilted, freak figured sapele, used for bushes, animal studies, portraiture.

85. **SATINWOOD, CEYLON** (H) India and Sri Lanka
Chloroxylon swietenia
Colour description: golden yellow to gold-brown. Mottle, roe, striped and 'beeswing' figure in quartered veneer. Special effects: crossbandings and inlays, cornfields, thatch, beaches. Sand shades for floral subjects, costume and drapery, and wild-life.

86. **SCOTS PINE (REDWOOD)** (S) Europe, Russia
Pinus sylvestris
Colour description: golden to light red-brown. Growth rings clearly marked by contrasting earlywood and latewood zones. Special effects: skies sand seas. Sand shaded for floral and costume subjects, beaches, feathers.

87. **SEPETIR** (H) Thailand, Malaysia, Philippines
Sindora spp:
Colour description: colour varies from pinkish-brown, golden brown to red-brown, with dark brown or black streaks, with growth ring figure on tangential surfaces. Special effects: sky and water effects, mid-distance fields, and foreshores in seascapes.

88. **SYCAMORE** * (H) Europe. W.Asia
Acer pseudoplatanus
Colour description: white to creamy-white. Quartered stock produces 'fiddleback' figure. Steamed for 'weathered sycamore' (pink-brown). Special effects: window-wasters, backgrounds, borders; skies, floral and costume.
Note: This is the principal veneer used for Harewood and produces silver, slate, and dark grey for water effects.

89. **TCHITOLA** (H) Tropical West Africa
Oxystigma oxyphyllum
Colour description: the log has three zones: the centre heartwood is red brown, the middle section is pale red, the sappy outer zone is yellow-brown with variegated stripes of black and yellow. Special effects: ornamental striped veneers are ideal for animals, birds, fields, hills and water effects.

90. **TEAK** (H) Burma, India, S.E.Asia
Tectona grandis
Colour description: golden brown to rich brown with chocolate markings. Special effects: borders,crossbands, trees, mountains, rocks, interiors, animal and bird subjects; shadows, boats, etc.

91. **TULIPWOOD, BRAZILIAN** (H) South America.
Dalbergia frutescens & Spp:
Colour description: pinkish-yellow, with variegated streaks and stripes of salmon pink, rose red, to violet. Special effects: inlays and crossbandings; dramatic sky and water effects, foregrounds, fences, striped awnings, floral subjects and costumes.

92. **UTILE** (H) West and East Africa
Entandrophragma utile
Colour description: reddish-brown to dark red. Grain interlocked, with irregular weak striped figure on quartered surfaces. Special effects: borders and crossbandings, roofs, foregrounds, reflections, shadows, wooden subjects. walls, doors, fences.

93. **WALNUT, AMERICAN** (H) Eastern U.S.A, and Canada
Juglans nigra
Colour description: rich dark brown to purplish-black.Straight, wavy or curly grain. Curls and burrs. Special effects: tree trunks, mountains and rocks, distant hills, borders, crossbandings, reflections, shadows, foregrounds, all wooden subjects, portraits.

94. **WALNUT, EUROPEAN** (H) Europe, Asia Minor, S.W.Asia
Juglans regia
Colour description: light grey-brown with irregular streaks of smokey mid to dark brown and attractive wild markings. Also in curls and burrs. Special effects: borders cross-bandings, foregrounds, mountains, rocks, portraiture, animals and bird subjects, wooden subjects.

95. **WENGE** (H) Zaire, Cameroons and Gabon
Millettia laurentii
Colour description: dark brown, with very close, almost black veins; hard and brittle. Special effects: borders, cross-bands; wooden subjects, interiors, houses, fences, boats.

96. **'WESTERN RED CEDAR'** (S) Canada, U.S.A
Thuja plicata
Colour description: variegated salmon-pink to reddish-brown with growth ring clearly defined. Special effects: crown cut for sky and water effects. Useful in landscapes for middle distance fields; sand shaded for floral and costumes.

97. **WHITEWOOD, AMERICAN** (H) Eastern U.S.A and Canada
Liriodendron tulipifera
Colour description: pale yellow-brown with variegated streaks and patches of olive green, grey and pink-brown and often with mineral stains of steel blue. Special effects: selected material ideal for sky effects and water, foreshores and foregrounds.

98. **WILLOW** * (H) Europe, N.America, N.Africa, Asia
Salix alba & spp:
Colour description: white to creamy-pink. Growth ring zones prominent. Moiré watersilk mottle. Special effects: snow scenes, skies, water effects. Shades for floral subjects and costumes.

99. **YEW** (S) Europe,W.Russia,AsiaMinor,N.Africa,India.
Taxus baccata
Colour description: golden orange streaked with purple, mauve and brown patches, with veins, knots and clusters of in-growing bark. Special effects: sky effects and water, portraiture, interiors, costumes.

100. **ZEBRANO** (H) West Africa
Microberlinia brazzavillensis
Colour description: golden-yellow with dark brown to black stripes. Special effects: crossbandings and inlays; fences, houses, wooden subjects, interiors.

SPECIAL FIGURED WOODS

The foregoing list of one hundred veneers will suit most pictorial marquetry purposes. But what brings a picture to life is the use of 'freak' or unusual figured woods.

Try to obtain some of the following species.

ROTARY CUT AND HALF ROUNDED

Bird's eye maple. *(Acer saccharum)*
Kevazingo. *(Guibourtia demeusei)*
Masur birch. *(Betula pendula or B.alba)*
Obeche, blue stained. *(Triplochiton scleroxylon)*
Pommelle. *(Entandrophragma cylindricum)*

STUMPWOOD (BUTTS)

Yew *(Taxus baccata)*
Willow *(Salix alba & S.fragilis)*
Olive ash. *(Fraxinus excelsior)*
Poplar *(Populus spp)*
Walnut, European *(Juglans regia)*
Walnut,American *(Juglans nigra)*

CURLS (Crotches)

Curls are usually obtainable in small sizes in ash, mahogany, sycamore, oak and walnut.

BURRS (Burls)

Amboyna *(Pterocarpus indicus)*
Ash *(Fraxinus excelsior)*
Cherry *(Prunus avium)*
Elm *(Ulmus procera)*
Eucalyptus *(Eucalyptus quadrangulata)*
Green Cypress *(Liriodendron tulipifera)*
Lacewood *(Platanus hybrida)*
Madrona *(Arbutus manziesii)*
Maidu *(Pterocarpus pedatus)*
Maple *(Acer saccharum)*
Myrtle *(Umbellularia californica)*
Oak *(Quercus robur)*
Poplar *(Populus spp)*
Thuya *(Tetraclinis articulata)*
Vavona *(Sequoia sempervirens)*
Walnut, Circassian *(Juglans regia)*
Walnut, Black American *(Juglans nigra)*
Yew *(Taxus baccata)*

4
Artificial Colour

SO FAR, we have been concerned with the limitations of natural woods in colour and tone.

Many marquetarians believe they are justified in crossing over the line between what nature can provide for their palette in natural woods, and what they can contrive to produce by their own ingenuity.

In times gone by, when logs for veneers were cut by pit-saw into boards of about ¼ inch (6mm) thick, the log was conditioned by soaking in artesian well pools, which contained traces of salts of iron in the water. The effect of these salts on various species was different. White sycamore turned silver grey; maple became grey-green; oak became purple and walnut, almost black. Wood which grew near artesian wells and chalybeate springs, also changed colour.

What they had discovered was that timbers coming into contact with iron compounds in the soil when growing, or when immersed, or even in damp conditions of use, are subject to severe black or blue-black mineral stains. These are caused by the chemical reaction between iron, and the natural tannin or related compounds such as polyphenols which are present in wood. The main timbers affected are oak, chestnut, afrormosia, idigbo, makore, kapur, obeche, walnut, etc.

When tannic acid is used as an astringent, and mixed with various metallic sulphates, the reaction forms a salt which rapidly oxidizes upon exposure to the air and causes the wood to change colour, chiefly blue or blue-black.

Harewood

The sulphate used to produce harewood is ferrous sulphate, (copperas) which will react with the tannin in certain woods at room temperature when in a water solution. It will convert white sycamore to silver grey by a process of oxidisation. It is similar to the ink making process, made by adding tannic acid to a solution of ferrous sulphate.

Alternatively, iron sulphate (blue crystals) can be used in conjunction with iron filings or nut galls (or in a metallic container) which will produce dark or slate grey.

Normally, sycamore is felled when the sap is at its height, not in spring or winter, as the amount of tannin in the tree also depends on the type of soil (sand, chalk, clay, peat) and the felling cycle.

The pre-conditioning of veneer logs for cutting draws the water-soluble tannin from the log and therefore logs for harewood have to be cut 'cold', and grown in locations where soil conditions are known.

Ever since those ancient days, sycamore has always been chemically treated to produce silver grey harewood.

It was extensively used on furniture and to this day, the Marquetry Societies around the world accept the use of harewood in their prizewinning pictures.

The classic argument is, that harewood can be created naturally. There have to be exceptions to every rule, therefore harewood is accepted, and regarded differently to all other dyed woods.

To produce silver harewood at home, the first essential is a non-metallic container. A plastic dustbin or fibreglass water storage tank is ideal for longer leaves which may be coiled around to fit inside.

Smaller leaves can be treated in a glass jar or even a small glass walled aquarium tank.

Make a solution of ferrous sulphate in water, using the proportion of 36 grammes to 4.5 litres, (1½ ozs to the gallon) in a separate container. Stir until completely dissolved before introducing the solution to the dyebath.

Obtain garden grade ferrous sulphate from your local garden centre, not the laboratory grade from the chemist.

The type of water used is very important, as tap water in your locality may contain purification chemicals and traces of calcium bicarbonate, calcium carbonate, nitrates, fluorides, carbon dioxide or ammonia etc., which may interfere with the tannin-ferrous sulphate reaction. Ideally, therefore, demineralised water should be used to make the dyebath, but rainwater, distilled water, or frost from a fridge-freezer melted down, would be suitable. If your local tap water contains traces of ammonia add a few drops of sulphuric acid to the mix to neutralise the ammonia.

Oxidisation problems can arise. Sycamore with very low tannic acid content which is left in the solution longer than necessary to convert the tannin may absorb some of the ferrous sulphate, which will oxidise on exposure to the air as the veneer dries, and leave a dirty brown sludge mark or stain.

Weight the veneers below the surface of the solution with a wooden weight. Remove the leaves after about an hour and wash off any sludge which may have formed on the surface with a sponge dipped in fresh water.

The strength of the ferrous sulphate solution and the time immersed has no effect on colour once penetration of the solution has occurred. There is only so much tannin in the wood, and once converted by chemical reaction, no further colour change will occur. The length of time this takes varies and can only be gained by experience.

The dye bath solution may also tend to oxidise and turn black if not sealed from contact with the air with the result that a dark grey colour will result and not pale silver grey.

Bubbling air into the mix with an aquarium type oxygenator, can also cause oxidisation and a sludge or mould will form on the surface. It is best to stir the dye bath and turn the veneers over.

I have produced harewood commercially for export around the world for twenty-five years, and my method was to immerse a complete bundle of sycamore on edge, containing up to 32 leaves, for an hour, giving the dye bath a stir occasionally. The leaves were separated below the water level, to ensure complete coverage and then reversed or turned over and left for another hour. Long leaves which were coiled around in a plastic dustbin or water tank, were coiled again in the opposite direction and re-immersed. The veneers were then removed from the dye bath and washed with a sponge in tap water before being hung up to air-dry in a warm atmosphere.

Complete penetration should take about an hour, but when the veneer is low in tannic acid, leave the veneer to soak for a further hour. The solution will work for weeks, but with each use the quantity will reduce due to absorption and evaporation and the mixture of ferrous sulphate and water needs to be topped up.

To produce slate grey or dark grey, heat the solution, or add washing soda to the dyebath. The more soda or the hotter the water, the darker the shade. Dark harewood may also be produced in an iron bath.

Cut off a sliver of the original veneer with a sharp knife and keep it for comparison. Cut a small test-piece from the dyed harewood, run it under the tap, and wrap it in paper and allow to dry thoroughly. If it is not perfectly dry, the knife will carry the solution with it and mislead you.

Break the test-piece in half and tear it across the grain. The fibres should be completely penetrated. It is the amount of tannin in the wood that decides the colour, not the length of time immersed in the dye bath.

Apart from sycamore, there are many other veneers that contain natural tannin and which can be treated by this process, such as ash, aspen, beech, birch, horse chestnut, maple, planetree, and poplar etc.

In addition to those veneers with a high, natural tannin content, it is possible to impregnate any permeable timber with tannic acid.

A tannin solution made from steeped tea, (or a solution made from old tea-bags), tannin powder or tannic acid, obtainable from any 'Home made wine' or 'Home-brew' store, will react with the ferrous sulphate and produce a change of colour, sometimes blue-black. But only a white veneer will produce silver grey.

Harewood should not be allowed to come into contact with acidic substances, or it will immediately bleach back to white. Anything with a pH factor below 7 will have this effect. Acid catalytic adhesives and finishing materials should be tested for compatibility before using harewood on a project.

Many amateur marquetarians exploit this by using diluted sulphuric acid (from a car battery, for example) to convert harewood back to white sycamore again, and applied carefully, can reproduce surf and waterfall effects and cloud formations.

Dyed Veneers

Apart from harewood, marquetarians have always used a limited range of dyed woods to create inlay motifs and bandings, which are still extensively employed for the repair of period furniture, reproduction furniture and on musical instruments such as guitar rosettes etc.

In the past, water-acid, spirit and oil dyes have all been used, with all sorts of recipies involving the use of saffron, turmeric powder, dragon's blood, logwood extract, Brazilwood raspings, malachite crystals, gall nuts and urine, etc.

The modern marquetarian, can widen his palette of colours by using fabric dyes on his veneers. Leaves can be coiled around inside a domestic pressure cooker, three quarters full of water (to cover the leaves) at 15 p.s.i and cooked for 45 minutes to produce excellent colours.

Those who argue in favour of using dyed woods in marquetry present a threefold case: firstly, it is traditional to use dyed woods. Secondly, natural woods such as padauk or purpleheart will fade in time and lose their original colour. Why not try to enhance the natural colour and make it 'fast to light' so that it can retain the colour in the years to come? Thirdly, if marquetry is ever to achieve its true status as an art form, the artist has to widen his palette of colour hues, or the medium becomes too restrictive.

There are others who claim that the only justification for using dyed woods in marquetry is to fill the missing gaps in the colour wheel, in the green, blue and violet sections, in order to make use of the abundant supply of natural red, orange and yellow veneers.

Whichever view you support, it is essential that these dyed woods should not be in brilliant, vivid hues, but in the lower tertiary range, having a brown tone and being more wooden in appearance.

Using modern chemicals, dyes and mordants for this purpose is not the same as staining the wood. A wood dye works differently to a wood stain, which adds a cloudy pigmented layer that conceals the grain and covers up the natural beauty of wood. A dye consists of a liquid medium, in which pigment particles are dissolved not merely suspended and is therefore more transparent. Better still are those which result from a chemical reaction in the wood itself.

Natural wood extracts such as logwood and Brazilwood available in powder form, can be applied by themselves to produce yellowish or reddish-brown tones, but when combined with mordants, produce a wide range of colours.

A mordant, from the French *mordre* 'to bite', helps the dye penetrate the fibres and achieve complete permeation. Dye creates colour with dissolved pigments, but mordants chemically react with other substances in the wood and can be used without dyes.

A widely used mordant is alum – the name given to double salts of aluminium and potassium and similar analogous compounds used as a mordant for fixing the colour in the dyeing process. Highly pigmented woods such as padauk and purpleheart, may be given an alum bath to 'fix' the colour and avoid the sanding dust from leeching to surrounding veneers. Other mordants like sodium sulphate increase the fade resistance of logwood and Brazilwood powders.

Sometimes the dye is applied first, and then dried before the veneer is returned to the mordant bath. For other colours, the process is reversed, but the dye and mordant are never mixed together.

A veneer can be progressively dyed to deepening strengths of colour. For instance, ash can be given a bath in tannic acid and dried. Followed by a 15% concentration logwood bath and dried, for an orange red colour,then a ferrous sulphate bath produces reddish-brown. After drying, a bath in alum turns the ash into a rich brown, and a final bath of potassium bichromate a lustrous dark brown.

When oak is exposed to fumes from heated ammonia solution (which requires use of vapour respirator with an ammonia cartridge) the tannin in the wood reacts. By applying tannic acid solution before fuming this can be achieved with other woods.

Dyed Black

This is the most difficult colour to produce, but is used universally for lines and bandings in marquetry.

Commercially it is produced in an autoclave with vacuum pressure to achieve penetration and re-circulation under high pressure, in a process using logwood extract, ferrous sulphate, and mordants with isinglass.

Another faking trick achieves surface penetration to a sufficient depth to permit a fixative sealing coat to preserve the colour, with the use of fabric dyes, artist's inks, or stains, but in some cases these may be incompatible with the solvents in the finishing process and may bleach out.

Tyloses

The major problems encountered with dyeing veneers are (a) penetration, in that the veneers must be dyed right through to enable them to be sanded; (b) fastness to light to prevent fading, and (c), the migration of colour to the surface which gives misleading results.

Many trees have a thin-walled secondary growth called tylosis, which produces a foam-like bubbly in-growth that fills the vessels during the changeover from sapwood to heartwood every year. This makes the heartwood of many woods impermeable.

A complete list of 276 woods of the world, and their permeability ratings is given in *World Woods in Colour*.

The Society of Dyers and Colourists have prepared a 'Fast to Light' set of eight standards, each one being twice as fast as the preceeding one. Most basic colours have a low rating, but acid dyes for wool and direct dyes used for cotton, achieve ratings of 6 or 7 and are best for veneers.

A good tip is to slightly heat the veneers before immersion which will reduce their moisture content and make penetration easier. Add 2 per cent urea to increase the solubility of the acid dyes, and add wetting agents such as *Lissapol N*, or *Perminal BX* and penetrating agents such as *Calsolene Oil HS* or *Turkey Red Oil PO* (all ICI products). ordinary dye bath with veneers immersed, should be brought to the boil and simmered for up to eight hours and left in the cooling liquid overnight. Rinse thoroughly before air drying.

The veneers chosen for dyeing are usually sycamore, but abura, agba, ash, aspen, beech, birch, bird's eye maple, boxwood, hornbeam, horse chestnut, maple, obeche, planetree, poplar and willow also dye successfully. Also most permeable species can be treated with a tannic acid bath and dried, and can be used for dyeing, and the sapwood of many impermeable species can be dyed too.

The mordanting and dyeing chemicals used are alum, aqueous ammonia, copper sulphate (blue vitriol), ferrous sulphate, isinglass, potassium bitartite (cream of tartar), potassium dichromate, potassium bichromate, sodium sulphate, (Glauber's salt), stannous chloride, and tannic acid. **Warning:** most of these chemical mordants and dyes are poisonous, toxic or carcinogenic, and all contact with them should be made with extreme care.

Protective goggles with an organic-vapour acid gas particulate cartridge vapour mask should be worn,as well as an apron and disposable vinyl gloves. A well ventilated room, preferably fitted with an extractor, should be used for the work. A secure lock-up cabinet is essential to keep these poisons away from children and pets.

The marquetarian who wishes to experiment should equip himself with a means of measuring the pH factor (like a pH meter used for a swimming pool).

Fig. 35 Anyone looking? (After Alan Fairbrass) (Intermediate class Highly commended) Joan Meadows

'Fineline' Veneer

In the 1950's, a mixture of constructional and decorative veneers, of varying thicknesses were bonded together to form a man-made flitch and then sliced into uniform width veneers, with a pre-determined straight striped pattern. This had limited uses for pictorial marquetry work in that it destroys the illusion of perspective. Some flitches were cut from injected wood and were far more useful for marquetry.

Injected veneer

LeRoy Frink, in America, successfully injected the living tree with wood dyes under pressure. Each tree was banded around its base with a probe of multiple hollow needles and piped a water based dye fed by ⅛th inch (3mm) hose from an oil drum reservoir. The tree's own active transport system circulated the dye throughout the tree through its sapwood to the leaves and needles.

A tree of 16–20 inches (400–500mm) diameter would take a month to syphon the contents of a 55 gallon (250 litres) drum! The process works best on fast growing Ponderosa pine *Pinus ponderosa*. More than 500 poplar (*Populus tremuloides*) trees have been dyed simultaneously.

It was found possible to force the dye through the tree and out through the buds! Howard W Fox, a consulting forestor of Oregon U.S.A., described how on one occasion he put too much pressure on an 8 inch (200mm) white pine tree and it exploded, drenching two men in green dye! Experiments are continuing!

Dyed blue is used to portray the Kingfisher with shades of harewood for sky and water (Fig. 35).

5
Veneer Defects

IF A TREE is forcibly displaced by land subsidence, or bent by the wind from its natural erect attitude, it develops a reaction to counteract the forces tending to deform it, as it strives to restore itself to its normal position. It develops 'reaction' wood.

Reaction wood

In hardwoods, this forms on the *upper* side of leaning or crooked trees and is known as *tension* wood This is quite common in logs of elm, oak, poplar, etc.

In contrast, softwoods are particularly affected and develop a reaction on the *lower* side and is known as *compression* wood. Abnormally high shrinkage along the grain causes transverse fractures and rough, woolly patches on the veneer surface, which tend to tear out.

Both impair the quality of the timber. In addition compression and tension wood can form above and below heavy branches where curls (crotches) are formed.

Compression or tension wood shows at the edges of veneer as fine strands similar to woodwool, or as a ripple of buckling, or series of blisters. Tension wood causes veneers to buckle or split due to collapse in drying.

Milling defects are quite frequent – not due to faulty machinery or workmanship – but due to the presence of reaction wood, and the machinery compensates for the unequal pressure through the log, resulting in 'wandering gauge' or in knife checks.

Knife checks

The more slanted the grain to the veneer surface, the greater the danger of checks which are particularly noticeable on end grain veneers such as burrs (burls), and on curls (crotches) which are cut from reaction wood. The exception to the rule is bird's eye maple. Because of the conical shape of the eyes, this veneer is always laid 'face' side down to ensure the eyes will not chip out. These tiny knife checks cannot be avoided in knife cut veneers, because the leaf is actually 'torn' from its natural position around the log and then flattened out, thereby opening its underside (see Fig. 36).

A is the tight side of the veneer with only minor compression knife checks on the surface. B is the loose or tension side, with knife checks running into the thickness of the veneer, up to about 25 per cent of its thickness. C is the veneer knife set at an angle, and D, the pressure or nose bar,

'Looseness' and 'tightness' refers to the relative depth of these knife checks. A good tip, when in doubt about the 'face' side, is to stroke the veneer against your cheek – you will feel the difference immediately between the smooth and rough sides. Bend a sheet of veneer along the grain. If the tension side is uppermost it will bend without audible cracking. But with the compression side up, the radius of the curve will be greater and you'll hear cracking before it breaks.

The veneer will feel stiffer when flexed to close the checks and limp when the checks

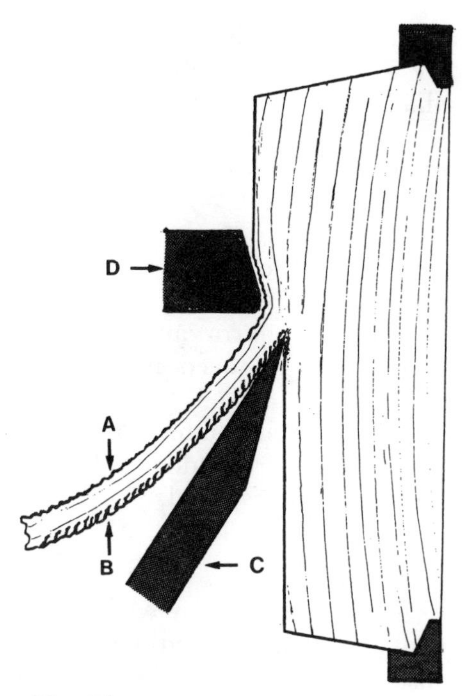

Fig. 36 The compression and tension sides of veneer

are flexed open. For the marquetarian, these parallel-to-the-grain checks in his veneers, can telegraph through to the surface and ruin his picture, and this can happen months or years after the picture was laid, (which probably appeared flawless on completion), as the checks migrate to the surface through the finish.
Also refer to Chapter 23 on cleaning up prior to laying).

It's worth repeating that for pictorial marquetry it is important that we use the tight, smooth, *compression* side of the veneers as the 'face' side and ensure that the knife checked tension or loose side is laid in the glueline.

Other defects

Look for scratch marks and surface scratches or scores across the leaf, caused by a dull knife. Or a chipped knife can form a hollow groove diagonally across the leaf on one side and a corresponding 'blip' on the other.

Woods with a pronounced ray figure, like oak, may become 'shelly' where the ray figure has been torn by the knife rather than cut. They feel like coarse raised bumps and tend to pluck out.

Shakes
The veneer should also be free from shakes along the grain, and 'thunder-shakes' across the grain, caused by tropical storms. These appear as though someone has tried to bend the veneer leaf and cracked it.

Iron stains
Wood in contact with iron compounds in the soil can suffer from black, or blue-black mineral stains. Chemical reaction between iron and tannin or related compounds such as polyphenols, which are present in woods, are likely to cause severe staining.

Mineral stains
Natural mineral stains are welcome for marquetry and can be found in afrormosia, ash, birch, chestnut, gum, idigbo, makoré kapur, mansonia, maple, oak, olive ash, 'Rhodesian teak', sycamore, walnut, willow and others. For example, 'blue-stained' obeche makes an excellent sky or water effect.

Softwoods such as Douglas fir and sequoia, are similarly affected by tannin-like substances or moist conditions. Reaction between iron compounds and other chemicals of a class known as tropolones cause red stains in western red cedar, and brown stains in yellow cedar. The presence of acetic acid in oak and sweet chestnut can cause corrosion of metals. (Also refer to Chapter 6).

False heart
Many species show a 'false-heart' caused by natural mineral stains, the black heart in ash and brown heart in beech, for example, but it is not a defect and the veneer is sound and decorative.

Bog oak, which is almost black, is caused by peat discolouration in logs dug up from the bogs of the fertile peatland of the East Anglian fens, part of a 70,000 year-old forest complex uncovered by wind erosion.

Chemical deposits
Gum pockets are found in many woods such as zebrano, and the resinous patches in agba, cedar and pine, should be avoided. White specks in the grain are caused by calcium deposits and are found in woods such as iroko.

Insect attack
All sorts of insects attack the living tree. In most cases they are very destructive,but in a few cases, in wood such as maple, oak, chestnut and birch, they can increase the decorative value of the veneer, for example, as in 'wormy-chestnut'.

One of the most treasured veneers is masur birch from Finland which is caused by the larvae of the *agromyzia carbonari* beetle which regularly attack and eat the cambium of the Scandinavian birch every year.

The rotary cut veneer reveals an entire surface covered with tiny brown clusters and pith flecks resulting in highly decorative black and brown markings in a swirling figure. It is a marvellous marquetry veneer.

Worm
A patch of tiny holes in a leaf caused by pin worm, can be ignored as they will fill in later stages. Signs of yellow dust called 'frass' can be ignored, but be on guard against any sign of white worm casts which indicate live worm and discard the veneer immediately, as this will not only damage your entire stock, but may also infect the workroom and furniture.

Fungal attack
A natural 'dross' forms on some woods. It is a fungus and is found on woods like canella, padauk, narra and maidu burr, etc. It is easily removed in the finishing processes.

Veneers stored in humid or damp conditions may suffer from 'doat' a form of wet rot and should be rejected.

Ingrowing bark
Burrs (Burls) and certain woods like yew may contain patches of ingrowing bark and may also be severely buckled and require flattening.

Sometimes burrs are dried to a higher moisture content to prevent them from cracking and breaking in storage and they form a silvery 'dross' which is harmless and wipes off easily. The 'decay safety line' is a moisture content of 20 per cent, as fungal decay or doat cannot develop below this moisture level.

Toxic veneers
The dust of certain species may be toxic and splinters can form allergies. Dark mansonia and Indian laurel are two examples.

Barrier creams or disposable vinyl gloves should be worn when handling these woods.

6
Storage and Preparation for Use

VENEERS ARE hygroscopic and will shed or absorb moisture from the atmosphere. If they have been kept in storage for a long time they may become overdry. In modern centally heated homes, or during a summer heatwave, they will tend to dry out and buckle.

It is best to store them off the floor away from any source of heat, in a well ventilated area with a good circulation of cool, *dry* air, around and below the veneers. They should be lightly weighted down with sheet of chipboard or blockboard to keep them flat and covered by a dust sheet from the effects of both natural and artificial light. White veneers like sycamore or horse chestnut will turn to a light tan colour if left exposed to strong light.

Veneers should also be kept away from contact with the walls or floor, and from any form of condensation or water. Water dripping from an iron roof would cause mineral stains in any veneer containing tannin.

Preparing marquetry veneers for use is a two stage process and there are various requirements to consider, beginning with the back or loose, open side, (which may possess knife checks).

The flatting process

As the name suggests, we need to flatten veneers prior to use. But there are many other reasons for this process. The requirements are:

(a) to flatten buckled, twisted veneers.
(b) to restore equilibrium moisture content.
(c) to render brittle or fragile veneers malleable and flexible to work with.
(d) to strengthen friable veneers and prevent splits from developing.
(e) to fill the knife checks on the tension side of the veneer.
(f) to ensure that the agents used in the flatting process are compatible with the adhesive used for laying.
(g) to draw out any natural resins or gums in the veneer which might affect adhesion or finishing.

To achieve (a and b), the simplest method is to sprinkle the back of the leaf with water from a previously wrung-out sponge, or use a garden spray, and wipe it with a damp clean cloth. Do not soak the surface, only slightly dampen it, or the veneer may turn spotty.

Place the veneer between clean paper to absorb the moisture and clamp between two boards and leave overnight. For this purpose sheets cut from a roll of ceiling paper are excellent. The boards can be of plywood, blockboard or faced chipboard and are called 'cauls'.

In practice, most of the veneers you obtain from specialist suppliers will be flat and ready for use and you need only carry out treatment to the face side. (See below).

However, you may often find some of the most interesting and valuable veneers are in what appears to be a buckled or distressed condition due to their natural short grain, such as burrs, or reaction grain, as in curls, or due to being in storage a long time.

The majority of burr veneers, and veneers like yew, contain small holes and patches of in-growing bark and tend to buckle very easily. Curl veneers are also inclined to be buckled and become wavy due to natural weaknesses in their structure caused by reaction wood. Oyster veneers are delicate due to their short grain nature.

These types will not respond to the 'dampening' treatment alone. We also need to deal with items (c, d and e).

This is achieved by coating the loose side of every veneer leaf with a weak solultion of glue size, made from one part glue, to nine parts water. Use the same glue for flatting as that used for laying the picture. (Refer to chapter 7 on adhesives and chapters 22 and 23 on laying).

The solution must be thin enough not to clog say, the nozzle of a garden spray.

Very brittle or severely buckled veneers can be rendered flexible and strong for safe handling by sizing with a mixture of adhesive for strength, glycerine for flexibility and alcohol for rapid drying. One tried and tested formula is:

Urea formaldehyde adhesive: 2 measures (1 part by weight). Flour (not self raising): 1 measure (½ part by weight).

Water: 3 measures (2½ parts by weight).

Glycerine: 1½ measures (1¼ parts by weight)

Alcohol (methylated spirit): ½ to 1 measure (⅓ to ⅔rds parts by weight).

The solution is used cold. All sorts of variations of this formula are used. For example, one American veneer mill recommends ninety per cent water and ten per cent glycerine.

The best approach is to try a diluted size of water and the adhesive first, and perhaps a touch of some of the other ingredients as necessary.

Lightly spray or sprinkle, sponge or brush a thin coat of glue size (or your preferred mixture) on the loose side of each veneer leaf and wipe off immediately with a cloth, cover with clean paper and clamp between boards.

Leave the veneers to stand for fifteen minutes for the moisture to penetrate and soften the veneers. For some of the fretsawing techniques it is advisable to glue a sheet of clean kraft or white paper to the back of brittle veneers, so that any splinters or tiny fragments which may break off during the cutting process will remain fastened to the backing sheet.

The paper is easily removed at the later cleaning-up stage. Never use newsprint against veneers, as the ink will offset, often with deep penetration in a heated press, and this is almost impossible to remove.

The outer veneers may be covered with polythene film to make certain that they will not stick to the two cauls overnight, but the polythene should be removed the next day as it could cause spottiness.

Many veneers are subject to severe black or blue-black mineral stains caused by the chemical reaction between traces of iron and the tannin or related compounds such as polyphenols which are present in wood in wet conditions. (Also refer to Chapter 5 Veneer defects).

These mineral stains can also result from tiny metal fragments picked up from the veneer mill knife in cutting, or from contact with metal in the workroom from a scraper iron or tool, reacting with the tannin in the wood. It is also possible when in contact with alumimum foil.

Should the black spot problem be encountered, they can be removed by touching the affected places with weak sulphuric acid (from a car battery for example). Do not use bleach as this will remove the veneer colour too.

The above treatments deal with requirements (a) to (e) but for (f) we need a press.

Simple home-made press

(Details of the construction of a simple press are given in Chapter 23 on laying.)

If you make a press, all the requirements (a) to (f) can be dealt with as most veneers will flatten in the home-made press. However, professionals use a *hot* press in which veneers are flattened overnight. It is possible for amateurs to use the same technique.

Let's assume you have a dozen 12 × 6 inch (305mm × 150mm) veneers which require heat treatment. To do this cut up a sheet of aluminium into four pieces about 14 × 8 × $\frac{1}{8}$ inch thick (350 × 200 × 3mm) or of sufficient size that will fit neatly into your kitchen oven. Next obtain two stout wooden cauls, 16 × 12 × $\frac{3}{4}$ inch (410 × 300 × 19mm) blockboard or chipboard to form a press, with the crossbearers or clamps as shown in Fig.37.

Coat the veneers and allow them to stand for a few minutes for the mixture to penetrate, before covering the loose side of each leaf with clean paper. The metal cauls are heated in the oven – just too hot to handle with the bare hands. Hot enough to require handling with oven gloves, but not enough to scorch the veneers. The heat will encourage the exudation of the resins or gums, and aid later adhesion.

Place the bottom wooden caul on the lower bearers of the press with a heated metal caul upon it and load four of the interleaved veneers on top. Continue in sets of four until all leaves and the four metal

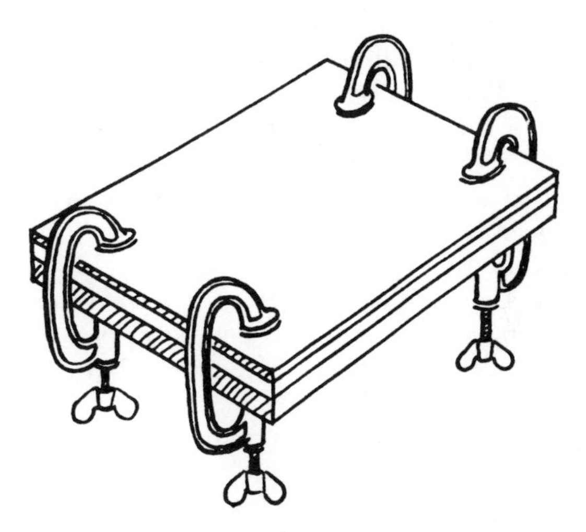

Fig. 37 A home-made press

plates have been loaded. The top wooden caul is then positioned and the press top bearers positioned and progressively tightened down in stages – centre bearers first and then at each end.

If the bundle was severely buckled, too much pressure at this stage could result in the veneers cracking. In this case only apply sufficient pressure to compact the veneers and allow time for the treatment to penetrate and soften the veneers before slightly increasing the pressure. In the case of stubbornly buckled, overdry veneers, the heat treatment may be repeated after twenty-four hours, and this time you will be able to tighten the press completely.

When removed from the press the veneers should be perfectly flat, strong and will spring apart when flexed, or will be easily separated with a flat knife or spatula. When perfectly flat and dry, the veneers are ready for their next treatment.

Face or tight side

This is the side of the veneer leaf which will eventually be seen in your finished picture. It is treated differently to the back or loose side. The requirements are:
(a) to reveal the true finished colour of the veneer to aid you in the selection process.
(b) to seal natural pigments or dyes in the veneer to prevent them from leeching into surrounding veneers in the assembly. Otherwise the sanding dust from a dark veneer may be ground into the open pores of a soft white veneer and spoil it, unless both are sealed.
(c) to ensure that the material used for this process is compatible with the chosen finishing material.

To achieve these requirements, the face side is given a brush coat of finishing material, diluted with its solvent in the ratio of about five to one. This has the advantage of revealing the true colours of the veneer before the time is reached for their selection. It is important that this treatment should be compatible with both the adhesive and the finish. (For a polyurethane finish dilute the lacquer with PU thinners. Refer to Chapter 26.) This will dry in a few minutes, and the veneers should be interleaved with clean paper and allowed to remain in the press overnight.

Allow the veneers to remain under weights after removal from the press, to acclimatise to their new environment, but with a free circulation of dry air around them.

Some of the burrs and woods like yew, although now flat, possess cracks that have opened wider, splits at the ends or around knots, or holes where knots have fallen out, or sections of in-growing bark which will have to be removed.

Repairing damaged veneers.

If, upon inspection, you find some of the veneers have split along the grain at the ends of the leaf, pull the veneer tightly together with a short 'strap' of gummed paper veneering tape, across the split and then another strip along it.

This defect will not show and will 'lose' itself in the grain when laid. The dampened tapes are placed *underneath* the split, and the veneer is vigorously rubbed along the split with a rounded piece of hardwood called a 'rubber' – which compresses the fibres of the veneer. The friction generated by rubbing, contracts the tape, pulling the join together more tightly.

It is good workshop practice to protect all veneers across the ends of each leaf, with paper veneering tape, to prevent splits from starting in handling.

To repair burrs or veneers with small holes, use another leaf from the same stock as a repair veneer.

With a sharp craft knife or a fretsaw, cut around the irregular contours of the burr's natural markings and cut a patch from a 'sound' part of the spare leaf. Insert it in the shape cut from the damaged leaf.

This 'inserting' process will be described in detail in later chapters featuring knife cutting and fretsawing techniques.

If you intend to use veneers to create veneer matches for borders or backs or applied marquetry tables and boxes etc., always keep them in matching sequence by chalking consecutive numbers on each leaf.

Professional craftsmen give *all* their veneers the flatting treatment and paper backing to render them flexible and easy to handle, while the majority of amateur marquetarians use their veneers untreated in the condition in which they receive them.

A cracked veneer can be repaired by taping over the face side and gently tapping the back with the rounded end of a ball pein hammer to crush the fibres together. Subsequent gluing and laying will conceal the crack completely.

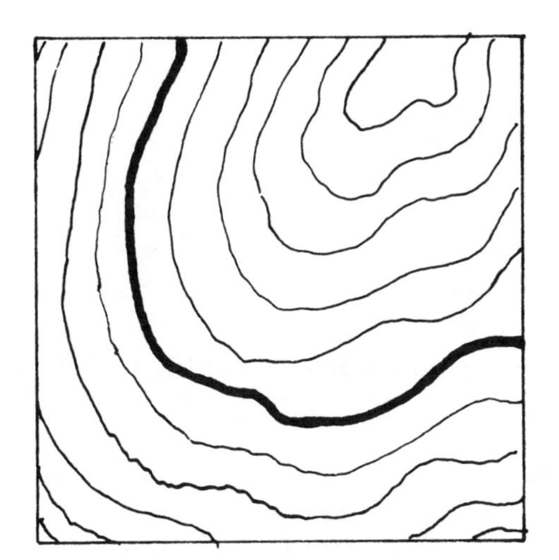

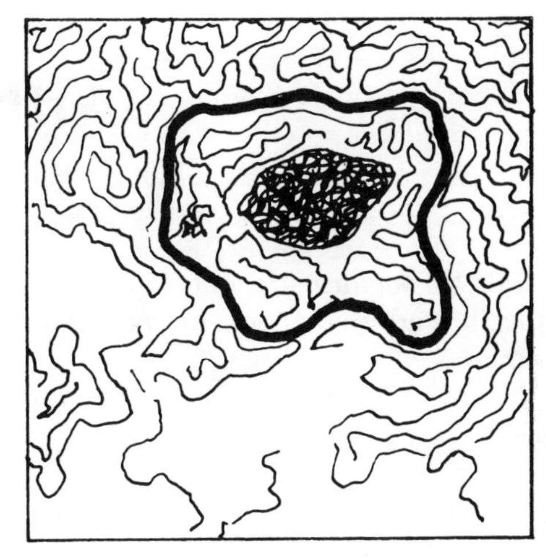

Fig. 38 Repairing burrs and veneers. Cut around a prominent feature of grain or markings.

7
Adhesives

ADHESION is caused in one of two ways, (a) specific adhesion or (b) mechanical adhesion.

Specific adhesion

When similar molecules are held in close contact, depending on their compatibility, natural attraction occurs and it becomes difficult to separate them.

For example, two sheets of optical glass or plastic will cling tightly together and cannot be pulled apart. They have to be slid apart.

But if the molecular attraction is impaired by foreign bodies such as dust, grit or grease settling on the surface, the two surfaces would pull apart easily. Wood falls into this category, as its surface is rough, uneven and porous, even after sanding, and would easily pull apart.

So we need an adhesive. This has two functions to perform. It needs to wet both surfaces and it has to solidify to hold them together.

To illustrate this, if we wet both surfaces with water, that would meet the first condition, but they would easily pull apart. But if immediately frozen, the water would become ice and the second function would be met and it would be impossible to separate the two surfaces

Mechanical adhesion

When an adhesive is allowed to penetrate the wood pores, either by natural absorption or when forced under pressure, microscopic examination would reveal thousands of vertical prongs in both directions penetrating the wood structure. In veneers, this 'mechanical lock' fills the open knife checks on the loose side of the veneer, if laid in the glueline.

The function of 'keying' a surface with a toothing plane is widely misunderstood. It is not for mechanical adhesion, but it actually increases the surface area, and cleans the surface of foreign bodies to prevent interfacial bond failure. Sanding the surface, on the other hand, creates dust and loose fibres which can actually encourage bond failure if not brushed or vacuumed away.

If two surfaces are flexed in service, shrink or swell due to humidity changes, or suffer bond creep due to sustained heavy loading, we have to use a *thermoplastic* adhesive which will yield to these changes. They can be re-heated after bonding for further work and then re-pressed for a repeat bond.

Thermosetting adhesives will crack, craze, or become brittle when subjected to loadings or stresses which they are not designed to cope with. However they set very hard and become impervious to boiling or extremely cold water, steam or dry heat, micro-organic or fungal attack and are used extensively for the manufacture of (WPB) 'Weather and Boil Proof' exterior and marine grade plywood.

Glueline

If the surface to be bonded is perfectly flat and smooth, such as high density chipboard, a thin, close contact glueline is required. The glueline should never exceed 0.13mm thickness.

But for porous, pervious surfaces such as 'keyed' wooden groundwork and marquetry assemblies, we need to use a *gap-filling* type of adhesive, which does not shrink when setting due to the addition of chemical additives in the mix, and may be applied slightly thicker. As a generalisation,however, the thinner the glueline, the better the bond. Timing is of the essence in the use of adhesives.

Shelf life and pot life

Some adhesives deteriorate in storage, others remain stable indefinitely, Careful storage in dry conditions is important. Once the lid of the container is opened, rapid oxidisation may occur giving the adhesive a limited pot life. Or when the adhesive is mixed, it will begin to coagulate and set and has to be discarded. Never make up more than required for the task in hand.

Assembly time

Sometimes known as 'open time'.This will depend on the type of solvent the adhesive requires and the workroom temperature. Adhesives with a very fast setting time due to the rapid evaporation of the solvent may only allow a few minutes for the groundwork and the assembly to be carefully loaded into the press.

For the marquetarian, it is important that he chooses an adhesive which provides sufficient assembly time. PVA cures in a press in 3 to 4 hours. Urea formaldehyde adhesives take from 5–6 hrs at 70°F (21°C).

Setting time

The faster the speed of set, the shorter the assembly time. Adhesives with very fast setting times should be avoided for this work as they can actually set faster than they can be spread by hand. Slow setting adhesives are best, therefore, for marquetry.

Press times

Some adhesives require a period of time to elapse to allow the solvent to evaporate into the atmosphere and the adhesive to tack before pressure is applied. Others have no tack period and rely purely on a chemcial reaction between catalyst and hardener.

If the glueline begins to cure before the correct pressure is applied, (the cause of blisters) this can be overcome by leaving the panel in the press for a longer period to allow the 'second phase of setting' to occur.

Curing time

The bond may superficially appear to be sound, but the panel will require a further period outside the press for the glueline to 'cure', harden and stabilise.

Working with adhesives is a question of being 'time concious'and acquiring a working knowledge of various timescales to suit your own equipment, project and working environment.

Temperature
For marquetry, choose an adhesive which will cure at room temperature of about 70°F (21°C), unless you have press temperature controls. A slight rise in temperature may assist the bonding time of some cold glues, but it will also soften the glueline, and the bond will have to remain under pressure until cold before it will cure, so there is little advantage in heating a cold glue.

Pressure
This depends on the equipment you have. For most home-made screw presses, clamps, car jack presses etc., we need an adhesive which will cure under low pressure over a timescale of hours rather than minutes.

Strength
The adhesive should be strong enough to resist the pulling power of the veneers, but also to hold surfaces which may have a residue of resinous, oily, gummy or calcious content on the back, without risk of delamination.

Discolouration
Many strong adhesives leave a visible dark glueline. This does not matter if the edges are to be covered but could spoil the appearance of a marquetry picture if the glueline penetrates open-pored, delicate veneers or burrs, or showed at some of the joints.

Types of adhesive

There is no such thing as the perfect marquetry adhesive. All types of glue and adhesives possess advantages and disadvantages. The most important factor which will decide on your choice of adhesive is the type of equipment available for laying the veneer.

The best adhesive for general veneering is not necessarily the ideal adhesive for multi-piece marquetry assemblies, which require only the groundwork to be coated, and allowed to dry before the veneer assembly is brought into contact and then held firmly under pressure.

Adhesives, generally, fall into two main groups. Hot or cold pressing adhesives. The same degree of heat required for hot pressing veneered panels would ruin a marquetry assembly. Cold pressing is always used.

The following is a list of adhesives for marquetry in order of preference. If you wish to pursue the subject of adhesives in greater detail in respect of hot pressing types of adhesives, such as epoxy resins, urea formaldehydes, melamine, phenol, resorcinol and various combinations; hot melts and glue films, etc., refer to *The Complete Manual of Wood Veneering* (Stobart & Son, Ltd, London).

COLD PRESSING ADHESIVES

Urea-formaldehyde

This is a pre-mixed powder of urea resin, plus catalyst, filler and flour extender, which is activated by the addition of water. It is a cold pressing type which relies on pressure alone until the glue has cured. It is non-staining and gap filling.
One pound of the mixture will cover about 30 sq. feet (lkg covers 6 sq. metres).

This type offers the greatest scope for enduring bonds under all conditions and the greatest resistance to heat, moisture and damage from other causes. Urea formaldehyde resins do not stain even the most delicate white veneers and possess tremendous resistance to changes in humidity and temperature extremes.

The most common fault with amateur marquetarians is to apply the adhesive too thickly, believing that the more that is applied, the better the resulting bond will be. The reverse is true. The recommended glue line is only five thousandths of an inch (0.127 mm) thin, and when this is exceeded the bond may crack and craze after curing.

To avoid this possibility, the product has been made gap-filling to make glue lines up to five hundredths of an inch (0.05mm) permissible without the danger of crazing. Once the bond has been made, it cannot be undone. It cannot be re-heated to repair blisters for instance.

Urea formaldehyde resin adhesives, with the water added according to the maker's instructions, have a pot life of only one hour. The ideal temperature of the workroom is 70°F (21°C) and after the application of the glue to the groundwork, allow ten minutes assembly time before applying pressure. The adhesive must be tacky to the touch before the press is tightened down and the press should be kept at room temperature for several hours for a perfect bond.

Warning: by increasing the press temperature the setting times can be drastically reduced to only four minutes at 200°F. (93°C). Never attempt this with a marquetry assembly as this heat will cause severe damage to the veneers.

The degree of heat cannot be compared to the little *gentle* heat, used in heated metal cauls in the press, which will draw the adhesive up into the pores of the veneer and reduce pressing time to four or five hours. The aim is to achieve absorption without penetration of the glue through to the veneer surface, which is why the *thinness* of the glueline is so important.

Polyvinyl Acetate adhesive (PVA)

As this 'white glue' is the first choice of the majority of marquetarians for edge-to-edge jointing of the assembly, many use it for laying the finished assembly. For amateur use for laying pictures which will be kept indoors at room temperature, PVA is ideal for another reason. If you have used diluted PVA as a size for flatting the veneers and for edge-to-edge butt-jointing the assembly, and also for making a woodfiller for the open joins on the back of the picture, when you use PVA also to lay the picture, all the adhesives used will be compatible and cause no problems.

Gluelines are invisible and PVA is non-staining. Brushes, equipment and hands may be cleaned with warm water.

It is used cold, undiluted, and is trouble free in application. The adhesive is an emulsion of particles of polymerised vinyl acetate in water, with the addition of plasticisers. The water disperses into the wood and the atmosphere leaving a thermo-plastic adhesive bond which has to remain under pressure until set. Extenders are added by the manufacturers to increase viscosity, thus preventing penetration but increasing spreadability.

There are various types of PVA, or white glue emulsions, available. Some contain a very low solid content in the emulsion. The danger with the *low solid* type is met when the veneer assembly is brought into contact with the adhesive before it has been allowed to tack and its high moisture content has had sufficient time to escape into the atmosphere. If the water content has subsequently to escape through the veneer pores, the veneers would absorb the water, and swell and then split when drying out. This must be avoided at all costs and could also lead to 'black-spot' problems.

Another problem with PVA is that the resulting bond is affected by moisture and humidity changes, excessive cold or some forms of stress.

Most PVA adhesives are non-waterproof. For this reason, PVA with high solid content is the best, such as *Evode Resin-W* and similar types specially formulated for woodworking, and they are also water resistant.

One advantage of cold pressing with white PVA glue is that if a blister should result, the glue may be re-heated and the offending blister relaid; however it has the disadvantage that the glueline is not gap filling, nor resistant to heat or moisture, or humidity changes.

PVA catalysed adhesive

Special formulations of PVA are also available which use a catalyst hardener to achieve a 'cross-linking' and speed up setting times when used with a heated press.

Gluelines are invisible, and PVA's are non-staining. Brushes, equipment and hands may be cleaned with warm water.

Aliphatic emulsions

Known as 'yellow-glue' to differentiate between the white PVA type, it is sold ready-mixed in cans and has a fast tack and short assembly time. It is a cream coloured ready to use resin adhesive of outstanding strength. It possesses the fast setting time and ease of use of white PVA, and has the tack, toughness and durability of liquid hide glue.

It is used at normal room temperature, and the panel may be pressed for two hours, before the panel is cleaned of squeeze-out. It is then returned to the press for twelve hours to cure.

For bonding backing veneers to very dense hardboard, chipboard and particle board surfaces, or for making corestock groundwork, sub-veneering, or applying edge lippings, it is superior to PVA.
It is not suitable for laying marquetry or parquetry as it has a tendency to stain light veneers.

Contact adhesives

There are two main types of contact adhesive, water based and solvent based. These synthetic or rubber based ahesives – often called 'impact' adhesives – rely on the volatile solvent evaporating into the atmosphere, and give off a heavy inflammable vapour, which must never be used near a naked flame, radiant fire, or pilot light etc. Good ventilation is essential.

The solvent based type is used for veneering as the volatile solvent evaporates into the atmosphere almost immediately. The water based type is never used for marquetry.

This material adheres to itself, therefore both surfaces have to be treated and allowed to dry before being brought together.

The 'thixotropic' type which is in the form of a gel for easy spreadability and allows sliding-time. These adhesives are ideal for specific adhesion as the two compatible gluelines adhere to themselves. The veneers may be applied to any type of *smooth*, clean surface, such as hardboard, chipboard. plastic sheets, metal or ceramics.

Marquetry assemblies can be applied around all types of shaped, curved or compound surfaces, or around corners, edges or places inaccessible to clamps or cauls. It is universally used for edge veneering, and for panel sizes too large for the home-made press.

Although these are excellent for veneering generally, especially for large surface areas which may be too large for your press, other types of adhesive are preferred for marquetry.

The glueline is slightly flexible, when cured, and it is advisable to provide panels laid with impact adhesive, with edge lipping or framing to avoid the veneers from lifting at the edges in the course of time.

The cured glue is 'rubbery' and the excess must be removed with solvent. Many finishing materials have solvents which penetrate through the veneer pores and may adversely affect contact adhesives. Test the intended finish on a scrap of veneer coated with contact adhesive.

These contact adhesives develop a strong bond with a shear strength in excess of 500 lbs p.s.i. (0.35 kg per sq. mm)

Liquid hide glue
This is sold in ready to use liquid form in cans and has the advantage that it may be used in a cold press without mixing. It is applied to the groundwork and allowed to tack before the veneer is brought into contact. The bond must remain under pressure for eight hours, with a further period for curing. The bond may be re-heated for the repair of blisters, but any further re-heating will deteriorate the bond. Flake white powder may be added, which will help to prevent surface discolouration due to glue penetration.

Fishglue
This is available either in liquid form in tubes, or in gel form in tins, and may also be used in a cold press and allowed to remain under pressure for 24 hours with a further period for curing. Further re-heating will deteriorate the bond.

Marquetry cement
Synthetic adhesives sold in tubes as 'Balsa cement' or 'Marquetry cement' are fast setting and have a restricted use for edge-to-edge assembly of marquetry pieces, mixing veneer dust to form a wood stopping for filling saw or knife cuts, or for inserting tiny pieces.

The early marquetry sets used these adhesives for the 'stick as you go' method, but its use has been superceded by PVA or impact adhesives.

Rubber cement
Known in the U.K. as 'Cow Gum', this artist's material is used for temporary adhesion only, such as fixing parts of the design on to the top of veneers for fretsawing, and for temporarily holding veneers together during the double cut, bevel cut and pad methods of fretsawing.

Another use is for the assembly of a picture to a thin card during the cleaning-up process (see Chapter 23).

After the cutting operation, the cement is easily rubbed with the fingers into a ball and removed without difficulty.

8
Tools, Presses & Equipment

THERE IS no such thing as the ideal marquetry knife. No two people can get the same results when using the same knife. They are personal tools, like pens. Each knife gives a different 'feel' and cut, from person to person.

Some people have a tight grip on the handle, others prefer to hold the knife more lightly. Others like to exert heavy pressure through their fingertips on the point of the knife without gripping the handle tightly; yet others like a long handled knife for balance and control.

The marquetarian should experiment and stock a few different types and use them according to the job in hand. There are a wide range of excellent commercial knives available.

Knives

The Swann-Morton craft knife has a small plastic handle with a knurled knob to tighten one of two blade-shapes, No.1, is straight and pointed, No.2 has a curved, rounded edge. Replacement blades 1 and 2 are sold separately in packs of 6. There is also a No. 3 hooked shape available.

This handle will also accomodate the specially fine pointed carbon steel surgical scalpel blades used by hospitals, of which the No.11 is the best shape for cutting intricate shapes and No.10a which is slightly wider for straightforward cutting, and the No.20 rounded blade which is useful as a scraper for removing tapes.

This is preferred to the surgeon's scalpel No.3, with nickel alloy handle, which leaves far too much of the blade exposed; when pressure is exerted the point of the blade may snap off. Much better for use with surgical blades is the round moulded nylon handle, circular in cross section, similar to the aluminium *Letraset* type, with a split chuck to grip the blades.

This means the blade position within the handle is variable and it can be gripped with only the cutting point protruding. It gives far greater rigidity (compared to the surgeon's scalpel handle), and enables greater pressure to be applied, safely.

Many marquetarians prefer to make their own knives.An engineer's high speed hacksaw blade, broken in half, with the teeth filed off, and a 45 degree or 60 degree cutting angle ground, sharpened and honed on the oilstone.

The blade is fitted into a hardwood handle into which a suitable sawcut has been made to receive the blade. The sawcut should only be $\frac{7}{8}$ths of the way through the handle. Drill through the handle and blade and secure with two rivets or countersunk bolts.

The end of the handle is then shaped to form a rounded knob – called a 'rubber' – which is used to 'rub-down' veneer joints on the underlaying veneer tapes, or small fragments of veneer which might lift or tear at the joins, or to coax small marquetry pieces into tight fitting assemblies.

The knife handle should cover and protect the back of the blade, with only the tip or point of the blade protruding.

Remember, it is the *width* of the hacksaw blade that provides the knife with its strength, so file away only the end of the blade at an oblique angle to a fine point to enable the maximum amount of pressure to be applied safely.

The single wane knife

When trimming veneers along the grain for jointing, the knife point wants to 'wander' in the grain of certain veneers like wengé. A long blade, *without* a cutting angle, and with one bevel ground and honed to one side only, will sever several thickness with a shearing motion, when the flat edge is held vertically against a straightedge.

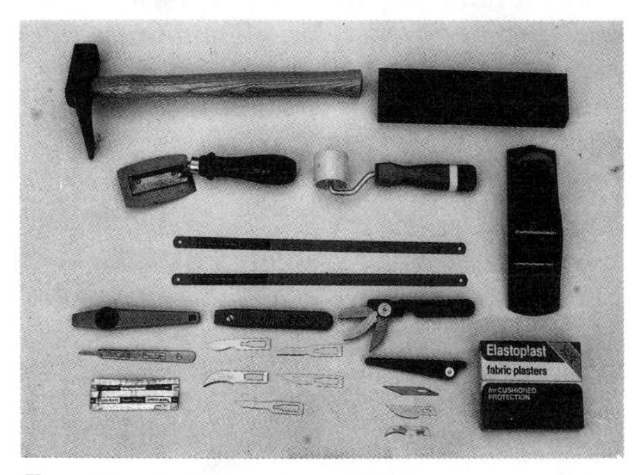

Fig. 39 A beginner's tool-kit

Sharpening stone

The ideal combination of stones for keeping the edges razor sharp, is a soft Arkansas medium stone to start the edge, and a hard fine stone to finish the honing. These stones actually polish the cutting edge as they sharpen and are used with plenty of oil.

Combination carborundum oilstones are another useful alternative, size 8 × 2 × 1 (204 × 50 × 25mm), with one side coarse and the other fine.

The rubberised *Craftex* 6 × 1 × $\frac{1}{8}$ inch (150 × 25 × 3mm) sharpening stone requires no oil or water.

Japanese water stones are also available. These man-made stones are manufactured from extremely tough abrasive material fused together under high temperature. They will cut faster and give a finer edge than most oilstones. They are simply soaked in water prior to use and can be re-surfaced by rubbing the stone on a sheet of 320 grit silicon carbide paper and water.

Sharpening and honing stick

This is home-made from a piece of $\frac{3}{8}$ or $\frac{1}{2}$ inch (9 or 12mm) plywood or hardwood, about 15 × 2 inch (380 × 50mm) wide. The actual dimensions are not important. Cover the stick with an abrasive paper.

Carborundum paper, emery, *Lubrisil* silicon carbide, garnet, or aluminium oxide paper can be used, in that order of preference, but glass paper or sandpaper are both unsuitable as they are too soft.

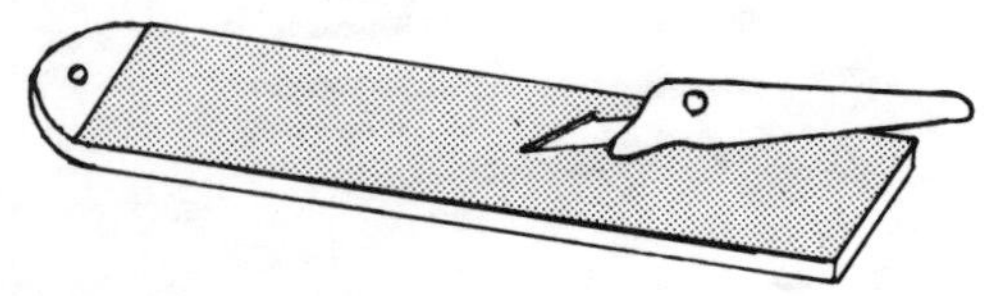

Fig. 40 A sharpening stick

Glue coarse 80 grit (or any coarse grade up to 150 grit) to one side and 220 to 320 fine grit to the reverse. The tip of the knife is kept very sharply honed on the smooth side. If the tip becomes worn or blunt, extend the blade from the handle as far as it will protrude when tightened, and draw the back of the knife blade along the coarse side of the sharpening stick, towards you in long strokes, with firm pressure, with the knife held at a low angle.

If the tip of the blade snaps off it can be re-ground on the stick to a new sharp point. Then honed razor sharp on the smooth side.

Cutting board

This is another home-made tool and can be made from a panel of blockboard 16 × 14 × $\frac{5}{8}$ inch thick (410 × 355 × 15mm). True the edges square, then pin and glue three strips 12 × $\frac{1}{2}$ × $\frac{1}{4}$ inch (305 × 12 × 6mm) to three edges, leaving a 2 inch (50mm) gap at each corner. Face with a vinyl tile or lino to save knife point. Fix another batten below to stop any movement, and so form a bench hook.

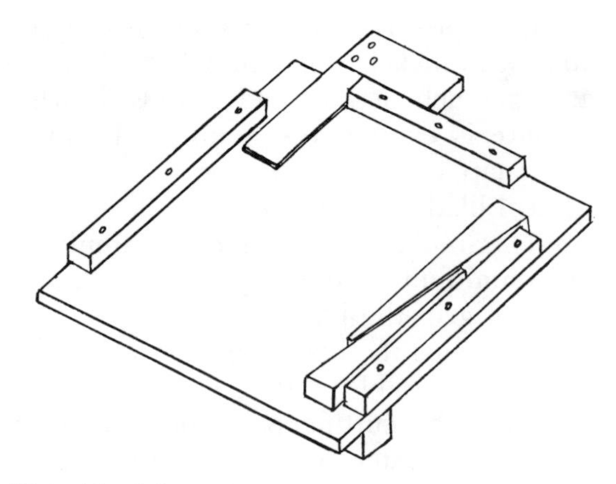

Fig. 41 The cutting board

The straightedge can be positioned through the 2 inch (50mm) gaps for perfect right angles when trimming off surplus veneer.

Cutting mats

These mats have a semi-hard rubber-like surface which allows the knife to bite into it – but the cut 'disappears' almost at once, as the mat 'self-heals'. Excessive pressure with heavy duty knives will cause permanent damage, but in normal use the mats will last for years. Two metric sizes are available, 450 × 300 mm or 600 × 450 mm.

Measuring instruments

Rulers

Use a ruler for measuring or lining up mitres, but never use a ruler to cut a straight line in a marquetry picture. There are three basic types.

1. *Sten-edge* rulers, are made of clear perspex but with a stainless steel edge bonded to them. Set squares are also made. This transparent plastic type of ruler is useful for checking vanishing points for perspective, source of light and shadow angles, etc; also for accurately spacing similar objects in perspective, in addition to cutting border mitres.

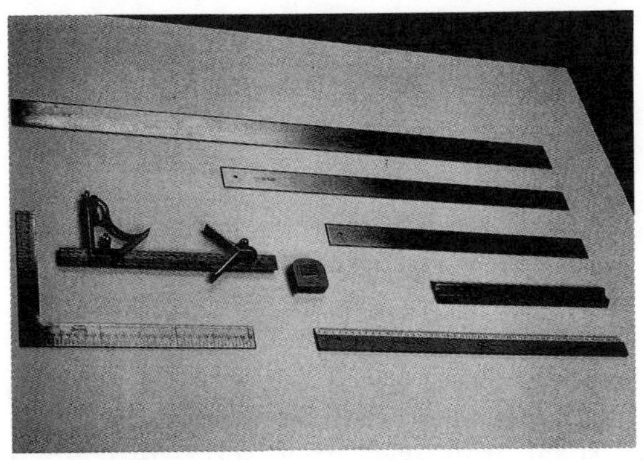

Fig. 42 Measuring instruments

2. *Maun* non-slip safety ruler, is pressed from sheet steel, and has an 'M' shaped section so that downward pressure anchors the ruler and prevents it from slipping. They are available in bright polished finish and graduated in inches and centimetres.

It is used outside the picture area for trimming off the surplus, applying the fillet strip and border surrounds, mitring the corners, and jointing the back.

3. Aluminium straightedges

This type are 300 mm long with a white edge graduated in millimetres and has a non-slip back. One edge is accurately squared for use as a cutting edge.

4. Steel straightedges

Flat straightedges of heavy duty steel with accurately machined smooth edges are available and I prefer these to the 'non-slip' type.

For pictorial marquetry an 18 inch (460mm) or a 24 inch (600mm) would be sufficient to cover most requirements. The thickness of the straightedge varies according to its length. Never use a wooden or plastic ruler as the knife will cut into it.

Cutting instruments

Veneer saw

This is widely used in America for cross-cutting 0.9mm thick veneers. There are two basic types.

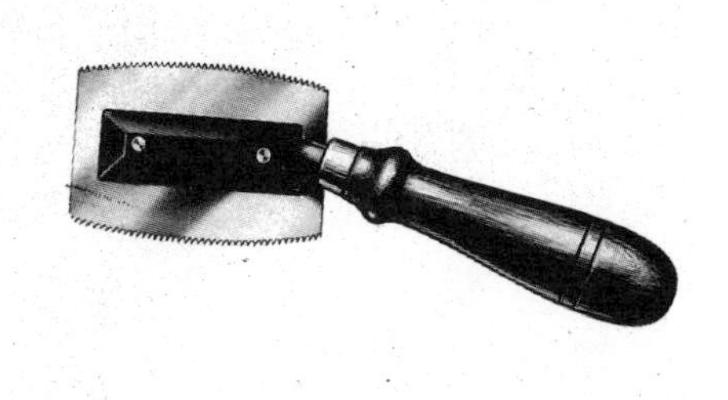

Fig. 43 A doubled edged veneer saw

One has a wooden saw-handle grip with a curved steel saw blade fixed to one face and with teeth pointing inwards from each end, and in the middle there is a single central tooth. When the veneers are compressed under a batten on the shooting board, the saw is rocked backwards and forwards and a clean, straight cut results.

The other has a 3 inch (75mm) blade screwed to a wooden tool handle, with different sized teeth on each edge. The blade is reversible to suit cutting with or across the grain. The saws have no set on the teeth to provide perfectly square edges suitable for jointing.

Cutting gauge

The gauge is used to cut a parallel line exactly true to the edge of the finished panel in order that the surplus veneer can be removed and the border veneers fitted accurately. The best types have brass strips on the face slide, and are adjustable up to about 6 inches (150mm)

Mortise gauge

This has two knives which can be adjusted to make a double cut of any width, and is ideal for both marking and cutting veneer to receive inlay lines, stringings or bandings. These should also have brass inlaid faces strips to prevent wear.

Veneer hammer
Another home-made tool made to any convenient size. It is not used like a hammer but like a squeegee. It is used for hand veneering of panels without pressure.

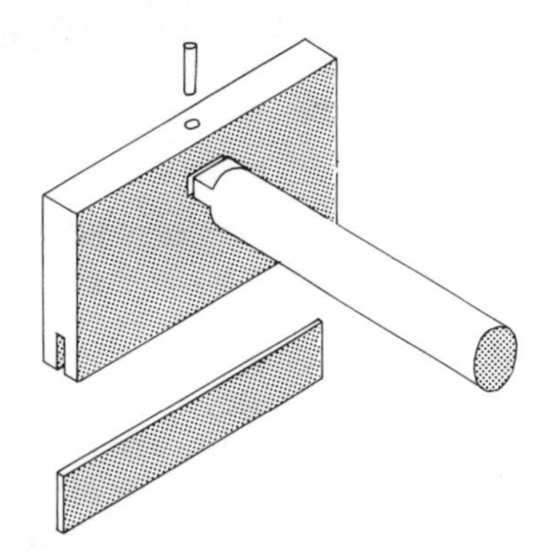

Fig. 44 Home-made veneer hammer

Scratch stock
This is a simple, home-made tool for cutting the grooves to accomodate inlay lines or bandings. It is made from two pieces of hardwood or plywood 6 × 3 × $\frac{3}{4}$ inch (152 × 76 × 19mm) screwed together with a

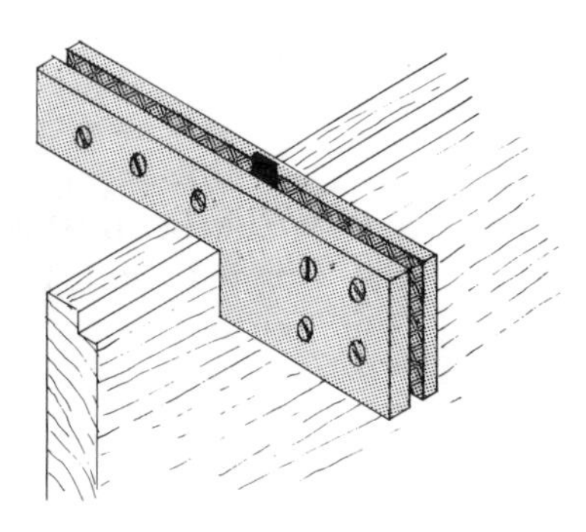

Fig. 45 Home-made scratch stock

notch cut out in both pieces to form a fence or shoulder.

The two pieces enclose a steel cutter, filed from a hacksaw blade, which is filed up square on all faces and edges to the exact width of the strip to be inlaid. (See Chapter 18 for methods of use.)

Small bullnose rabbet plane
Used when a square inlay line is to be inlaid on an edge. The cutting gauge is used in both width and depth dimensions and the waste removed with a rabbet plane.

Toothing plane.
This is a wooden plane with an almost vertical iron with tiny serrated teeth at the cutting edge. It is used for levelling groundwork prior to laying.

Ulmia 1061 Prepared scraper blade.
The veneer scraper is a rectangular flat steel blade about $4\frac{1}{2}$ × $2\frac{1}{2}$ inch (114mm × 63mm) with the long edges burred over to form a cutting edge. This is an indispensable tool for removing veneer tape, levelling the back of the picture and finishing the surface.

Ulmia Scraper Burnisher
A special tool which enables an absolutely even cutting edge to be formed on an ordinary steel scraper blade. The wooden handle contains a pivoting steel disc, with an angle section of steel with a recessed corner to protect the formed cutting edge.

Ulmia 1067 Scraper blade sharpener.
A triangular tool for restoring the cutting edge of a scraper without having to reform the edges. (See Chapter 23 for a full description of scraper technique.)

Fluorescent Illuminated Magnifiers

An essential piece of equipment. It provides an exceptionally good light to work in, plus excellent magnification. The viewing head is illuminated with a 22 watt 'cool' fluorescent tube. The standard lens is moulded from high impact strength ABS polymer and fitted with a hinged lens cover.

Fig. 46 Toothing plane

Fig. 47 A selection of cramps

A typical U.K. make is the 'Luxo' with specifications as follows:

Focal length 13 inch (330mm); magnification 3/4× (times larger than the object appears to the naked eye). Lens diameter 5 inch (127mm).

The head is mounted on a spring balanced parallel movement arm, fitted in a bench clamp. An auxilliary clip-on 7 diopter lens can be supplied with a 5½ inch (140mm) focal length and with 1.3/4× *Coil* aspheric magnifiers.

These eliminate the image defects of ordinary magnifiers and give a flat image free from distortion edge to edge. They are available for hand use, chest, fixed or flexible stand, or adjustable with magnification, illuminated etc. up to 3×.

PRESSES AND CLAMPS

'G' clamps

Ideal for clamping together heated cauls in the flatting process; holding steel straightedges in place when making joints; holding the cutting table to the workbench.

Also for clamping heated wooden blocks for the repair of blisters.They are available from 2 inch (50mm) upwards.

Marquetry Presses

The minimum pressure required for laying veneers is between 15lb/p.s.i., (1.05kg/cm^2) (the approximate pressure of a vacuum press) and 30lb/p.s.i., (2.10kg/cm^2) although commercial screw presses operate at 60lb/p.s.i. (4.21kg/cm*2*)

For laminating curved and compound work, pressures from 150 to 300lb/p.s.i., (10.54kg/cm*2* to 21.09lb/cm*2*) are required. Translated into practical terms for pictorial marquetry panels, based on the 15lbs/p.s.i. minimum, a 10 × 8 inch (250 × 200mm) picture would require over half a ton (0.5 tonnes) of pressure, and a panel of 24 × 18 inches (610 × 460mm) would require 2.89 tons (2.93 tonnes). It is obviously impossible

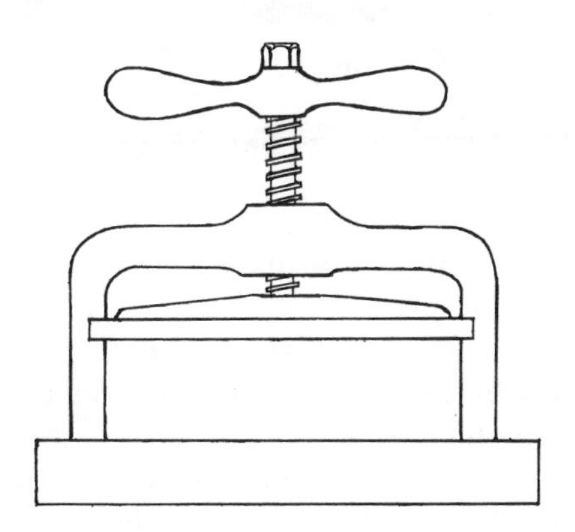

Fig. 48 A book press

to exert that much pressure by placing the panel under say, a pile of books!

There are suitable presses available for all veneering needs. Many marquetarians acquire old book presses with a central screw of the type found in solicitor's offices. These may be extended to take longer pictures by using angle iron on top and bottom of the two pressing cauls, aided by G-clamps placed at intervals.

Simple home-made press

A press of this type should be large enough to cover most requirements of flatting veneers and laying marquetry pictures, but the dimensions can be increased or reduced to suit your own purpose. (See Chapter 25 on Laying, for details of construction.)

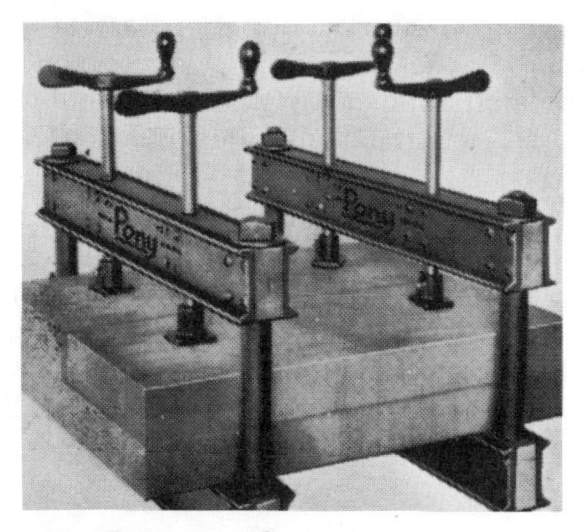

Fig. 49 Pony press frames

PONY PRESS FRAMES AND SCREWS

Convenient ready-made press frames are also available, complete with Jorgensen cold-drawn steel press screws. The inside width of these frames is 18 inches (457mm), inside height 6 inches (150mm), screw diameter 11/16 inches (17mm). There are two screws per frame, and the total weight of frame with screws is 36lbs (16 kilos).

Fig. 50 Jorgensen press screws

Two such frames have a capacity of 18 inches by 18 inches (457 × 457mm) panel size, sufficient for most picture needs.

Jorgensen Press screws

These cold-drawn steel press screws $\frac{11}{16}$ inch (17mm) diameter, are available separately, in 9 inch (228mm), 12 inch (304mm) and 18 inch (457mm) lengths.

The size of your panels will decide the dimensions of your frame members, the quantity, diameter and length of the Jorgensen press screws.

For every 9 inches (228mm) of work *width* you require one press screw in each frame. And for every 9 inches (228mm) of *length* you require one complete frame. The height of the side members of your home-made press is governed by the distance the screw will travel through the top cross member, plus the thickness of the work panel to be pressed, the press bed, and the cauls.

Hydraulic Car Jack Press

Many marquetarians make an excellent home-made press by using a three ton car jack, which would cover most marquetry needs, as originally mentioned in *The Art & Practice of Marquetry* in 1971.

Fig. 51 Pressing a larger panel with Jorgensen press screws

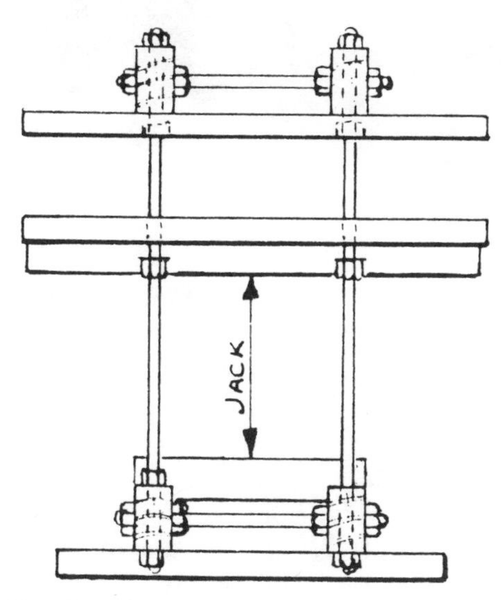

Fig. 52 Hydraulic car jack

The drawings are reproduced here by kind permission of the Editor of *The Woodworker*, which contained full constructional details in the December 1983 issue, from an article by Ernie Ives, editor of *The Marquetarian*.

The illustrated car jack was made by Peter White of the Marquetry Society, to whom acknowledgments are also due.

Cutting list

1. Bearers. (Hardwood)
   4 off 24 × 3 × 2 inch
   (600 × 76 × 50mm)
2. Cauls. (Blockboard)
   2 off 24 × 20 × 1¼ inch
   (600 × 508 × 31mm)
3. Top pad. (Hardwood)
   1 off 20 × 6 × 1¼ inch
   (508 × 150 × 31 mm)
4. Bottom pad. (Hardwood)
   1 off 11 × 8 × 1½ inch
   (280 × 202 × 37 mm)
5. Feet. (Hardwood)
   2 off 16 × 2½ × 1¼ inch
   (404 × 63 × 31 mm)
6. Uprights. (BSF/BSW Steel studding
   4 off 24 × ½ inch
   (600 × 12 mm)
7. Crossties (BSF/BSW Steel studding)
   4 off 12 × ½ inch (300 × 12 mm)
8. 3 dozen nuts and washers to suit the steel studding.

Tapes

Veneering tape
Special ½ inch (12mm) tape is available which is extra thin and double gummed, and will not leave a residue when removed. This 'friction' tape will stretch slightly when rubbed and will exert a pull on the joints as it dries.

It is cut into 'straps' about 4 inch (100mm) long, and applied across the joints to pull them tightly together, then applied along the length of the joint as a 'hinge' tape to enable matched pairs of veneers to be folded.

Protective tape
Stronger brown paper parcel tape, in 1inch (25mm) widths is applied to the ends of veneer in storage to prevent splitting in handling.

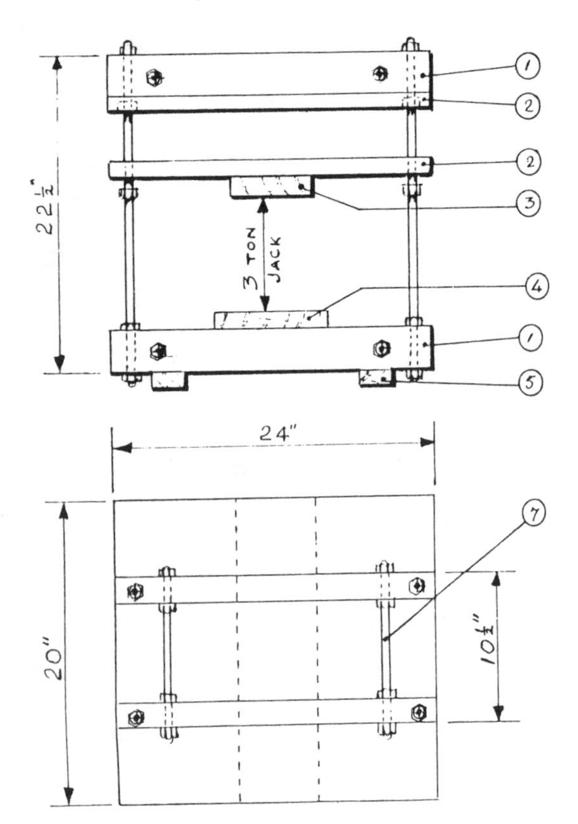

Fig. 53 Car jack press dimensions
(For key to numbers used see p. 65 Cutting list)

Fig. 54 Front view of car jack

Location tape
Applied across the grain of a veneer before it is cut through to ensure a clean cut without splintering. The tape is about 1½ inch to 2 inches (38 to 50mm) wide. Edges

Fig. 55 Side view of car jack

Fig. 56 Rear view of car jack

to be cut after the panel is laid are also taped, or where possible splits are anticipated when laying curls, or in shaped veneering.

Masking tape
Available in various stretch and strength categories. It is used as a temporary hold only and is immediately replaced with veneer or protection tape. If allowed to remain, it leaves a residue which will form into balls and tear the grain when sanded.

Pressure sensitive tape
The familiar transparent type of Sellotape in ½ inch (12mm) widths. There are various types. The 3M type (sold in Woolworths) is less fierce and easier to remove. Some brands leave a stubborn residue.

It is used for hinging the design to the waster, and also used as a temporary hold in small ½ inch (12mm) squares to hold tiny inserts in the assembly, until it can be removed and replaced with paper tape. All traces of this tape must be removed either with a touch from the tip of a domestic iron, or with lacquer solvent or lighter fuel.

Double-sided self-adhesive tape
As sold in most stationers shops for repairing books or albums. Also available in the form of plastic sheets. It is used for fastening over a design for the assembly of parquetry components.

Tweezers
One pair of fine-point and a pair of flat-point tweezers are useful when locating tiny fragments of veneer into the assembly, or holding veneer parts for sand-shading when immersing the shaped veneer into the hot sand. And for removing splinters!

Brushes

A medium size glue brush, (available in sizes from 6 up to 24) and a natural hair mop brush for applying the polish will be required.

Avoid synthetic bristle brushes. A decorator's soft brush for keeping the work free from sanding dust and the cutting board from grit and veneer splinters and fragments.

A comprehensive list of veneering tools, equipment and presses etc. (with a chapter on low voltage heating) including full instructions for the construction of the Jorgensen press, is featured in *The Complete Manual of Wood Veneering* (Stobart & Son Ltd).

9
Knife Cutting Techniques

THE BEST and most inexpensive way to start marquetry is with a beginner's kit. Any make of commercial kit will do.

The one I've chosen is generally available and has proved very popular. You will also find a 'Test Piece' supplied with the kit, which will enable you to practice many of the cutting techniques you are likely to meet in marquetry, before attempting the kit.

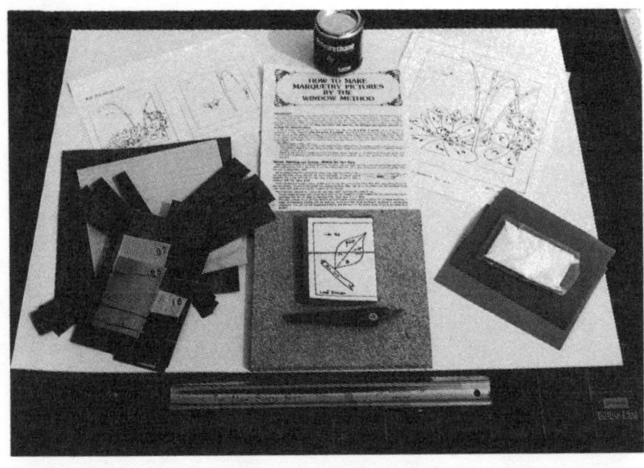

Fig. 57 Marquetry kit 'Evening on the Broads' including the 'Test Piece'

The only other items you'll need are a reel of Sellotape, a ruler and a small carborundum stone.

Anything else are items normally found around the home, such as the domestic electric iron or rolling pin.

I'll make you a promise. If you persevere through the following chapters of this book, step by step, you will learn all the 'tricks of the trade' to equip you to become a competent marquetarian.

You'll learn that marquetry is not so much a challenge of your skill and patience, but more a matter of 'know-how' and technique which will enable you to discover your hidden talent for creating pictures of enduring beauty from natural, rare and exotic wood veneers.

If you prefer to buy a different kit, simply copy this illustration of the test piece and obtain a leaf of two contrasting veneers such as sycamore and walnut from your veneer supplier.

'Getting Started'

We are going to learn the "Window Method" – the traditional knife-cutting technique of creating marquetry pictures, adopted and taught by the Marquetry Society, which has enabled thousands of amateur craftsmen and women to take their first steps in this rewarding craft.

The name is derived from the simple process of cutting a hole or 'window' in a soft 'waster' veneer, which then acts as a templet for cutting the veneer required to fill it.

Before we start you will need a suitable surface to cut upon. The ideal surface should be firm but soft to enable you to keep a sharp point on the knife.

Suitable cutting surfaces are, in order of preference, a vinyl floor tile, lino, thick cardboard, or plywood. Do not use chip-board as the resin in the surface blunts the knife.

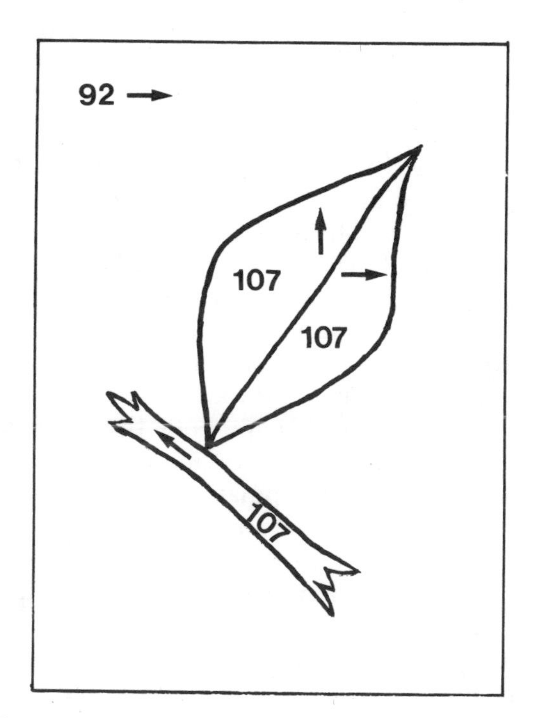

Fig. 58 The Test Piece

This apparently simple leaf design has been carefully contrived to introduce you to various cutting skills which you will encounter when we work together on 'Evening on the Broads'

Just imagine that I'm sitting at your elbow as you read and work your way through this test piece. I'll try to anticipate your questions and provide the answers and, from time to time, I'll ask you to stop for a moment while I explain some critical point for you to watch before you continue.

Begin by fastening the design like a hinge to the top edge of the white sycamore veneer,

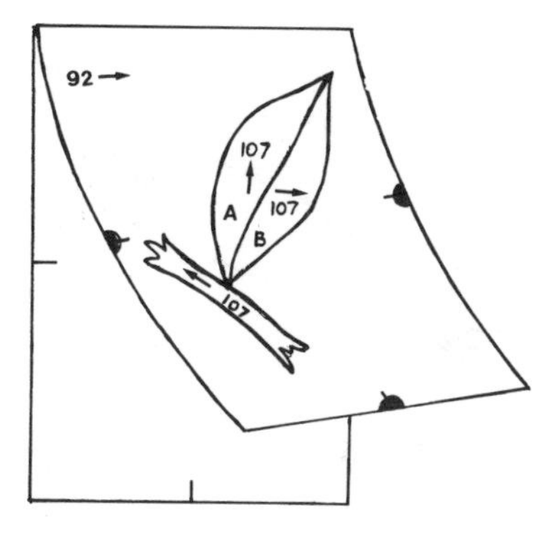

Fig. 59 Registration marks on design taped to the waster veneer

with a piece of Sellotape. Using the black carbon paper and a sharp pencil, make a mark or short registration line at the bottom

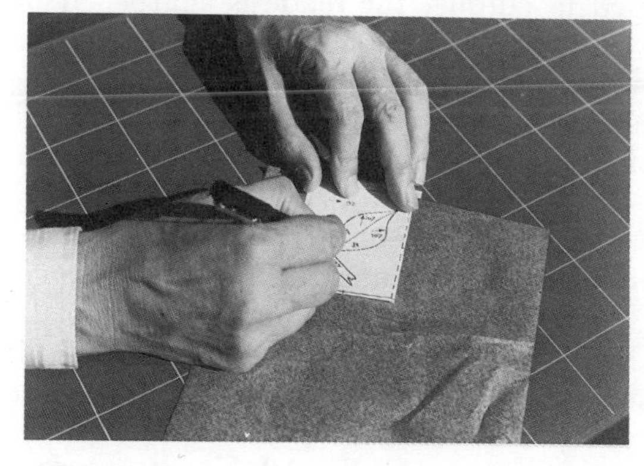

Fig. 60 Trace the design to the white veneer

of the design to ensure correct alignment as work proceeds, as shown in Fig.59.

Now trace the outline of the leaf design on to the sycamore veneer, as shown in Fig.60.

When assembling the Swann-Morton craft knife, (which is included with the kit), note that the clamp screw in the plastic handle does not go through the slot in the blade. The blade passes between the screw and the rounded back of the handle and is held in position by tightening the clamp screw.

For accurate cutting it is essential to use a very sharp blade and to sharpen the blade

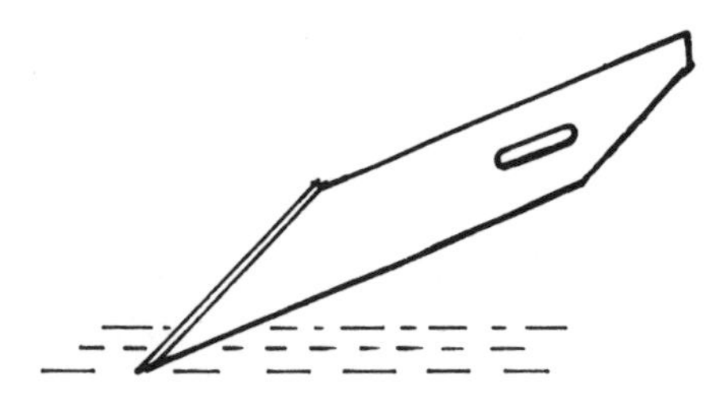

Fig. 61 Sharpen the back of the blade

point frequently. *You will rarely cut yourself when using a very sharp knife.* Only when the knife edge is blunt and cannot bite into the wood fibres, is it likely to slip on the surface. So keep the blade razor sharp at all times.

Since it is the tip of the blade that is mostly used in cutting, the blade is sharpened by wearing away the back of the blade on an oilstone or sharpening stick. This moves the cutting tip progressively further down the blade, as shown in Fig.61.

It is also a good idea to have a piece of candle at hand, and occasionally draw the knife across it to lubricate the cutting edge.

Before we actually commence cutting the veneer, remove the carbon paper and lift and fold the design back. Place the white veneer on the cutting surface ready to make your first cut, as in Fig. 63. Now let's pause

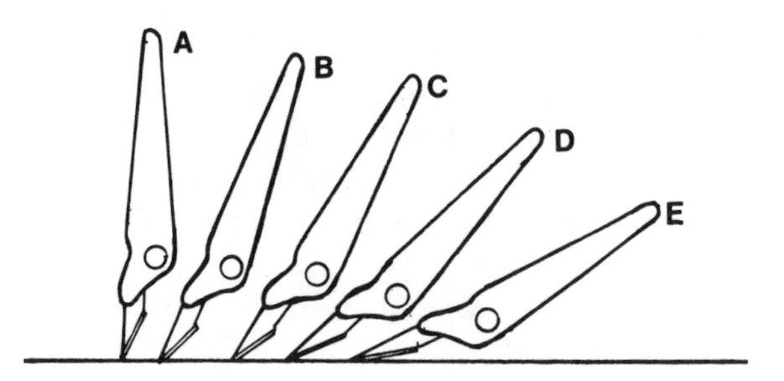

Fig. 62 The five knife positions A to E

for a moment because I want to explain something about the use of the knife in marquetry.

A is the **stab-cut**, B is the **step-cut**, C is the **sweep-cut**, D is the **score-cut** and E is the **straight-cut**.

Remember these catchwords *Long and low!* The longer the cut the lower the blade. The shorter the cut, the higher the knife handle is raised.

I call them the five 'S' cuts, to make them easy to remember. Let's see how each of these special cutting techniques is used.

The score-cut (D)

This is the first type of cut you will make. It is a very light tracing cut made without any pressure. The idea is to ensure that you have a clearly visible outline marked on the surface of the veneer to establish the line. A 'tramline' to run the knife along.

Rest the wrist comfortably on the cutting board and check that the knife is held square to the workpiece. Don't hold the knife as you would a pen. Learn to roll the wrist over slightly. Manipulate the knife with controlled short finger movements, turning the workpiece towards the knife so that all the cutting is done by drawing the knife towards you.

If you commence cutting at a point furthest away from you, it is likely that your hand will obscure your line of vision.

Fig. 63 Cutting a window in the waster

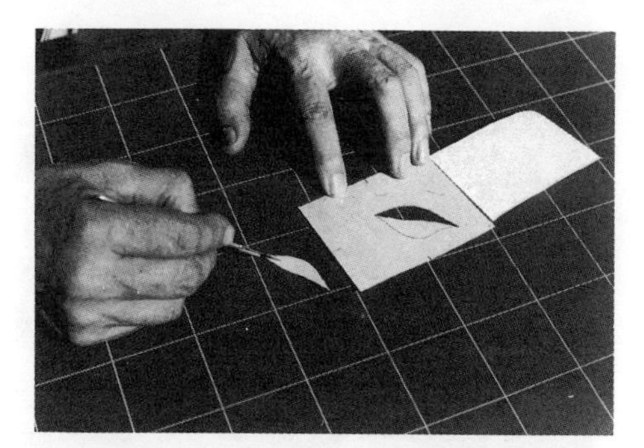

Fig. 64 First section of the leaf removed

Fig. 65 The walnut veneer beneath the window

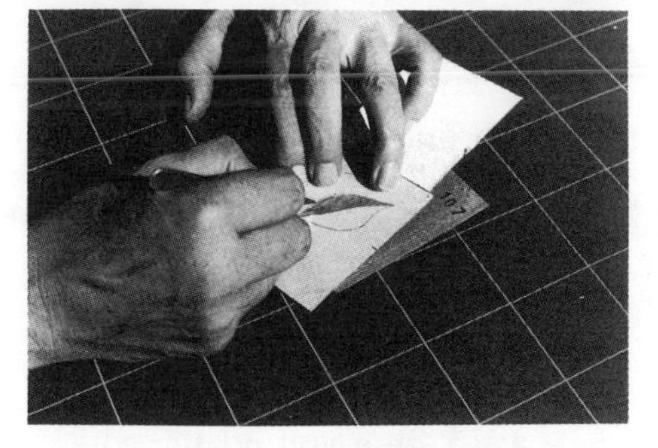

Fig. 66 Scoring the outline to be cut

Position the veneer so that you have a clear view of the line.

Carefully work around the outline of one half of the leaf shape, shown as A in the white sycamore veneer. *Lightly!* Not a deep, heavy cut. Don't try to cut the veneer out with one cut – only just enough to mark it.

Try to keep accurately to the traced design line.

The sweep-cut (C)

The second type of cut is also used without heavy pressure. This is used to cut the gently curving half-leaf outline and the centre line. These simple flowing lines can be cut in one continuous sweep of the knife.

Gently does it. Coax the outline by making two or three stroking cuts with the handle raised slightly. It is better to use several contolled strokes with light pressure than try to sever the fibres of the veneer with one heavy cut.

Fig.64 shows the 'window' or hole cut in the white sycamore veneer and the half-leaf discarded.

Now place the dark walnut veneer underneath the hole and arrange the 'flow' of the grain in the direction shown by the arrow on the pattern to obtain the correct leaf effect as in Fig.65. When you are satisfied with the position of the darker veneer, hold both veneers firmly and turn them over face down on to the cutting surface.

Temporarily fasten them together with a small piece of Sellotape to avoid movement during the next score-cut. Mark the outline shape of the half-leaf accurately on to the surface of the dark walnut veneer, by running the knife point carefully around the edge of the hole, using it as a templet with another light tracing score-cut, as in Fig.66.

If you look at the pointed ends of the leaf design you will see that the grain tapers to a fine point. There may be a tendency for the veneer to split and break away there due to the short cross grain. To avoid this, cover each pointed end of the half-leaf shape with a piece of Sellotape.

The heavily scored shape and the pencilled line clearly show where to affix the tape and also assists the subsequent knife cut. It is a good idea to fasten a 6 inch (150mm) strip of Sellotape on the cutting board, and cut it through into ½ inch (12mm) pieces.

Cut through the tape and separate the two veneers. place the dark walnut veneer on the cutting surface

The next cut will be made through the veneer and taped together so that the tape reinforces the wood. This will help prevent the cross grain from splitting, or if it does, will hold the fragments together safely, as in Fig.67.

Now pause again. This time we are going to use another type of cut.

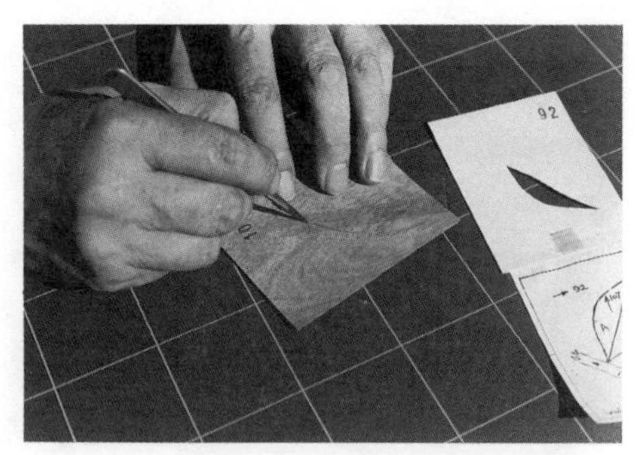

Fig. 67 Cutting the shape on the cutting mat

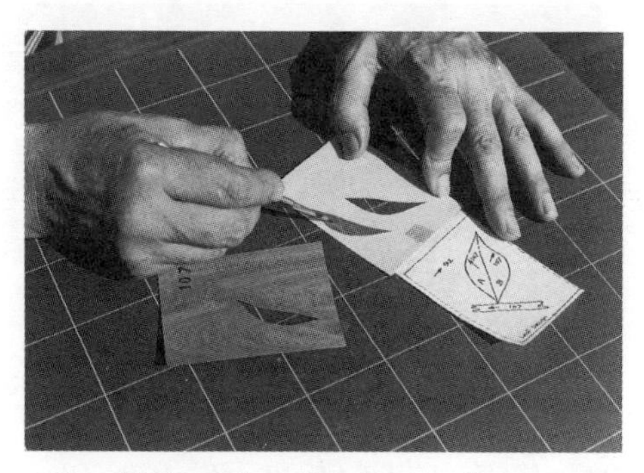

Fig. 68 Fitting the shape into the waster

Fig. 69 Step cuts being made in the waster

The step-cut (B)

This is used when you encounter a veneer which is hard to cut or a design outline which has sharp or twisting curves. Break this down into a series of short cutting movements with pauses between them. This gives far better directional control and produces a smooth cutting line.

The step-cut is made in short steps of about ½ inch (12mm) each. Slightly raise the knife handle to a higher position and make a series of small step cuts towards you, pausing between them, and then repeat the process. As shown in Fig.69.

Now work over the step-cuts for the second time linking them together by cutting from the middle of one cut to the middle of the next.

See how the work is turned so that all cutting is done towards you.

Using a combination of the step-cuts and the sweep-cut, coax out section A of the dark veneer. Now pierce a fine hole with a pin through one of the two shaped corners of the sachet of PVA adhesive, and squeeze the sachet carefully to exude a small bead of glue. After use, the pinhole seals with glue making the sachet air tight, ensuring the adhesive doesn't harden.

With a sliver of veneer, smear a few spots of white PVA glue around the edges of the dark walnut half-leaf and insert it into the hole in the white sycamore.

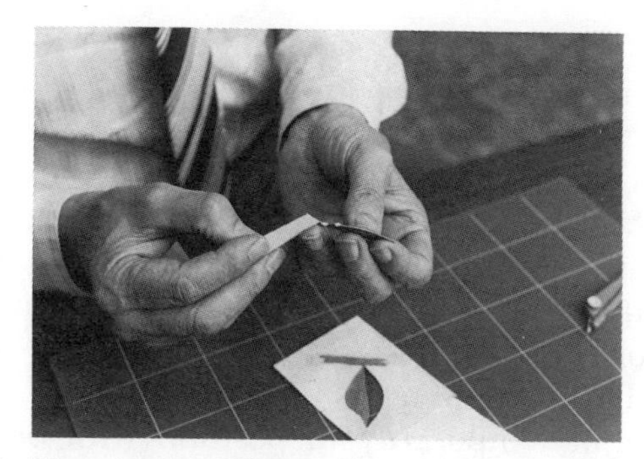

Fig. 70 Apply PVA to the edges

Fig. 71 Rub the joint with the knife handle

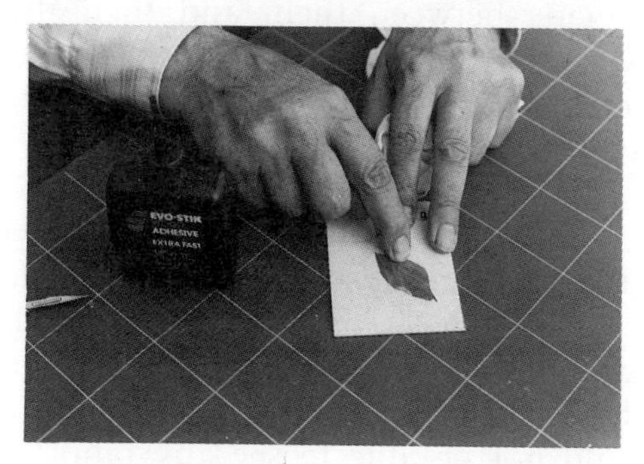

Fig. 72 Clean the face side of PVA glue

It should be a tight fit. Coax it gently into position by rubbing around the join with the rounded end of the knife handle. Also squeeze a small dob of white PVA adhesive into the join on the back side of the test piece, rubbing it gently into the join all around with your finger-tip until the surface is almost dry to the touch.

The glue is water soluble and will wash off your fingers. The first piece of the pattern has now been butt-jointed into the assembly edge to edge. Clean off any traces of glue from both sides of the veneer and leave this to dry for about five minutes.

Now repeat the process with the other half of the leaf marked B, by making a light score-cut into the white sycamore veneer. Cut out the half-leaf shape from this as in Fig.69. For ease of illustration I have indicated a series of step-cuts which show up better on the white sycamore veneer.

Position the walnut veneer under the 'window' as before and notice that the grain direction has changed for side B. Arrange the walnut in its required direction and turn the two veneers over to secure them temporarily with Sellotape.

Make a score-cut into the walnut and follow up with a very sharply pointed H pencil. Work around the score-cut outline again to indicate where to affix the protective strip of Sellotape, at each end of the pointed leaf shape, as in Fig.70.

Separate the two veneers and cut out the shape using short step-cuts, taking special care at the two ends, cutting from the tip of the leaf point towards you. Apply white PVA glue around the edges of the leaf; insert the piece into the window and rub gently around the join with the smooth rounded end of the knife.

If necessary, rub in some more adhesive with the finger tips. Clean off any traces of PVA from both sides of the leaf. Now put the test piece aside under a light weight and wait for it to dry for a few minutes.

While it is drying let me explain about the stab-cut

The stab-cut (A)

This fourth type of cut is used for small, intricate jagged points, complex shapes, or on very hard woods. This time the knife handle is held almost vertically. The shape is cut out by stabbing or pricking through

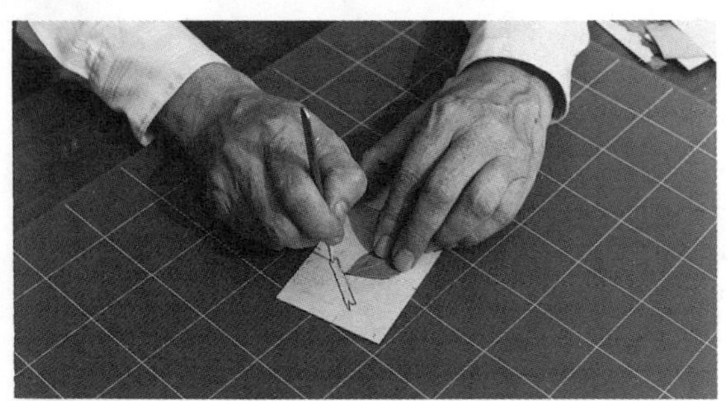

Fig. 73 Using a combination of stab-cuts and step-cuts to cut around the ends

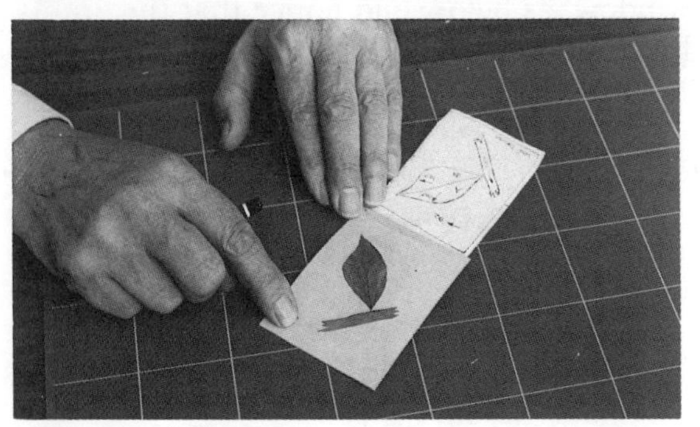

Fig. 74 The stem in position

the veneer with the sharp tip of the knife blade.

With each stroke, jab through the veneer; withdraw and move a fraction along the line and stab through again. A continuous cut is now made by linking together a series of overlapping stab-cuts.

When making a stab-cut it is good practice to cover the cutting line in the veneer with Sellotape to control cracking or splitting of any cross-grained fibres and to retain the small detail or tiny fragments.

We will use the stab-cut on the next part of the test piece.

First, re-sharpen the point of the knife, and begin by tracing the outline of the stem on the white veneer, taking care to ensure correct alignment of the registration marks, as shown in Fig.73. Then make a light score-cut. Now use a sweep-cut along the two sides of the stem. Put a small piece of Sellotape across each end of the stem where there are jagged points to cut out in case cross-grained pieces break off.

Use a combination of stab-cuts and step-cuts to cut around the ends and remove the stem. Position the walnut beneath the window and align the grain direction as shown by the design arrow.

Turn the veneers over and fasten the walnut temporarily in position with Sellotape. Now flip the veneers over and make a score-cut around the hole as before and mark with the hard pencil.

Separate the two veneers and cover the ends of the stem outline with Sellotape to prevent losing tiny fragments. Sharpen the knife point on the stone again.

Now for the tricky bit! Start at the end of the stem furthest away from you. Don't let your wrist obscure the line to be cut and begin with stab-cuts from a pointed tip of the stem, cutting towards you.

Turn the work around when you cut the other end. Link these stab-cuts with more stab-cuts between them and then slightly lower the knife's attitude to make a few linking step-cuts. Don't apply pressure, just keep the tip of the knife sharpened and coax the shape out.

Again, apply white PVA glue to the edges of the stem and insert it into the assembly. Rub it into position with the rounded end of the knife.

Hold the test piece up to the light. You should not be able to see any pinpricks of light or open joints around the shapes you have inserted. Rub a little more PVA into the joints with the fingertip. If you can see any open joints or bad cutting, and you have any part of the walnut veneer you can use to try again, remove the offending part and cut a replacement.

Now you can see why I wanted you to practise your cutting skills on a test piece rather than on your first kit. There's still one more cut you have to meet.

The straight-cut (E)

This is the last of the five basic cutting techniques and is used for trimming straight edges on veneers for jointing.

Hold the knife blade as low as possible against a straightedge. Place it across the top of the white veneer and after a score-cut to establish the line, make a straight-cut, with one or two light strokes to sever the Sellotaped design from the veneer.

When the test piece is dry and cleaned of all traces of glue and Sellotape, place it under a light weight such a book, to keep it flat, until we learn how to cut the central vein into the leaf with a fine sliver-cut.

In addition to the five "S" knife positions (stab, step, sweep, score and straight) you have already practised, we now meet a few more.

Vertical cutting

Most knives have blades which have a double wane or bevel. Fig.75 shows what happens to a veneer when the knife cuts through it. The wood fibres are pushed aside as the knife ploughs through.

A slightly raised lip occurs on the surface and a 'V' cut results. In Fig. 76, 'A' represents the picture veneer, 'B' shows the window aperture being cut, with the tip of the blade making the score-cut into the veneer to be inserted; 'C' shows the insert being fitted back into the picture, and 'D' shows a series of V cuts which result on the side being worked upon. The side with the best joints is underneath, shown by the arrows in 'D'. This is not what we want at all!

The best side, which we know as the 'face' side, is the side we want to see when the picture is finished.

That means, if we glue the open V cut side to the baseboard, the face side will be in reverse and show a picture around the wrong way.

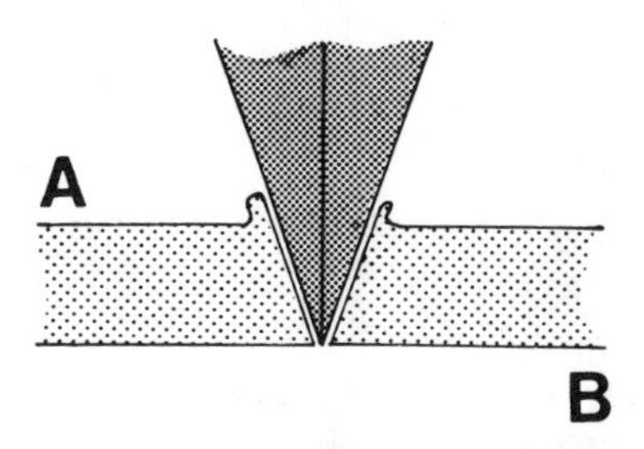

Fig. 75 The knife makes a 'V' cut and forms ridges on side A of the veneer

That doesn't matter with some subjects, but if the picture was of a particular view which you need to show the correct way around – not a mirror image of it – we would have to begin by *reversing* the design. Reverse designs are widely used in both knife and fretsaw techniques.

Bevel cutting

The way to resolve this problem *without* reversing the design, is shown in Fig.77, where 'A' is the picture veneer,'B' shows the window aperture being cut. Notice how the double bevelled blade is held at an angle with the handle of the knife tilted *inwards* towards the centre of the hole and one bevel held vertically against the edge to be jointed.

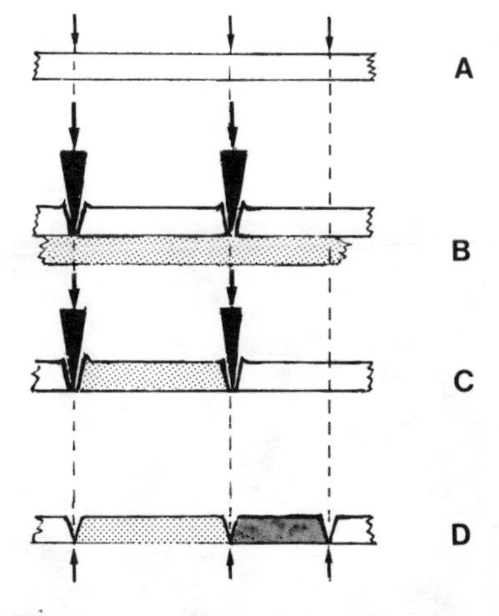

Fig. 76 The top surface of the veneer has open V joints visible

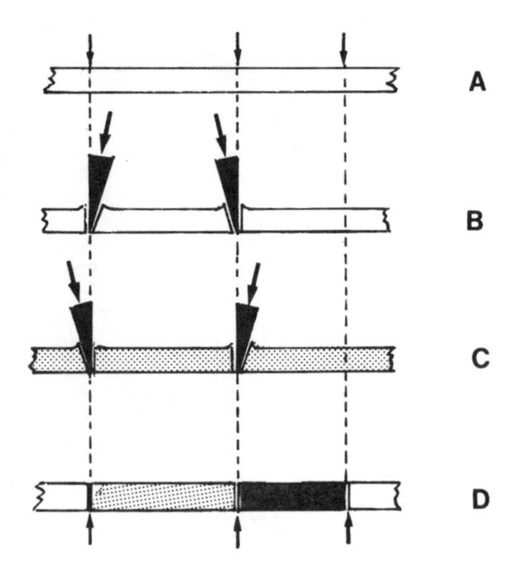

Fig. 77 Bevel cutting results in invisible joints

'C' shows the insert veneer being cut. This time the knife handle is tilted *outwards* with the blade bevel held vertically against the edge of the veneer to be jointed again.

'D' shows the resulting joints between two inserted veneers in the surrounding picture.

Let us put this new cutting technique into practice on another cutting problem you will meet in marquetry, known as 'sliver cutting'.

Most pictures have a few very narrow lines to be inserted, for example as window sashes and frames, rigging and masts on ships, branches of trees, etc.

Even the test piece had a central vein on the leaf, which we did not attempt to cut in until you have learned about 'sliver cutting'.

Sliver cutting

Practice sliver cutting on a piece of scrap veneer. A long, curved thin line is marked on the background veneer. The score-cut is made towards you, angling the blade so that the left-hand edge of the window slot is cut vertically. The handle of the knife tilted to the right as shown in Fig.78. (The angle is slightly exaggerated in the illustration for purposes of demonstration.)

The knife is held at an angle to the left, when scoring the right-hand edge of the window slot, as in Fig.79. The sliver is then cut out on the cutting board in the same way, and the waste sliver of veneer removed.

Here we meet a departure from the normal window method procedure. When cutting a sliver, we do not put the veneer to be inserted beneath the narrow slotted picture veneer, as a good fit would be difficult to obtain.

The insert veneer is cut against a ruler edge in a straight-cut, as in Fig.80. Make a trimming cut, holding the vertical bevelled edge of the blade against the ruler to get a square cut edge. The ruler is moved a fraction to the width of the sliver required,

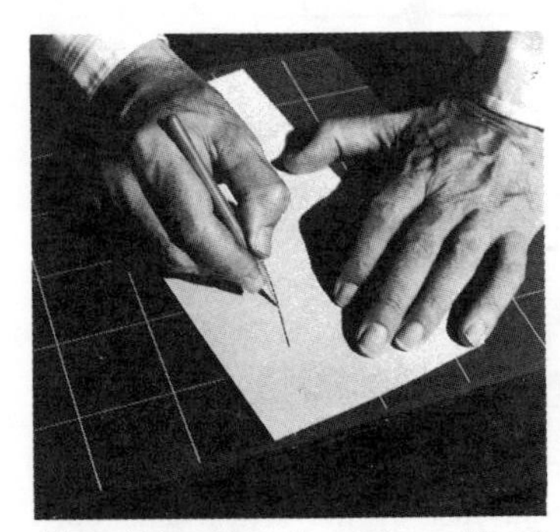

Fig. 78 Bevel cutting. Knife handle tilted to the right

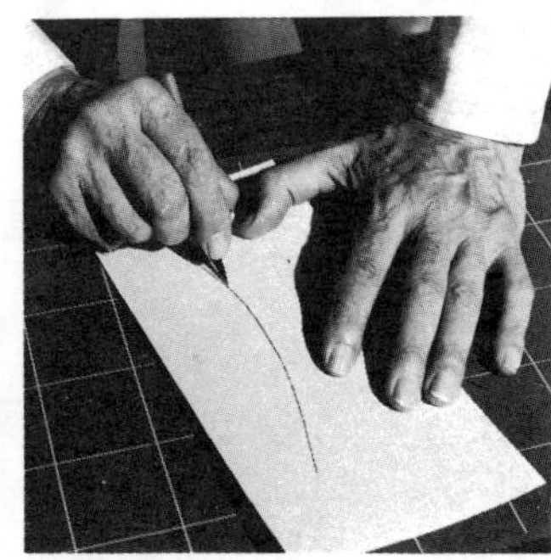

Fig. 79 The knife handle tilted to the left

Fig. 80 The sliver trimmed with knife handled tilted but blade held vertically

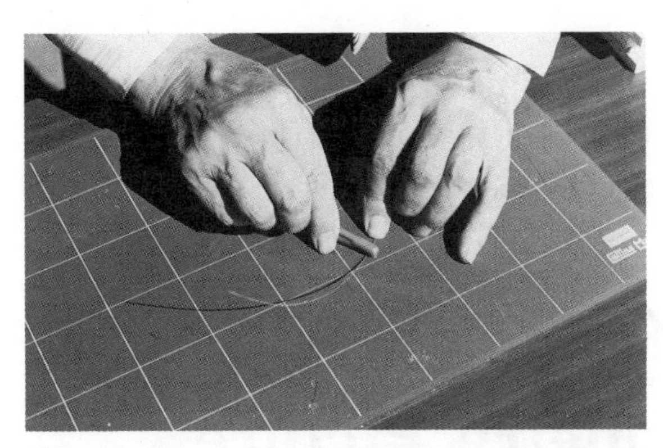

Fig. 81 Flatten the sliver with the rounded end of the knife.

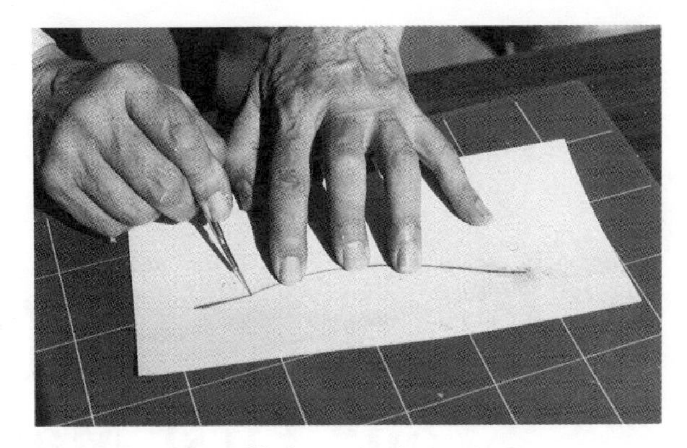

Fig. 83 Nip off the end of the sliver

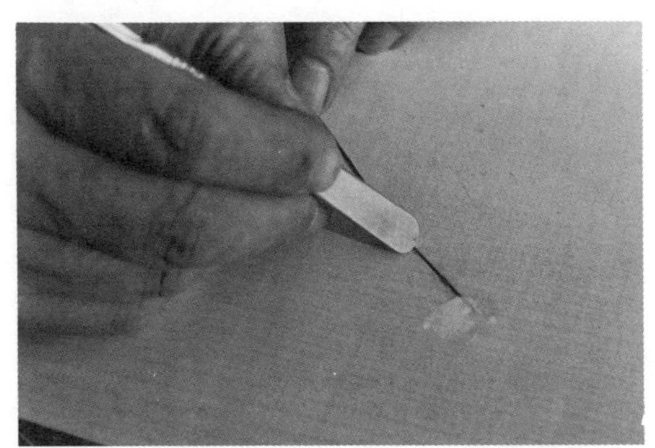

Fig. 82 Fasten one end of the sliver in the slot and coax into position

and the knife angled outwards to keep one bevel of the blade vertical. Practice cutting several narrow slivers and see how fine you can cut them.

The finer they are, the more they will curl up. Remember to lightly score-cut the line first before you use the heavier straight-cut.

Rub the sliver with the rounded end of the knife handle to flatten it as in Fig.81. Do not attempt to put any white PVA glue either on the sliver or in the slot or it will not fit. First position the end of the sliver in the far end of the slot. Next, put a tiny spot of PVA on the end, (or temporarily fasten it with a small piece of Sellotape), and gently coax the sliver into the slot. Hold the sliver in position and snip off the end as shown in Fig.82. Rub the sliver tightly in position with the rounded end of the knife handle.

Now PVA adhesive can be rubbed into the join, the surplus wiped off, the surface covered with a piece of polythene and placed under a weight until dry.

Now cut a fine sliver in the central vein of the test piece leaf before we tackle the marquetry kit.

10
Your First Marquetry Picture

'Evening on the Broads'

THIS IS a very popular beginner's picture and is ideal for our purpose. The manufacturer has included an instruction leaflet for you to follow, but I will amplify those instructions and try to anticipate any points where you may need help.

You may prefer to photocopy the design and order the veneers from your supplier so that you have a stock of spare veneers. Here is the list of veneers required to make the picture, numbered to correspond with the design. (Fig.84)

List of veneers required

12. Aspen
15. Ayan
16. Obeche
35. Padauk
38. Mansonia
49. Harewood
57. Mahogany
59. Honduras mahogany.
62. Sapele
85. Planetree
89. Indian rosewood
92. Sycamore
96. Weathered sycamore
103. American walnut
106. African walnut
107B Figured walnut

Also required is a border veneers packet containing a fillet border strip of sycamore; border veneers, edging and backing of sapele.

Alternatives: No. 11 olive ash may be substituted for No. 49 harewood; or a leaf of any orange-red veneer such as American gum (satin walnut) or rosa peroba can be subsituted to form an effective one piece 'sunset' background.

Apply a piece of tape to the surface of any veneer which feels brittle or hard to cut, also when you have small curves and intricate shapes to cut.

If any of the veneers are buckled, overdry or split, before using them read Chapter 6 on flatting veneers.

The 'Waster'

Marquetry pictures can be broadly classified in two groups according to their background veneers.

One group comprises pictures with one or two-piece backgrounds. The test piece was in this category with a one piece sycamore background. The complete design was cut directly into it.

When two pieces form the background – such as sea and sky – these two are tape-jointed together first to form one background

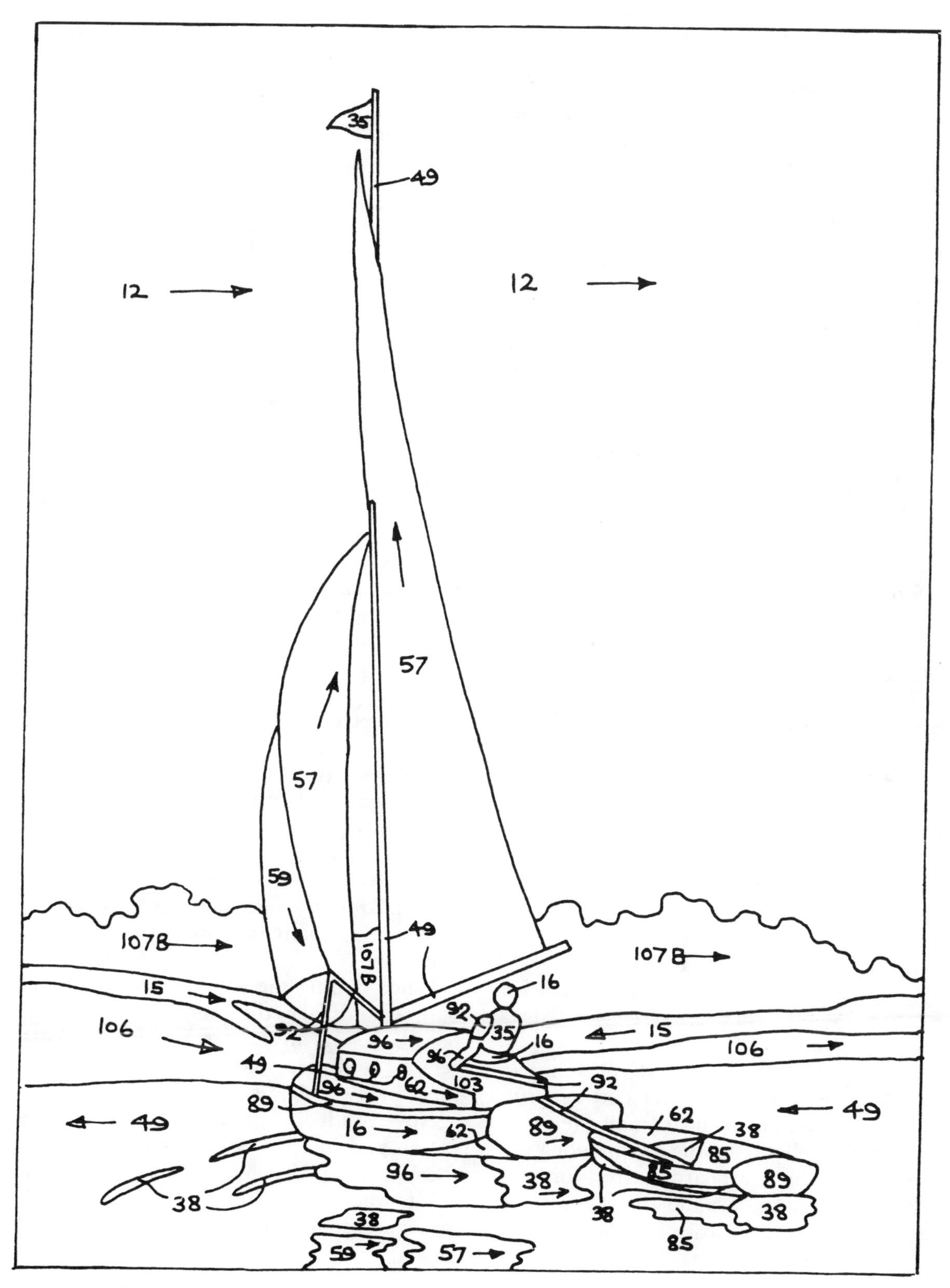

Fig. 84 Marquetry set No. 401. 'Evening on the Broads' (Avco)

veneer, and the design is then traced directly on to these veneers. The picture is cut into them, exactly as you did with the test piece.

The second group of pictures have more complicated multiple-piece backgrounds. This doesn't mean that they are more complex and advanced to make, simply that the picture subject requires several pieces to form the background.

That's why I have selected this kit which has a five-piece background. Instead of attempting to join all these veneers together to form the background, it is simpler and easier to use a separate sheet of veneer or cardboard which is known as a 'waster' to trace the design upon.

The kit has been provided with a sheet of white cardboard for this purpose. The card is cut away one piece at a time as before, with the hole being used as a templet.

All the card *in the picture area* is cut away and replaced by the various veneer shapes, so that when the basic picture is completed it is held within its cardboard 'frame'. This can be trimmed off later when we are ready to lay the picture.

But here's the important difference in technique between pictures using a veneer background waster, and pictures using a *cardboard* waster.

The first veneer shape is *taped* back into the hole in the *cardboard, not glued*, as this would make the cardboard soggy.

As subsequent shapes are fitted, *veneer-to-veneer* edges are *butt jointed* together with white PVA glue, and *veneer-to-cardboard* edges are *Sellotaped.*

If you find a few 'whiskers' or splinters on the edge of a veneer after cutting, trim to size with an emery board nail file.

Begin by Sellotaping the design along the top edge of the cardboard waster, forming a hinge. Also tape around the other three edges of the card to protect it from tearing as work proceeds.

Fig. 85 Target style registration mark

Mark registration lines on the design and on the cardboard, at the bottom, as you did with the *test piece*. This time, try a more sophisticated registration mark by drawing a circle with cross-hairs on the design and trace them on the card; cut out the circle from the design but not from the card, so that you can see through the hole in the design, and align the crosshairs in the target with those on the design as in Fig.85.

The short cut

There is another cutting technique to learn before we tackle the kit. This will make cutting marquetry pictures much easier for you.

It is used when the design requires you to cut around curved, jagged or craggy outlines, especially in hard, thick or difficult woods.

When cutting the window, first score the outline and take the piece to the cutting board. Using an easy series of step-cuts, remove a simple shape from the centre of the window hole, as shown in Fig.86.

Now you'll find it much easier to stab-cut around the curves in a loop and remove them individually by returning the knife cut to the centre section which you have previously removed, as shown by the shaded area.

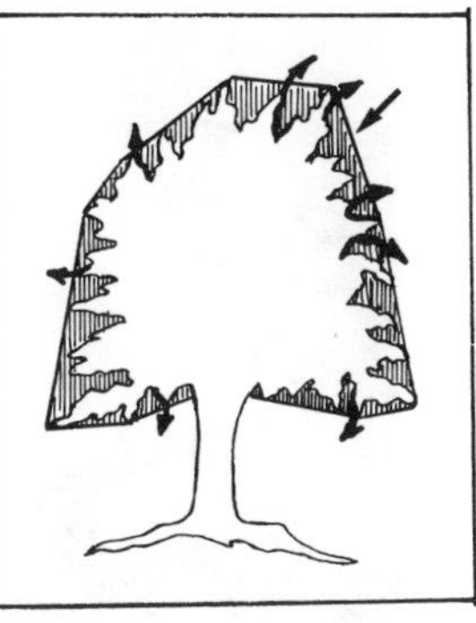

Fig. 86 Cut a simple shape in the window and nibble the jagged outline back to it

Fig. 87 Cut the insert veneer to a simple shape and nibble out the outline

You'll soon learn the knack of making the most of these short cuts along the grain. Reverse the process when cutting out the insert required for the picture, as shown in Fig.87.

Score-cut the design outline into the insert veneer. Now cut around the simple line which encloses the pattern.
It is then much easier to 'nibble' away (like a mouse around a cheese!) at cutting out the small loops and curly shapes and remove them individually, as shown by the shaded area.

Sometimes tiny fibres may have avoided the knife cut and will still hold the piece together. When you try to lift out the required insert, it will break or crack. Dip the point of the knife in a spot of glue and pick up the small piece with the point of the knife.

Apply a piece of tape to the surface of any veneer which feels brittle or hard to cut, also when you have small curves and intricate shapes to cut.

THE CUTTING SEQUENCE.

There are three rules to remember when cutting any marquetry picture:

(1) Always *first cut the items furthest away in perspective* and work towards the foreground. In this case we have five pieces forming the background: (a) the sky down to the skyline at the horizon, which is the first section to be worked upon; (b) the distant shoreline, comes next; (c) fields next; (d) then the bank, and (e) finally, complete the background by cutting in the water in the foreground.
(2) *Omit any design component, which is completely within another part of the design*, such as the portholes on the side of the yacht, as they cannot be cut in until the correct background veneer has first been fitted.
(3) *Omit any detail which runs through or across other parts, such as the man in the boat and the sails.* This makes it easier to ensure grain continuity in those parts which are separated in the final design.

With experience you will also learn to cut the soft, easy veneers, into the picture first and let the harder brittle or more difficult veneers into them.

The picture will be worked in three separate stages. The first stage is to complete the background, for which we will need veneers number 12, (aspen) 107B (figured walnut), 15 (ayan), 106 (African walnut) and 49 (silver harewood) from the kit.

Before we start cutting, sharpen the point of the knife. Always keep the knife point razor sharp by sharpening the back of the blade and honing the *cutting* edge on the garnet paper or sharpening stick. Learn to recognise a dull knife. If you look at a knife blade under reading glass and you see a contrast in the light reflection, then the blade needs resharpening.

When you commence cutting the kit, work *slowly*, coaxing out the shape with perhaps four or five cuts, working through the knife positions. Strengthen frail veneers by taping the back. Insert the tip of the knife into candle wax before each cut. Always cut away from any fine pointed shape.

This kit is made in three stages:

Stage One

Place the black carbon paper between the white card and the design and trace the outline of the sky veneer (No.12) down as far as veneer 107B, extending the design lines along the top and both sides of the picture area, about $\frac{3}{16}$ inch (5mm) into the surrounding border margin. Use a hard pencil, stencil stylus, or used ball point pen and a ruler to trace the border lines. Also insert the registration marks to ensure the design will always be aligned correctly. as in Fig.88.

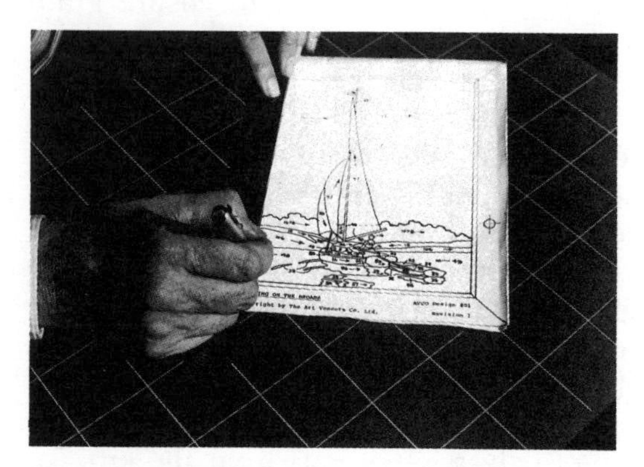

Fig. 88 Tracing the border outlines

The veneers which form the edge of the picture are allowed to overlap into the border margin.

By making the picture oversize, and retained within its cardboard 'frame', it can be trued square and to its correct size along the border lines with straight cuts against a ruler. This will provide accurately cut edges for the completed picture.

Having established the border margin and the net picture area, next trace the sky outline. Lift the design and place the cardboard waster on the cutting board. Lift the design. Cut out the sky shape from the cardboard and discard it.

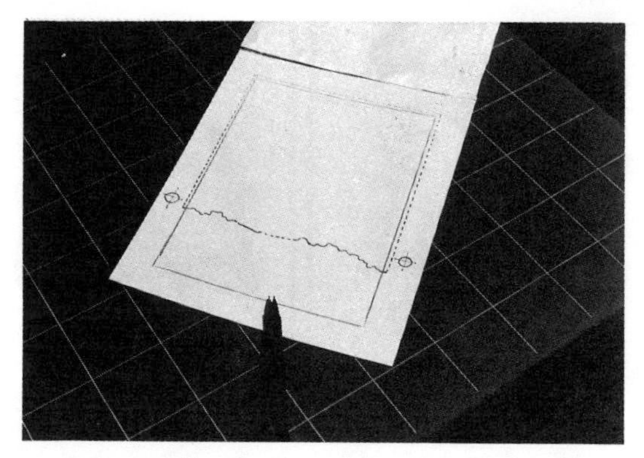

Fig. 89 Trace the skyline

Place the No. 12 veneer under the window and align the grain direction as shown by the arrow.

The advantages of the window method are now apparent. When the veneer is placed beneath the window we can see exactly the effect of grain, figure, tone and marking that the chosen veneer provides.

The veneer can be moved around to test various sections of the wood for better effects, watching the changing pattern through the window.

You can actually see the result you will obtain in the finished picture and can therefore experiment by trying and testing all sorts of alternative sky-effect veneers under the window, until you find one with just the right effect.

For example, test the effect of the sapwood side of the leaf towards the horizon line, and position the pinkish heartwood at the top of the picture. Swivel the leaf slightly so that the streaks of figure appear to climb to the top right-hand corner of the picture, rather than simply run horizontally across.

Hold the veneer and card firmly and turn them over. Sellotape the No. 12 veneer temporarily to the card on the back so that it cannot move.

At this stage, we are going to completely ignore the boat and dinghy and omit them from the first phase of cutting.

Fig. 90 The sky veneer in position

The dotted lines indicate the line of cut to ensure grain continuity and will eventually be cut away as other parts are added.

Now return to the design side and score-cut around the outline into the sky veneer. Remember the five knife handle positions.

Take care around the skyline where it meets No. 107B veneer. Release the No. 12 veneer from the back of the card and place it on the cutting board.

You can use either of the cutting techniques that suit you best, vertical or bevel cut. Using the stab and step-cuts, work around the outline a couple of times to cut through the soft sky veneer.

Position it within the cardboard frame, and Sellotape it to the cardboard along the top and two side edges. Fig.90.

Now bring down the design and align the registration marks and trace the 107B area – ignoring the yacht.

Lift the design and cut out the 107B outline from the card and discard it. Place the veneer below the window and adjust it to determine the best grain direction. Turn the veneer and card over and secure them on the back with tape to prevent movement.

Score-cut the line as before. Release the veneer and place it on the cutting board; use stab and step-cuts to cut out this piece, with a sweep-cut on the join with No. 15.

Before you position No. 107B back into the picture assembly put a few spots of white PVA glue along the join with the sky veneer No. 12, but Sellotape it at the two sides which have been extended into the cardboard border margin.

Rub more PVA glue into the join between No. 12 and No. 107B. Repeat this process with veneers No. 15, 106 and 49. Remember to keep the knife really sharp and to use tape between veneer-and-card and glue between veneer-and-veneer.

At the end of stage one your picture looks like this, with the window already cut in for the boat hull. Fig.91.

Fig. 91 Stage one background completed

Stage Two

Now you are ready to trace, cut and fix the hull and superstructure of the yacht into the picture assembly, omitting the mast and sails.

As the original border margin outlines have been discarded and replaced by background veneers which overlap into the margin, the next thing to do is to restore the border outline from the tracing and trace in the next section to be cut.

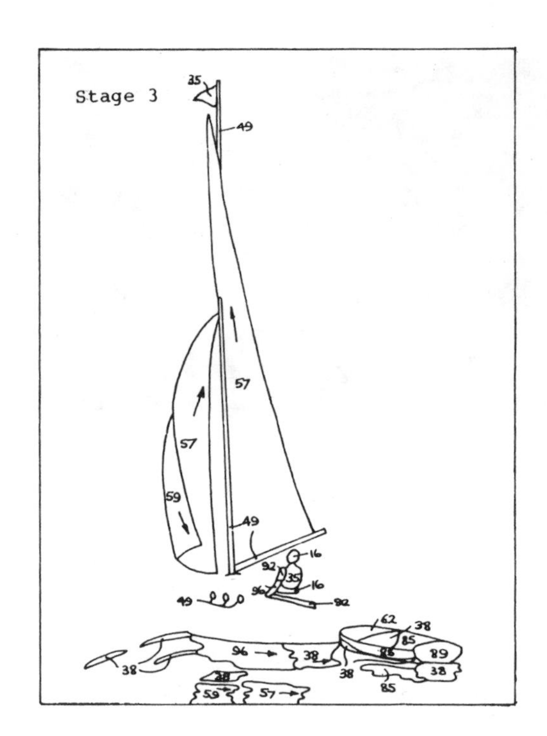

Fig. 92 Stage 2 and Stage 3 Drawings

Cut in veneers Nos. 96 and 62, for the top of the boat, 96 again for the deck, 16 for the side of the boat, 103 for the cabin interior, 89 for the stern, 62 for the shadow, and finally insert the sliver No. 89, as in Fig.93.

Stage Three

The sails are cut in next. First the right-hand sail No. 57, and then the left, followed by No. 59, and the masts and flag. (Fig.94).

Now replace the design, check the regist-ation marks and trace the inner border line to the picture.

With a ruler, accurately measure the nett picture area and make sure each of the sides are exactly the same size, also the top and bottom lines are precisely at right angles. With a straight-cut, (knife held at a low angle) trim the surplus veneer and cardboard frame from the edges of the picture. Fig.95.

In the kit you will find (a) one strip of white veneer, to be cut into narrow strips about $\frac{1}{8}$ inch (3mm) wide to form a fillet border to be positioned around the picture area. (b) Four strips of veneer for the picture borders, (c) four narrower strips of the same

Fig. 93 Cut in the boat hull

veneer for the edges of the baseboard; (d) one sheet of veneer for the back of the panel, about $\frac{1}{2}$ inch (12mm) larger all round than the size of the baseboard.

Place the white strip of veneer (a) on the cutting board, and measure four $\frac{1}{8}$ inch (3mm) strips for fillet borders. Cut them carefully to the correct width, with a straight-cut using the ruler as a straightedge.

Now take the four border veneers (b) and the four fillet strips (c), and Sellotape them around the trimmed edge of the picture allowing them to overlap at each corner.

One piece of tape can be used to hold both border and fillet strips to the picture. The borders should extend about $\frac{3}{16}$ (5mm) beyond the baseboard to allow for trimming down to size when mounting the picture to the baseboard.

If you used the more advanced 'bevel-cut' method in which the bevel of the knife is held vertically and the knife handle is tilted, the face side of the picture will have tight, close joints.

Hold the picture assembly up to a strong light and see if there are any badly cut or open joints. Examine the surface and see which side you prefer.

Measure and mark with pencil two centre lines on the back or loose side of the picture to be laid in the glueline on the baseboard. Also measure the two diagonals across the

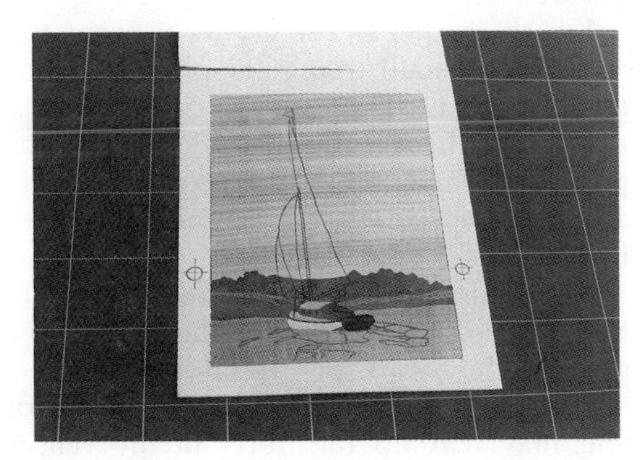

Fig. 94 Trace in the sails and dinghy

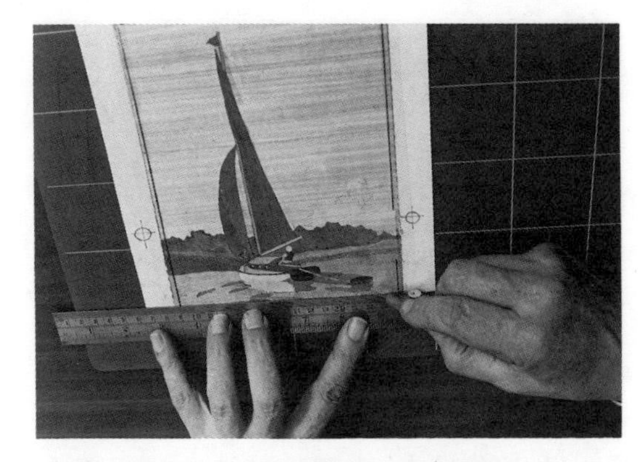

Fig. 95 Trim off the picture surplus

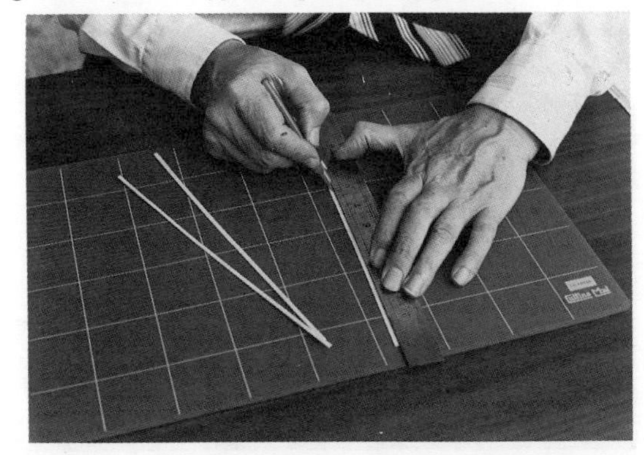

Fig. 96 Cut four fillet strips

Fig. 97 Check the measurements carefully

kit baseboard, check that it is perfectly rectangular, and add these pencil lines to the picture assembly, as shown in Fig.98.

Check that the pencilled centre lines and the outline of the baseboard are correct by placing the baseboard temporarily in position on top of the picture assembly, and

Fig. 98 Check baseboard registration

Fig. 99 Carefully mitre the borders

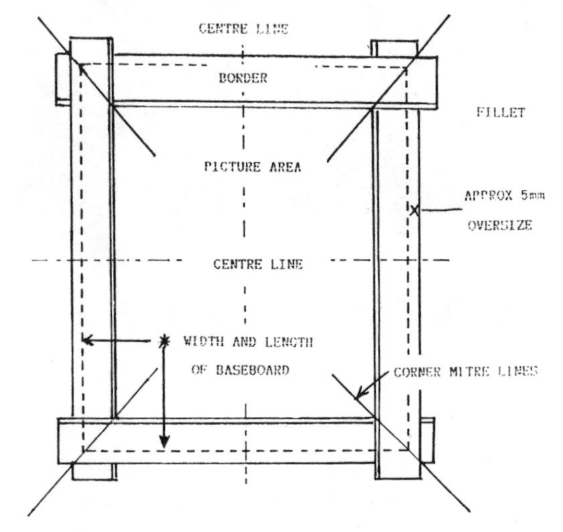

Fig. 100 Back view of veneer assembly

drawing a pencil line around it on the picture borders.

Pencil around the board on the border veneers. Write 'back X-top' on the board so it goes back the same way.

Remove the baseboard and place the ruler diagonally across the back of the picture at one corner. Fig.99.

Line up the pencilled lines representing the corner of the baseboard and the corner of the fillet border and cut the mitres through both border and fillet strips where they overlap. Take care to cut from the outside inwards, towards the picture to avoid 'break-out' of the cross grain at the edges of the border strips.

It is a good tip to glue a strip of sandpaper or double sided tape to the bottom of the ruler to prevent it from slipping. Do not attempt to sever both thicknesses of veneer at one stroke. Remember to make a light score-cut first to establish the line and then a few firmer straight-cuts at a low angle.

This time it is essential that you use the bevel-cut, angling the knife handle, so that the mitres are perfectly square cut and the joint is tight.

If you are nervous about cutting towards the picture area, cut from the outside borders towards the fillet border, and then turn the assembly around and cut from the fillets out
towards the borders.

Lift the corner of the border veneers and remove the small triangular piece from the lower border. Tape these corner mitres tightly together on the face side. Repeat the process at each corner. The border veneers are left oversize to be trimmed off after laying.

Now remove all traces of Sellotape from the back of the picture – the side to be glued to the board. Be careful how you peel off the tape. Sometimes it can be stubborn and may tear up the fibres of the veneer surface, especially on soft veneers. This can be overcome simply by applying a touch from the point of an ordinary domestic electric iron at a low heat setting. The tape will curl up and can be peeled off easily.

Examine the picture against a strong light and see if you have made any bad joints, open cuts, or if there are any missing fragments. Now is the time to replace any poorly fitting parts before the assembly is laid.

Place the picture 'lay-on' assembly on a flat surface and secure the edges temporarily with tape. Now wrap a piece of garnet paper around a wood or cork block and give the back a superficial, light papering to remove any traces of tape or glue, fingermarks, etc. from the side you will glue to the baseboard.

Cover the assembly with a sheet of polythene (a polythene bag will do), which will not adhere to the PVA and put the assembly under a weight to dry out overnight.

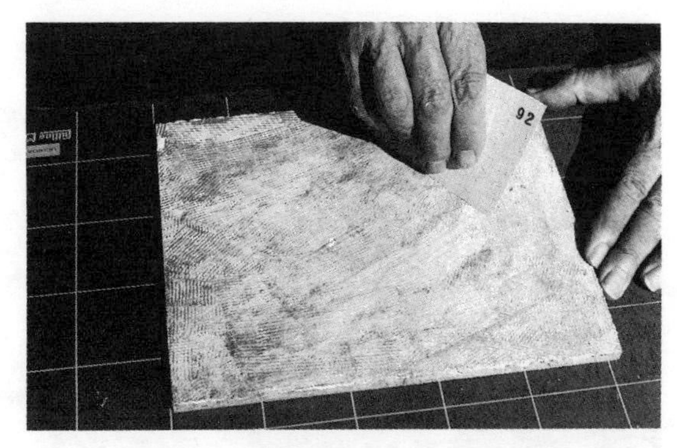

Fig. 101 Apply the adhesive to the baseboard

Fig. 102 Laying the backing veneer with a veneer hammer

Laying the picture

First, accurately check the measurements of the baseboard with a ruler and ensure that it is perfectly rectangular. Then proceed with the following steps:

1. With the edge of a scrap piece of veneer scrape the PVA glue *thinly* over one side of the baseboard, covering the panel in all directions, from side to side, end to end and diagonally. *Do not use a plastic comb as the resulting glueline will be too thick.*
2. Allow this to dry thoroughly for ten minutes or so. If applied thinly enough, it will be transparent when dry.

Have at hand, either a block of wood (or a boxwood seam roller, or rolling pin) and an ordinary domestic electric iron. Also a sheet of kitchen foil and brown wrapping paper.

3. Fasten a couple of short lengths of gummed paper tape to each side of the backing veneer and place it on a flat, clean surface or cutting board, 'true-face'

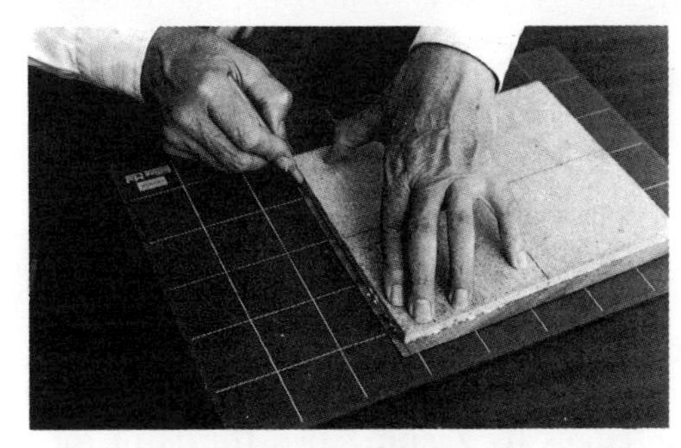

Fig. 103 Trim of the backing veneer surplus

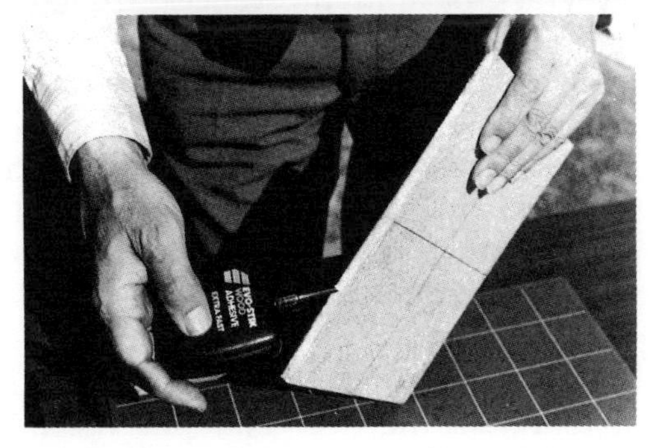

Fig. 104 Apply PVA to the edges

Fig. 105 Press the panel on the edges

Fig. 106 Trim off the edge veneers

(smoothest side) downwards, with the tapes underneath.

This backing veneer should be about ½ inch (12mm) larger all round than the baseboard. Now apply a second coat to the baseboard, as before, taking care not to miss a spot, and allow this to tack.

4. Position the coated baseboard on the back of the veneer, check the pencilled alignment marks, showing a margin all around to be trimmed off later, and fasten the tapes on the back of the panel to secure it.

5. Carefully turn the panel over and work on the backing veneer. With a rolling pin (or veneer hammer), work from the centre of the panel outwards towards the ends and edges to exclude air from the bond.

Take care not to allow the tool to run off the edges by keeping two thirds of the tool on the flat panel at all times, otherwise you may crack or split the veneer around the edges.

6. The PVA glue relies on the evaporation of the solvent into the atmosphere. Therefore, place the brown paper over the veneer and work over the panel with the iron set at its lowest setting. Not too hot or this could cause shrinkage. Again, work from the centre outwards.

7. Now cover the surface with the kitchen foil to retain the heat and put the panel under a heavy weight, a pile of boards or books, for half-an-hour.

8. Examine the veneered surface for blisters. (See below). Replace the brown paper and repeat stages 5, 6 and 7.

9. When the glue has hardened, trim off the surplus backing veneer around the edges and clean off the tapes.

Take care when cutting across the cross-grained ends by making a light score-cut first, cutting from the outside towards the centre, then a heavier straight-cut. Fig.103.

10. Wrap coarse garnet paper around a cork or wood sanding block and paper the edges flush.

Examine the four narrow strips of veneer supplied for the edges and arrange these with their smooth sides downwards on the flat surface.

Carefully repeat the sequences from 1 to 10 with the four edging strips. Veneer the top and bottom edges first, then the two sides. Fig.104.

By now you will have gained the confidence to tackle laying the picture. Place the veneer picture assembly face down on the flat surface. You will remember that there are pencilled centre lines on the back of the picture.

Position the baseboard temporarily over the assembly to make a final check to ensure that the corners of the baseboard coincide exactly with the mitres of the border mounts

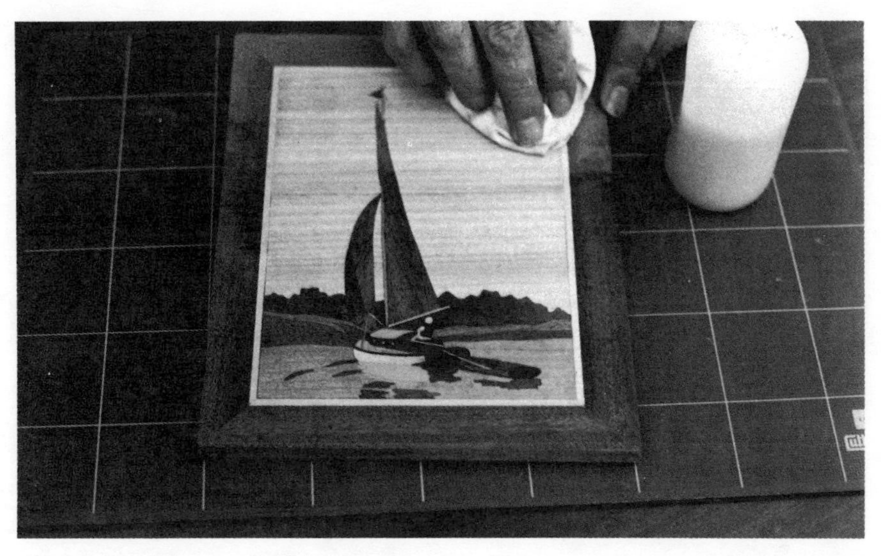

Fig. 107 The completed picture

(which should be fractionally larger all round than the baseboard).

Repeat the sequences from 1 to 10 as before and leave the completed panel, suitably protected, under a weight to thoroughly cure for a few days before finishing the picture.

As this is perhaps your first picture and you may be anxious to see a quick result, rub on a coat of sanding sealer using a cloth wrapped around a finger tip. Give the surface a superficial papering with grade 4/0 and then 6/0 garnet finishing paper wrapped around a sanding block, between the first two coats, allowing each coat to dry for half-an-hour. Lightly rub down the final coat with grade 9/0 garnet paper.

Finally, apply white siliconised furniture wax polish with grade 0000 wirewool and burnish the picture with a soft cloth.

Congratulations! I hope you are delighted with your marquetry picture. Now let us move on to learn more about the fascination of marquetry.

11
The Templet Method

THE TEMPLET method is often described as the 'stick as you go' method and is widely practised throughout Europe and the Mediterranean countries, especially in Granada in Spain and Sorrento in Italy, and north Africa where marquetry is hand-made by small family cottage industries.

It is especially useful for parquetry and applied marquetry work, or for picture assemblies too large for the available means of pressing.

The process is very simple. In the example shown in Fig. 108, the sky veneer (A) is selected to match the design, and arranged so that the flow of the grain direction and figure are correct to suit the picture.

The design outline is traced on to the selected veneer and cut out on the cutting board. A surplus is left at the bottom of the 'sky' veneer where it meets the 'mountain' veneer (B) to be trimmed off later.

The mountain section (B) is overlapped on top of (A) and used as a templet to cut around through the surplus of the sky veneer (A) which is then discarded. A surplus is left at the bottom edge of (B) where it will meet veneer (C).

Similarly, when the sea veneer (C) is cut accurately to shape along its top edge, it is laid overlapping the surplus of the mountain veneer (B) and used as a templet around which to cut veneer (B) to obtain a perfect fit. The foreground veneer (D) is cut to size and overlapped over the sea veneer and inserted.

As each part of the picture is cut, it is overlapped on a veneer that has already been laid, and used as a templet. The surplus is then prized off and discarded.

The baseboard may also have a copy of the design traced or printed on it as a location guide for assembly.

Care has to be taken to scrape away any glue 'squeeze-out' from the edge of each piece as it is laid, to ensure a good fit for the next piece.

Using a fast-setting marquetry cement, only finger pressure is used to lay the picture and there is no need for weights or cauls. However, it is important to ensure that the baseboard is of sufficient thickness to resist the tendency to warp as the assembly is glued direct to the board, if making the picture over a prolonged period. Also the

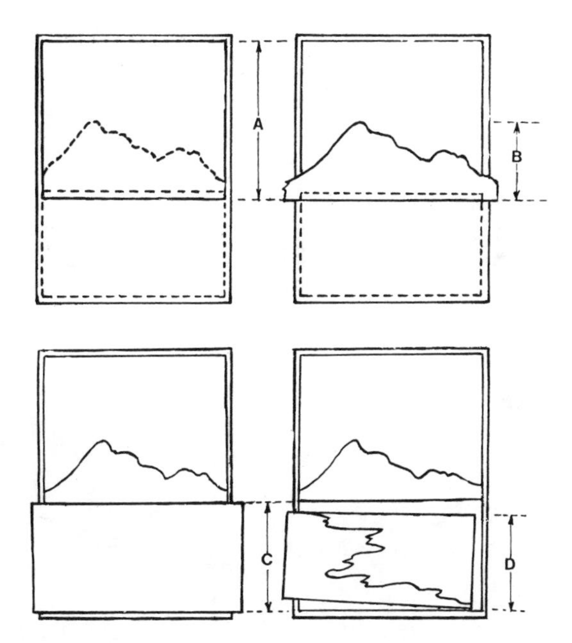

Fig. 108 Each veneer is used as a templet to cut the next

panel must be veneered on the back to counteract the pull of the veneers and so keep the panel balanced.

The advantage of the templet method is that a beginner can see the picture growing piece by piece.

The disadvantages of the method are that all the work is carried out on the face side which will show any open or poor knife joints, knife cuts or scratches, contain any black carbon from tracing, glue remainders, etc., which are difficult to remove.

To avoid these problems, leading exponents of this method prepare a *reverse* design and cut the picture on the back or loose side of the veneers.

Reverse design

A reverse design is made on very thin white cardboard, by placing it immediately beneath the design, and a sheet of carbon paper with the carboned side uppermost, under the card.

The picture is then cut in reverse. A little of the rubber cement (Cow gum) is spread thinly over the card and allowed a few minutes to dry. A second fresh coat is then spread over the section of the design to receive each veneer piece in turn, and while it is still wet the veneer piece is placed in position.

It is the back of the picture which is visible now, and any minor defects can be remedied. Pieces can be removed and replaced; tiny cracks or open joints can be filled with sanding dust and PVA; and the whole asembly can be levelled with a cork sanding block and garnet paper before being laid in a press.

The thin, white card is then peeled off the face veneers, and the rubber cement easily rubs off the face side of the picture without trace, leaving a clean, flat, dry surface ready for finishing. This method is often used in combination with the 'window method'.

12
Fretsawing: Flat Table

THE THICKNESS and the hardness of the material to be cut governs the type of tool used and over the years, as the craft developed, marquetarians have used many different tools.

The knife and the saw

In the days of the 'shoulder-knife', veneers were actually thin boards up to $\frac{1}{4}$ inch (6mm) thick. Later on, when the pitsaw was mechanised by the watermill, the veneers were cut only $\frac{1}{8}$ inch (3mm) thick, and the marquetry was cut with the fine bow saw. The fretsaw was invented in 1562 and revolutionised marquetry cutting.

The circular saw enabled thinner veneers to be produced up of about $\frac{1}{16}$ inch (1.5 mm). According to the archives of the French guild of Maîtres et Ébénistes in Paris, the 'donkey' or French Horse was invented in 1780 and has continued in use by professionals to this day. Students at l'Ecole Boulle des Arts Appliqués in Paris are taught how to make their own saws and produce exquisite work on the 'donkey'. (Fig 109.)

With the advent of knife-cutting machinery to produce rotary cut and sliced veneers (from .01mm up to 5 mm) veneers of two main thicknesses are used. In Europe most veneers are cut $\frac{1}{40}$ inch (0.65 to 0.7mm) in thickness, which permits the use of knife. As a direct result advanced knife-cutting techniques have evolved.

Fig. 109 Ecole Boulle student cutting on the 'Anc' (Donkey) or 'Chevalet de marqueterie'

But in the Australia, Canada and the U.S.A., and in countries which export veneers for consumption in those countries, veneers are cut $\frac{1}{28}$ inch (0.9mm) thick, so that marquetry has continued to be cut by hand-held and power fretsaws and scroll saws. Therefore, the choice of tools is largely determined by the thickness of the available veneers and it is for this reason that the craft has developed along two different paths.

Those using the thinner veneers in Europe have perfected both knife-cutting and fretsawing techniques as taught by the Marquetry Society, and those who have access mainly to the thicker veneers, use the fretsawing techniques taught by the Marquetry Society of America.

Flatbed Techniques

It will soon become apparent that although some really beautiful pictures are knifecut, if the marquetarian restricts his choice to the thinner European veneers, knife-cutting has its limitations for a number of reasons.

The first is that tricky, undulating contours and jagged outlines such as tree foliage, require a lot of stab and step-cutting. This is even more difficult to do when the ideal veneer for the part is a burr (burl) veneer, cross-grained, very hard, brittle, a thicker gauge, or perhaps a combination of all of these.

Next is that veneers such as ayan, wenge, laurel, are particularly difficult to knife-cut. Also you may only have access to $\frac{1}{28}$ inch (0.9mm) thick veneers which are too difficult to cut with the knife.

The 0.9mm thickness is easier to work and handle by fretsaw, and enables craftsmen anywhere in the world to utilise an almost limitless variety of species including local native woods.

Many species such as Gabon ebony, greenheart, lignum vitae etc., are not available in knife-cut form and small dimensioned trees such as holly and laburnum for example, are not commercially viable for saw cutting.

However, the amateur woodworker can re-saw on a bandsaw a wide range of attractive woods from small sections.

The advantages of using bandsawn veneers are:

(1) they retain their original colour, tone and vividness, as they have not been subjected to steam treatment.

(2) by using the fretsaw on these woods, the most elaborate and detailed contours can be cut, which are impossible with any knife cutting technique in this thickness.

(3) pictures can be cut in a fraction of the time involved with knife-cutting, and will produce excellent results with invisible joins.

(4) the marquetarian can repair, restore or reproduce period furniture with the correct timbers and be able to use many of the traditional materials such as tortoiseshell, mother of pearl, ivory, brass and other metals; or venture into the use of acrylic sheeting.

There are advantages and disadvantages in using saw cut woods. The teeth of the saw leaves teeth marks across both sides of the veneer concealing the true figure, markings and colourtone of the wood. If these teeth marks are not planed, scraped or sanded off, the marks will telegraph through to the face of the panel as the action of the glueline will pull the veneer down and 'telegraph' the pattern to the face side.

But there are compensations, because the picture assembly can be scraped and power sanded with far more confidence than a picture assembled from 0.7mm sliced veneers, without the attendant danger of 'rubbing-through'. Again, the thickness or hardness of the material to be cut governs the type of tool used.

Hand-held fretsaw frames

The easiest way to start is with a hand-held fretsaw frame. Your introduction to fretsaw marquetry can be inexpensive. There are

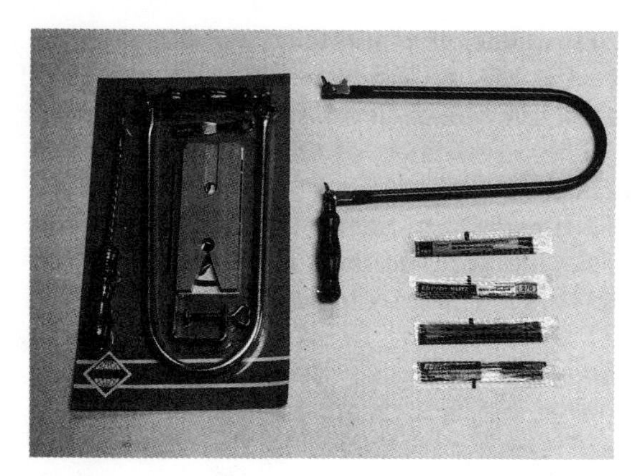

Fig. 110 A complete fretsaw outfit

mm) sewing machine needle held in a bottle cork, or pin vise to make the pricker, as this only pushes the fibres apart and does not remove veneer like a drill. The tiny hole will close up later.

Another 'pricker' can be made by jamming a needle into a wooden plug inserted in an empty ball point pen case and glued with epoxy resin.

The veneers are pierced where two or more design lines meet, or in a part of the design which will subsequently be discarded.

various commercial fretsaw frames available, such as the F.S.701 Eclipse lightweight tubular fretsaw frame which has an 12½ inch (320mm) throat. Although this limits the overall size of the marquetry assembly to below 24 inches (600mm), it is usually sufficient for all normal marquetry purposes.

The deeper the throat, the more scope for turning the picture assembly without having to work in smaller sections. It is widely available and is ideal for a beginner to try his hand and take the first steps in fretsawing.

The bird's mouth or V cutting table usually supplied with the fretsaw outfit is not suitable for marquetry as there is very little support for the veneers at the point of cutting. Small pieces fall out and get lost.

Initially let us begin with flatbed cutting to get used to handling the fretsaw. Make a simple wood cutting table, as shown in Fig.111, supplied by John Sedgwick of Canada. Some marquetarians convert these 9.5mm holes into tiny triangles. The idea is to prevent cutting into the saw table.

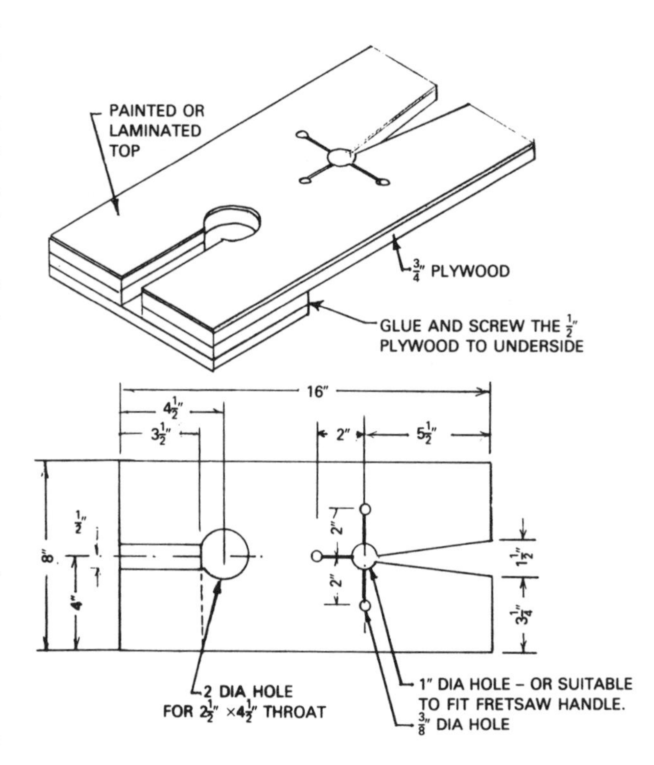

Fig. 111 A multi-position type fretsaw table

The Pricker

A simple home-made tool is required to make a tiny hole through veneers to receive the fretsaw blade.Use a .020 inch (0.50

Fretsaw blades

There are four basic types:

(1) Single tooth blades for general veneer cutting, with rounded backs.

(2) 2/0 Double teeth blades for marquetry, each with a special set to allow for sawdust clearance, and with rounded backs to enable the blade to swivel around tight curves without stress.
(3) Jeweller's metal-piercing blades, with single teeth.

All these fretsaw and piercing saw blades are available in sizes varying from Grade 3 (coarsest) to Grade 1 (robust), 2/0 (medium) 4/0 (fine) 6/0 (very fine) and 8/0 (extremely fine).
(4) Helical spiral piercing blades in Grades No. 1, 0 and 2/0, used for metal inlays, and 'roughing-out' pads for series cutting.

For your introduction to fretsawing, begin with a strong No. 3 blade until you are proficient, and then progress to a 2/0 double toothed, rounded back marquetry blade.

These saws are available in packets of dozens or grosses, and can be stored in 6 × $\frac{3}{8}$ inch (150 × 9mm) diameter rigid plastic tubes with cork stoppers, as sold in aquarium shops. Aluminium cigar tubes also make excellent storage containers.

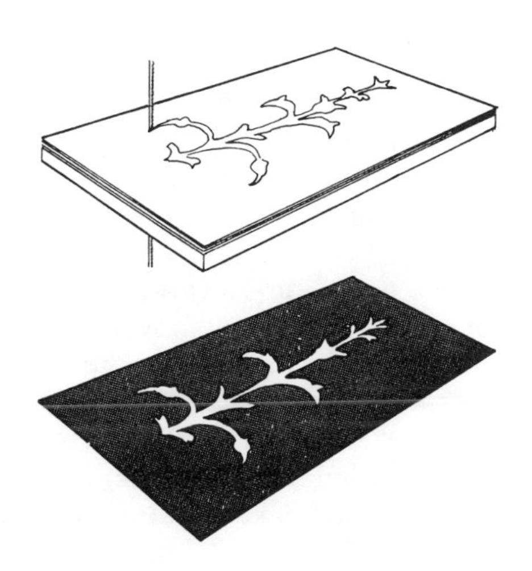

Fig. 112 A typical interchange pattern

Some fretsaws adjust to use broken blades like jeweller's blades, down to only $2\frac{1}{2}$ inch (65mm) long.

THE DOUBLE CUT

This is the simplest of all fretsawing methods by which two contrasting veneers are cut simultaneously and the parts interchanged to provide two identical patterns; one with a light motif in a dark background and a reverse pattern in the other.

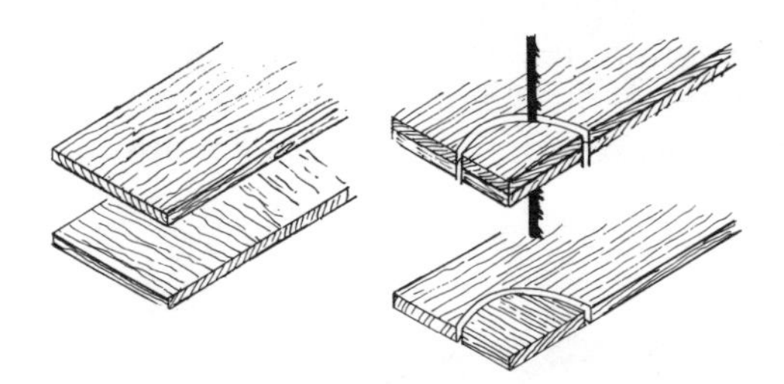

Fig. 113 The simple 'double-cut' interchange method

The test piece used in the introduction would make an ideal practice piece. The two contrasting veneers to be interchanged, have a third 'waste' veneer (which may be thicker than the other two), placed beneath them to take the swarf of the saw and prevent the veneer from splintering by the downwards pressure of the saw.

The grain direction of the waste veneer should be opposite to that of the veneer above. The three veneers should be slightly larger than the design.

Put a few spots of rubber cement (Cow gum) on each leaf of veneer to hold them together temporarily in a sandwich which will not move during cutting. Alternatively, bind them together with veneer tape, Sello-tape or masking tape as a temporary hold. Or they may be stapled together through the working margin with an office stapler.

The working design is fastened to the top of the sandwich with rubber cement. With the needle pricker, pierce a hole in the working margin, where a design line meets the margin, about $\frac{1}{4}$ inch (6 mm) from the beginning of each line.

Usually only a few piercings are necessary. However, any 'island' parts within the design need to be pierced separately rather than sawing across to them from the margin. The arrows show the point of entry of the saw in Fig.114.

Inserting the blade
Examine the fretsaw blade. As the teeth are so small, to tell which way they are pointing rub the ball of your thumb up and down over them. They will feel smooth to the touch in one direction and will grip and catch in the other.

Fig. 114 The arrows show the point of entry for the fretsaw

Press the top of the frame into the V of the sawing table for support. Fasten the fretsaw blade into the bottom clamp (at the handle end of the frame), with the teeth pointing downwards towards the handle so that it cuts as the saw is pulled downwards through the workpiece. The rounded back of the blade is towards the back of the frame.

Now carefully thread the loose end of the blade through the workpiece and tighten the top clamp of the frame, allowing the veneer sandwich to hang harmlessly out of the way at the bottom end of the blade. If necessary use pliers to tighten the clamp wing nuts. If your fretsaw has a tensioning toggle this should be adjusted. The blade should make a high toned sound if flicked with the finger nail.

Sometimes the ends of the blades may have a small burr where they have been cut to length which can be easily removed on a sandpaper file.

To prevent these delicate blades from breaking too easily, stretch a cord across the fretsaw frame to act as a tourniquet, with a small piece of wood resting on the back of the frame. By adjusting the number of turns on the tourniquet, the tension of the blade may be increased or decreased to suit your cutting style.

Now guide the saw blade through the slot in the table, until the back of the blade nestles in the apex of the V slot. Hold the fretsaw frame handle loosely in the right hand, and rest the rounded end of the frame against your right arm.

The veneers on top of the table should be pressed down with the left hand, using the fingertip of the left forefinger to exert firm pressure downwards at the point of sawing to prevent the work from rising on the upstroke of the blade. (Vice versa if you are left-handed) as in Fig.112. The cutting occurs on the downstroke. A thimble can be worn to protect the forefinger, or a thimble soldered to a flat metal plate called a thimble-plate is a very useful aid.

Turn and feed the work towards the saw which must be held perfectly vertical, in both front and side elevations. Work the saw up and down in easy movements of less than an inch (25mm) or so, in its V niche, without turning the blade. Move the veneers towards the sawteeth and turn them to follow the design line. Let the saw cut at its own rate and make no attempt to force the cut or the blade will break.

Be especially careful when meeting sharp corners of the design or jagged points. Do not attempt to turn the saw, but gently joggle the saw as you turn the workpiece. Sometimes you'll find it best when turning a really sharp corner, to back out along the cut just made and approach the corner from the other direction.

If you use a jeweller's sawblade, some types have graduated teeth at the ends, and by using the top ¼ inch (6mm) of the blade it enables the work to be turned at tight corners within the sawcut.

A good tip is to spread a newspaper on floor beneath the sawtable, to catch any tiny pieces that may fall. Also occasionally wipe the teeth with candlewax to lubricate the blade.

Commence cutting any small 'island' pieces in the centre of the design first, to prevent the design from falling apart at an early stage, and work outwards towards the edges.

When you complete sawing the assembly, do not release the blade by loosening the clamp wing nuts or the blade may snap due to the springing action caused by the sudden release of tension. Hold the handle in one hand, press the top of the frame gently against table, to relieve the tension, while releasing the lowest end of the sawblade first.

This way, the release is gentle. Slide off the veneer sandwich, and bring the top of the frame down to the table when undoing the top clamp wingnut to avoid breaking the blade.

If the pattern is small, the three veneers comprising the sandwich will separate easily. If they are still held together with rubber cement, they will spring apart if prized open with a wide flat kitchen knife.

Assembly of the motifs.

Place two reverse copies of the design on a flat surface and pin a sheet of transparent self-adhesive film, of the type used in photo albums and book covers, over each of them, adhesive side uppermost.

The sawn parts can now be assembled directly over the designs. The open sawcuts will be visible around each part and these are filled in with a paste made from sawdust and PVA adhesive which dries transparently.

The filler may match the backgound veneer colour tone, or may be a deliberate contrast, for example to emphasise the veins in a leaf.

The advantage for the beginner, is that even with these first steps in fretsawing, there will be no difficulty in making the parts

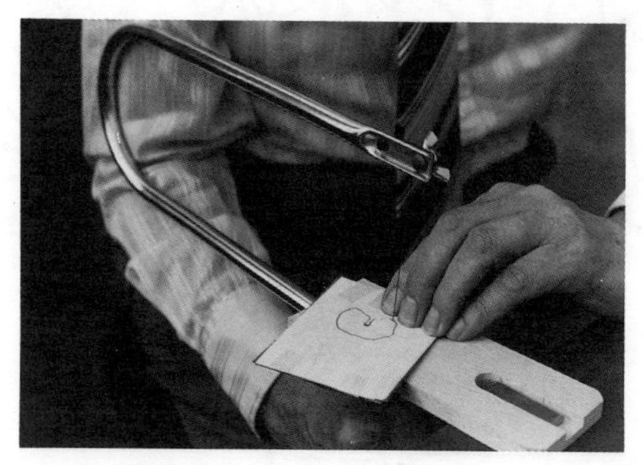

Fig. 115 Fingertip pressure applied close to the blade

fit. Even now at this stage of development, it is possible for you to cut a complete marquetry picture on the flat table, from one single sawing operation, using the 'Pad Method'.

THE PAD METHOD (Flat table)

This method is extensively used in America and allows a considerable margin for error in sawing in early fretsawing attempts, with freedom to wander off the design line without undue concern. It also enables the beginner to cut very brittle, hard or thick woods, including a wide range of species bandsawn from the solid.

Perfect joints will result, to within the thickness of the sawblade, and it is possible

Fig. 116 'The Needles' design for fretsawing by the 'Pad method'

to fill these with a matching background filler or accentuate them for artistic effect.

The picture will fit togther without difficulty if you can be certain that you are able to hold the fretsaw *exactly vertical*. The saw cuts the line between two adjacent pieces which ensures that the parts must fit together perfectly as they are cut simultaneously. If a geometric design is required, the method permits several design combinations from one single sawing.

Master control design

1. For your first attempt, the first step is to prepare a master control design, with information as to choice of veneers and their grain direction etc.

Leave a working margin of about ½ inch (12mm) around the net picture area to allow for a trim off. Insert centre lines and a 'target' registration mark in the margin at the bottom of the design.

2. Next, cut out a piece of acetate or transparent plastic film, to the exact size of the master control design including border margins. Make a tracing of the design in black India ink, using a fine pen, omitting all the veneer details and grain directions etc. This is the working design which we will call the 'finder' (viewfinder).

3. Now have two photocopies made from the finder to use as working drawings. One to fasten on to the top of the pad as the cutting design, and the other a *reverse* photocopy for the assembly of the cut out pieces.
4. Obtain a few leaves of scrap, soft, easy-to-cut veneer such as obeche, sycamore or poplar, the same size as the transparent finder. It is important that these 'wasters' are all of the same thickness.

Many marquetarians prefer to use white poster cardboard the same thickness as the veneers, as their wasters.
5. Draw centre lines on each waster for registration purposes and also the 'target' crosshairs, because you may get the centre lines in perfect register but have one inverted accidentally.
6. Obtain two pieces of stout white poster card to form the top and bottom of the pad.

Patching the wasters
Begin by selecting one of the background veneers, farthest away in perspective, such as the sky veneer,by reference to the master control design sheet. The finder is placed over the veneer and moved across the leaf to determine the most suitable flow of grain direction and figure markings for the picture.

Hold the finder down on the veneer with one hand, and with the other, mark the extremes of the skyline of the design, upon the sky veneer, *allowing about ½ inch (12mm) all around the section to be cut.*

Slip a leaf of black carbon paper between the finder and veneer if necessary. With practice the carbon can be dispensed with and the pencilled line made directly to the veneer. Place the finder back over the sky veneer to check that the pencilled lines you have drawn are correct and completely cover the sky area and margins. Remove the finder.

The rectangular pencilled shape (which is known as a patch) is now cut out from the sky veneer leaf, on the cutting board, using a straightedge and knife.

The finder is placed on top of the waster and checked to see that the register lines coincide. The newly cut sky patch rectangle is then slipped in between the finder and the waster, located in position, showing the patch to be overlapped about a half inch (12mm) all round.

The finder is removed, and the exact position of the patch is pencilled around on the waster. The waster is then placed on the cutting board. With a straightedge and knife, cut a rectangular hole into the waster, and insert the patch of sky veneer.

The patches are inserted into the wasters, and held with small pieces of gummed paper veneer tape of about 1 inch (25mm) in length, with all tapes on the underside of the wasters to keep the face side clean and free of tape.

This prevents a build-up of criss-crossing tapes. Consecutive layers of the pad are then bonded together temporarily with spots of rubber cement applied on the veneer surplus margin areas. It is easily removed later.

Where several parts of a design call for sky veneer – for example in a picture featuring a tree where the sky shows through the foliage and branches – cut all the pieces from the one leaf to preserve continuity of grain and figure flow.

Patching

Patching may be done in any convenient order, as the overage around each patch, prevents adjacent veneers being patched together in the same waster.

If one veneer completely fills the picture as the background, this can form one complete patch or layer.

In a sea or landscape with a two-piece background, the overage will ensure that they are patched in consecutive layers.

The first layer, which may comprise four or five patches, is placed on the bottom of the pad.

During this patching phase, the pad should be held in register in a simple bench jig, which can be a few nails driven into a plywood sheet at each side.

Similar patches are prepared for every part of the picture, endeavouring to get as many patches into one waster as possible. The fewer wasters used when making up this sandwich-like saw-pad, the easier and more accurate will be the result. But it is important to note that you should always *patch adjacent parts of the picture design in consecutive layers* to minimise the risk of open joints. The farther apart adjacent pieces are in the pad, the bigger the risk of an open joint.

List of veneers used in the picture 'The Needles'

11 Olive ash	62 Sapele
12 Aspen	85 Planetree
34 Horse chestnut	92 Sycamore
35 Padauk.	103 American walnut
39 Dark harewood	104 Walnut
49 Silver harewood	134 Slate harewood
56 Macassar ebony.	Sapele borders & back

In waster No. 1, patch in veneers No. 12, (aspen), 39 (dark harewood), 62 (sapele), 85 (planetree) and 92 (sycamore).

Waster No. 2 comprises Nos. 11 (olive ash), 56 (Macassar ebony), 92 (sycamore) and 104 (European walnut).

Waster No. 3 consists of Nos. 35 (padauk), 39 (dark harewood),49 (silver harewood), 92 (sycamore) and 134 (slate harewood).

Waster No. 4 is the top layer and is patched with 34, (horse chestnut), 35 (padauk), 103 (American walnut) and 104, (European walnut).

As you can see, some veneers are used more than once in different patches either because they are required in different grain directions (No 35) for example, or they would be adjacent in the picture.

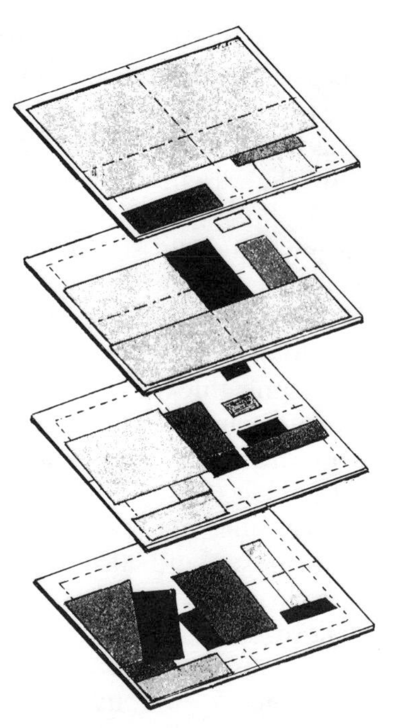

Fig. 117 An exploded view of a four layer sandwich for 'The Needles' picture

In practice, wherever the design lends itself, you will find it simpler to allow the outside patches to run right across the working margin to the outside of the pad, rather than cut a patch *including* a surplus plus a working margin.

Most pictures can be sawn from a six or seven layer sandwich. If the picture cannot be fitted into seven layers, it would be better to make two separate pads and join them together in the final assembly stage.

If the picture is too large for the throat of the fretsaw frame, saw along part of the design line and cut the pad in halves. Securely bind each half-pad with Sellotape or masking tape along the cut edge and continue with the work.

When all these layers are complete, place the two pieces of stout white poster card at the top and bottom of the pad. Fasten the design to be cut on the top layer of the pad with rubber cement and check the registration with the finder.

The pad is now compacted by placing

plywood panels on top and below and clamped together with two edges of the pad protruding. The outer edges are then bound tightly together while under pressure, using masking tape, Sellotape, gummed veneering tape, staples or nails. Then the other two edges are compacted and bound.

The pad is allowed to remain under pressure for an hour until the rubber cement between the layers has dried.

Fretsawing the pad.

Tiny holes are drilled through the pad to accomodate the saw, using an Archimedean-type fine drill bit, where a design line meets the surrounding border margin, about $\frac{1}{4}$ inch (6mm) from the beginning of each line.

Usually only a few drillings are necessary. However, any island parts within the design need to be drilled rather than reached by sawing across to them from the margin. Where possible use an awl to pierce this hole which will close up later and be 'lost'.

Alternatively, any tiny detail can be omitted from the sawing, leaving it to be 'let-in' by other fretsaw techniques.

Most pad method cutting is done with the woodworking 2/0 blades with double teeth and rounded backs. Blade size is determined by the size and shape of the pieces, not the depth of the pad. With a little practice, even finer 4/0 jeweller's metal-piercing blades may be used for small intricate shapes.

Sometimes the 2/0 blades flex as work proceeds, and layers may tend to bind against the blade. Relax your grip on the pad, and the blade's motion will move the pad and straighten the blade.

Assembling the picture

The *reverse* photocopy of the design is fastened to a flat surface such as a stout poster card, with Sellotape. There are various ways of assembling the picture. Either, coat the surface of the design evenly with Cow gum or rubber cement, allowing it to dry thoroughly. Use the edge of a piece of veneer to apply the cement. When sawing is completed, a fresh squeeze of rubber cement is spread over the section of the design to receive the veneer, which is then pressed down on the design with finger pressure.

Alternatively, fasten a sheet of transparent self-adhesive film over the design, adhesive side uppermost.

The sawn parts can now be assembled in jig-saw fashion directly over the designs and they will fit easily together.

As the picture is assembled face-down on the *reverse* design, it is the back of the picture with the gummed paper tapes and rubber cement spots that is now uppermost and this is then cleaned off. The joints can now be filled with a wood stopping made from a mixture of sawdust scraped from the back of the veneer parts, mixed with a little white PVA adhesive, which dries transparently, to butt-joint the picture together. The filler may match the backgound veneer colour tone, or may be a deliberate contrast, for example to emphasise the veins in a leaf.

The assembly is released from its anchorage and turned over, face side up, the reverse design is peeled off and all traces of rubber cement rolled off with the finger tips.

By this method, the picture is made from the face side, which most marquetarians prefer, and a reverse design is used for the final assembly. The use of PVA adhesive in butt-jointing the picture has practically eliminated the joins.

Without Wasters

With a little practice, you will soon find it possible to dispense with the use of wasters altogether.

By studying the design and allowing sufficient overage around each part, the patches are placed together to form a complete layer and rubber cemented to sheets of clean paper. Six or so of these sheets are arranged into a pad with a waste veneer at the bottom of the pad to take the saw swarf and the design rubber cemented on top. The pad is then compacted as before and sawn.

Light box

An interesting innovation is to make a light box comprising a simple wooden frame with a glass top enclosing a fluorescent tube.

The reverse design is placed on top and fastened with sellotape at the corners. The surface is then covered with self-adhesive transparent plastic film, or even shelf covering material such as 'Fablon'. The light will show the design through the adhesive material, and after the picture is assembled, the material is easily peeled from the face side.

There are advantages and disadvantages with the 'Pad Method'. Freedom to wander from the design line and yet produce a picture that will fit together perfectly is its greatest advantage.

Most pictures can be sawn from a six layer sandwich, but an advanced technique is to cut a six layer pad and assemble it and use this as layer No. 1 in a second pad of six layers – a process which lends itself to the creation of really advanced pictures.

The major disadvantage is the open joints which result, at least until you are able to use very fine saws – and that takes practice. Another is the need to keep the sawblade precisely vertical in both front and side elevations.

This is achieved by mechanising the fretsaw frame in a home-made rig-up, which will be described in Chapter 13. But before we examine mechanised fretsaw frames, we should now progress to angled tables and bevel cutting of marquetry pictures with *invisible joints*.

13
Fretsawing: Angled Table

Bevel Cutting

THIS REQUIRES the saw table to be inclined to an angle, either to the left or right, by sufficient degrees to make allowance for the thickness of the material being cut, plus the thickness of the sawblade.

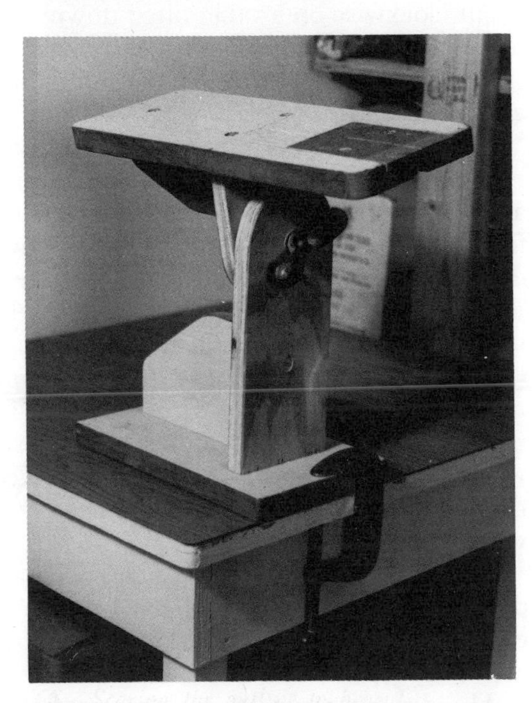

Fig. 118 Angled fretsaw table

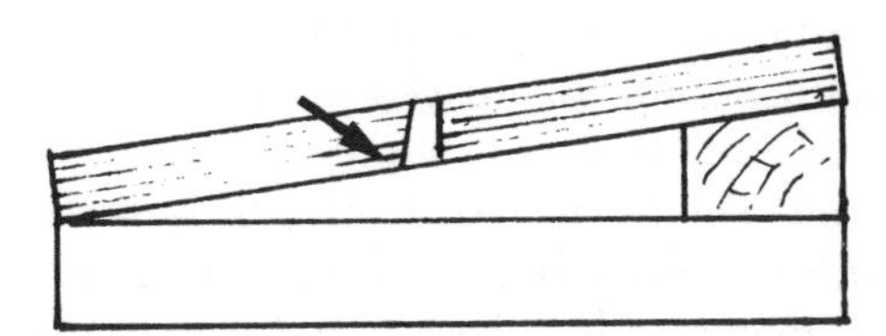

Fig. 119 The underside of the table is cut to allow for the angle of tilt

We will require a worktable which can be used both as a flatbed table and also capable of being angled to right or left at varying angles as shown in Fig.118 for bevel cutting.

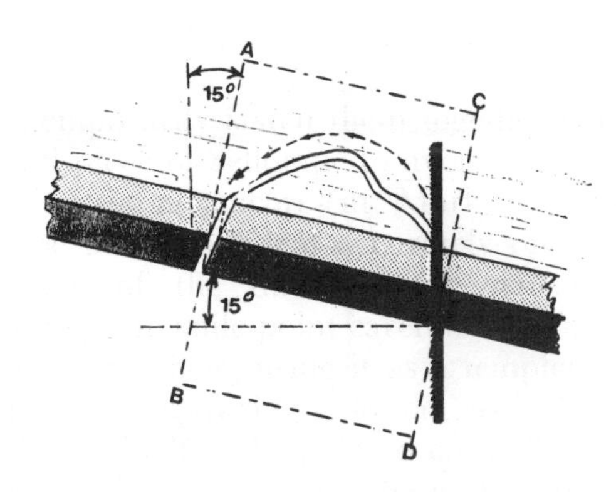

Fig. 120 The insert being let-in from below. The table angled at 15 degrees

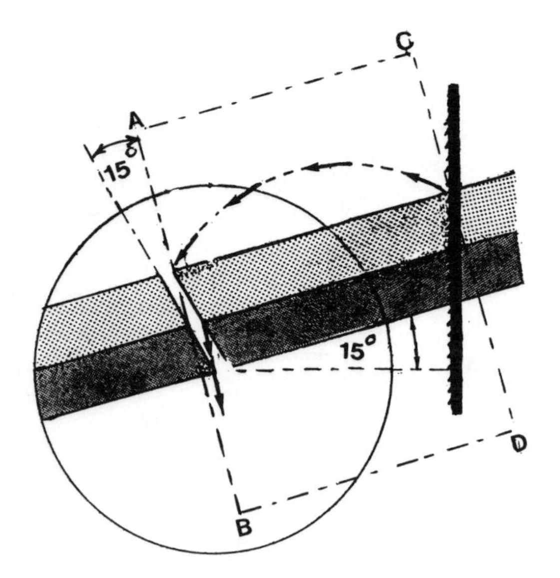

Fig. 121 The insert being let-in from above. Table angled in the opposite direction

The saw cut slot will have to be tapered wider below to enable the table to tilt up to 15 degrees right or left for bevel cutting. The V slot must also be undercut at an angle to allow the blade to remain vertical when the table is tilted. Fig.119.

Fig.120 shows the theory of the bevel cut technique, when the piece is required to be inserted from beneath the assembly.

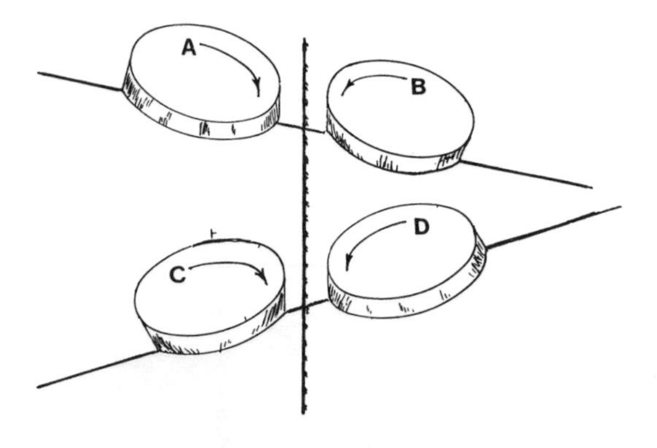

Fig. 122 The direction of feed depends on the angle of tilt; if the insert is let-in from above or below and if the saw teeth are pointed away from or towards the workpiece

Fig.121 (overleaf) shows the insert being 'let-in' from above. In both cases, for the purpose of this example, the table is angled to 15 degrees, and the distance between A-B is identical to C-D.

This shows we have to consider (1) the rotation of feed, (2) the direction of cut and (3) whether the piece is to be inserted from above or below the main picture assembly.

When the angle of incline is matched to the thickness of the sawblade and of the material to be cut, the joins will be invisible, *if the rotating direction of cut is correct.*

The direction of cut (whether the work is rotated in a clockwise or anti-clockwise direction as it is fed to the saw teeth), will depend upon whether you wish to insert the piece being cut from the face side or the back of the picture.

In Fig.122, (A) is rotated clockwise on a table angled downwards to the right, and the insert will be let-in from below; (B) is rotated anti-clockwise on the same angled table, to be let-in from above. Similarly, (C) is cut clockwise on a table tilted downwards to the left, and inserted from above, and (D) is fed anti-clockwise on the same table, and inserted from below.

As all hand-held fretsaws (and many home-made rigs) have their teeth pointing away from the craftsman, the work must be fed *towards* him and the saw. But power driven fret and scroll saws have their teeth *facing* the craftsman, and the workpiece has to be fed away from him, into the saw.

This reverses the direction of feed. It sounds more complicated than it is, and a few moments practice with either type of saw will quickly demonstrate the point. Keep the following table pinned up near your workbench.

This guide to the table angles will also depend on the thickness of the work being cut, and is a matter you will quickly discover after a few practice cuts.

The direction of feed option may help if you are either left-handed, or your saw table

HAND HELD FRETSAWS AND HOME RIGS

(Teeth of blade pointing away from the operator)

Table angled downwards to the left.	
Insert to be let-in from beneath:	Feed anti-clockwise
Insert to be let-in from above:	Feed clockwise
Table angled downwards to the right.	
Insert to be let-in from beneath:	Feed clockwise
Insert to be let-in from above:	Feed anti-clockwise

POWER FRET OR SCROLL SAWS

(Teeth of blade pointing towards the operator)

Table angled downwards to the left	
Insert to be let-in from beneath:	Feed clockwise
Insert to be let-in from above:	Feed anti-clockwise
Table angled downwards to the right	
Insert to be let-in from beneath:	Feed anti-clockwise
Insert to be let-in from above:	Feed clockwise

Fretsaw blades sizes

The following blade dimensions will vary according to the supplier, but average:

Blade size		Thickness		Width		Angle of tilt
		Inch	mm	Inch	mm	
No. 3	course	.034	.863	.016	.406	20 degrees
No. 1	robust	.028	.711	.013	.330	18 degrees
No. 2/0	medium	.022	.558	.008	.203	14 degrees
No. 4/0	fine	.016	.406	.0075	.190	12 degrees
No. 6/0	very fine	.015	.381	.0066	.167	10 degrees
No. 8/0	extremely fine	.012	.304	.006	.152	8 degrees

is already tilted in one direction and you do not wish to change it for one small insert.

Before tackling a picture, a simple cutting exercise will enable you to become familiar with the technique.

We will 'let-in' a motif from underneath and then insert a smaller detail within the new motif, this time from the top.

Begin by drawing the outline of tree foliage as shown in Fig.123, on to a piece of white veneer.

Sellotape this to a dark veneer, pierce a needle hole through a point on the line, and

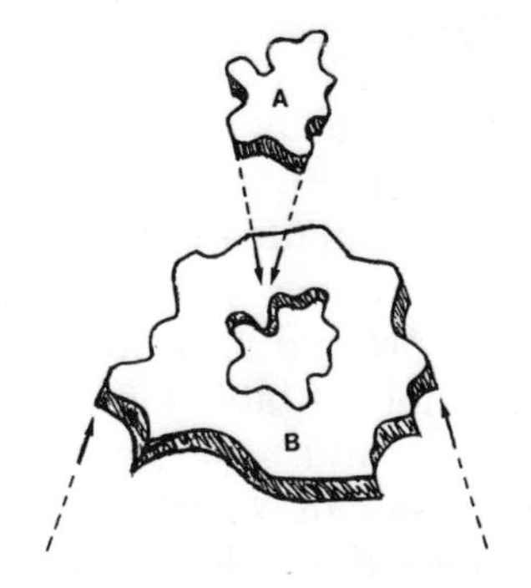

Fig. 123 The insert B to be let-in from below, will have insert A let-in from above

threadle the workpiece on to the hand-held fretsaw and tighten the top clamp of the frame.

We want to insert the larger piece from below. If you refer to the table you will see this requires you to tilt the angled table 12 degrees downwards to the left and *feed anti-clockwise*.

Saw around the outline, separate the two veneers and insert the piece from below. Secure it in place with a trace of PVA glue around the edges.

Now we want to insert the small section of the sky veneer through the tree foliage from above. Just for the sake of experiment tilt the table by lowering the right-hand side 12 degrees.

The chart shows that we need to feed anti-clockwise again. This time the sky insert will fit snugly into the foliage shape from above. The value of this exercise is very important when you come to make pictures. You will want to insert a house wall, for example, from underneath, and possibly need to insert windows and the door from above.

Combined methods

In practice, it is possible to combine both flatbed and angled bed cutting methods. For example, as a cutting exercise, you could cut identical motifs for six coasters – of any simple design of your choice – by the flatbed double cut technique.

This time, cut the motifs fractionally oversize or slightly larger than the final drawing. The motifs are assembled and then temporarily cemented directly on top of the background veneer with its underlaying waster and pressed until dry. Now they are cut on the angled tabled and bevel-cut with a 2/0 blade and inserted into the background, by sawing accurately to size on the required design line, for a perfect fit without visible joints.

Although hand-held fretsaw frames are the ideal way to start and to learn the techniques, you will soon discover the disadvantage is that one hand must feed the workpiece while the other operates the fretsaw. As you progress through the various fretsawing techniques, you will want to adapt your tool to make the task easier as the projects become more ambitious. This is overcome by making a home-made 'rig-up' which is a half-way step between the simple hand-held frame and power machines.

Home-made rig-ups

The magazines of both the Marquetry Society and the Marquetry Society of America contain numerous articles about how to improve fretsaws and, as in the case of knives, there are many ways of adapting the fretsaw to suit the individual.

This may be prompted by the cost of commercial machines or by the need to incorporate features not found in commercial saws.

Most home-made rigs incorporate certain advantages to suit one type of marquetarian which others would claim as disadvantages! These are some of the universally desired essentials:

(a) The home-made rig-up should be light in weight, portable and easy to store away.

(b) It should be capable of use on any worktop or table surface, with or without G clamps to anchor it.

(c) The first improvement is to extend the throat to cope with larger picture assemblies, by the use of dowelling as at 'A' in Fig.124.

(d) The depth between the upper and lower frame can be reduced by cutting the frame and fixing aluminium plates as at 'B' to enable broken blades to be used.

(e) Next comes the need to control the tensioning of blades. If the end of the frame is removed, its springiness can be replaced

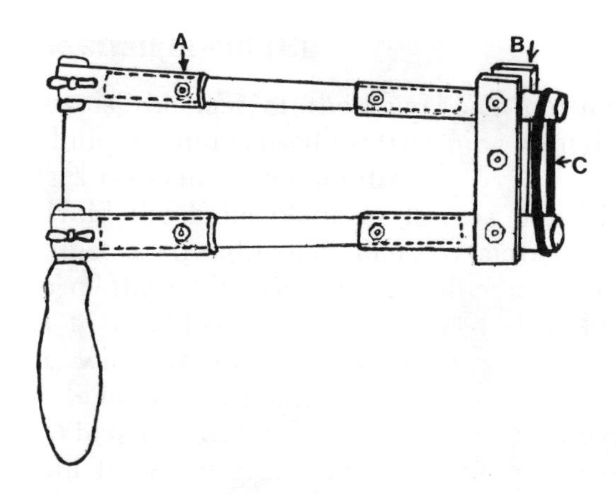

Fig. 124 The fretsaw frame throat can be extended with dowels or tubing

by either a coil spring or heavy duty rubber bands, as at 'C'.

Some of the older type of 'Hobbies' fretsaws, and some other makes are fitted with blade tensioning toggles, operating through a simple cam.

(f) The throat plate should be capable of inverting and have angled slots to suit table angle and bevel cutting.

(g) The throat plate can be removed easily when the slot becomes worn.

(h)any adaption can be made from readily available materials and the cost inexpensive.

(i) The next logical step is for precise and sensitive control, with instant speed changes to suit the design line being cut, through a hand-operated wheel.

(j) A foot treadle – working through either rubber bands or a spring – would leave both hands free to guide the work.

(k) The introduction of power: making use of small motors, worm drives and simple gearing.

Quite elaborate home-made rig-ups can be made, depending on other skills the marquetarian may possess, such as wood-working, metalworking, or engineering, etc.

First of all, here's a very elementary rig which will enable you to clip the frame on to a block to hold it upright while you change the blades and threadle the blade through the veneer. The dotted line in Fig.125 represents the veneer. Another simple rig, as shown in Fig.126, ensures the saw frame remains vertical.

Here are two excellent fretsaw devices which have been proved to be successful in recent years and have enabled hundreds of American amateur marquetarians to take up fretsawing.

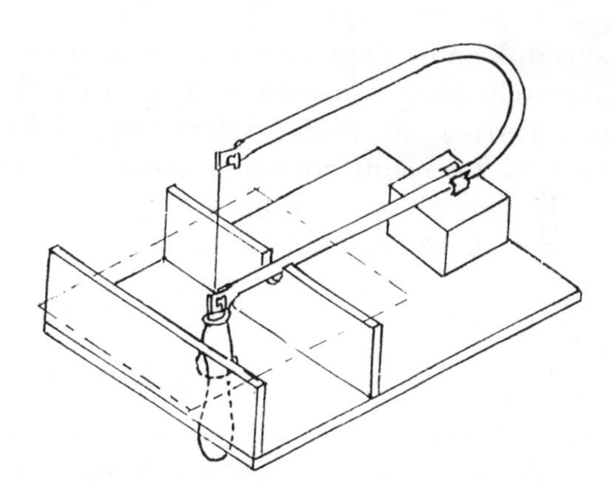

Fig. 125 A bench jig to hold the frame while changing blades

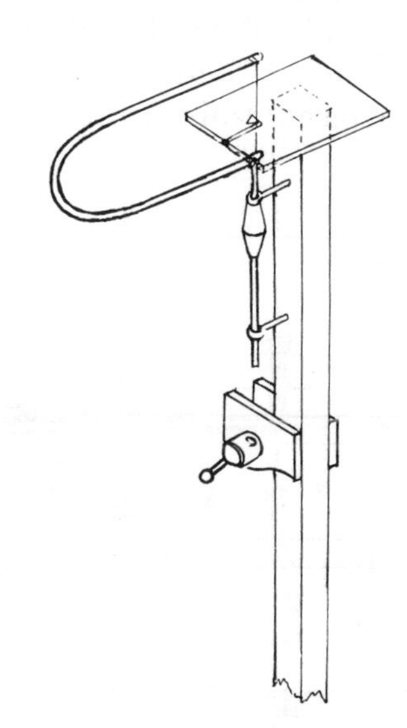

Fig. 126 A jig to ensure the saw cuts vertically

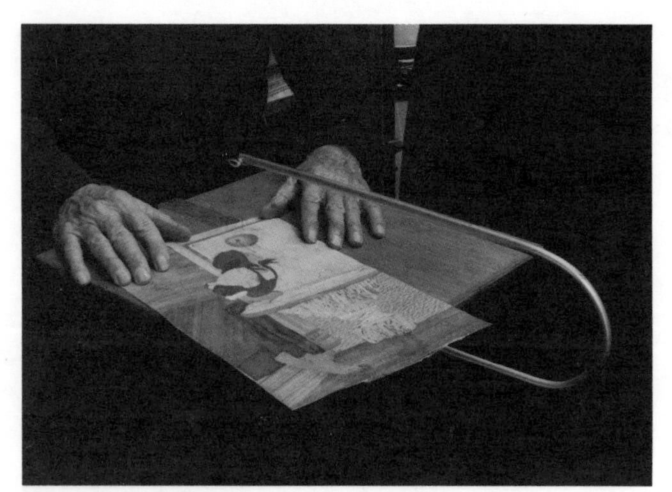

Fig. 127 Cutting a marquetry picture on the portable rig-up

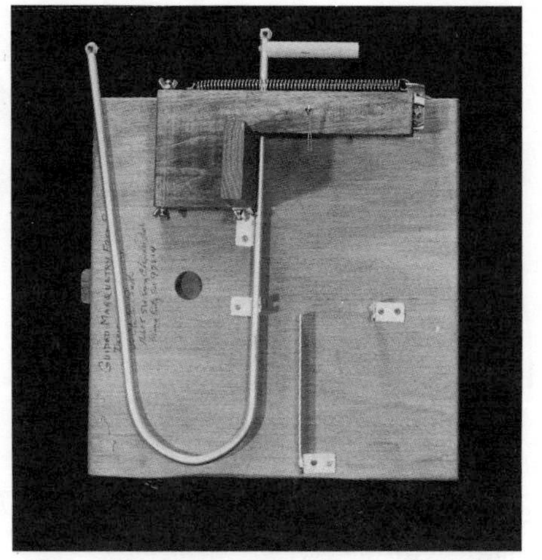

Fig. 128 The portable rig folded for carrying and storage

The first is from G. Clifton Baxter, of King City, Oregon, U.S.A., the National Chairman, Chapter Organising Committee of the Marquetry Society of America.

Fig.128 shows the portable rig-up in the carrying and storage position with the main frame secured under the table top with a wing nut.
This is shown diagramatically in Figs.129 and 130.

By releasing the wing nut (A) the saw will slide out of the slot. With the saw frame

Fig. 129 Diagram of the folded rig

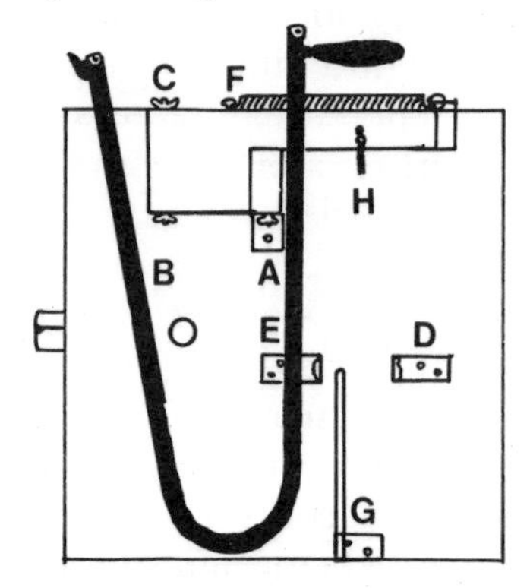

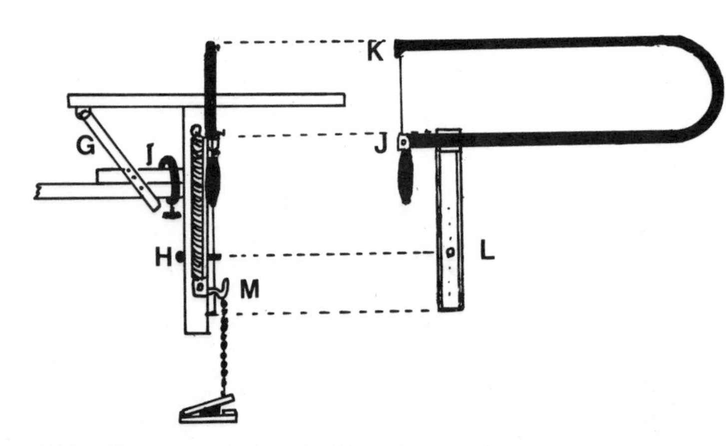

Fig. 130 Diagram of the rig from front and side

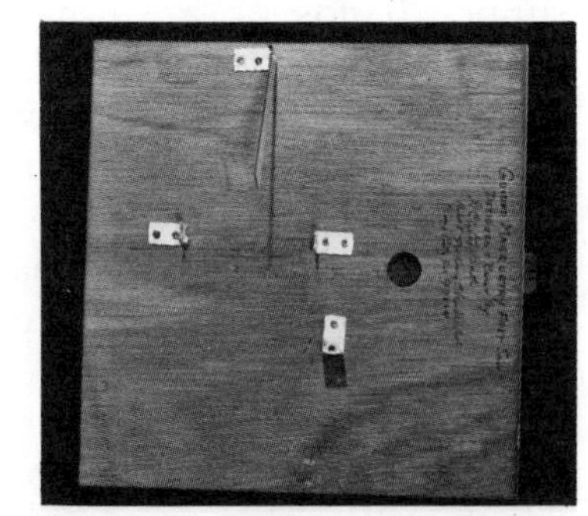

Fig. 131 The base of the dismantled table showing the bracket supports

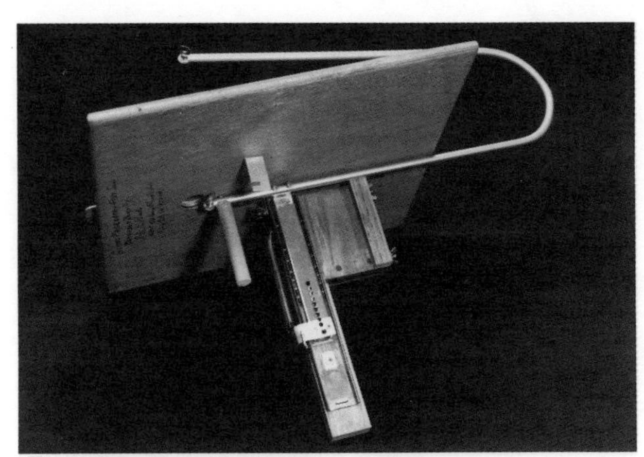

Fig. 132 A right-hand view showing the drawer slide, with the table tilted left

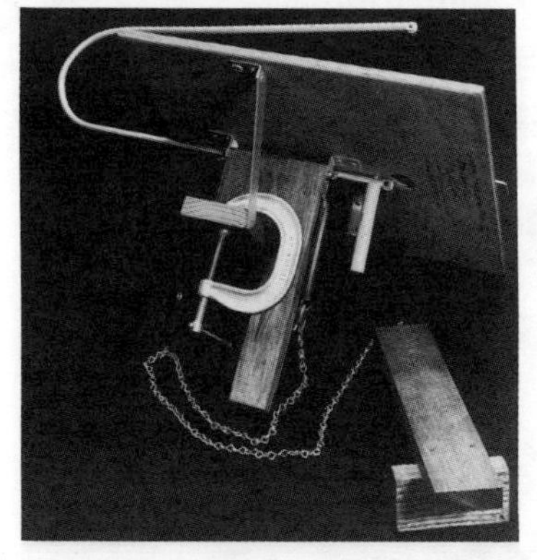

Fig. 133 The left hand side of the rig with table tilted down to the right

Fig. 134 A front view, table tilted to right, showing a foot treadle and chain

positioned over and under the table top, place the slotted brackets (E and D) over the bolted wing nuts (B and C) and tighten firmly.

Fasten the base as shown in Fig.130 (I) to the worktop table with a G cramp. Hook the coil spring over the screw head (F) (Fig.129) . Place the chain on the foot-feed over the hook (M) and adjust to the proper height for the full action of the saw.

Position the adjustable tilting bar (G) over the peg. The centre hole is for flatbed working, and the other holes are made for various degrees of bevel cutting.

Insert a blade, teeth pointing downwards and away from the operator, tighten in the lower clamp (J). Raise the saw as high as it will go and the insert cotter pin (H). Push the dovetail throat-piece into place with the sawblade in the slot. Fasten the blade in the upper clamp (K). Note: when the table is tilted to the left, keep the workpiece on the right side of the sawblade. When the table is tilted to the right, keep the work on the left of the saw.

On completion of the cut, raise the sawblade to the upper limit and push the cotter pin through the sliding mechanism (L). This is shown in Fig. 132 and is a smooth riding 'Accuride' ball-bearing drawer slide.

Release the blade from (K) and remove the workpiece. Fig.132 and Fig.133 show the underneath of the rig from both sides, and the table tilted at 12 degrees in each direction for bevel cutting. Fig.127 shows both hands free to guide the workpiece and the saw in use.

I am also endebted to Dr. Donald E. Winchell, of Lancaster, Ohio for details of his fretsaw rig.

The ordinary 12 inch (305mm) throat tubular fretsaw frame was lengthened by soldering in two lengths of ½ inch (12 mm) copper water pipe, to create a 24 inch (610 mm) throat. It can be made to any length

Fig. 135 A general view of the fretsaw rig-up

Fig. 136 View of the right hand side, showing the table set for 9 degrees cutting

to suit your needs. It may be necessary to shim the joint for a good fit.

Fig.135 shows the table in the flatbed position for vertical cutting with a simple hook in the top of a series of three screw eyes, on each side of the machine. Upon closer inspection there is a small wooden bar (held in place by simple pegs) marked '9° left'.

With this bar in place the table tilts to the left, and the hook reaches down to the middle screw eye. The hook on the opposite side hangs free. A similar wooden bar on the other side enables the table to tilt 9 degrees to the right. The bar is pegged with nails for easy lift off. When the wooden bar is removed, the table can now tilt to 12 degrees and the hook reaches the bottom screw eye.

Continuously variable tilt angles could be achieved by fitting a protractor, and a slotted metal strap, wing nut and washer to hold the table at any angle. The basic cranking mechanism and slotted saw frame guide are also shown. This needs to be fitted carefully to allow smooth movement, yet prevent the saw frame from wobbling.

Also shown in Fig.135 is the simple storage for replaceable throat plates for different bevel angles, which are slotted at

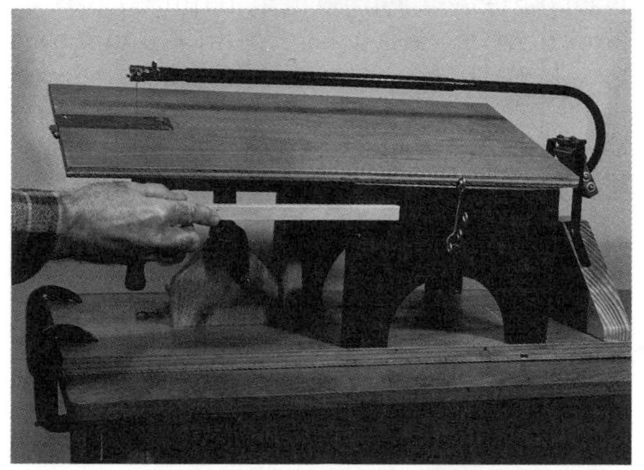

Fig. 137 The wooden plate removed and table fully tilted downwards to the right

Fig. 138 The table tilted 9 degrees left with the right hook hanging free

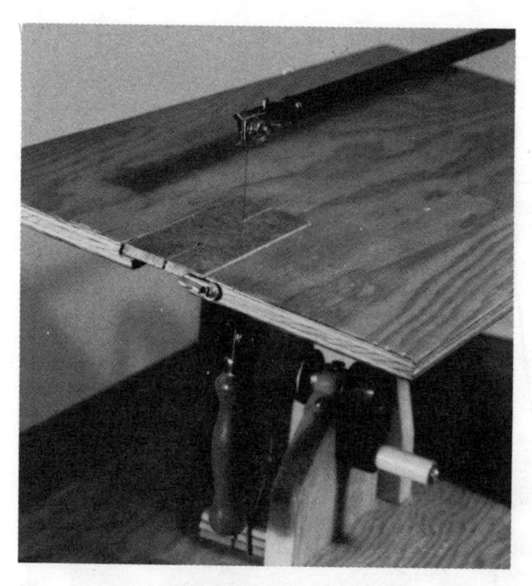

Fig. 139 The throat plates are slotted at each end for vertical and bevel cutting

Fig. 140 The cranking mechanism seen from the left side showing the three bolts

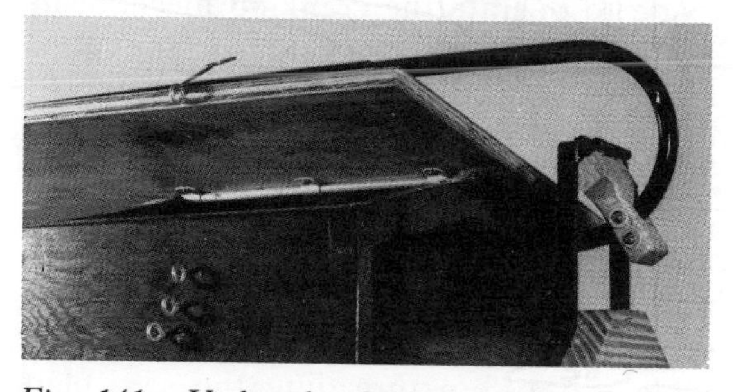

Fig. 141 Underside of table showing the steel pivot rod and mounting straps. Also hinge mechanism

each end and slightly undercut to suit left- and right-hand tilts.

The narrow saw slots prevent tiny pieces falling out. These throat plates are made from $\frac{1}{4}$ inch (6mm) plywood scraps or hardboard. They are dovetailed and held in place with a thumb button. The throat-plates can have slots and triangular V's to allow the table to be tilted in either direction.

Fig.136 shows the table tilted 9 degrees to the right with the hook in the middle screw eye. Fig.137 shows the wooden bar removed and the table tilted to 12 degrees, the hook in the bottom screw eye. In Fig.138 the table is tilted 9 degrees to the left with the hook hanging free on the right side.

The replaceable throat plate is shown in Fig.139. These are made for vertical cuts, 9 degrees and 12 degrees right and left cuts. One throat plate can have one end for a left tilt and the other end for a right tilt. This keeps the saw slots narrow so that tiny pieces can be cut out without dropping through wider slots. As the plates wear in use, they are easily replaced with $\frac{1}{4}$ inch (6mm) hardboard.

Fig.140 shows the cranking mechanism from the left side. The three bolts holding the blocks of wood to the saw frame are important. The centre one goes through the frame and prevents it from changing position. By adjusting the tension on the upper and lower bolts, the fit of the crank arm can be adjusted.

Fig.141 shows the underneath of the saw table which pivots on a $\frac{1}{4}$ inch (6 mm) steel rod. This is mounted at each end of the base frame with metal straps and is then turned on its back and the three pivot straps are fitted, one at each extreme end to prevent table movement, and the table is then mounted on the base frame

Here is a vital measurement: the pivot bar is $8\frac{1}{2}$ inches (216mm) above the base-board, to allow the table to tilt without interfering with the other mechanisms.

The saw frame must be $6\frac{1}{2}$ inches (165mm) above the baseboard, in order to clear the cranking mechanism; the fulcrum of the hinge is 9 inches (228mm) above the base, assuming the table top is made from 1/2 inch (12mm) plywood.

Fig.141 also shows the hinge mounting. It is essential that the fulcrum of the hinge is exactly at the centre of the saw frame, and at the level of the table top surface, and the frame positioned so that half is above and half below the hinge fulcrum. Otherwise the saw blade will travel forward and backwards in the saw slot, as well as the up and down movement.

Fig.142 shows the disassembled hand cranking mechanism. The crank shaft is a length of $\frac{1}{2}$ inch (12mm) copper water pipe joint, which should slide freely on the pipe (not the type that has stops in the middle), with a flat steel washer soldered to its end. A hole is drilled in the washer into which a short length of $\frac{1}{4}$ inch (6 mm) steel rod is soldered to form a crank.

A flanged length of $\frac{1}{4}$ inch (6 mm) copper tubing is used as an oil hole and is soldered in place to keep the bearing from rotating. The knob of the crank handle is drilled larger than the screw by which it is mounted, to allow it to turn freely on the screw.

In Fig. 143, the critical dimensions are from the centre of the crank axle to the baseboard (B); allow 2 inches (50 mm) from the centre of the axle to the tip of the crank arm to allow room for fingers when the crank is turned, and (A) 2 inches (50 mm) center-to center of the metal strap connecting the crank to the saw frame clamp, so the frame clamp will clear both the crank mechanism and the table top when in operation.

The entire crank mechanism can be eliminated and the saw handle used directly if preferred.

For foot treadle operation, either (a) a chain connects from the fretsaw handle to a foot pedal. Or (b), a treadle could be made to operate the cranking mechanism.

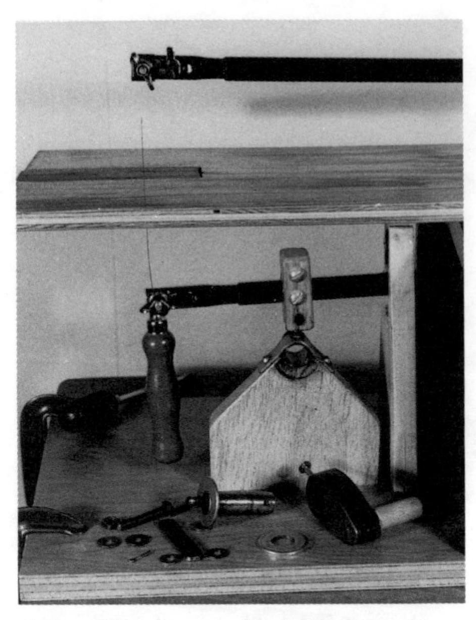

Fig. 142 The disassembled hand cranking mechanism

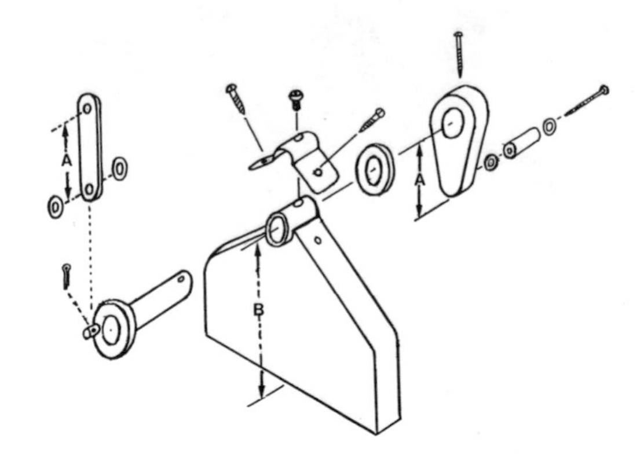

Fig. 143 A diagram of the hand cranking mechanism

If you wish to motorise the operation, Fig.144 shows the fretsaw frame connected to the crank mechanism, which would operate through a worm drive and gear wheel, to a small continuous duty rated motor running at about 300 strokes per minute. Control the motor with a foot-actuated 'on-off' switch. If using a tilted table, tilt before threading the saw blade into the chucks.

Although the rig-up can be adapted for foot treadle or motorised foot control, Dr.

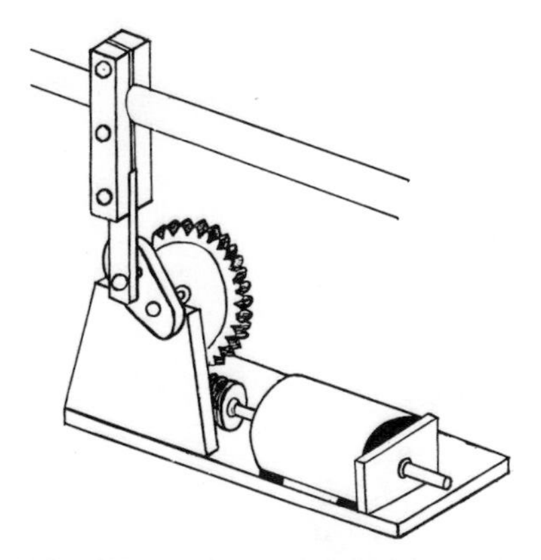

Fig. 144 Worm drive motorised cranking mechanism

Winchell is against modification. With a hand crank, the marquetarian has infinite and immediate control of cutting speed, starting and stopping. When making very intricate cuts with sharp pointed pattern lines, the hand crank can be grasped between thumb and fingers and gently rocked back and forth, as the blade slightly 'nibbles' its way very precisely. It can stop *instantly* if the cut begins to wander.

A light 'jogging' of the blade as the workpiece is turned sharply, also prevents the blade from binding or breaking.

Dr. Winchell is left-handed, and says it is a simple matter to locate the crank support mechanism to the right or left of the saw frame.

There is a wide variety of fretsaw rigs, many incorporate the ideas of the marquetarian, from the adaptation of old sewing machines to 'Heath-Robinson' contraptions, which all have similar features.

Professionals often eliminate the throat altogether and rig up the top clamp with a self-centring chuck from the ceiling to enable marquetry of any size to be handled. Other modifications include replacing the tubular steel frame by a wooden saw frame, swivelled at the closed end, and fitted with rubber bands to return the top of the frame after the down stroke. Also, wooden frame supports and side steadies at each side of the lower frame are added to eliminate side wobble.

The top arm may be fitted with a cam-lever toggle device as a means of tensioning the blades. The lower saw clamp is contrived to enable the blade to be inserted through the workpiece, before being placed on the table, and clamped to the lower arm of the saw frame, leaving only the top clamp to be tightened.

For further information on home-made rigs, contact your local branch of The Marquetry Society.

14
Advanced Fretsaw Techniques

The professional technique

THIS IS the 'batch' method, adapted from the traditional 'donkey' or French horse and used by professional marquetarians today, either on a mechanised rig-up, power or scroll saw.

The work is carried out on a flat saw table and requires great accuracy. By this method either a single insert for a picture may be cut or a batch of as many as the saw will cope with.

Usually a designer produces a water colour design in veneer tones, of the marquetry picture called a paramount. From this, a master 'show' drawing is prepared on strong parchment, vellum or strong cartridge or crystal paper.

A piece of lino or thick card is placed on a flat surface with the paper sheet for the 'show' drawing. The paramount design is then weighted down with metal bars, and pinned in the four corners.

A 'pricker' – a very fine No. 12 needle held in a pin vise or bottle cork – is worked over every inch of the master drawing, piercing holes through the paper as closely together as possible. The needle protrudes about 2mm. This seemingly tedious task is amply repaid by the accuracy of the resulting work.

Fig. 145 Frommia Precision fretsaw Type 187: Available for fixing to bench or on a separate stand

Professional craftsmen use a 'pouncing head' rather like an adaptation of a dentist's drill or a 'pricking machine' like a sewing machine. Amateurs have to do this by hand.

When the master 'pricking' is completed, it is held against a strong light to check that no part of the design has been missed. The back of each copy is rubbed lightly with a pumice stone to remove the burrs.

Pouncing the design

Next, a sheet of white paper is placed on a soft surface – either a cloth or lino – with the pricked design stretched tightly over it, held securely with metal bars and pinned at each corner.

A 'pounce' is a piece of felt rubber about 3 × 1 inch (75 × 25mm), or a piece of felt tied with string to form a hard pad.

The pounce is charged with fine bitumen or asphaltic powder and worked in circular movements on a piece of flat marble to ensure the rubber is well charged. It is then lightly worked over the pricked design and the powder is tapped or pounced through the tiny perforations.

The design is carefully unpinned and the weights removed. Now the pounced design is carefully removed without disturbing the powdered outlines and held over a diffused heat source, such as a hot-plate. This causes the paper to yellow slightly but permanently fixes the powder.

In this way, exactly as practised for centuries, any number of identical original or reverse pouncings can be made.

Alternatively, make a 'master control' tracing of the design with a very fine pen and Indian ink on transparent plastic film. From the master you can obtain photocopies in face or reverse from your local stationers, but the traditional method can produce fine needle-sharp lines to follow and are much cheaper to produce as so many copies are required.

Make separate pouncings of the complete design in reverse, for every part of the design, (not just for every veneer in the design.) Also for the cutting sequence: one is required for each of marquetry assemblies to be produced. Each part of the design is accurately cut out with a sharp knife to within 2mm of the pricked design line, and laid out in the form of an 'exploded' design in a felt lined tray.

Now make pads of the selected veneers, of the required number to suit the batch of assemblies in production.

If only six veneers are to be cut at one time, no waxing of the blade is necessary, but for larger pads it is usual to interlay a sheet of waxed paper, suet paper or paper coated with Russian tallow or candle wax to lubricate the saw. Oil is never used as this will discolour the veneers.

A sheet of paper is coated with candle wax on one side and then folded in half to form a double thickness of paper with the wax inside, to prevent contact with the veneers. The veneers are kept papered sides uppermost and all in the same grain directon.

If a picture insert segment is required, the veneer with the design on top, and a waste veneer to take the saw swarf, is all that is required for a 'pad'.

The pads can vary in size, from a small batch of three veneers for a marquetry

Fig. 146 A bundle prepared for sawing on a power saw

insert, to a bundle of 24 or 32 veneers, as in Fig.146.

If a quantity of say, six motifs are to be cut, the pad would have a 2mm veneer, with the design fastened to it on top, and a 3mm veneer waster underneath to take the saw swarf. The pad may be simply stapled together with a commercial type stapling machine.

Small pads can be pierced with an awl for the saw blade to enter, which forces the wood fibres apart; they will close up later as no wood dust is lost as is the case with a drill.

Larger pads have their outside edges coated with glue and are allowed to set in a press until dry. Compact the pad between two thin pieces of plywood, and secure with panel pins.

For drilling 'island' parts of the design within the pattern, a 2mm diameter drill is made which has four flats ground on the sides tapering to a point. This can be made from a broken drill shank. It prevents the drill from wandering.

Large pads are nailed together with very fine steel wire nails. Ensure that the plywood cutting pad is ½ inch (12 mm) larger in each direction to allow a working margin for pinning or nailing. As a precaution against splitting the veneers, drill a few tiny holes where the nails are to be inserted. Nip off the points before nailing through the drilled holes against the steel plate, as the pointed ends will bend over. Also nip off the protruding heads.

The edges of the complete pad are trimmed on the bandsaw and the bottom of the pad touched with talcum powder for ease of handling on the saw table.

The saw table must be perfectly flat and the saw vertical in both front and side elevations.

Each part of the paper design is now taken from the tray, and glued on top of the pad and allowed to dry.

If necessary panel pins are driven in at 1 inch (25mm) intervals to strengthen the pad, away from the design line. If panel pins or nails are inserted within the design area, they must be driven in vertically or there is a risk of breaking the saw. Draw a pencilled ring around them as a warning.

Sawing technique

1. *'Split the line'.* For this method the accuracy of sawing is critical. It is carried out at 'half-mark'. As the line to be sawn is needle thin and a fine sawblade is used, great accuracy is possible. Try to split the line in two. With practice, try to leave a hairline fraction of the needle sharp cutting line visible. As cutting proceeds, the waste between pieces is secured with gummed taper tape to keep the pad intact.
2. *'Male and female.'* By this method the saw cuts to the *inside* of the line when cutting the background veneer, and to the *outside* of the line when cutting the parts to be inserted, remembering the old adage that 'it is easier to take a bit more off than to put a bit more on!' This method enables a more robust sawblade to be used with far less breakages. Accurate cutting is only achieved after a great deal of experience.
3. *'The nibble'.* This allows for a really tough sawblade, such as a helical shaped scrollsaw, which can cut in any direction.

First an easy shape is cut around well away from the required curved or jagged design line to remove most of the waste veneer. Then the design line is approached in a series of swooping 'bites' rather like nibbling the edges of a biscuit. This works very well but if carried too far, results in the 'cart-wheel' shapes around foliage, visible in many professional pictures!

As each part of the design is cut out, it is placed in a felt lined sectional tray until the sawing of the design components is completed.

Assembly of the background

Many designs include parts which require special treatment, such as sand shading, to create the effects of folds or shadows in ribbon or floral subjects and in segmented sunburst designs, fans, urns etc. This process is described later, in Chapter 16.

It is carried out before the background of the motif is dealt with, to allow time for the sand shaded pieces to regain the moisture lost in the process and be restored to their shape.

A reverse copy of the master control design is pounced on to a sheet of lightweight kraft paper and fastened on to a flat smooth surface – known in the trade as an inlay board – in preparation for assembly. It is wiped with a damp sponge and allowed to dry.

Carefully following the master control sheet, the background veneer is placed in position face down. Then the numbered parts are picked up with tweezers and assembled jigsaw fashion. The trick is to complete the outer parts first and work towards the centre. If work begins at the centre it tends to come out larger than intended. If the picture is a large one, a flat heavy weight is placed over each newly assembled part to keep it flat as work proceeds, and as each assembly is completed it is placed in a press.

It is often necessary to moisten the glue or add fresh glue. To avoid this problem a favourite method used by the old inlay motif makers, was to place the kraft paper, brushed with glue, on a metal hot plate over a constant heat source – a candle!

This kept the glue tacky, and when the motif was complete and the kraft was removed from the hotplate, the glue set rapidly

Allowance has to be made for human error and fatigue. To compensate for this tendency to wander from the line, the pouncings are made for cutting all the components of the motif or design, but an identical pounce is *not* used for the background.

Instead, the sawn motif parts are cut out and separated into trays, then temporarily fastened individually to the top of each background veneer, and the actual contour followed by a fine sawblade, using the bevel cut on an angled sawtable.

If this is not practical due to the size of the piece, the motif is placed over a sheet of plain paper with a leaf of carbon paper between. When rubbed over with a smooth tool, such as the pene of a hammer, the slight swarf on the underside of the veneer prints an impression on the paper. This is sometimes done with heelball, as in making a brass rubbing.

This outline is then used as a cutting line for the background veneer, thus compensating for any sawing errors.

Modern marquetarians use edge-to-edge butt-jointing with white PVA adhesive. If the veneers are papered on their back or loose side, the assembly may be rubber cemented to a reverse design. The design is then peeled from the face side, and the rubber cement rolled off. The assembly is scrutinised against a strong light to check for flaws, which can be rectified at this stage.

The motifs are filled and scraped level on the back and, if they are for sale, it is trade custom to supply them with the face side covered with brown kraft paper, ready for insertion into the main veneer assembly.

POWER SCROLL SAWING

By using the three techniques previously explained, the power scroll saw can easily deal with the simple double cut for interchange marquetry; the pad cut to create pictures from a single cutting operation, and professional batch cutting, all carried out on the level table.

For bevel cutting, we move to the angled table. Apart from the angle of tilt and the direction of feed, the actual cutting of a marquetry picture is the same as in hand-held cutting.

Only two pieces of veneer need be cut at a time. The degree of table tilt will depend on the saw thickness, and this will vary from about 8 degrees to 15 degrees. If the table angle is too great the veneers will tend to feather at the edges, and if the tilt is too small they will not fit tightly.

A few moments of experiment with a some scrap veneers will determine what is best for your method of work. It may be necessary to modify the bird's mouth of your cutting table to suit the table tilt, but most power saws with angled tables have taken this into account.

Power sawing has many distinct advantages but at first you will have to learn how to benefit from them.

No waste veneer is necessary to take swarf of the saw. The workpiece gets better support from the narrow opening in the saw table. The power saw has a much bigger throat.

Many marquetarians prefer to remove the hold down 'foot' device to enable them to see the line more clearly, and to make a simple thimble plate to prevent the veneers from lifting on the up-stroke.

Now both hands are free; the table can be set at any desired angle accurately and will remain constantly at that set angle, yet can be changed at will.

To remove a blade, loosen the top chuck first, then the bottom chuck. When the design requires a sharp pointed shape cut or a U turn, pivot the veneers with the saw running, and while pivoting ease the veneers back slightly so that the pressure comes to bear on the rounded back of the blade and you will hear that the saw is not cutting. Now gently swing the workpiece around to its new direction and continue cutting.

If the blade breaks, do not try to insert the new blade in the saw kerf. It is best to return to the original drill hole to insert the new blade and then to restart the cut. When you have changed the blade, the workpiece may have moved fractionally. The easiest way to re-align it is to tilt the saw table the opposite way, and saw around in the opposite direction to meet the original sawcut and the bevel will match where the lines meets.

When you are new to power sawing, breaking saw blades can become a constant and annoying problem. The choice of blade is a compromise between a thin saw kerf and freedom from breakages.

The 2/0 veneer cutting double-toothed blade with the rounded back is suitable for marquetry work, as they have a slight set and clear the sawdust, but the more robust, single-teeth, jeweller's metal-piercing blades, No 1 or 3 can also be used by this technique.

When these metal-piercing blades are used on very hard species such as ebony or rosewood, they tend to clog and overheat and are likely to become brittle and snap more readily and the blades need tempering.

Tempering the blades

Jeweller's metal-piercing blades have a high carbon content and are tempered to only 230°C to suit metal cutting. For marquetry, we need less brittle blades and can temper them to suit. Lead melts at 330°C, which, coincidentally, is the ideal temperature to temper blades for marquetry. We need only heat some lead in a shallow tin over a hotplate, immerse the blades for only half a minute, remove and allow them to air cool. This will give them a far longer life with less breakages.

Tempered blades are available from Marquetry Society suppliers.

Combination Methods

In practice, a combination of both flat and angled table methods are used when the design lends itself.

For example, as a cutting exercise you could cut identical motifs for six coasters – of any simple design of your choice – by the flatbed double cut or batch cut techniques.

First of all, a multi-layered pad of veneers is cut with a robust blade on the flat table using either the simple double cut or the batch series cut.

The periphery of the decorative marquetry motifs cut by this technique are cut fractionally oversize or slightly larger than the final drawing. The motifs are assembled and then temporarily cemented directly on top of the background veneer with its underlaying waster and pressed until dry. Now they are bevel cut on the angled table with a 2/0 blade and inserted into the background, by sawing accurately to size on the required design line, for a perfect fit without visible joints.

Fretsawing by the window method

Remember, there are two ways to work when cutting the window method on a power saw. The required piece for the picture may be inserted from beneath or from above. Let us examine the differences between knife-cutting and fretsaw cutting by the window method.

In knife-cutting, we cut an aperture in the assembly to the shape of the required insert. The edges of this hole acted as a templet to guide the knife when cutting the actual insert.

In fretsawing, the technique is slightly different. Cutting is normally carried out on the back of the picture from a reverse design and the workpiece inserted from underneath – the face side – up into the picture assembly.

The first step is to cut the window about $\frac{1}{16}$th to $\frac{1}{8}$th inch (2–3mm) undersize. This need not follow the contours of the design line, but may be any simple shape which would allow the underlying veneer to show through.

When the veneers have been tested for suitability, grain direction etc., they are fastened to the back of the assembly with small pieces of gummed veneer tape, or Sellotape or a few spots of rubber cement between them to prevent slipping. (Small segments can be simply held with finger pressure only.)

The hole is then pierced and the blade entered. Sawing is carried out on the angled table exactly on the design line and the insert fitted up into the assembly from below.

Most pieces will be cut from the reverse design, on the back (or loose, tension side which will eventually be glued to the groundwork), and inserted from the underside, (tight, compression, face side which will be polished).

However, those small inserts of the picture which have another piece within them, (such as the tree with the sky showing through the foliage) need to be cut in from both directions.

Whenever you need to let-in a piece from above, (with a reverse shaped bevel) the required veneer is simply laid over the picture in its required position and the design brought down over it and the outline marked. The table and direction of feed chart will show how to tilt the table in the opposite direction and adjust the direction of feed to suit.

This is obviously a much more simple method than cutting a window first, since it involves only one cutting. For this reason, many marquetarians prefer to cut a 'true' design 'face' side up, (not from a reverse design) so that they can actually see exactly what they are producing.

In this case the veneers cannot be tested for grain direction using a window aperture, but a 'finder' design is used, as in the pad method, to mark the selected veneer first and this is laid on top of the picture, tested for accuracy of register, and with a single cutting operation, let-in from above.

The most difficult lines to fretsaw accurately are straight or gently curving ones. A good fretsawing tip to overcome this is to either make the aperture by the window method, or make a wooden, metal or plastic templet, and score around the templet with a knife cut. Then use a sharply pointed HH pencil to follow the scored line and the saw will tend to follow this 'railway line' groove without wandering.

After you have practised all these techniques and decide to take up marquetry seriously, you might well decide to indulge yourself with the aquisition of a marquetry machine.

Fig. 147 Hegner Multicut 2. Fretsaw

Fig. 148 Frommia Precision fretsaw Type 187B: with 2 metre throat

Fretsaw Machines

Hegner Multicut 2

Ideal for the amateur marquetarian. This is a high performance universal fretsaw. Technical data: Maximum cutting height 1.97 inch (50mm): depth of throat, 14.37 inch (365mm), adjustable worktable calibrated up to 45 degrees.
Cutting strokes, 720 per minute. Motor, 90 watt 110/120v, 60Hz, or 90 watt 220/240v, 50Hz. It is possible to introduce a sawblade through a pre-drilled hole in the workpiece, with the blade remaining installed in the machine.

Hegner Polycut 3

This is the ultimate machine for the professional marquetarian. A four speed high performance saw, which can cut a smooth straight line as well as the most intricate, twisting lines on internal or external radii as small as 0.5mm. A 'V' belt drive provides 4 cutting speeds, that takes only 30 seconds to change, with a maximum output at 1,600 rpm.

Technical data: Maximum cutting height 2.16 inches (55mm). Depth of throat 19.69 inches (500mm). Adjustable worktable: calibrated up to 45 degree angle of tilt each side. Cutting stroke 24mm.
Eccentric speeds 1600, 1270, 1100, and 700 rpm Motor, 180 watt 110/120 or 220/240v 60Hz. Uses 5 inch (130mm) fretsaw blades.
Optional extras:
Speed control unit. User can adjust cutting stroke rate from maximum to almost zero, essential for advanced marquetry cutting. *Workpiece hold-down arm.* Supplied with adjustable height control and guard. *Foot switch.* Leaves both hands free to control the workpiece. *Machine stand.* For vibration free mounting. *Adjustable Lamp and magnifier.*

Frommia Precision fretsaw
Technical data.

Table size $68\frac{5}{8}$ inch (2,200 mm). Throat capacity of $39\frac{1}{2}$ inch (1,000 mm) each side of saw total 2,000 mm. Cutting stroke $1\frac{5}{32}$ inch (30mm). Strokes per minute 500/775/1000. Motor 0.18kW (0.25 H.P). Motor speed 1,500 rpm.

Table tilts to either side 30 degrees and is vertically adjustable to use broken saw blades. Blower removes sawdust. Accomodates standard saws. Suitable for cutting softwood $1\frac{1}{4}$ inch (30mm), hardwood $\frac{3}{4}$ inch (20mm) synthetics $\frac{5}{8}$ inch (15mm) aluminium $\frac{1}{3}$ inch (8mm) brass $\frac{1}{5}$ inch (5mm) tin, zinc and copper $\frac{5}{32}$ inch (4mm).

Fig. 149 Hegner Polycut 3 Scrollsaw

15
Advanced Cutting Techniques

The Window Method

WE HAVE already met the window method in the test-piece and in making 'Evening on the Broads'. It is the traditional professional knife cutting technique which has been used for the hand cutting of marquetry pictures for many years.

The advantages of this method are:

(a) The effect of each piece of veneer in the picture can be seen before it is cut.

(b) Several alternatives can be offered to the 'window' and tested for suitability.

(c) Accurate fitting is achieved as each piece of veneer is cut from, and fitted snugly to, the adjacent parts in the picture and not from the design line.

(d) Despite inaccuracies of cutting to the original design line, the veneer parts will fit accurately.

(e) As the picture develops, modifications may be made to the design to suit the freak figure, markings or other characteristics of the veneer as the overall effect of the composition emerges.

(f) For pictures with a predominating background comprising only one or two veneers, it is easier to use these actual veneers as the waster and cut the picture directly into the background.

(g) Poorly fitting parts can be easily removed and replacements parts cut and fitted.

(h) By PVA butt-jointing the assembly it is possible to make up component parts of a picture, such as individual roses, place them on different backgrounds to test the effect, and in various positions, to effect a balanced floral arrangement, *prior* to 'letting them in' to the selected background.

Most knives have blades which have a double wane or bevel, (as we met with the 'sliver cutting' exercise, and the fibres of the veneer are pushed aside as the knife ploughs through them.

A slightly raised lip occurs on the surface and a 'V' cut results, with open joins on the side of the picture you are working on. The side with the best joins is underneath on what should be the 'tight' or 'face' side of the picture.

This is the best side, and is the side we want to see when the picture is finished. This means we have to glue the 'loose' or open 'V' cut side to the baseboard. The snag is, the side we are working on will show the picture the wrong way around, and the face side will be in reverse.

Now that doesn't matter with some subjects, but if the picture was of a particular view which you need to show the correct way around – not a mirror image of it – we would have to begin by reversing the design.

Reverse designs are widely used in all techniques. However, there is a more advanced way of both working on the face side (the correct way round) but at the same time eliminating those open V cuts.

Single wane, bevel cutting.

The way to resolve this problem without reversing the design, is shown in Fig. 154

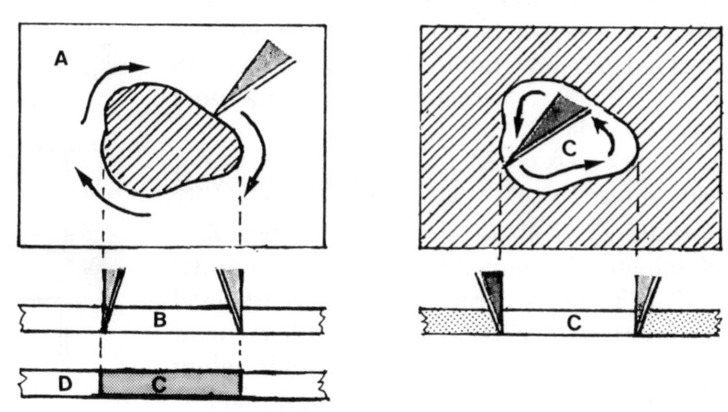

Figs. 150–154 Bevel cutting with single wane knife

where 'A' is the picture veneer, 'B' shows the 'window' aperture being cut, and 'C' shows the insert veneer being cut.

Notice how the single wane blade is held vertically but with the bevel of the blade sloping *inwards* towards the centre of the hole and the flat side of the blade held upright against the edge to be joined.

This time, the wane of the knife blade slopes *outwards* with the flat side of the blade held vertically against the edge of the veneer to be joined again, resulting in a square edged insert and a square edged hole, as shown at D. *But the direction of cut has to be reversed.*

The knife is tilted *inwards* with a clockwise cutting direction for the window and tilted *outwards* with an anti-clockwise cutting direction for the insert.

The window method is also used for fretsawing techniques.

Fretsaw bevel cutting on the flat table

Advanced marquetarians can also achieve fretsaw bevel cutting on the flat table and make joins which are invisible.

Until you are proficient in using a hand-held fretsaw frame you are advised to work on an angled table.

Using a flat table, the saw is held at an exact angle to the vertical, to compensate for the thickness of the saw, plus the thickness of the veneer sandwich. The angle of tilt will vary from about 9 degrees to 15 degrees depending on the saw thickness being used. It is a matter of trial and error.

Right-handed people sit to the left of the saw table and left-handers sit to the right. If the saw is inclined towards the centre of the piece being cut out, the workpiece is rotated towards it in an anti-clockwise direction if the piece is to be inserted from below, and in a clockwise direction if the insert is from above.

If the saw is tilted outwards from the centre of the piece being cut, inserts from above are fed in an anti-clockwise direction and from below in a clockwise direction.

I am greatful to John Sedgwick of the Marquetry Society of Ontario, Canada, for supplying the following sequence. He has developed his own technique of fretsawing in which he uses a fretsaw with the throat extended to 30 inches (762mm) and supports the end of the frame by bending a wire coat-hanger over the back of a chair!

John does all his work on a flat table on which he can undertake either flat or bevel cutting with ease. He holds the fretsaw in a completely unconventional way. Instead of having the saw throat facing his cutting arm and shoulder immediately in front of him, he leaves the saw in the conventional position relative to the workpiece, but sits at ninety degrees to it, resting his cutting arm along his thigh. He can sit comfortably for long periods, and can see and follow the line more clearly.

He angles the saw at about 11 degrees and cuts a bevel in either a clockwise or an anti-clockwise direction, depending on whether the insert is to be let-in from the top or bottom. The angle can be varied to suit the thickness of the veneer sandwich being cut.

To illustrate the technique, here is a portrait silhouette design using two contrasting veneers.

Begin by fastening the design across the top of the dark veneer with Sellotape and applying pencilled registration marks. Using white or yellow carbon paper, trace the outline with a sharp HB pencil or stylus. (Fig.155 and 156). Place the light, contrasting veneer of the same size beneath the dark veneer. (Fig 157).

Tape the top and bottom edges of the sandwich. Now cover the pattern lines on the top, (dark) veneer with clear Sellotape. Cover the back of the light veneer with paper veneer tape to prevent accidental breakage during cutting, (Fig.158). Pierce through both veneers with the point of a knife. Thread the fretsaw blade though both veneers and tension the blade (Fig.159). Cut along the design line of the largest piece (Fig 160).

Note the position of the fretsaw frame. Remove the unwanted dark segment (Fig.161). Now hinge back the light veneer and apply PVA adhesive to the interior perimeter edge of the dark veneer (Fig.162). The light veneer piece, cut simultaneously, can now be inserted from below to fit exactly into the dark veneer and rollered into the assembly (Fig 163). The assembly is covered with a perspex tile and weighted down until dry, (Fig.164). The light veneer is hinged back into position in the sandwich and the cutting is continued (Fig.165).

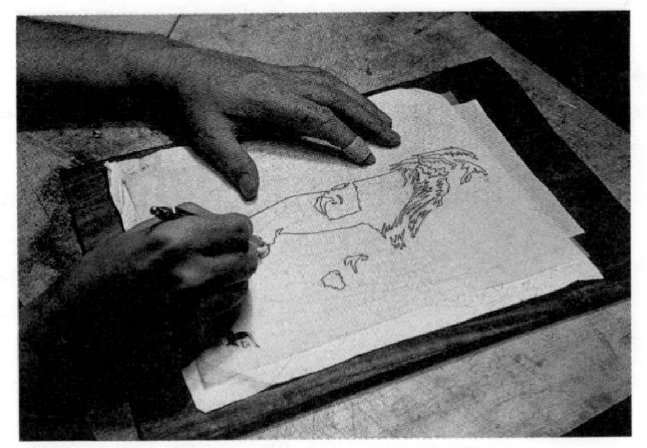

Fig. 155 Tape and trace the design to the dark veneer

Fig. 156 Use a yellow carbon on dark veneer

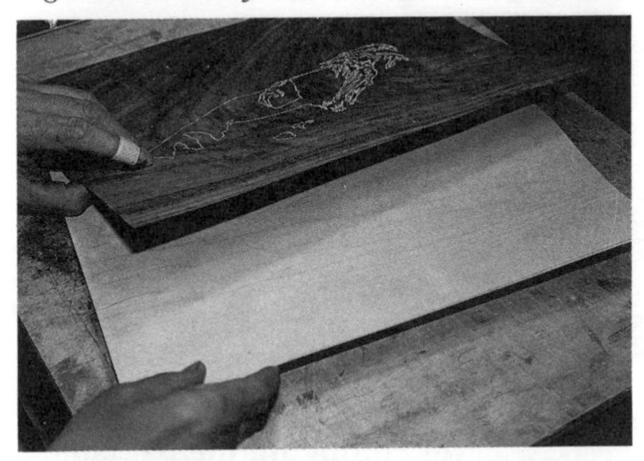

Fig. 157 Place a contrasting veneer below

Fig. 158 The top and bottom edges are taped

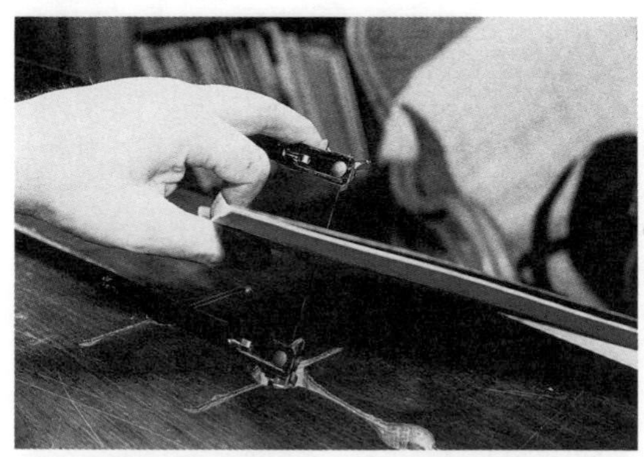

Fig. 159 Threadle the blade through both veneers and tension the saw blade

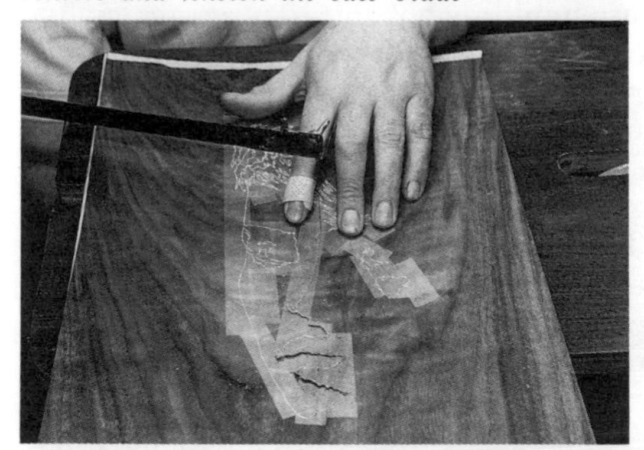

Fig. 160 Cut out the largest piece first

Fig. 161 Remove the dark veneer window

Fig. 162 Hinge back the light veneer and apply adhesive to the dark veneer edges

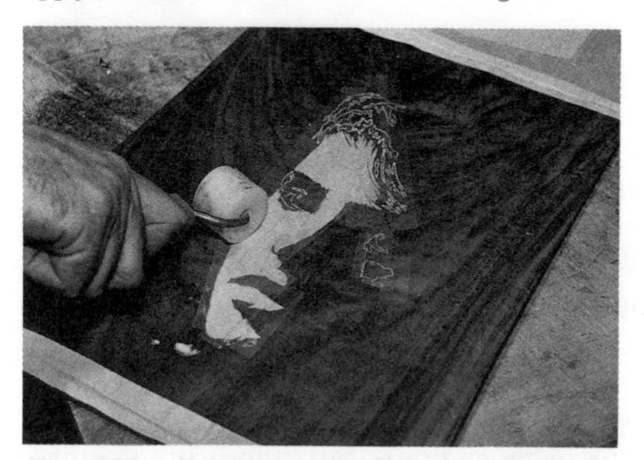

Fig. 163 Position and roller the insert

Fig. 164 Place under a weight until dry

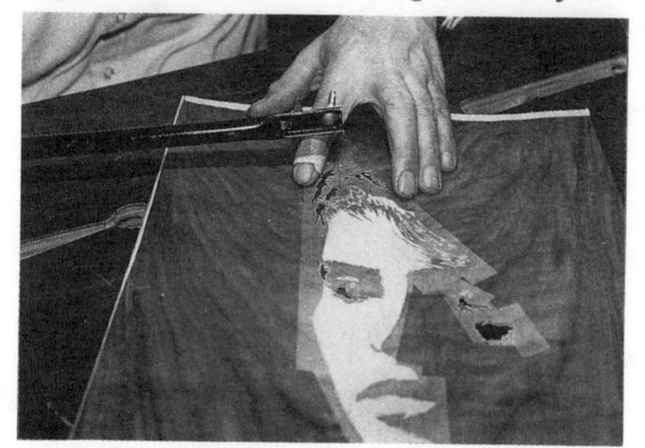

Fig. 165 Hinge the light veneer back

By this method, John has won many prizes in international exhibitions. His picture *Harbour Sunrise* won 1st prize in the 1983 Canadian National Exhibition. *Rocky Mountain High* (See colour plates section) won 1st prize in the Marquetry Society of America's Californian show, and also second prize in the Marquetry Society National in 1987. *Creation* won 1st prize in the North Carolina MSA and third in the Marquetry Society National in 1987.

Overstep Technique

We can now bring together everything you have learned about knife-cutting and fretsaw cutting and combine them to produce a first class picture. But first we have to understand progressive stage drawings for sequential cutting of the overstep technique.

In the same way that an experienced musician can 'sight read' a new piece of music, or an engineer can read a blue-print, so an experienced marquetarian learns to read a complicated marquetry design.

The advanced 'overstep' method requires the marquetarian to 'think one step ahead' and plan the sequence of cutting from his master design.

You will recall how we overlapped the picture veneers into the surrounding border margin, so that we could trim them off neatly afterwards and get the picture square? The same overstep – sometimes called the 'overcut' technique – can simplify the shape of the piece to be cut and also make it less fragile, which is very important with irregular cross-grained pieces.

Even more important is what happens if we *don't* use the overstep technique. If we cut a piece to exactly the right shape, to be butt-jointed to an adjacent piece already in the assembly, we are obliged to cut along the common joint between them through the PVA glueline.

The new piece has to be glued to an edge on which the glue has dried on the original piece. This is not ideal, as it will affect subsequent gluing.

As the knife or saw cuts along the glueline it is quite easy to leave behind a fragment or splinter in the old glued joint, which goes undetected until the picture is polished, when it will show up and spoil the picture. And no matter how accurately you make this 'double-cut' along the common joint for the second time, it will not be such a perfect fit as a single cut.

Therefore, the rules to remember are:

(1) *Never cut along an existing glueline.* To avoid doing so in practice requires us to 'think one step ahead' and contrive to bring the design line of the piece to be cut, below or within the line of the adjacent piece, to be trimmed off later.

(2) Always cut the piece furthest away in perspective.

(3) Omit all detail which falls completely within another larger part of the design; for example, omit the windows and doors of a house until it is possible to insert them after the wall has been fitted.

(4) Omit any parts of the design which runs through or across other pieces, and cut these in later. (For example, the bridge in Fig.166.)

This also makes it easier to ensure grain continuity in those parts which are separated in the final design (i.e., the sky peeping through tree foliage).

Obviously this does not apply when you are obliged to cut across a glue joint when inserting detail, or when tracing and cutting-in small detail within a background.

It's quite simple when you get the hang of it! Once you master this 'overstep' technique your pictures will be enormously improved, because every veneer joint will be freshly cut.

Advanced bevel cutting of marquetry pictures requires us to observe the same rules and to plan the sequence of cutting.

With knife cutting, this entailed cutting only the topmost outline of the first piece correctly, and allowing the lower sides of the piece to overlap into the adjacent areas so that the next piece would be cut to its correct shape where the two parts meet, and the edges of the second piece would be cut to overlap into the position of the third piece, and so on. With fretsawing, the logical place to begin and pierce the blade hole is in the next segment to be cut (which will remove the hole).

Each time the pattern line is cut away, bring down the design, check the registration and restore the next design line to be cut.

To clarify the thought processes involved in reading a design properly, we will follow the reasoning step-by-step with a new design.

Let us put into practice this 'overstep' technique on 'Stillwaters'. This is a multi-background picture for which a cardboard waster is supplied for knife-cutting. If you use the card waster, remember to Sellotape the outer veneers (which overlap into the border margin), to the card, and to butt-joint all veneer edges together.

For this reason, fretsaw craftsmen prefer to use a veneer waster on a multi-background picture and use PVA adhesive throughout.

During the course of the work, if you use black carbon paper to trace the design, and white PVA adhesive used on the joints,(and you may make a few knife cuts and scratches into the face of some of the veneers too) the side you are working on will look grubby and not be the best side.

Therefore you should avoid this by making a reverse design to start with. By working on the back of the picture, that side will show the signs of the work and can be filled and levelled before laying, keeping the underside – the face or tight side – in perfect condition.

If you wish to obtain the veneers direct from your supplier and copy the design from this book, here is the list of veneers required:

11 Olive ash
14 Avodiré
15 Ayan
38 Mansonia
41 Eucalyptus
49 Harewood
54 Lacewood
62 Sapele
66 Makoré
92 Sycamore
97 Teak
101 Sappy walnut
103 American walnut
104 Light figured walnut
107B Dark figured walnut
113 Zebrano
122 Lacewood burr,
106 African walnut borders and back

A baseboard size 10 × 8 × $\frac{3}{8}$ inch (255 × 205mm × 9mm) is required, plus a sycamore waster, and No. 106 backing veneer. 4 matching leaves of No. 106 border veneers 11 × $1\frac{1}{2}$ inch (280 × 40mm) are required for the borders and edges. Four narrow $\frac{1}{8}$ inch (3mm) fillet strips can be cut from the edge of the leaf of sycamore.

If you do not wish to use the waster, (remember *not* to use PVA edge-to-edge veneer to cardboard) you may prefer to dispense with it and join No. 14 and No. 11 veneers together to form the background.

Stage 1

(1) Use Sellotape to hinge the design to the top of the card waster and make the registration crosshair marks.

(2) Cut in the No. 14 sky veneer and No. 11 water veneer to form a rectangle, overlapping into the border margin about $\frac{1}{4}$ inch (6mm) all around.

Stage 2

Let's begin with the distant hill No.122 as this is furthest away in perspective. (Rule 2).

Only the top section of No. 122 against the skyline is accurately cut. The rest of the piece can be left as a rectangle, overlapping the left and right-hand sides into the 107B positions, and the bottom below the top of the bridge (Fig. 167).

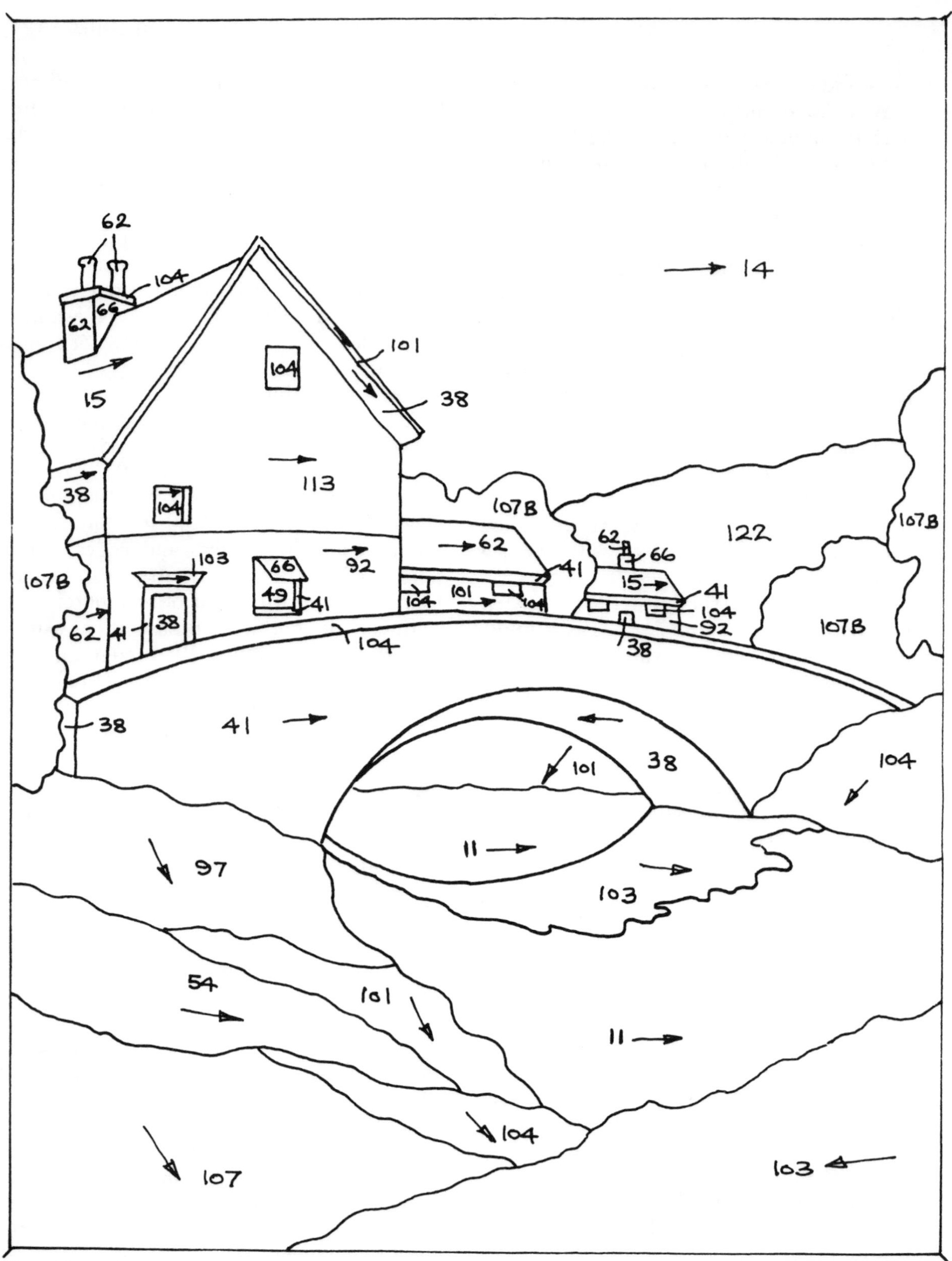

Fig. 166 'Stillwaters'

(3) Next, cut in the foliage 107B which touches the bridge parapet along its top-left outline, but allowing it to run off into the border margin at the right, and below in the bridge position.
(4) Now you can cut the tall 107B piece on the edge of the design which trims off both the 122, hill and the lower 107B foliage.
(5) We can also cut in No. 15 forming the roof of the house on the bridge, overlapping into the 92 space and also the 107B tree.

Notice how the shape of each veneer is simplified and the cutting made easy, in Fig.167.
(6) Then the No. 92 wall of that house, which can also overlap the 107B tree and the bridge, ignoring the No. 41 sliver.
(7) Now the 107B tree foliage can be inserted, which will trim off the 122 hill veneer, the roof No 15, and wall No. 92. It is allowed to overlap both the Nos. 113 and 92 parts of the end wall of the house.
(8) Now the 62 roof can be cut in, (overlapping the house wall) and into the 101 position.
(9) Followed by the 101 house wall, overlapping the No. 92 base wall of the house and the bridge. (Ignore the 41 sliver.)
(10) Next cut in piece No. 15 forming the roof of the millhouse, allowing it to protrude past the 107B tree into the border margin to the left and into the 113 position to the right.
(11) Now fit the 101 veneer as a triangular shape, trimming off the No. 15 roof veneer on the left and cutting accurately into the No. 14 skyline.
(12) Next cut in the shadow under the eaves No.38 overlapping into the 113 position.
(13) Now cut the No. 38 side wall, overlapping into the 113, 107B and 62 positions.
(14) Cut in No. 62, trimming off No. 38, overlapping 107B, 92, and the bridge.
(15) Now the 113 veneer is inserted, trimming off the surplus 101 and 38 veneers at the top, also the 107B foliage over the

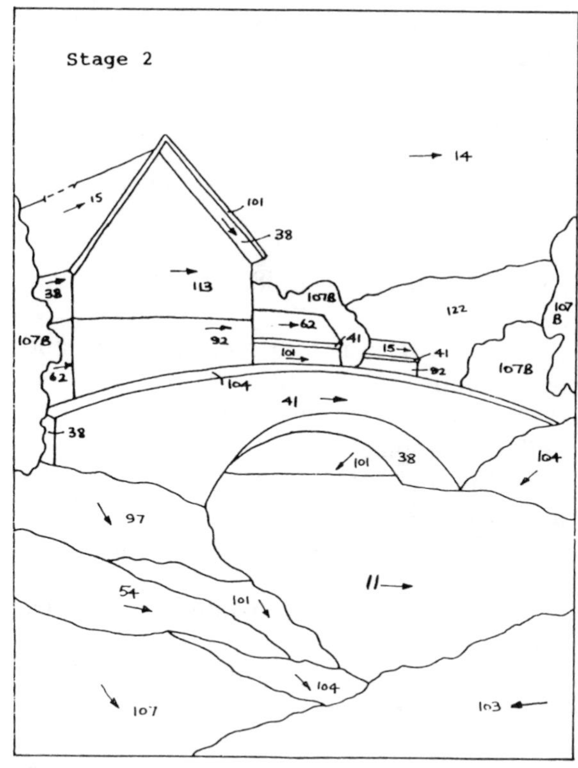

Fig. 167 'Stillwaters' Stage 2

bridge; overlapping down into the 92 position, trimming off the 62 roof of the house.
(16) The 92 veneer is next, trimming off the 113 above, the 62 at the left, the 101 on the right and the bottom overlaps on the the bridge.
(17) The parapet of the bridge No. 104 is next, trimming off all the protruding veneers above, from 62 at the left across to 107B at the right. The bottom part of 104 is now brought down into the bridge position.
(18) The 38 end wall of the bridge is next, overlapping the 107B on the left, also the 41 and 97 positions.
(19) Now the 41 bridge veneer is inserted, trimming off No. 38 and overlapping the 104 right-hand bank.
(20) No. 101 beneath the bridge follows, fitted accurately on the waterline, but protruding up into the 38 position.

(21) Next No. 38 shadow and trimming of 41 and 101 veneers. .
(22) No. 104 right-hand bank can be inserted next, trimming off No. 41 and 107B.
(23) No.97 riverbank is next, overlapping the 107B, 54 and 101 positions.
(24) Now 107B at the left can go in, trimming off Nos. 15, 38, 62, 104, 38, and 97.
(25) No. 101 is next,trimming off 97 and overlapping 54 and 104.
(26) Now 54, trimming off 97 and 101, and overlapping 104.
(27) No. 104 veneer trims off 101 and 54 and overlaps 103 and 107.
(28) No. 107 trims off No. 54, and 104, overlaps 103.
(29) No. 103 is next, trimming off Nos. 104 and 107.
(30) The slivers of No. 41 forming the eaves of the two houses on the bridge can be fitted.

This step-by-step example of the sequential cutting, has completed Stage 2 of 'Stillwaters', as shown in Fig.167. The remainder of the detail to be cut in (rule 3), is shown in Stage 3, Fig. 168.

Sequential Cutting

You now see the difference between the stages of cutting as shown in the Stage 2 and 3 drawings, and the sequence of cutting from the viewpoint of overlapping technique.
(a) Although the advanced marquetarian does not produce separate drawings, but works from one master drawing and learns how to 'read' it, the beginner will find it simpler to break down a complicated drawing into stages with all the major components in Stage 1, medium sizes pieces in Stage 2 and minor pieces in Stage 3.
(b) He may also decide, which stages can be cut with the knife and which ones by fretsaw. Knife-cutting drawings can be separated from fretsaw drawings.
(c) Some may be 'face' drawings and others 'reverse' to suit the technique – all in perfect register – and can easily be supplied from photocopies of a transparent film design.
(d) Flat table cutting may be separated from angled table cutting.
(e) Pieces to be inserted from the face side can be on separate design overlays from those required to be let-in from the back.
(f) Parts requiring shading or bleaching can be separated.
(g) Areas can be separated which need fragmentation, sliverisation, or mosaic treatment.
(h) Where a small window is to be filled 'freehand'.
(i) The marquetarian can adapt a design to suit his own level of competence, by

Fig. 168 'Stillwaters' Stage 3

eliminating detail or demands the design may make on his skill that he feels may be beyond his present level of attainment.

(j) It enables him to scrap, change, amend, transpose or adapt a stage drawing, if he discovers features in his veneers which could be brought into the design.

(k) If he felt, at any stage, he was satisfied with the resulting picture, there would be no need to continue with more detailed or difficult cutting. Simplicity is the keynote to success. His purpose is to allow his creative talent and artistic flair to display the wood to best advantage.

Overlay stage drawings

A 'master control drawing' of the complete design is prepared and kept for reference.

A tracing is made from the master drawing on transparent film, using black Indian ink, of the parts to be cut in the first 'Stage 1 overlay' which show:

(1) a thin outline of the exact shape of the veneer pieces *to be fretsawn* (not their final shape in the picture), extending into adjacent areas,(which are to be cut in later stages);

(2) the adjacent parts of the picture can also be shown as a series of dotted lines for reference only;

(3) any pieces where grain continuity is essential;

(4) accurate registration marks.

Photocopies – either face or reverse – are made from the film and these are used for the first cutting phase in Stage 1 and for the assembly of the picture.

When that phase of cutting is complete, another photocopy of the master control drawing is prepared on film in which the parts to be cut in Stage 2 are shown, together with dotted lines showing the adjacent pieces to be cut in subsequent stages.

The Stage 2 overlay, which would include the medium detail, is photocopied and overlaid on the assembly and brought into accurate register. This overlay should show only those parts which will be cut at this stage omitting the pieces already fitted unless they fall into the categories mentioned at (a), (b) and (c) above.

Any of these stages can be cut with the knife or fretsaw. But a change of tactics may now be required if this is the point when you intend to use both the knife (for cutting the window aperture in the assembly) and the fretsaw on cutting and inserting difficult, intricate curved or serrated parts of the design, requiring the use of hard, brittle or end grain burrs.

Combination overlays

The advantages of cutting and letting-in the insert from above the assembly means (a) the work can be carried out on the face side with a normal design (not reversed), and (b) there is no need to cut a window aperture in the assembly.

(1) A design is made on transparent film, through which the veneer can be tested for correct grain flow, and marked out. Then it is knife-cut on the cutting board to an approximate 'polygon' shape.

This 'patch' is then located directly on top of the assembly and the stage drawing of the design is brought down and registered. The outline shape to be sawn is traced on the veneer (*not the design line to be seen in the final picture, but the overstep line* to be sawn).

(2) If the picture is cut on the back, in reverse, with the 'face side' underneath, and the insert made from below, the procedure is different.

The overlay drawing should show a *dotted line* for the window aperture to be knife-cut on the cutting board, and this should be about ⅛th inch (3mm) smaller in outline than the actual fine design line to be fretsawn and of an easy polygon shape, sufficient to show the veneer below.

The design is brought into register, and a simple window traced and knife-cut on the cutting board. It is then fastened on the underneath face side, of the assembly with tape. Sawing is carried out on the 'overstep' line and the insert let-in from below.

These two techniques are combined when some pieces are to be let-in from above and others from below.

Here is another interesting picture for you to try, titled 'Red Roofs', size 10 × 8 inch (255 × 200mm). Make your own master control drawing on film and copy the seven stage drawings shown in Figs 170–172, or make as many stage drawings as you need.

Here is a list of the veneers required:

11 Olive ash — 66 Makoré
14 Figure avodiré — 92 Sycamore
26 Brown oak — 90 Rosa peroba
35 Padauk — 101 Light sappy walnut
38 Dark mansonia — 107 Figured walnut
45 Cedar — 107B Dark walnut
49 Harewood — 122 Lacewood burr
62 Sapele (Also for borders and back)

Think ahead and plan the cutting sequences. Remember the golden rules! Take care to preserve grain continuity of the sky seen through the foliage and trees in Stage 3

Notice how the tree No. 107 is inserted into the small sky piece within the tree foliage which was let-in during Stage 3. Another tree trunk is added in Stage 4 which cuts across the gate inserted in Stage 3.

This enables you to practice inserting the medium pieces from below and the tiny inserts from above. The detail of the fence at the bottom left-hand part of the picture and the sequence in the order of cutting is shown in Stages 5,6 and 7.

Fig. 169 'Redroofs'

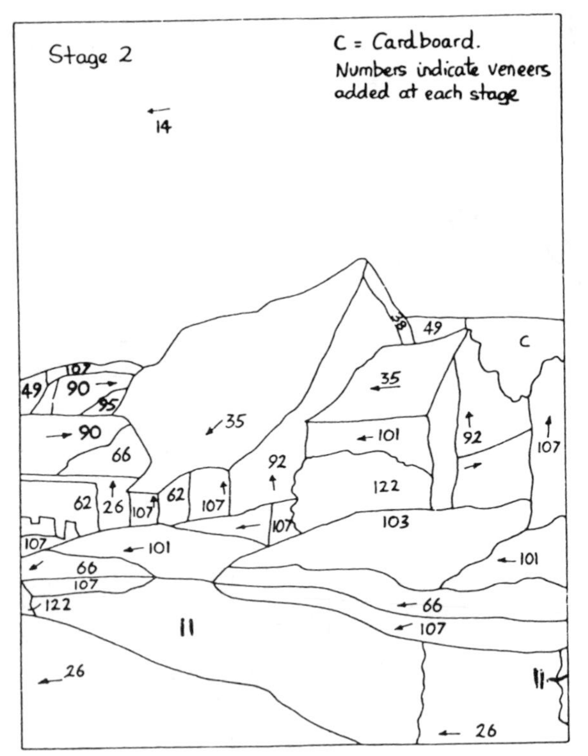

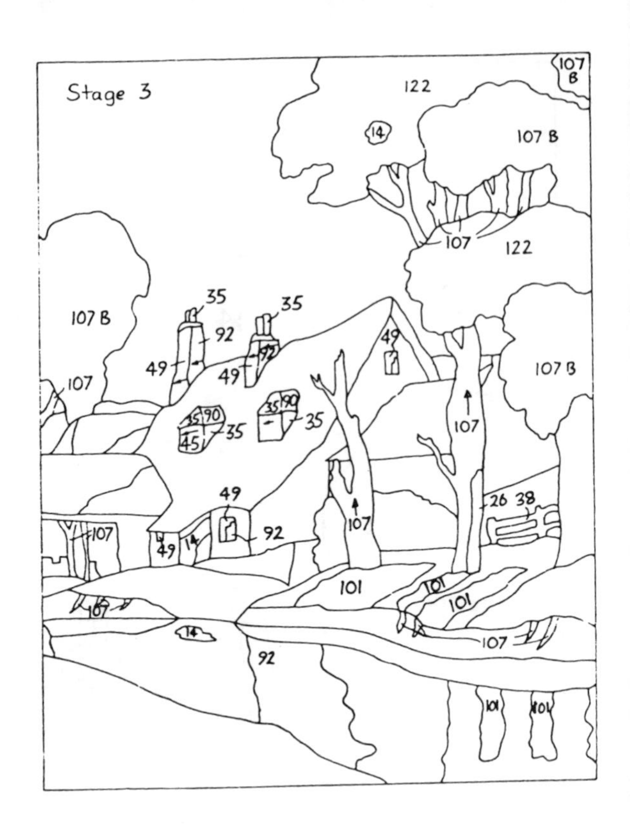

Fig. 170 'Redroofs' Stages 2 and 3

Fig. 171 'Redroofs' Stage 4

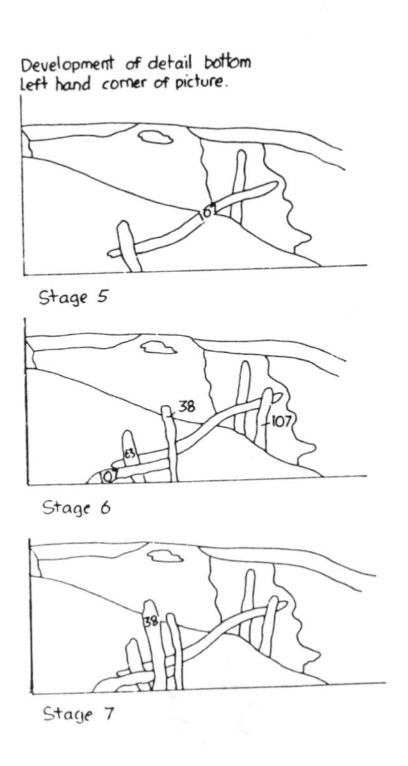

Fig. 172 'Redroofs' Stages 5, 6 and 7

16
Tinting and Shading

THE ARTIST tints his true colours by the addition of white and creates shades by adding black. The marquetarian changes the natural hue and tone of his woods – his form of tinting – by bleaching.

TINTING

I am indebted to George Monks, an English wildlife artist living in California, for a practical example of what can be achieved by bleaching.

He was fascinated by the humming-birds – those tiny jewel-like creatures flashing in the sun, which the Indians called 'The Tresses of the Day-Star'. He had tried many times to capture in marquetry, the illusion of the movement of their tiny wings, without success.`A humming-bird's wings move so quickly, the human eye sees them only as a blurr. Even a camera with a 1/2000th of a second shutter speed cannot completely arrest the movement. The impression to the human eye is that the wings are transparent.

George decided to try to bleach the background veneer to lighten its tone but still show the original grain and markings. Here is a list of the items he used for bleaching wood in order of strength.

Bleach.	**Neutraliser.**
1.Peroxide (hair bleach).	water
2.Laundry bleach: (Sodium hypochlorite)	water
3.Oxalic acid crystals	borax and water
4.Commercial wood bleach.	(Parts A & B)

Equipment required:
Two plastic containers to hold the bleach and neutraliser rinse, large enough for the veneer pieces to be dipped. Stainless steel tweezers, blotting paper, a lamp or low level heart source, a watch and a note pad.

Bleach is dangerous to the eyes and lungs and can cause severe skin reaction and allergies. The safety rules to follow are: 1. Avoid all personal contact. 2. Wear vinyl gloves, a face mask and goggles. 3. Use

Fig. 173 Sand shading a piece of veneer

synthetic fibre brushes as bleach will decompose natural bristles. 4. Neutralise the bleached veneer before inserting it into the assembly. 5. Always work in a well ventilated room.

In the humming-bird picture, after tracing the overall outline of the wing on the back, the complete wing is covered with Sellotape which will hold the pieces together thoughout the process, before the individual wing sections were cut out, using a reverse design, and bleached separately

The golden rule: test, test and test again. Remember when you tackle the actual part for the picture there is no room for error. Take several scraps of the same veneer as the pieces to be bleached. Every species will react differently, so make no assumptions. Test each scrap in the bleach for a different length of time and note this accurately.

Bleach each piece for the pre-determined time then rinse thoroughly. Follow the manufacturer's instructions if using a proprietary bleach.

The rinsed veneer is blotted to remove excess moisture. The rinse time is not critical but must be long enough to neutralise. Heat from the lamp will quickly dry the pieces. Each piece will fit back exactly into its original position and can be edge glued with PVA.

Next, complete the whole process of scraping, sealing, sanding and applying the final finish to the scrap pieces. With the bleached area completely sealed, the finish will now only penetrate the rest of the picture. The final result will show an increase in contrast, making the bleached part more apparent. Without sealing properly, the bleached area would virtually disappear in the finishing process.

The lessons George learned from the first two experiments were: (a) after bleaching and neutralising, the veneer has to be sealed against the finish, or the effects of bleaching disappear. And (b), this meant removing each piece to be treated from the background assembly.

The best results are obtained by making a reverse design and cutting the parts to be bleached from the back (even if the actual picture was cut from the face side).

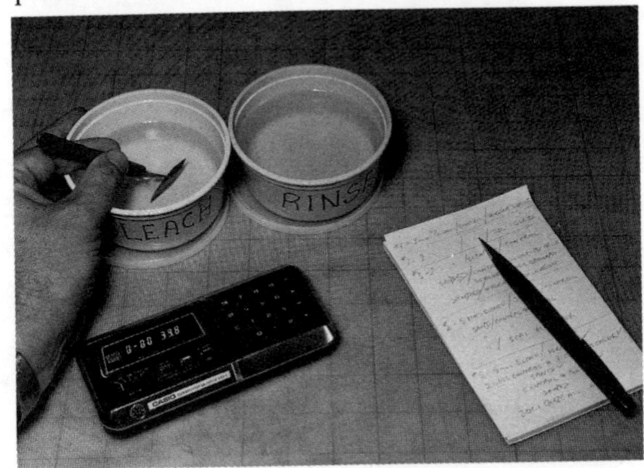

Fig. 174 The equipment for bleaching

Fig. 175 Detail from 'Frilled cocquettes' shows the background through the wings

The third attempt was successful and achieved the transparent wing effect with the grain continuity of the background veneer showing through the wing.

The picture *Humming-bird with hanging vines* has won many prizes, including the 'Best in Show' at the International Creative Marquetry Exhibition.

Now that the technique was mastered, George Monks worked on another picture *Frilled Coquettes*, illustrated in the colour section, which won an award in the San Diego Wildlife Art Show – a juried show open to all forms of art media.

This technique is ideal for creating reflections and shadows in pictures, by scraping away the outer skin of the veneer to reveal the darker colour beneath, which would still show the grain and figure of the original colour tone. Do not scrape the bleached areas when finishing.

SHADING

The opposite of tinting or lightening a veneer is to darken it by carbonising the wood with heat. There is tremendous scope for the use of artificial shading to create three dimensional realism, as in the roundness of columns, folds in costumes and drapery, still life and floral arrangements and especially in portraiture.

There is a need for shadows and shading in almost every picture to convey solidity. The marquetry artist often needs gradations of tone to set one piece of veneer against another, cut from the same leaf as, for example, in creating the petals of a rose.

Sand shading is always used for making inlay motifs such as fans, shells, urns, ribbons, classical figures and sunburst oval patterae.

Sand shading

Traditionally, this task has always been held to need a woman's light touch! Its application is an aesthetic one, calling for personal judgment. Successfully shaded work is one which, at first glance, does not appear to have been shaded at all. If you can see the darkened contrast, it is overdone. Subtle tones which blend, harmonise and fade into natural wood tones are preferred to dark scorched tones.

Obtain some clean, sharp-edged fine silver sand from a local pet shop for this purpose. Pour it into a flat-bottomed metal baking dish and place it over a heat source, preferably an electric hotplate, over which one can work even in warm weather without discomfort.

The depth of sand is not critical about $1\frac{1}{2}$ to 2 inches (37 – 50mm) is about right. Soft, light woods react to the heat more quickly than harder or darker species, and pointed or tapering parts also shade quickly. In a crescent shape, the ends would shade first, so scoop up the hot sand with a spoon from the bottom of the tray and pour it over the veneer, as in Fig.178, using stainless steel tweezers.

The sand is brought to the desired temperature and the control adjusted to provide a constant heat.

Fig. 176 'Humming-Bird with Hanging Vines' George Monks

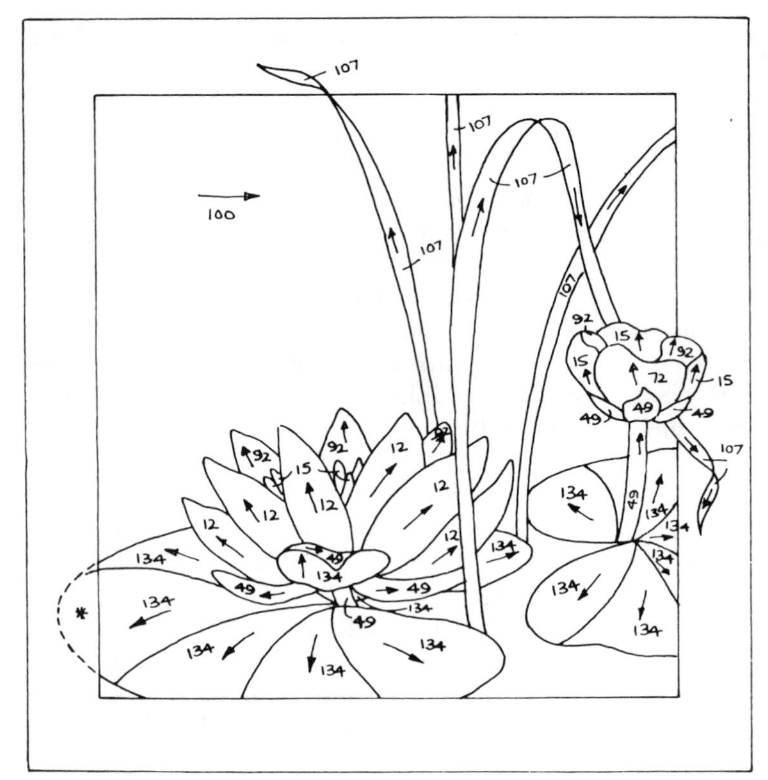

Fig. 177 'Waterlilly'

Here is another marquetry kit for you to practise on, with a list of the veneers required:

12 Aspen
15 Ayan
49 Silver Harewood
72 Quilted willow
92 Sycamore
100 Castello
107 Figured walnut
134 Slate harewood
Sycamore borders and backing veneer.

Where fairly deep tones are required the sand may be shallow and of greater heat than for the delicate, softly gradated tones, for which the sand is heaped into a mound and the heat lowered. More time is allowed for the veneer to shade.

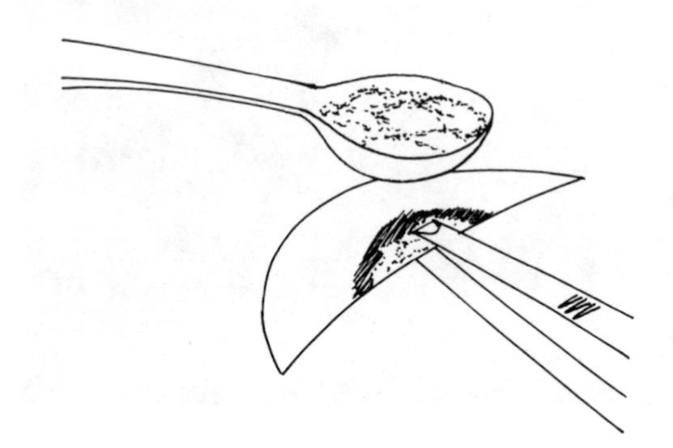

Fig. 178 Pouring hot sand with a spoon

The timing of the operation is quickly learned by experience after a few experiments with scraps of waste veneer. Use either a silent count or a stopwatch, allowing various lengths of time at a given temperature.

Most shading effects are reached in a few seconds. It is rarely necesssary to have to count more than ten seconds.

After that time, the surface of the veneer above the sand should appear unchanged, but with a gradual tonal change through the veneer in the sand.

The surface of the veneer tends to carbonise more quickly than the inside, which is a good fault, as this is removed in the finishing process.

A skilled sand shader would insert twelve segments of a sunburst oval into the sand, on edge in pairs, face sides in the centre,

Fig. 179 65 Watt soldering iron with copper tin for sand shading at controlled heat

Fig. 180 A veneer petal being shaded

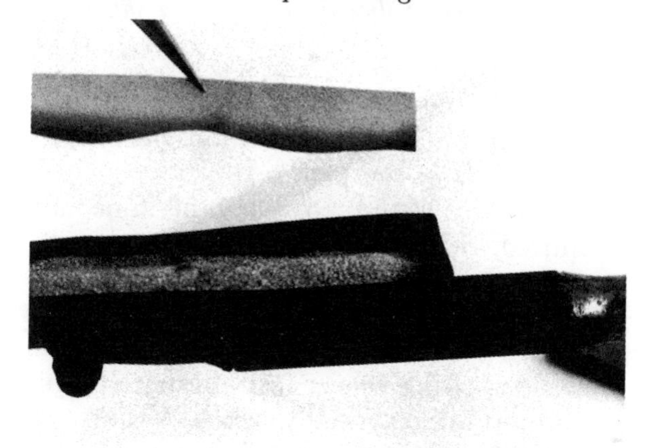

Fig. 181 Shading the edge of a veneer

one pair after the other, and immediately begin to remove them again in the same order, and they would be shaded perfectly.

Never attempt to shade wet or moist veneers, nor to shade too many pieces at one time. If you stop when you believe it is just about right, the finished result will be just a tone lighter! A common fault with beginners is to over-scorch the work. It is always better to increase the heat than the immersion time. The veneer should never be allowed to touch the metal bottom of the tray or it will char. It could, in the event, burst into flames.

The normal practice is to hold the veneer with tweezers, insert it on edge and count. Then withdraw the piece and check its progress and re-insert it, rather than risk over-shading. A greater subtlety of shading can be achieved with lighter hued veneers than with the red and browns which darken quickly.

Tonal chart

Construct a tonal chart with the veneer you intend to use. Fix the heat at a comfortable constant setting and using the tweezers, insert a few scraps of veneer on edge, with a silent count of 6, 8, 10, 12 seconds, etc.

As you remove each piece in turn from the sand, sandpaper the scrap and lightly 'mist' the surface with a lightly dampened sponge to restore the veneer's natural equilibrium moisture content and no shrinkage will occur.

This will remove the surface charring and approximate to the tonal effect when polished. It is advisable to cover them with paper and place them under a light weight to keep tham flat until they are normalised.

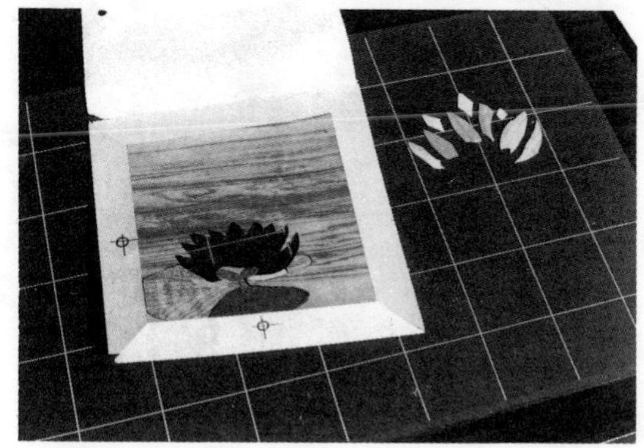

Fig. 182 Petals removed from the 'Waterlilly' picture for sand shading

Glue the test pieces of scrap to the tonal chart for future reference.

Angle of entry

This governs the pattern of shading on the leaf. If inserted vertically there would be a marked tonal gradation across the leaf; if slid beneath the sand horizontally, the whole piece would revieve a uniform shade.

The height of the sand is an important factor. A half inch (12 mm) of sand will darken veneer more quickly than a heaped up mound about 2 inches (50mm) high.

There are five methods of working.

(1) When you have actually cut out the shape to fit the picture, or removed a piece from it, dip the piece into the sand and bring it out quickly, lightly dampening with a moist sponge and place under a weight.

(2) A crescent shaped piece would require you to heap or mould the surface of the sand so that the inside of the crescent shape can be pushed over the mound.

(3) A whole leaf of veneer to suit part of a picture is shaded around its edges to varying depths of shade, then tested for effect under the window of the picture.

Fig. 185 'A Belvedere for Escher', (2nd Premier class). Notice the use of sand shading on the building. *Peter J. White*

Fig. 184 The completed 'Waterlilly' picture with accentuated corner mitres

(4) Where 'island' patches of tone are required within a leaf, hot sand is repeatedly poured on to the veneer leaf from a spoon and tossed back into the tray until the required tone is achieved. Pour the sand on *both* sides of the veneer leaf alternately. This is important, especially when testing the effect through a window when cutting from the back of the picture and not from the face side of the veneer.

(5) Mask the veneer with a cut out scrap,or a coat of polish, so that only the exposed area is affected by the sand, which is poured over the mask, and tossed back into the tray repeatedly. The mask is removed when the desired tone has been attained.

Remember, it is the face side that will be seen in the picture even if you are cutting a reverse design.

The hotplate
Another technique used by marquetarians who prefer to eliminate any possibility of the abrading action of sand particles being left in the open pores of the wood, (especially in some veneers which have a natural resin content) is as follows:
an aluminium plate of about 12 × 12 × $\frac{1}{4}$ inches (305 × 305 × 6mm) is placed on an electric hotplate and this provides a whole range of temperatures.

The intensity of heat radiation varies inversely to the square of the distance from its source.

The plate becomes hot in the centre and less hot at the edges. Mark the area when doing uniform shading for fan inlays. The closer to the heat source, the narrower the band of shading. Aim at 6 to 8 seconds before removing the veneer. Too long exposure will dry out the veneer and cause charring and shrinkage. Too short a time risks failure to penetrate.

Experiment with the degree of heat, time, distance from the centre, differences between species and the tone penetration achieved. Record this on a tonal chart.

Ironing

Another technique is to use an ordinary domestic electric iron in one of two ways:
(a) Keep it moving across the leaf continuously and have a scrap of the original veneer beside the worktable for comparison. This can be used to gradate a sky veneer from its natural tone at the horizon to make it a tone darker at the top to increase aerial perspective.

Even more important is the opportunity this affords to use the same veneer species for sky and sea, as ironing the leaf enables the sea veneer to be shaded all over to a darker tone than the sky.
(b) Sandwich the veneer between the aluminium plate and the iron and form a shaded gradient on both sides of the veneer simultaneously.

Fig. 186 'Wrens' P. White (First prize in secondary class). Excellent use of sand shading

Sand shading, hot plate and ironing methods of shading are carried out while the picture is being cut and assembled. But there are also shading techniques to apply to the picture after it has been laid.

Shading after laying

Pyrography
From this separate artform, the use of pyrographic pens are used to shade marquetry pictures. Using a wide variety of points which are interchangeable, shading and details are burned or branded into the veneers.

Pyrography machines with controlled heated points and wire knibs can be used for hachured shading and fine detail etching.

A background 'blow-lamp' technique can be used to darken a complete area, to provide large areas of flame washed tones, which can then be scraped away with fine pointed scraper board engraving tools, to reveal the original wood tone beneath the shading in order to highlight certain features.

There is a valid argument in favour of using artificial aids to complete a picture using these techniques, rather than to discard a valuable freak veneer because of some minor defect, only to search in vain for a replacement.

Brushwork
A technique still used today in Paris, is the application of *Lapis infernalis* (silver nitrate) prepared in several dilutions with distilled water. The required strength is applied by brush and at first there is no apparent tonal change, for it takes time for the water carrying the silver nitrate to penetrate the veneer cells and the effect makes its appearance slowly.

The strength of the solution and number of applications is a matter of experiment.

Exquisite results have been achieved by this process with floral subjects and costumes which are given a far more natural appearance than by other methods.

India ink
In Sorrento, Italy, widespread use is made of Indian ink etching on finished pictures to create fine detail. This is applied by pen, fine brushwork and with feathers.

Back faking
Another widely used professional trick is to dye or stain the back of the veneer before the picture is laid, using dyes which are compatible with the finish, which causes the dye to diffuse naturally up into the thin layer of veneer and appear on the face side as a natural pigment streak.

Artist's colours, inks or dyes are used to paint the back of the veneer by brush or mixed with PVA glue and applied to the back of the leaf to alter the appearance of the face veneers.

Touching-up
When harewood is touched by a brush or sponge with a polyurethane catalyst, it immediately bleaches back to become white scyamore again. This trick can be turned to advantage when trying to achieve 'white water' effects of turbulence around rocks, waterfalls, etc.

Dusting
A method known as 'dusting' is to sprinkle powdered dust scraped from a red pigmented veneer such as padauk, for example, over the unsealed surface of an open grained, soft veneer, such as aspen, required for a sky effect.

It would be applied with a bronze brush. When the face is polished, the red pigment would be diffused through the sky veneer by the finishing medium and would appear as a natural streak.

This 'dusting' method should not be confused with 'micro-dusting' used to create man-made textures which is dealt with in Chapter 17.

Some marquetarians might feel that these 'tricks of the trade' are a retrograde step and a form of cheating, especially as such techniques, skilfully executed, are virtually impossible for exhibition judges to detect.

Others claim that such techniques are justified if they enable them to increase their restricted palette of veneers, utilise freak species and to tackle far more artistic subjects.

17
Textures and Templets

THIS TECHNIQUE, originally pioneered by a friend of mine, the late Norman Macleod of South London, is now widely used throughout the marquetry world.

Some marquetarians have found the search for freak woods to represent a desired effect has proved fruitless, and have turned to this method of achieving their purpose. Many unusual and beautiful effects can be obtained, almost as limitless as the craftsman's ingenuity.

Sometimes a picture calls for a pattern or texture such as cobbled streets, brick walls, bird's feathers, animal fur, bushes, grass or tree foliage. In the absence of a freak veneer to suit a special requirement, the only answer is to create the veneer texture. For a bush or tree foliage, several *different* burrs and other veneers are cut into minute splinter-sized fragments of various colour tones.

Fragmentation

The technique is very straight forward. First, the veneer is cut into 2mm strips (or finer) across the grain, so that they are fragile and will break easily in this very brittle cross-grained width.

A bunch of these strips is then cut *with* the grain on the cutting board, with the rounded blade of a craft tool, chopping the strips into tiny lmm fragments. One enthusiast puts the strips into a food mixer to churn them into tiny fragments!

The different colours are carefully kept in separate small 'baby-food' jars for mixing as required.

Application of the fragments

Cut a 'window aperture' into a separate waster, larger than that required for the final shape of the bush or tree, and fasten gummed paper tape on the underneath of the opening. Place it on a hard, smooth surface such as melamine surfaced chip-board, and pour PVA glue into the hole. The fragmented veneer chips are piled high into the aperture, rammed tightly into it and pressed firmly down with a rounded tool.

Cover the surface with a wood block and pound the surface with a hammer to squeeze out excess glue. Keep the in-fill level with the top and cover with wax paper or polythene. Put a board on top and clamp for an hour for the glue to set.

Remove the board and if necessary apply more PVA and add another layer of fragments, proud of the surface, close up any gaps and press until smooth on the top with a knife blade dipped in hot water.

Cover with wax paper or polythene and clamp again, this time leaving two days for the mixture to harden completely. When dry, sand the fragments level with the waster and position the waster under the window in the main assembly and treat as an ordinary veneer insert.

The fragments may be of one wood if that is the overall tone required for a life-like appearance for cobbles or a stone wall, or multi-coloured, like a mosaic, where necessary for a natural setting like the autumnal colours of tree foliage or a forest path

Where a bright dyed green veneer would look incongruous and shriek aloud to spoil a picture it may be mixed with natural fragments and impart an overall green-ness which looks much more natural.

Many 'high noon' subjects which demand greens and blues which were not possible with normal veneers, become possible. An ivy coloured wall, part in sunshine and part in shadow, can be produced by mixing tones of dyed green with the natural gold, reds, browns and yellows.

A past master at the technique was Richard Shellard who has won the Marquetry Society Rosebowl three times, and whose work is featured in the 'Gallery of Marquetry Prizewinners'.

Micro-dusting

Mr. Harry Hulls introduced this technique to create atmospheric mists, distant heat haze and special cloud effects. The face side of the finished picture is worked over with a scraper, to make a recess a few thousandths of an inch deep. Powdered veneer dust mixed with glue is applied, and when dry the surface is levelled and finished in the usual way.

In one picture this was used effectively to depict the blurr seen when looking at the revolving propellers of an aircraft.

Sliverisation

Another technique pioneered by Norman McLeod which has since been named 'sliverisation' is used in many different ways.

The idea originated when he used the Excelsior woodwool I had used for packing when sending him veneers by post! We called it the 'Excelsior technique'. The techniques are as follows:

(a) The fine woodwool shavings are dyed to suit the project, mixed with PVA and rolled into a ball and then pressed flat in the aperture. This produces a marbled effect which is different from the mosaic effect of fragmentation.

(b) In turn, this led Norman Mcleod to experiment with natural wood veneers. Thin slivers are trimmed from the edges of a variety of veneers, as fine as it is possible to trim them either with a knife against a straightedge, or planed with a finely set iron. The shavings curl up into coils and in this form can be used as 'Excelsior' for marbled effects.

(c) The strips are rubbed on a flat surface with a knife handle and flattened. In this form they are used for very fine detail such as ship's rigging, or as 'accent lines' between masonry, window glazing bars, and for fine lettering.

(d) When movement is required in the picture, to represent sea waves for example, a hole is cut into the picture to the outline shape of the waves required. It is taped underneath and PVA applied. The 'combed' shavings are arranged in waves in the window.

The picture *Brief Encounter* by Cliff Daniells featuring a family of deer in a sunlit woodland glade, used a combination of these methods. (See page 167.)

The main picture elements *omitting all tiny detail* were cut and assembled using the window method and laid. Next he turned to the templet method (or 'stick as you go') to inlay the fragments and slivers. The slivers were cut and arranged into colour groups. The fragments were made up in segments in spare wasters, in various colours required for the project.

The required overall shape of the insert was cut from a prepared 'patch' of fragmentation veneers and used as a templet. The outline was scored into the face of the picture with a knife, then the contour cut around and the underlying waste picture piece was prized up and discarded. (When you try out this method avoid digging into the groundwork.)

The aperture was coated with a thin application of adhesive, as was the back of the fragmented insert, and when tacky the insert was pressed home.

The slivers were treated differently. First, the overall aperture was scored into and prized up from the picture and a thin coating of adhesive applied to the baseboard.

The slivers were laid in strips according to colour and the required flow, and nicked to length with the knife. They were then rammed into the aperture with a rounded tool. The aperture was filled slightly above the face of the picture and a wood chisel, held flat, used to scrape off the excess material.

Bear in mind that any misaligned fragments will spoil the picture, so take care with your efforts.

Combinations of both methods are now in vogue and have proved immensely popular to depict hair in portraiture, fur for animals and feathers for bird subjects; thatched roofing, bulrushes and reeds in streams, weeping willow trees, ploughed fields, and for superb water effects.

The combination of white, various harewoods, dyed greens and blues, are especially suited to depict highlights on front-lit water subjects, lapping waves, surf, waterfalls, and for moonlit subjects.

TEMPLETS AND JIGS

Most branches of the woodworking crafts use some form of templet or jig. The 'window method' aperture makes use of the templet principle.

This can now be extended to create endless versions of profiled jigs to accomplish various effects in pictorial, geometric marquetry and in parquetry, when repeating patterns are required such as cobblestones, drystone walls, various sizes of rock formations etc. Whenever a picture demands repetitive cutting, which can be tedious, a jig can be an enormous time-saver and greatly enhance the realism.

The overall 'window' conforms to the peripheral outline, but the individual profiles cut with the use of the jig are inserted within the window by guesswork. They are laid in visual proximity in a reasonable order of assembly similar to fragments.

For a practical example of the technique, I am indebted to Mr. Gene Weinberger, the President of the Marquetry Society of America for permission to reproduce the jig he used to create the *Golden Eagle* in what he calls the 'sticker technique'.

Knife cutting jig

The jig is made from thin plywood and fitted with any shaped handle to suit you, as shown in Fig.188.

Profiles

1. For feathers below neckline.

2 and 3. Each represents half of one of the larger feathers, $1\frac{1}{2} \times \frac{3}{8}$ inches (37 × 9mm) at its widest.

4 and 6 profiles and interior profiles are for random feathers which can be worked in.

5. Small feathers for the head and neck area.

Draw a paper pattern of the profiles and glue each to a $\frac{1}{4}$ inch (6 mm) plywood base. Glue 180 grit sandpaper to the base to prevent slipping.

Fretsaw the jig base using a 2/0 fretsaw blade, and drill $\frac{1}{8}$ inch (3 mm) hole in the centre and in the handle knob to receive a dowel and glue to the base..

To begin, prepare a *reverse* drawing of the *Golden Eagle*, as this will be cut from the back, by making a photocopy of the design, Fig.187.

Make a master design, put in the registration marks and cut the picture in the

Fig. 187 'The Golden Eagle'

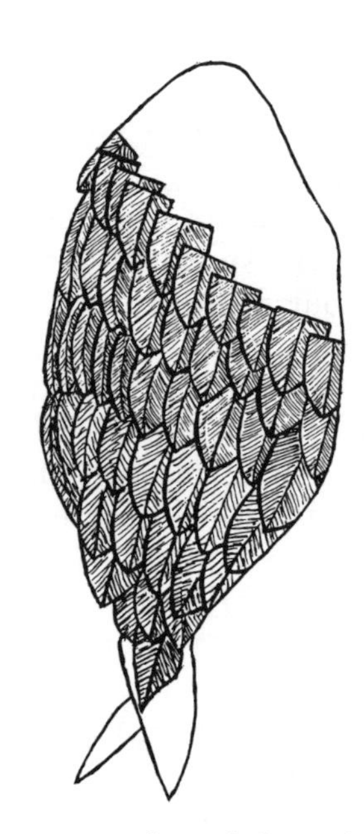

Fig. 190 Feathers are overlapped from the bottom upwards

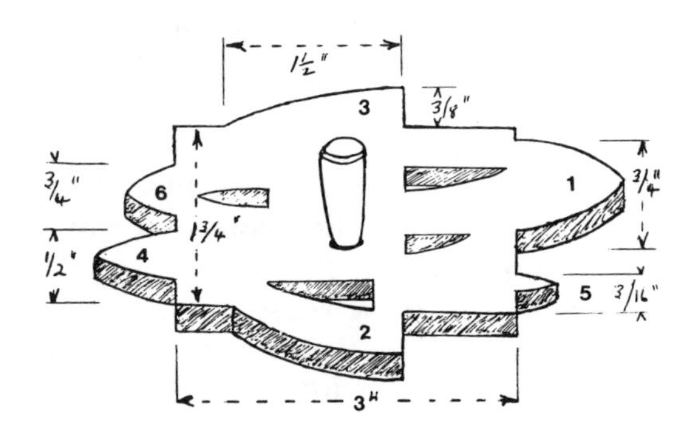

Fig. 188 Profile jig for eagle feathers

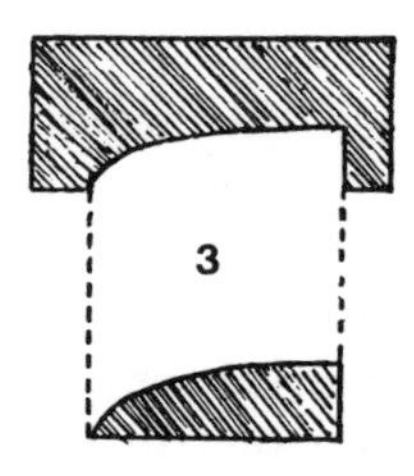

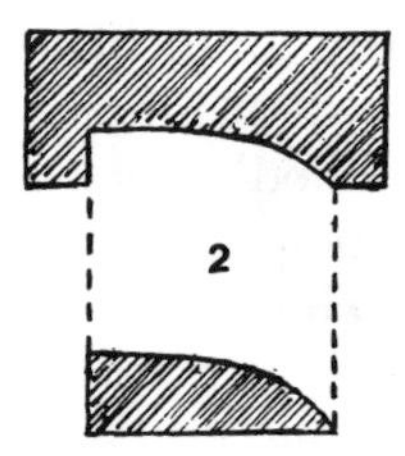

Fig. 189 Alternate grain direction for profiles 2 and 3

normal way, completing the major segments. Now make a window opening in which to create the feathers.

Veneer selection
The natural colours of the eagle are as follows: the head is golden, the body is deep brownish-purple and the feet are yellow. The right-hand side of the body is in deep shadow, and the tones lighten to the left. The highlights are in white. The upper tail feathers are dusty white to pearl grey; the beak is yellow with a black tip and the claws are black.

This is the opportunity to test your own judgment in the selection of the veneers. As a guide, here is a list of possible veneers in colour groups:

Golden-yellow
Ayan, gold peroba, iroko and satinwood for the head.

Golden brown
Amboyna burr, afrormosia, igibgo, teak, thuya burr, African walnut, parinari and opepe.

Purple-brown
Kingwood, dark mansonia, purple-heart, Indian rosewood, American walnut.

Remember that some of the highlights should show reflected light and be yellow to cream-white, such as avodire and afara. Direct highlights could be in sycamore. Sand shaded sycamore and harewood for the white feathers

Bird subjects break all the rules about starting at the top and from parts of the picture farthest away in perspective. The trick with bird subjects is to *cut the bird from the bottom up*. All feathers overlap those below them and *also from right to left* in the 'face' design. Remember, if you are working in reverse to clearly mark the design so that you are working from the bottom up *as well as from left to right.*

Fig. 191 Feathers cut using the templet

Fig.190 shows the outline in reverse, viewed from the working side, with a few feathers in place, some showing the join line. Each row overlaps the one below, and each feather overlaps the feather to the left.

Cutting sequence
Begin with the log, then the lower leg of the bird. This has to be cut in first before the thigh, because the feathers in the thigh have to overlap the feathers in the lower leg. Commence sticking the feathers into the aperture from the bottom left, working across to the right, return to the left in the row above and start the next row in turn.

The long tail feathers are next using two or three compatible shades of veneer, working upwards to the head. Trace and cut out the window aperture for the right wing.

It is not necessary to follow a precise pattern line for the feathers. In the same manner that an artist would transpose a given line visually on to paper an approximate visual orientation is enough.

The veneers and burrs should all be flattened first, preferably with paper on the back to prevent any tiny fragments chipping off.

The jig is placed over the required veneer, on the cutting board, selecting the desired profile. The handle is pressed down, and the knife used to make score-cuts around the shape which is then cut out. Remove the jig and cut across the two ends of the profile to free the segment.

Half profiles are handled differently. The long feathers have quills and the grain in each half is oriented to a 45 degree angle, reversed to each other. Fig. 191 shows individual feather segments cut from two veneers joined at an angle, the joint forming the feather quill.

Long feathers

Use profile No. 3 to cut the left half of the feathers and profile No. 2 for the right side. Both halves are cut from the straight edge of the veneer. The two halves are butt-jointed together with PVA, the join line portrays the quill of the feather.

Turn the veneer over when cutting the opposing half feather. As the feathers are cut they may be sand shaded before being butt-jointed into the assembly.

Large feathers

The first large feather is allowed to overlap into the position where the tail feathers will be overlaid later. Notice that the feathers get closer together on the left side; also that some of the large feathers overlap those on the right *and on the left.*

Smaller feathers

Many of these may be cut as one piece, unlike the large feathers. Others have a quill and reverse angled grain direction.

Shadows

Some of the feathers can be given the appearance of overlapping by the use of sand shading. In each case, it is the side of the feather that appears to be overlapped by its neighbour that is sand shaded. To accomplish this, sand shade an edge of a leaf of veneer and obtain a choice of parts from which to cut profiles.

Highlights

The source of light originates from the left rear of the bird. Cut a large feather using Nos. 2 and 3 profiles, but this time cut the hole in the waster as a one-piece feather. Cut the actual feather from the white or grey veneer but only the lower portion of the feather.

Insert and glue in place. Position the jig over it and trim off all but a tiny sliver about $\frac{1}{32}$nd of an inch (0.8 mm). Now cut a full size feather as before from the normal feather veneer using the two half profiles, 2 and 3, and glue them together.

Place the complete feather into the aperture *from the face side.* Turn the assembly over and cut away that portion of the complete feather that is overlapped by the sliver of highlight veneer.

Ensure that the grain direction of the highlight is the same as the feather. The beak is inserted last, sand shaded. Highlights in the eye are made by inserting a sliver through a hole pierced with a needle.

18
Inlays

Bandings, Lines and Stringings

A WIDE range commercial inlay bandings are available today, sold in 1 metre lengths: stringings; flat lines; square lines; purfling and inlay bandings.

Stringings, flat lines and bandings are supplied in veneer thickness, but square lines and purfling are usually sold in imperial wire gauge (WG) measurements:

WG	Inches	Mm.
22	.028	0.711
20	.036	0.914
18	.048	1.219
16	.064	1.626
14	.080	2.032
12	.104	2.642
10	.128	3.251
8	.160	4.064
6	.192	4.877
4	.232	5.893
2	.276	7.010

Stringings

These are veneers, sawcut into square section in 20 or 22 gauge, usually from boxwood or dyed black. Guillotined stringings can be produced from $\frac{1}{32}$nd to $\frac{1}{64}$th inch (0.79 to 0.39mm). They are useful for marquetry as they may be twisted or curved easily, and inserted like slivers.

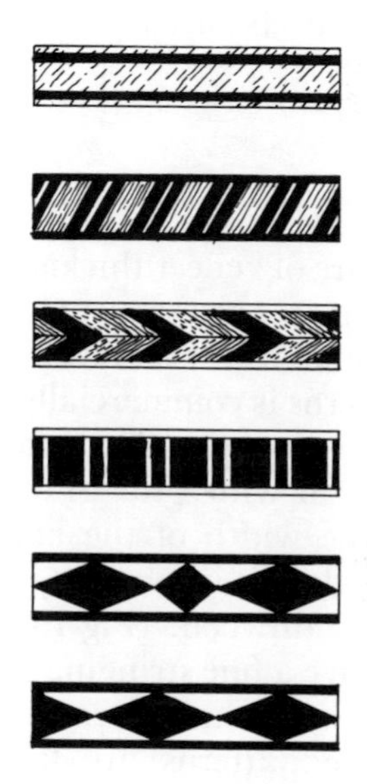

Fig. 192 Traditional banding patterns

Flat lines

These are narrow strips of veneer, supplied in 1 metre lengths, and in all the various widths, available in boxwood or dyed black. Narrow lines or stringings are used in conjunction with crossbanded borders to form a fillet border, or with border mount veneers around a marquetry picture. The marquetarian can easily cut his own lines from a wide variety of veneers.

Square lines are also available in these sizes. The most popular sizes stocked at $\frac{1}{16}$, $\frac{1}{8}$ and $\frac{1}{4}$ inch (1.6, 3.2 and 6.3mm).

Purfling
This is used for musical instrument decoration and comprises a three line 'sandwich' cut into square section. Purfling is ordered by specifying 'white-black-white' or 'black-white-black'. One layer of boxwood or sycamore, and two layers of ebony, rosewood or dyed black veneer, or in reverse order, usually available in $\frac{1}{16}$ or $\frac{1}{8}$ inch (1.6mm or 1.8mm) square section.

It is used extensively for the decoration of violins, guitars, mandolins, lutes etc., and is also supplied in pearl acetate, imitation tortoiseshell and ebonised plastic strips.

Bandings

All bandings are of veneer thickness. Widths vary according to pattern usually in 4mm, 6mm and 10mm widths, or wider. A wide variety of patterns is commercially available. One of the most popular types is the 'crossbanding' in which the grain direction runs across the width of the banding and are usually offered in walnut, rosewood, tulipwood or satinwood. (Fig.192)

Bandings have a fine stringing of boxwood or dyed black, or both, at each side. Feather or herringbone patterns are favoured for bending around curves as any pattern slip does not mar the work. Ladder, rope, arrowhead, lozenge, diamond, elongated diamond, chess-checker, and Grecian key patterned bandings are all popular.

Three line bandings are also supplied to match with purfling. Purfling is usually set in at corners or edges, and any bandings used to decorate the face of the instrument are in the form of bandings.

Application
There are several points to note on the application of lines and bandings on a veneered panel.

1. The stringing or line is used to *divide* two surfaces, not necessarily to form a contrast. For example, a walnut curl centre panel, with a striped walnut crossbanded surround might be sufficient to form a panel, but there is the risk that the top of the curl might 'lose' itself in the straight striped grain of the crossbanding, and a fine walnut line would divide the panel tastefully.
2. A panel may be completely covered with a veneer match, without a crossbanded border, but the *effect* of a border can be achieved by the use of a banding.
3. On a very plain panel, the banding itself could be the main decorative feature by using an intricate design incorporated into the panel.
4. The outer edge of bandings is usually white or box or dyed black. On a rosewood background, the boxwood outer stringing of the banding would provide too stark a contrast, but a black line would still make a tonal contrast to the lustrous dark brown of the rosewood, as the idea is not to form a contrast but to mark the divide between two surfaces.
5. On a walnut panel, a sap walnut line is preferable to a sycamore or boxwood line, and an American walnut line preferable to dyed black.
6. The craftsman has to exercise his aesthetic sensibility in the choice and application of lines and bandings. They can be used to dignify and grace the work, or can ruin or spoil the work if overdone.

Bandings should be used with restraint and always be subordinate to the decorative veneers and serve to enhance them rather than compete with them for attention. They should compliment the panel by accentuating the harmony of the design.

7. True face. It is important to examine lines and stringings to determine their 'true-face', (tight side up) as they will present a different appearance when finished if they are accidentally turned over in assembly.

Cutting and inlaying

There are various tools used to cut the inlay groove for lines and bandings into already veneered surfaces.

(a) *The scratch stock.*

The shoulder-notch or fence runs along the side of the panel, and the cutter is worked backwards and forwards scraping away the wood to form a groove of the required pattern and depth pre-set on the cutter, which should be slightly less than the thickness of the inlay banding to allow for pressure to be applied when it is laid.

When the cutter is set near the notch it is used for shaping edge lippings, and when set further out, it is used for scratching grooves for stringings, lines and bandings.

For crossgrain inlaying, cut the two outer lines of the groove with the cutting gauge to sever the fibres cleanly, and then use the scratch stock between the two cut grooves. The fence may be rounded for use around curves. Although the modern router plane can be used for this work, the scratch stock is still extensively used by craftsmen.

(b) *Small router plane*

Used for removing parts of the groundwork when inlay motifs are to be inlaid into the solid.

(c) *Mortise gauge*

This cuts twin lines and the unwanted strip is removed with a firmer chisel.

(d) *'Ulmia' inlaying gauge*

This has a third cutter to remove the unwanted strip.

(e) *Cutting gauge*

(f) *The double knife*

This is a home-made tool. A piece of the line to be cut is inserted between two knife blades in a wooden handle and the adjusting screw tightened. Or a washer of the desired width can be used as a separator or spacer between the blades.

The double knife can be used against a straightedge for straight lines or free-hand, when the design requires curving or intricate outlines. It can also be used to cut the actual lines from suitable veneer and, at the same setting, the required groove to receive them.

Fig. 193 'Ulmia' 728 inlay gauge

Bending the line around a curve

When bending a stringing or square section line around a curve, as in an oval panel, the line is formed to the correct shape either by steaming it or immersing it in hot water and bending the line over a dowel or heated tube, working it backwards and forwards gradually increasing the curvature of the line. When it dries out it will retain the new shape.

To cut a curved geometric line (as opposed to free-hand cutting with the double knife), use a pair of dividers, of which one point has been flattened and sharpened into a cutter. Do not place the other point on the work, but put a scrap of veneer beneath the point, taped to the surface to stop it moving.

When a banding is needed for a curve, select a feather or herringbone type, and use a knife to separate the banding down the middle. This allows the two 45 degree feathered angles to slip to the curvature without disturbing the grain pattern, as shown in Fig.194 at (A). A mis-match, as shown at (B) is avoided.

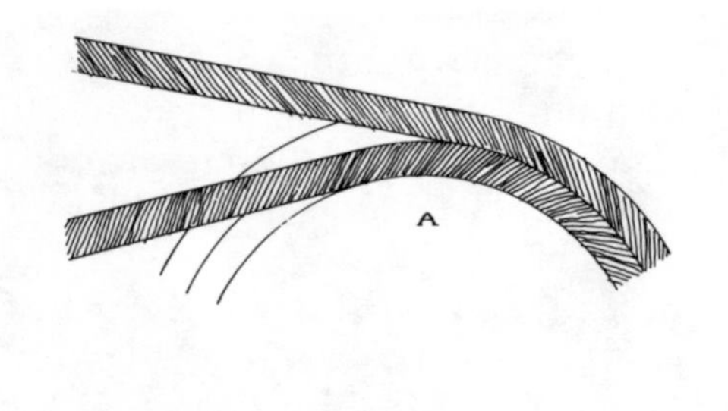

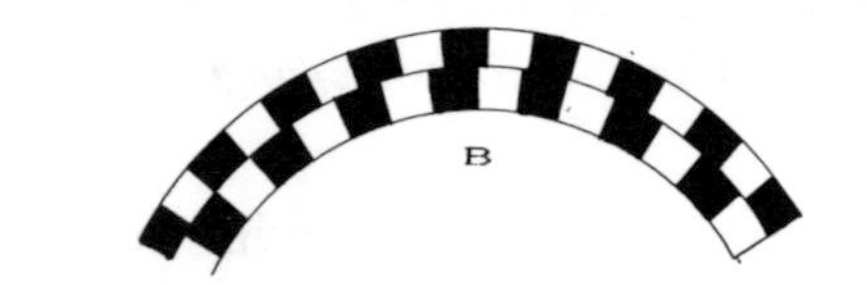

Fig. 194 Pattern slip around a radius

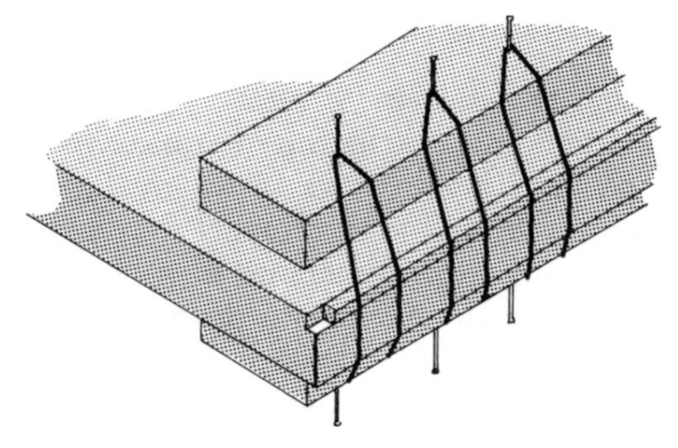

Fig. 195 Lacing a square line into a rebated edge

Criss-cross lines

When cutting a pattern of lines which criss-cross each other, always tape or glue in one line at a time and allow one to dry before cutting in the intersecting line. Never attempt to cut criss-crossing lines in the veneer assembly, which may result in tiny cross grained pieces breaking off and becoming lost.

Pattern balance

Care should be taken to match the pattern of the banding. It is incorrect to begin by

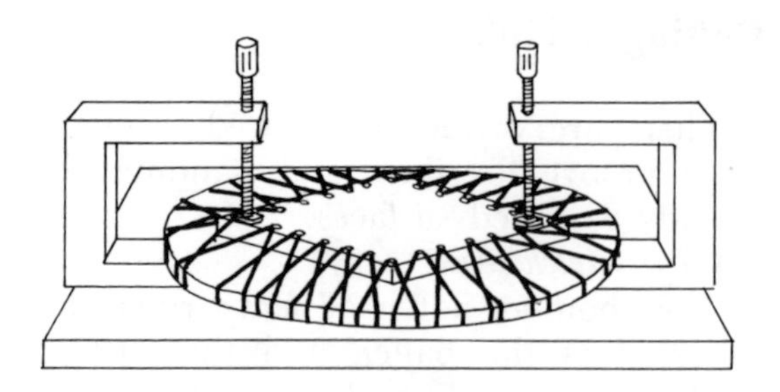

Fig. 196 How to lace edge veneers on a circular panel

laying one length of the metre banding from one corner of the panel and then continue along the next side using the offcut, join the next banding to it, etc. The result would be unbalanced.

The correct method is to start at one corner. Select two bandings and adjust the ends so that the patterns coincide.

Now mitre those two bandings into the corner of the panel allowing the other ends of the bandings to overlap the centre-lines of the panel. Repeat this in each corner overlapping at the centre-lines again.

Now cut through the bandings at the centre-lines, checking that the pattern is equal and symmetrical on both sides of the cut.

Inlaying at the edge of a panel

Very often a square section line is required right at the edge of the panel to be seen from above and from the side. This is best achieved by using the cutting gauge, first from the top and then from the side. Then use a chisel to start the rabbet at the corners, and finish off with the small bullnose or rabbet plane.

Lacing the edge

Clamp battens near to the edge at both sides of the panel. Drive nails into the battens at regular intervals, around which wet string is wound, alternately from above to below, binding upon the square section line. As the string dries it presses the line tightly into position.

Inlaying bandings into a panel
If your marquetry assembly has been laid and trimmed square without a banding, and you now wish to inlay a line or banding, select a router cutter or make up a scratch stock that is the exact width of the banding and set it to cut a groove slightly less in depth than the thickness of the banding.

If you have not got a cutter of the required width, use a narrower width cutter, set to the *inner* edge of the groove marked out by the cutting gauge, and then run a second groove with the cutter set to the outer edge. Do not use a router cutter into the corners. Mark the corners with a chisel and remove them.

Laying bandings and lines
It is modern practice to insert the banding or line into the veneer assembly which is then laid in one operation in a press. For this reason, bandings, lines and stringings to be used as components of a veneer assembly must all be of the same thickness as the main veneer assembly.

If commercially bought bandings or lines are slightly thicker than the marquetry assembly, they must be rendered level with the surface on the back, by scraping and sanding before the assembly is laid.

As a safeguard against blisters, use a yielding wad of paper or baize, felt, thick card, linoleum, plastic or rubber sheet in the press to allow for slight variation in thickness.

If the line or banding is to be inserted into solid groundwork or an already veneered panel, providing the groove is slightly less in depth than the thickness of the inlay, it may be laid with a veneer hammer or in a press.

Laying with crossbandings
When the marquetry has a crossbanded border surround, it is a wise precaution to lay the assembly without the crossbanded border mounts, fillet border or bandings.

The assembly is laid oversize and the borders and bandings are fitted in a separate operation. This is because the slightest 'press-slip' would result in the grain of the crossbanding not being parallel with the sides of the panel.

The assembly surplus is marked with a cutting gauge and removed, and the stringings, lines or bandings mitred in position and held temporarily with tapes. The tapes are run the length of the join to form a paper hinge. The crossbandings are fitted and mitred next.

Each side of the surround is hinged back and glue applied to the groundwork, and the corner mitres well taped. Tapes are also brought around the oversize crossbandings to the back of the panel. To prevent the cross grained borders from splitting, a few small wooden glue-blocks are placed against the panel around the edges, beneath the tapes.

How inlay bandings are made.

This is a fascinating and challenging craft, but the principles are quite basic. The trick is to contrive the composition of the banding so that the *end grain* is never exposed. It is the *side grain* that is seen in the banding.

For example, to make a walnut crossbanding, with a sycamore and black walnut stringing at each edge, you would require two leaves of black walnut 36 inches by 10 inches (914mm × 254mm); two leaves of sycamore of the same dimensions, and some solid walnut 8 inches (204mm), as *thick* as you can find, by any *width* that you can rub-join together to make up 10 inches (254mm) overall width.

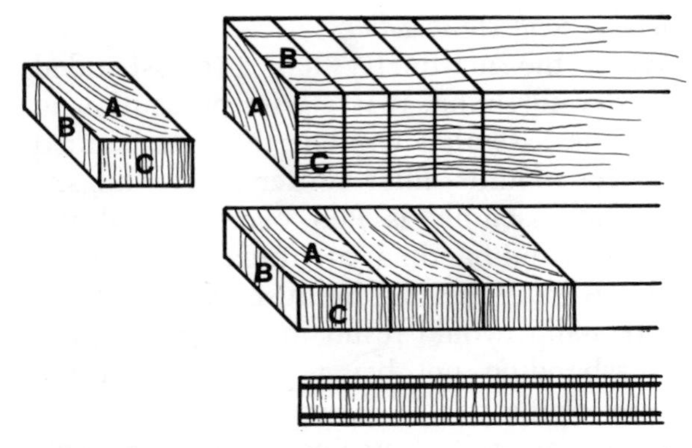

Fig. 197 How bandings are cut from the solid to display the side veneer face

Saw the walnut into ¼ inch (6mm) *long* strips, 10 inch (254mm) *wide* by 1½ inches (38mm) thick. Now turn the strip on its side. Cut, assemble and edge glue twenty-four such strips together, and you have a banding 36 inches (914mm) long, ¼ inch (6mm) thick and 12 inches (305mm) wide. (Fig.197).

The assembled blocks are bound with wide Sellotape, securely tied with string protected with polythene, and have temporary end-pieces fitted to take end clamps, and three sash clamps are applied. They are placed under pressure until dry. The 'block' as it is now called, is untied, and the wrapping removed. When dry, both sides are cleaned of glue traces.

The black walnut and sycamore veneers, suitably coated with glue, are laid in the press with the core blocks, followed by the other two leaves of veneer and pressed.

When dry, the panel is sawn into bandings of veneer thickness with a fine toothed hollow ground circular saw or bandsaw. The saw should have the absolute minimum sawcut, and the actual sawing be most accurately executed to avoid wandering. Every cut with the saw produces an identical banding.

In modern banding mills, roller fed multiple gang-saws are used, with washers fitted to the required banding thickness.

Making veneer bandings

Many marquetarians make their own bandings from veneers. For example, ebony and sycamore veneers can be glued together to form a plywood, and then sawn into veneer thickness. In their turn, these are turned on their sides and glued together again, to form miniature chessboard patterns, when re-sawn once more.

If you follow the simple rule that it is the *sidegrain* that is displayed in the banding, it is possible to cut and assemble triangular, rhomboidal, rectangular or other profiled sticks to form lozenge, feather, rope, ladder, domino, diamond, and geometric shapes such as hexagons, octagons, etc, and as many as your imagination and inegnuity can conjure up.

Soundhole rosettes

Used to decorate musical instruments these are made in the same way as bandings, except that they are assembled around a centre core or mandrel, and tightened in a steel 'Flexiband' type of clamp. Mother of pearl, or pearl acetate in veneer thickness is often included in the design.

19
Borders, Edges and Backs

Border Veneers

THE BORDER surround you choose can make or mar your picture. The wrong type of border can completely spoil the effect of a well-designed and executed panel. Conversely, a suitable border enhances the unity and distinction of a picture. Some subjects, such as portraits and oval floral subjects for example, do not require borders at all. The background of the picture extends to the edge of the panel.

To decide on the best type of border, many points have to be considered. Firstly, whether the overall impact of the picture is light, dark or monotone. It is usually found that neutral-toned woods enhance light or dark pictures, while lighter or darker borders are best with medium toned subjects.

The aim is to seek a harmonious blend, rather than a stark contrast. The subject matter of the picture is also a factor. If the picture is of a religious nature or solemn in intent, the border should be similarly subdued; more colourful treatment can be given to a calypso scene.

The attention of the viewer must never be diverted from the picture by the competing claims of the surround clamouring for attention. A simple picture relying upon its charm may need a plain, figureless border, but a scene depicting plenty of life, colour and vigorous action can 'carry' a border of more robust character.

The temperature of a picture also plays a part. If the predominating scene in a picture is a low horizon seascape or landscape and a sky using veneers in the golden-yellow range, a border in a yellowish veneer would be entirely wrong, as would a reddish toned border for a sunset or sunrise sky.

However, the same scene may have a very dark walnut foreground, for example, for reasons of aerial perspective. This would not rule out the use of a dark walnut border, in an otherwise light toned picture, provided the grain of the border is not in the same direction as the foreground, or, if it is, a contrasting fillet strip is inserted to form a break between the two walnut veneers.

Similarly, a winter snow-laden landscape would not require a plain white sycamore border, but this would greatly enhance a vibrantly coloured Carribean scene.

Highly figured woods are seldom used for borders. Quarter-cut, straight grained, ribbon striped or plain veneers make the best borders and include ash, cedar, elm, Douglas fir, mahogany, oak, pine, Queensland maple, rosewood, sapele, sycamore, teak, utile, African walnut or wengé.

A favourite ploy, to lend three dimensional realism to a picture, and to heighten the dramatic effect, is to allow part of the subject to pierce or overlap into the border surround. For example, the tail feathers of an eagle, or a leaping gazelle's foot would seem to add to the desperation of the animal's leap from an attacking tiger.

The traditional border surround comprises four consecutive matching leaves of veneer as shown in Fig.199, precisely mitred at each corner. It is important that the figure matches exactly and the mitres have invisible joints, as poor mitring is one of the most common faults of the amateur

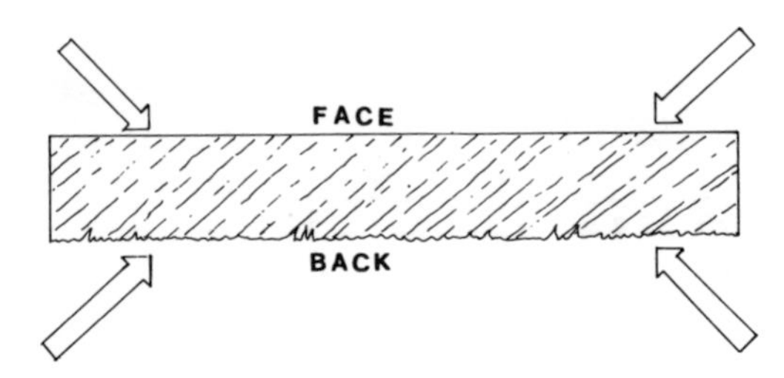

Fig. 198 Four different tones of veneer due to light refraction

marquetarian, especially where the border and fillet borders fail to coincide.

This type of border also causes differential light refraction as the four border veneers are laid both 'true face' and 'loose face', with the resulting effect of four different tones and loss of harmony.

To understand this better, let us begin by considering the problems of supplying the picture with a suitable backing veneer, in the form of a veneer match. The hallmark of a master marquetarian is the care and attention paid to the back of the panel as part of the whole.

Veneer Matching

The fascinating subject of veneer matching is fully described in *The Complete Manual of Wood Veneering* (Stobart & Son Ltd) but the basic principles are given here, as they apply to border veneers and the back of the panel.

Every leaf of veneer can be displayed in four different ways. The smooth 'face' side, viewed from top and the bottom and vice versa on the reverse side, viewed from the same two directions.

This will provide four different tonal values due to light refraction, and these will be particularly contrasting when the grain of the veneer is interlocked.

Book match

Two consecutive matching leaves are opened in book fashion, and jointed along the centre line to form a mirror image. It is important to 'open' the pair of leaves at the edge with the maximum figure.

Four-piece match

Select four matching consecutive leaves, and mark them each in chalk, 1F, 2F, 3F and 4F on the face side, and 1R, 2R, 3R and 4R on the reverse side. Take leaves 1F and 2F and open them in the direction of the maximum concentration of figure, into a two-piece book match.

If the best figure was at the bottom right-hand corner of the top leaf, open 1F to the right, forming a match 2F+1R. If the most

Fig. 199 Traditional border mount from four matching leaves

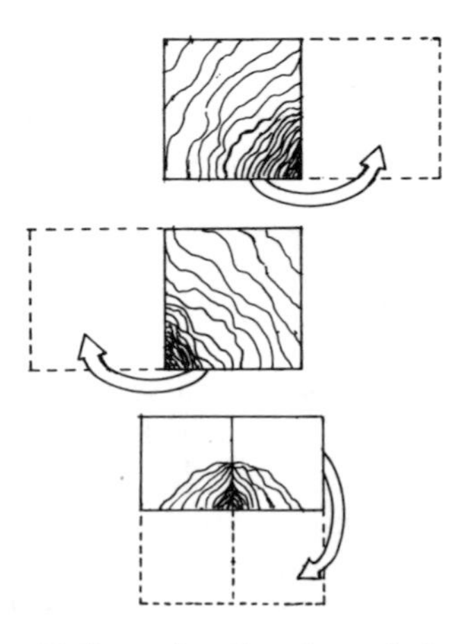

Fig. 200 Follow the direction of the maximum concentration of figure

attractive figure was at the bottom left-hand corner, the match would become 1R+2F.

Now take leaves 3 and 4 and open them to form either 4F+3R or 3R+4F. Reverse the second book match by turning it over on its horizontal axis. You now have a four-piece match which is either:

$$\frac{2F + 1R}{4R + 3F} \text{ or } \frac{1R + 2F}{3F + 4R}$$

Pattern jump

In both cases the pattern jump is one in the horizontal direction and two in the vertical direction, with opposite corners balanced for light refraction.

Angled mirrors

To test the best effects of a four-piece match, without cutting into veneer stock, hinge a pair of handbag mirrors together. When held at 90 degrees,they will display the effect of a four-piece match. At 45 degrees, the mirrors will show the effect of an eight-piece match.

The Diamond match

This is a popular match for the back of marquetry pictures. It enables narrow striped veneers to be used, such as sapele, rosewood, teak or walnut.

Assume you intend to use four such narrow leaves. They are 'slip-matched' by 'dragging-over' the leaves sideways, all showing their true face side, and jointed into one full width veneer, which you number 1F on the face side. Repeat this with leaves 5, 6, 7 and 8, to form leaf 2F; leaves 9, 10, 11 and 12 form leaf 3F, and leaves 13, 14, 15 and 16 form leaf 4F. The pattern jump will be only four between each newly formed leaf. Chalk 1R, 2R, 3R and 4R on the reverse of these leaves as in Fig.201.

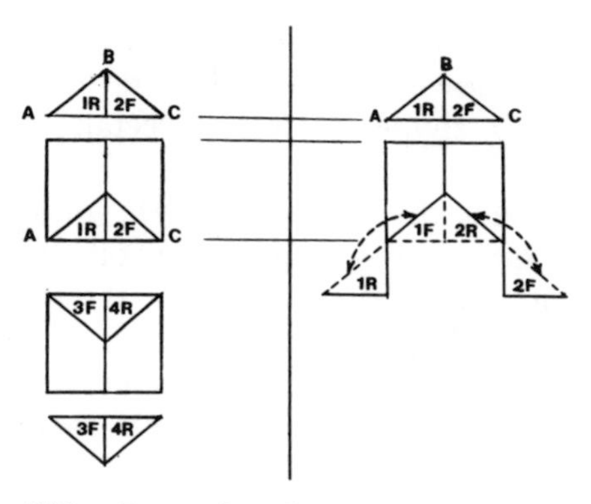

Fig. 201 Lettered and numbered veneers for a diamond match

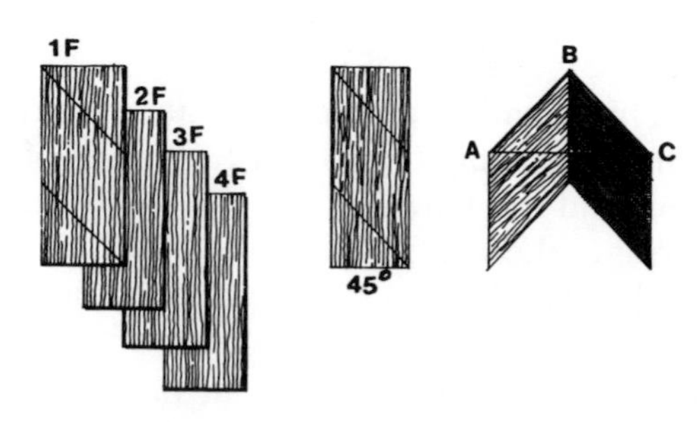

Fig. 202 Diamond match. The triangle A-B-C is fitted in the space below

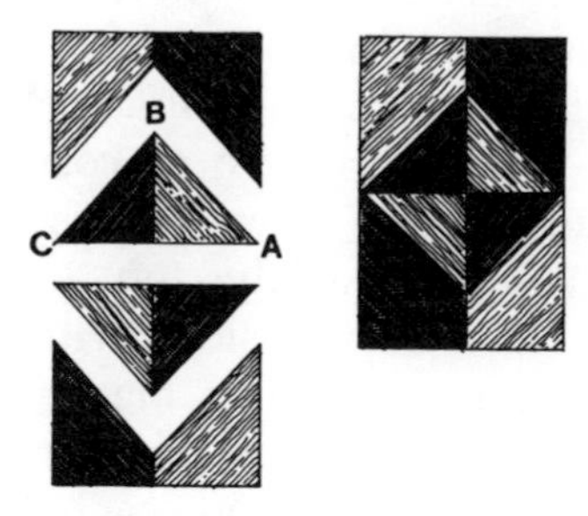

Fig. 203 Reverse diamond match. The triangle is reversed C-B-A

Cut through all four wide leaves at 45 degrees at each end, to form a rhomboidal shape as shown in Fig.202.

Now form a book match between 1R and 2F by cutting and taping a joint along the mitred edges. Next place a straightedge across the two leaves at A-C and trim off the top triangle, A-B-C, which is then brought down and taped into the lower triangular shape to form a rectangle with the baseline A-C.

Now take the pair 3R and 4F, joint them along the mitred edges, cut off the top triangle, and tape this into the bottom triangular shape to form a second rectangle.

Next, turn this rectangle over along its horizontal axis and tape both rectangles together.

The completed match reads:

$$\frac{1R+2F}{3F+4R}$$

This forms a correctly balanced pattern jump, with light and dark corners of the diamond match in opposite corners. By turning the centre triangles over, to form C+B+A (1R becomes 1F and 2F becomes 2R), a reverse diamond match can be formed as shown in Fig.203.

Crossbanded borders

These are usually eight-piece matches cut across the grain into short lengths, kept in matching sequence, and all kept 'true face'. They have either centre or corner mitres. The 'Queen Anne' style has the grain in the vertical direction at the top and bottom, and horizontal at both sides, with 45 degree corner mitres, as at B in Fig. 204.

Another style has a straight joint in the centre top, bottom and each side, and arranges the grain to run in the same direction as the 45 degree mitred corners, forming an eight-piece match, as at C.

This type is more decorative, as it possesses an 'explosive' effect with its grain flowing outwards from the centre, giving the picture maximum impact. Type A has the advantage that the crossbandings may be cut from veneers which are not straight grained along their entire length but are straight in sections.

Crossbandings laid around a radius, (circular or oval panels) need to have the grain direction of the veneer flowing outwards uniformly around the curve. This is achieved by cutting a number of consecutive lengths of short *width* veneers, and fan them around the curve so that the grain direction turns through 90 degrees in small steps. Use a minimum of four veneers, each with a pattern jump of 22½ degrees or six veneers, each with a pattern jump of 15 degrees.

For a multi-corner assembly of crossbandings, compress a small bundle of suitable narrow striped veneers between battens and shoot the edges. Joint them on the shooting board, tape them together and lay them in a caul.

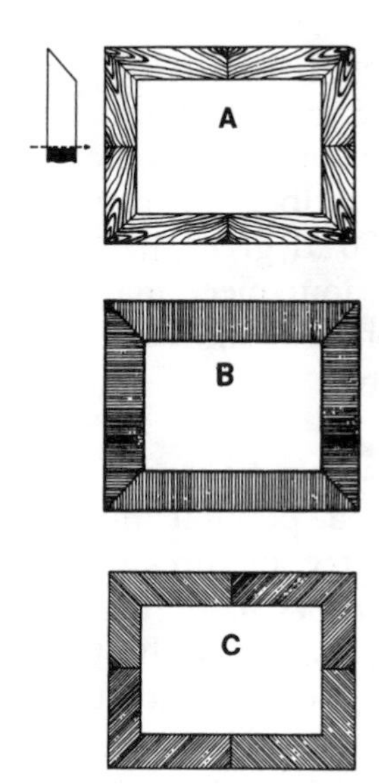

Fig. 204 Crossbanded border mounts

Many expert marquetarians prefer their finished panel to create an illusion of solidity and resemble a solid board, not with the intention to deceive, but to preserve the natural appearance of a hand-made wooden picture.

To achieve this, the true face of the veneer is determined to provide the same overall

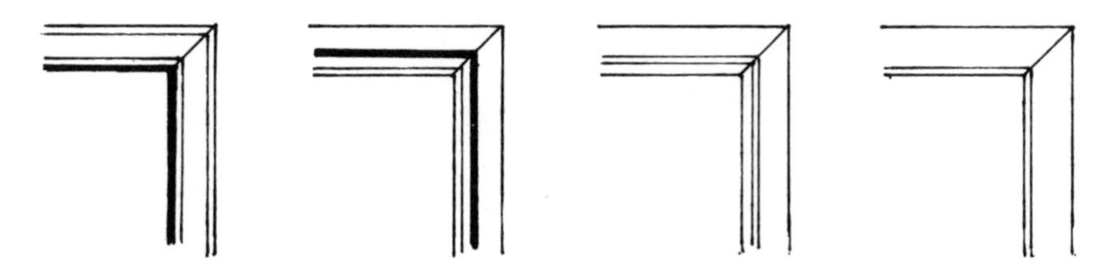

Fig. 206 Four different fillet borders

tonal value by reflected light. Matching leaves are cut to create the effect of a picture let-in to one single veneer. The matching veneer on the back of the panel is also laid without joints, and the panel's edges continue the illusion by being cross grained on the top and bottom edges and long grained on both sides, as in Fig. 205.

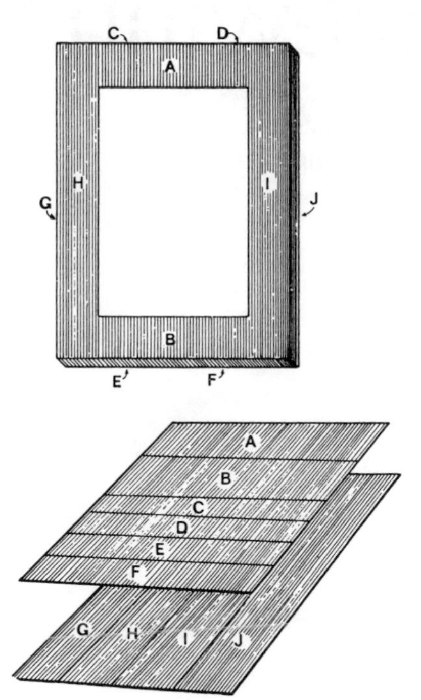

Fig. 205 Border mount with a solid panel effect

Fillet Borders

The conventional format is to fit a narrow strip of veneer up to ⅛ inch (3mm) wide, mitred at the corners, adjacent to the picture area, surrounded by the border framing of your choice.

The fillet border has to be chosen carefully as its purpose is to stand out in contrast between the picture veneers and the borders. The main consideration in selecting the best veneer for this purpose is that it should contrast with the veneers nearest to the border, and also the selected border veneers.

Traditionally, dyed black and boxwood were used and are still obtainable as stringings or lines in veneer thickness. Today, most marquetarians use white or black (sycamore or walnut) or neutral brown or grey, chosen from either extreme or centre of the tonal values scale (see Chapter 29).

Decorative mosaic bandings are also used for pictorial marquetry. Simple; narrow 'ladder', or 'rope' types are used on smaller pictures and the 'feather', or 'chevron' types on larger pictures. The fillet strip may be inset inside the border veneer, so that the border itself forms the fillet. For decorative purposes, sometimes two fillets are used, either of the same veneer or contrasting with each other and of varying widths.

Other subjects lend themselves to the treatment where the background veneer continues to the edge of the panel, without a border, but a break is indicated by a fillet set inside the picture area. (Fig. 206).

Yet another idea is to use one of the main veneers in the picture (either the sky or foreground) and use that as a fillet border, which shows up on only three sides of the panel.

A Gallery of Marquetry Prizewinners

A selection of some of the finest
work by contemporary craftsmen
being produced today (pp. 161–176)

Savage Splendour *P.J. Levens*

Radio Times *A.D. Lord*

Our Mutual Friend
A.M. Townsend

Mask from the past
A.M. Townsend

The Reverie *T. H. Turton*

Craftsmen *P.J. Levens*

Ma Gu *Peter J. White*

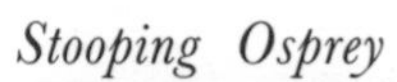

Stooping Osprey *Peter J. White*

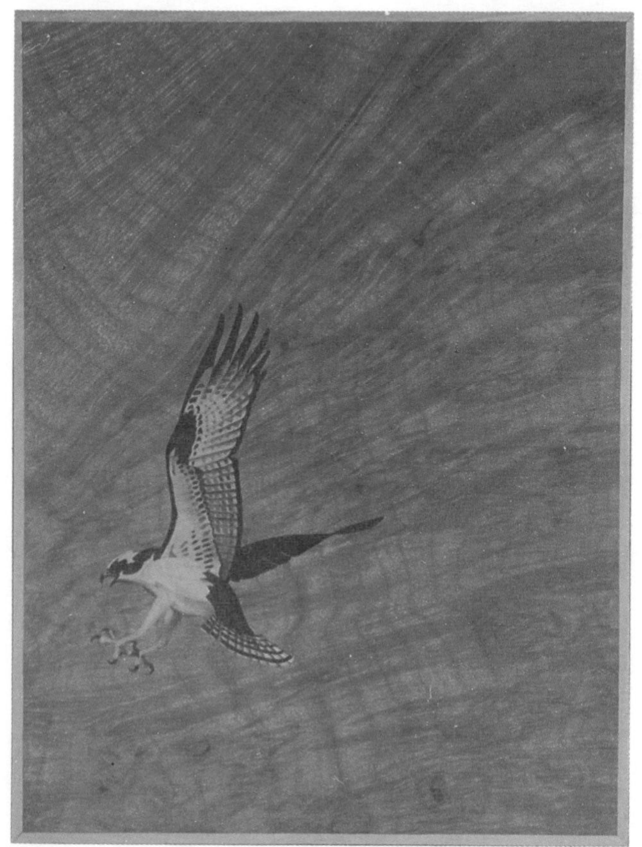

Monogram of entire alphabet
Eric Horne

Lazy Moments — *Andrew Smith*

Lazy Susan — *T. Chandler*

Coat of Arms, J. Jelley

Early Spring, John May

Musical Maestros, J. Secker

On the Riverbank — *Peter J. White*

Plain turnery with marquetry decoration by Dennis J. Hunt

Reflections in Maple Peter J. White

The Woodcutters W.A. Spinks

Newlyn, Cornwall Peter J. White

Sweetie Jar Alan Townsend

Charles H. Good
Forget me not (after Graham-Johnson)
(2nd Premier class winner)

Gordon Baker *Winter in Town*
(2nd Advanced class winner)

Richard Shellard Fruits of Nature
(Premier class and Rosebowl winner)

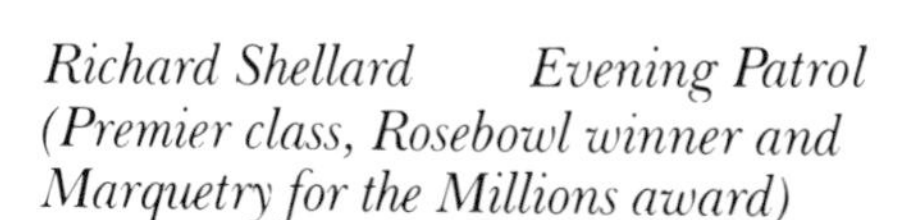

Richard Shellard Evening Patrol
(Premier class, Rosebowl winner and
Marquetry for the Millions award)

George Monks (USA) Frilled coquettes
(Marquetry Society of America winner)

D. Middleton *A scene from Hard Times*
(Advanced class winner)

R. Thomas *Love from Katie*
(Class 2 winner)

M. D. Kelly *Where's the Children?*
(Highly commended beginner's picture)

G. Baker *Feathered Friends*
(Highly commended)

Mrs P. Davies
(Artistic award) *The Washerwoman*

Alan Townsend *Bluebell wood*
(Class 3 and Rosebowl winner)

Bluebell wood (detail)

C. Daniels *Brief Encounter*
(2nd Intermediate class winner)

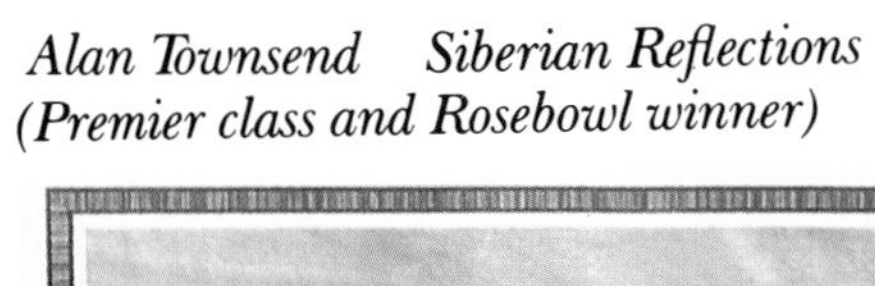

Alan Townsend *Siberian Reflections*
(Premier class and Rosebowl winner)

Siberian Reflections (detail)

Emanuela Marassi (Italy)
Scultura In Legno E Tarsia
Sculpture in marquetry, exhibited at Il Bosco di Arianna,Fondazione Bevilacqua La Masa, Venice

Silas Kopf (USA) *Azalia cabinet*

Contemporary marquetry cabinet
by Stephane Robino, Didier Pujal and
Pierre Marie Boisset,
Ecole Boulle des Arts Appliques, Paris

Eddie Stevens White Moon (after S. Nardini)
(Intermediate class and Artistic merit award)

W. A. Spinks Springtime
(after a stained glass design by Grasset)

Frank Taylor Abseiling
(Highly commended in the Three Veneers class)

A. Pedder
(Artistic merit award) Cutty Sark

Cornfield Scenario (Detail)

Alan Townsend *Cornfield Scenario*
(Winner of Marquetry for the Millions award; 2nd prize in the Premier class)

Tawny at the Wheel (detail)

Peter J. White *Tawny at the Wheel*
(Premier class and Rosebowl winner)

Cliff Daniels *Come on!*
(Advanced class winner)

H. A. Pedder *Still life*
(2nd Advanced class winner)

Poul Middelboe (Sweden)
World woods
Contemporary geometric marquetry

B. Bedford *Tunbridgeware ball (125mm diameter)*
(Winner, Advanced applied marquetry)

Andrew Smith *Zodiac table*
(Winner, Advanced applied marquetry)

Andrew Smith *Indian Fur Trapper*
(Rosebowl winner)

John Sedgwick (Canada) Rocky Mountain High
(Intermediate class and Marquetry Soc of America winner)

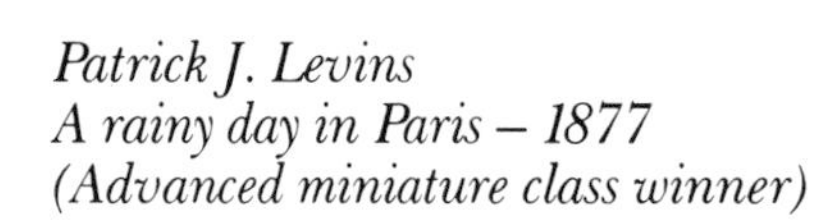

Patrick J. Levins
A rainy day in Paris – 1877
(Advanced miniature class winner)

Eddie Stevens
H.R.H. The Queen Mother
(Highly commended, Premier class winner)

J. Beattie *Chipping Camden* *(Artistic merit award)*

Rothenburg
Siegfried Klotsche, Canada

Morning Calm *Jeff Herbert*

Wrens and blackberries

Pineapple Table *Andrew Smith*

Long-tailed Tit
R. Shellard

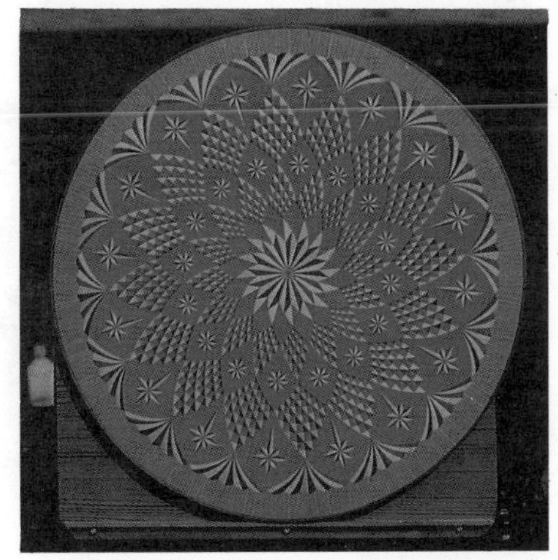

The Busker *Joan Meadows*

Homework *Silas Kopf*

Maltravers Street, Arundel *D. Middleton*

The Tailor *H. Beecher*

Backgammon Box *D. Middleton*

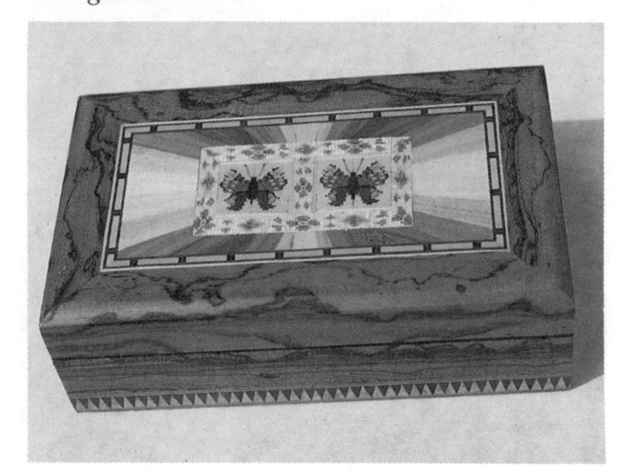

Tulip Hadley Chest — *Silas Kopf*

Two plus one — *Ron Gibbons*

On the Beam — *R. Mehew*

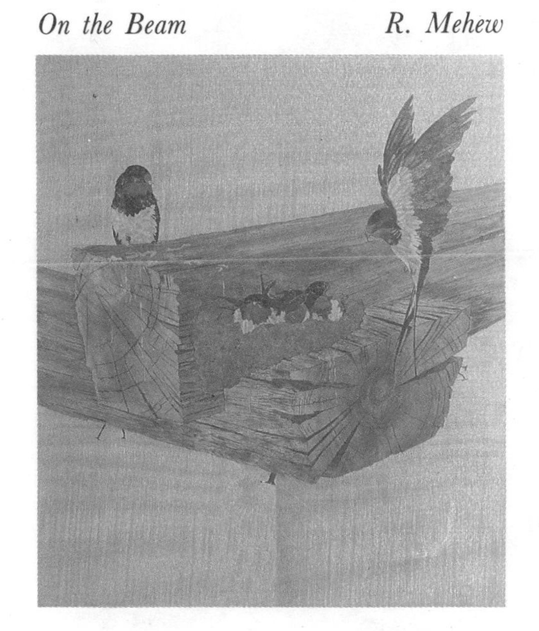

Five Waits — *Charles Good*

Eight Course *Charles Good*

Charles Good won the Lincoln Open International Exhibition in the 70's, and the 'Marquetarian of the Decade' award. He won the Marquetry Society Rosebowl four times and excels in every class from minatures to murals.

Approaching Dawn *Charles Good*

The Priory  *Charles Good*

 *Hawfinch* *Charles Good*

20
Applied Marquetry

'APPLIED MARQUETRY' is the colloquial term used to describe all forms of marquetry applied to the decoration of boxes, trays, furniture etc., and similar applications such as the ornamentation of wood turnery.

The marquetarian needs to know the best methods of tackling the traditional forms of marquetry furniture decoration, as he may wish to restore or repair a genuine antique or create a modern reproduction.

A knowledge of the techniques may also inspire the craftsman to create new forms of decorative ornamentation for modern furniture.

Inlay motifs

Most traditional forms of marquetry decoration are available today, including such favourites as round and oval patterae, shells, fans, corner pieces, (all sand shaded), floral bouquets with knotted bows, ribbons and garlands, urns, vases, musical instruments, military trophies, grotesques, chinoiseries, figure studies in classical Greek art or mythology and the beautiful and intricate scrolls and entwined English sea-weed marquetry. Regency motifs in brass set into rosewood or mahogany backgrounds are also available.

These motifs are already assembled and sold with a kraft paper backing covering the face side with the reverse side toothed ready for laying.

Sometimes these motifs are left in their waster veneer backgrounds for protection and this needs to be trimmed off before use, but in most cases, the ovals, fans, shells, etc., are supplied already released from their background wasters.

Motifs are applied in two different ways, either being 'let-into' the veneer assembly and laid as part of the whole, in which case there may be a difference in thickness to be removed from the back before laying. Alternatively, they may be inlaid into a routed aperture in the solid groundwork as a separate operation, such as when repairing an anqtique, or into an existing veneered panel. The motifs are laid paper side uppermost.

Inlaying a motif

When an inlay motif has to be let into a veneered or solid base, many marquetarians use power routers for the task. It is safer for the amateur to use hand methods which require a diligent but limited level of skill.

Cover the area to receive the motif with 1 inch (25mm) masking tape and press down securely.

For round or oval motifs, draw center register lines on the project and on the paper covered face of the motif. Apply rubber cement (Cow gum) to the masking tape within the pencilled line, also about an inch (25mm) around the edge on the back of the motif and allow a few minutes to dry.

Place the motif in position and secure to

Fig. 207 Cutting around the motif taped in position

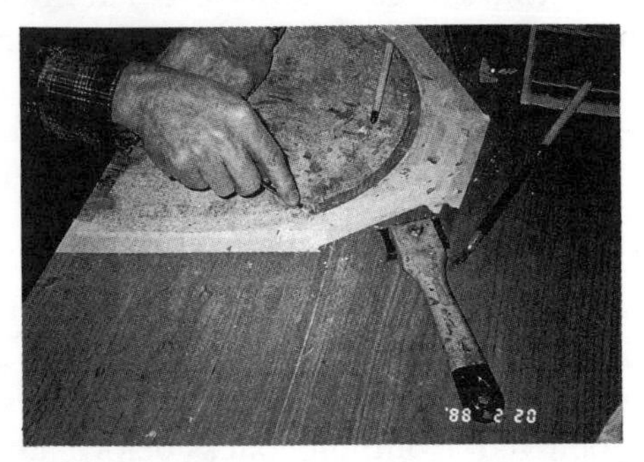

Fig. 208 Remove the waste from beneath the motif

the base using a boxwood roller to prevent movement. To cut the motif in, first use stab-cuts around its edges to prevent the next cut from following the grain. (Fig. 207). Increase these into $\frac{1}{4}$ inch (6mm) step-cuts with a $\frac{1}{4}$ inch (6 mm) gap between them and then go back to the previous cut to link these cuts together.

Remove the motif by slipping a steel ruler beneath it. Rub off the rubber cement from the back of the motif with the fingertips or use a scraper. Now peel off the masking tape inside the area to receive the motif. Use either a hand router plane or power router to within $\frac{1}{16}$th inch (1.5 mm) of the pencilled line with a $\frac{1}{4}$ inch (6mm) straight bit, and use a curved carving gouge or the back of a paring chisel to remove the remaining waste veneer in the designated area. For most veneered surfaces the router can be dispensed with and the waste removed with chisels. A scraper is also useful for this purpose.

The depth of the routed contour should be slightly less than the thickness of the inlay to allow for finishing level. (Fig. 208).

Fit short 3 inch (75mm) lengths of gummed paper veneer tape as straps around the motif. Apply glue to the scraped base,

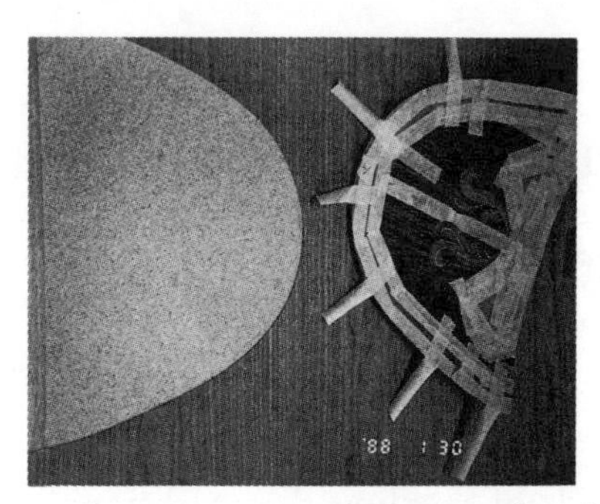

Fig. 209 Fit tapes around the motif and apply adhesive to the base

Fig. 210 After pressing, dampen and remove the tapes

Fig. 211 Scrape the protective kraft paper from the face of the motif

not to the inlay. When tacky, quickly position the motif and check that the registration pencil marks coincide. Dampen and fasten the veneer tapes. (Fig. 209).

Apply pressure with cramps or in a press. When dry, remove the panel from pressure and dampen the paper tapes. Fig. 210. Scrape off the protective kraft paper from the face of the motif and level the motif with the surrounding panel, and carry on with the finishing treatment. Fig. 211.

For the repair of antiques, take care to ensure that the main grain direction of the motif runs in the same direction as the solid groundwork. On veneered furniture the background veneer of the motif should run opposite to the grain direction of the underneath case veneer. Inlays of this type may be left smooth and level, or engraved and filled with a contrasting wood stopping to suit the period.

Layer relief inlays

A modern variation of this ancient form of inlay is to make a relief marquetry motif in ebony, satinwood and rosewood, and also use the rosewood as the face veneer of the panel.

A decorative pattern would be fretsawn in the three veneers, but not interchanged as a normal marquetry motif. The ebony and satinwood veneers would be allowed to show at two different levels below the rosewood surface, forming a two-tone pattern, at various positions according to the design. For example, parts of the rosewood would show the satinwood at the layer immediately below the surface – possibly with ebony inserts within the satinwood – and at other positions, ebony decoration two layers below the surface, which may also have satinwood inserts.

Metal inlays

In the Regency period, brass motifs inlaid into rosewood or mahogany backgrounds enjoyed a popular vogue and is still one of the forms of marquetry widely practiced today for reproduction furniture and on chairbacks.

Brass sheet is hard, and most professionals use a composition bronze in the proportion of sixty to forty of brass and copper.

Robust grades 3 or 1, jeweller's metal-piercing blades are used for this work. The brass and the rosewood veneer are held together with a temporary adhesive (such as rubber cement) for the sawing process, and are easily separated afterwards.

Boulle work

André Charles Boulle, (1642–1732) rediscovered an ancient Italian technique of interchange marquetry and developed a fascinating style of his own using tortoiseshell and metals such as brass, copper, tin, zinc, pewter and silver.

To enhance the effect, he underlaid the almost transparent tortoiseshell with red or green paper or silk, and the metal parts were richly engraved and filled with a contrasting paste.

Boulle work consists, for the most part, of sheet brass inlaid into a tortoiseshell background called the *première-partie*, or inlay of the first part, and its reverse, tortoiseshell inlaid into brass, known as *contre-partie* or counter-inlay. The inlay of the first part is considered by connoisseurs to be the most highly valued.

On a piece of ebony furniture, both the first part and counter-inlays were often combined, and this is generally known as 'counter-change marquetry'.

Because counter-change marquetry had to be cut on a flat sawtable, leaving a join around each section to be filled with a contrasting paste, for the very best work it became fashionable for only the *première-partie* to be used and the metal parts were inserted using the bevel cut.

The *contre-partie* would then be unusable as a counter-change and would have to be saved for another project. Tortoiseshell was prepared into small plates and are brittle when cold. They were then heated and rendered supple in hot water.

Today, this work can be created using plastic sheets of imitation tortoiseshell and pearl acetate with sheet brass.

Epoxy resin adhesives must be used for gluing metal to wood, as with heat the metal will expand and wood contract.

Traditional furniture marquetry

Marquetry has always been used to enhance the furniture it decorates, and as a general rule, should never be allowed to become the focal point of interest. Whenever, throughout history, the decoration became more important than the piece of furniture, the style declined and led to a change of style. Splendid examples of traditional marquetry cabinet reproductions are made by students of Professor Pierre Ramond, at the famous Ecole Boulle in Paris, one of the finest schools of marquetry in the world. The students also produce remarkable pieces of contemporary applied marquetry.

Contemporary furniture marquetry

Silas Kopf of Northampton, Mass., U.S.A., a professional marquetarian, has deliberately set out to be the exception to the rule. He creates 'virtuosity' furniture by making the picture the focus and then designs the furniture to best display it.

His furniture is highly original in concept, whimsical and humourous in style, and are provocative, conversation pieces.

Silas has been given a 'one man show' at the prestigious Gallery Henoch in New York, where his *Azalea cabinet* (featured in the coloured plates section), aroused great interest. Although Silas has a thorough understanding of perspective drawing, he claims that a mathematically correct perspective drawing is only true from one viewing angle and height.

He tries to achieve a feeling and illusion of depth and solidity by the use of shadows and highlights, rather than attempt strictly accurate perspectives, by overlapping and juxtapositioning objects to suggest or emphasise depth. (Figs. 212 to 215).

Eye-level application seems best, as horizontal surfaces such as tables soon tend to become cluttered in use, but cabinet doors and door panels are more suitable for this treatment.

Other applications

There are many other very popular applications for pictorial marquetry, from the decoration of boxes to tables of all kinds. Perhaps the favourite application is for the decoration of jewellery boxes.

This leads to the challenge of creating marquetry jewellery. There is a wide range of jewel mounts obtainable, and many marquetarians create brooches, ear-rings, pendants and cameos in a variety of woods decorated with marquetry.

Fig. 212 An imbuyia and oak burr cabinet featuring a self-portrait on the door. Silas Kopf.

Fig. 214 Trompe-l'oeil cabinets; a wine cabinet in maple and amboyna burr, and a tea cabinet in quilted mahogany. Silas Kopf.

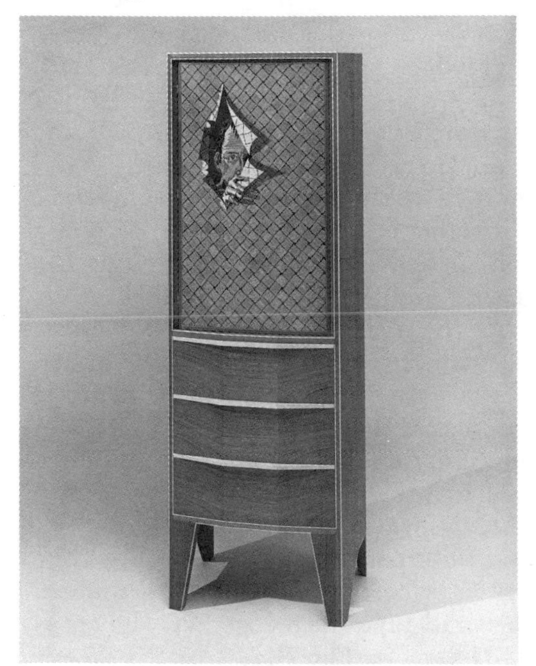

Fig. 213 Self-portrait, breaking through a sand-shaded basket-weave parquetry cabinet door. Silas Kopf.

Fig. 215 A mahogany and rosewood tromp-l'oeil fall front desk and chair. Silas Kopf.

21
Parquetry

THE TERM parquetry actually derives from a pattern of wood flooring, but today it is colloquially applied to the cutting and assembly of wood veneers to form a geometric marquetry pattern.

It has a mathematical basis and is also governed by the laws of symmetry. The veneers are chosen for different reasons than those selected for marquetry. Either plain, or narrow striped veneers with parallel grain, are best. In this type of marquetry, all the lines are cut against a straightedge into small geometric shapes to form a decorative pattern. These are assembled and laid as a normal marquetry assembly.

Fig. 216 The chess board is a simple form of parquetry

Chessboard

One of the simplest forms of geometric marquetry, and excellent practice, is to make a chessboard.

To begin, select two contrasting veneers, (not black and white, which will prove to be too tiring for the eyes in play). There is an infinite number of choices to be made depending on your own preferences. For example, you may choose to select from the dark brown or red tones of walnut or rosewood, and contrast with golden yellow satinwood or avodire, for the light tones.

Purpleheart and ayan, or mahogany and harewood make good contrasts. More highly figured contrasts such as walnut burr and bird's eye maple are popular and thuya and ash burr, or pommelle and quilted maple are other possibilities.

Accurately cut nine strips, $1\frac{1}{2}$ or $1\frac{3}{4}$ inch (38 or 45mm) wide, by 14 or 16 inches (355 or 406mm) long, from the light veneer, and 8 strips from the darker species using a straightedge and a sharp knife. As an aid, file up a strip of alumimium as a templet to the exact strip size, to ensure all the strips are precisely the same width.

Now join the alternately light and dark strips together edge-to-edge with PVA white glue or impact adhesive, or tape along the joints with gummed veneering tape.

Rotate the assembly through 90 degrees. Check with a try square that the metal templet is positioned exactly at 90 degrees, and cut across the grain into eight strips in the opposite direction. If you did not use a templet, ensure these eight strips are sanded to the same width.

Move alternate strips forward by one square, to bring the light and dark squares together and tape them together, shown as A-B-C-D etc., in Fig. 217.

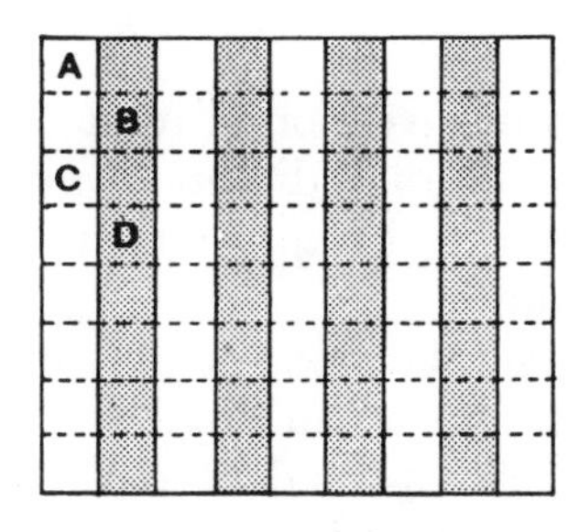

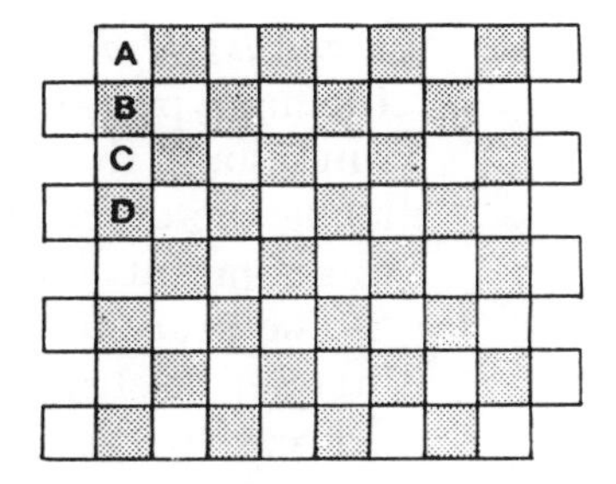

Fig. 217 Move columns A and C forward one square

Fig. 218 Cutting strips accurately with veneer saw and steel straightedge

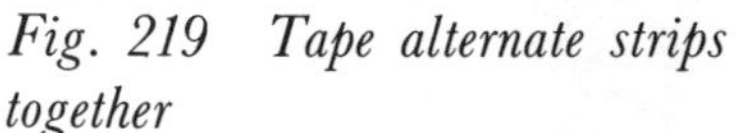

Fig. 219 Tape alternate strips together

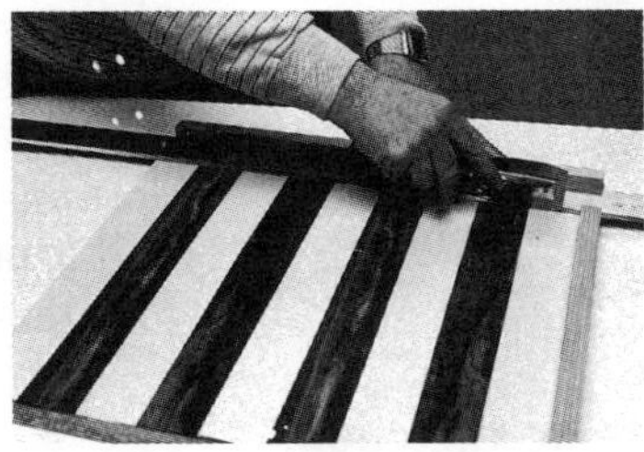

Fig. 220 Cut strips in the opposite direction

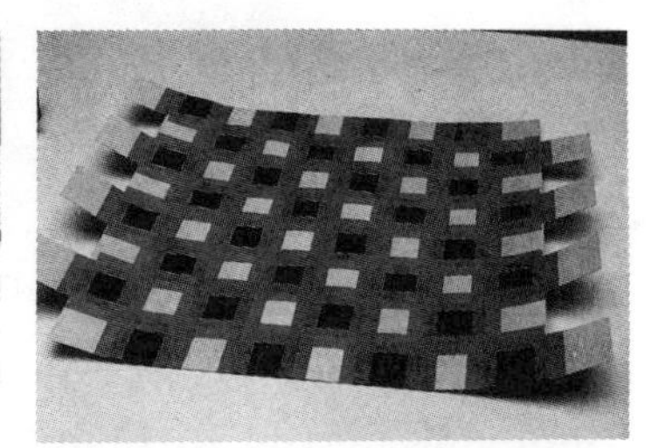

Fig. 221 The taped assembly with alternate rows staggered

Trim off the unwanted ninth squares which protrude at the end of each row. Now the fillet border, inlay banding or lines and the border veneers are fitted.

It is usual to tape these to the assembly on the face side. The normal sequences of preparation for laying and finishing are then carried out as described for a pictorial marquetry assembly.

From this simple start a great many variations can be made. For example, the veneers may be all of the same species, but the pattern is achieved by alternating the grain direction which is made to run parallel to alternate pairs of sides.

Diamond parquetry

There are almost unlimited geometric combinations possible in creating parquetry patterns. For the best effect, select quarter-cut closely striped veneer, such as pencil striped sapele or African walnut, which has an interlocked grain with a high degree of light refraction, and a natural lustre which, when polished, adds to the surface interest and appeal of the wood. Or use veneers with a pronounced natural stripe such as zebrano, tulipwood, kingwood or rosewood which rely more upon the striped marking of the figure.

The tools required are a knife and straight-edge, a protractor, tee-square, set squares, compass, and a scale ruler, a pocket calculator and a special type of cutting board, (see Fig.224.)

There are several different types of diamond parquetry:

Diagonal diamonds.

(a) In this type, the grain direction is contrived to run parallel with the left-upper and right-lower sides of the vertically elongated diamond, alternating in adjacent

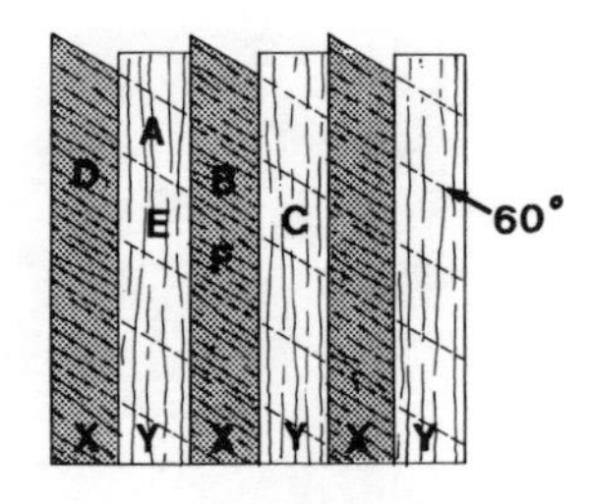

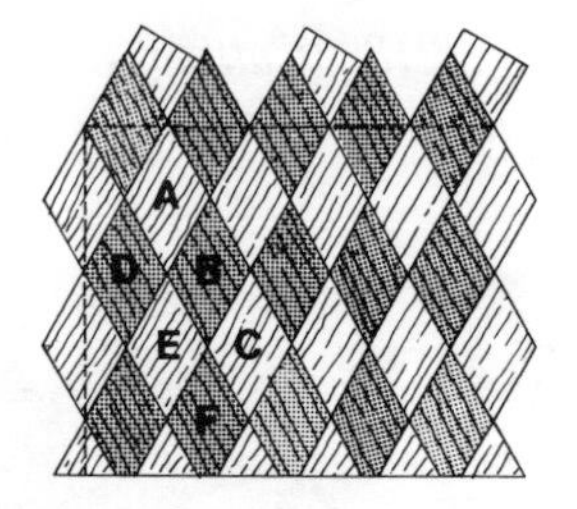

Fig. 222 After a 60 degree cut, A-B-C is moved forward by one row

diamonds to run in the opposite direction, (i.e. right-upper and left-lower sides of the diamond).

Cut a straight grained leaf of sapele veneer into three $1\frac{1}{2}$ inch (38 mm) strips, with the grain parallel to the edges. Cut another matching leaf into another three strips of exactly the same width (X), but this time cut diagonally across the grain at 60 degrees from the vertical, (Y). Compress both sets of strips together and rub them gently on a sandpaper file to ensure clean edges.

Assemble these six strips together alternately and tape them together. Now cut across this taped assembly at 60 degrees from the vertical into strips of exactly the same width.

Note the position of rhomboidal shapes A, B, and C, in relation to D, E and F. The strip containing D, E and F is moved downwards one space to align with A, B and C.

Tape the assembly together again. Place the straightedge along the top of the first row of diamonds, and remove the odd surplus shapes to reveal a pattern of alternating diamonds.

Right angled diamonds

In this type, the grain direction is made to run along the axis of one diamond and along the other axis at right angles to it on the adjacent diamond.

The procedure is similar, except that the first set of strips are cut at an angle of 30 degrees to the vertical, instead of parallel to the grain, and the second set are at 60 degrees as before. The alternate strips are taped together. The assembly is then cut at an angle of 60 degrees as before, into strips of the same width.

When these strips are moved forward by one space the pattern formed will reveal diamonds with alternating grain in vertical and horizontal directions in adjacent diamonds.(See Fig.223.)

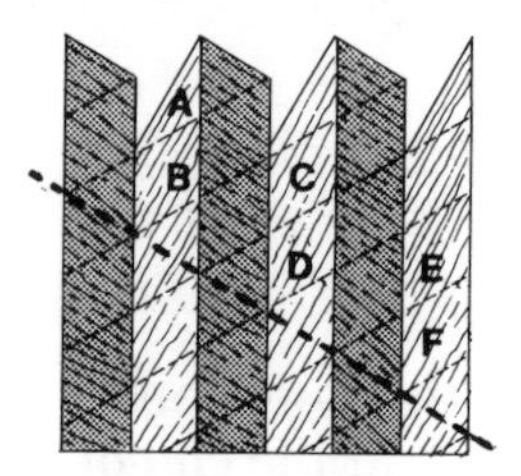

Fig. 223 How right angled diamonds are cut

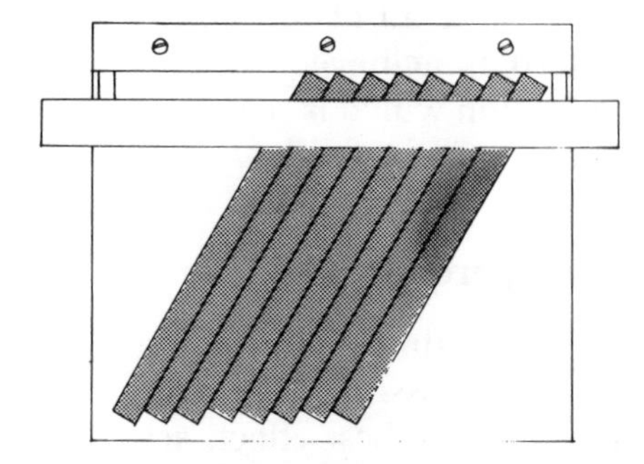

Fig. 224 A diamond cutting board

Checkers
As a further experiment, if you now cut through this assembly again, this time cutting the diamonds in half along one of the diagonals, and moving the strips forwards one space, a multiplicity of triangular designs is created.

Regular and irregular polygons
When a *regular* polygon is required in a pattern, all the angles must be *constant multiples* of an angle, which itself is a multiple of 180 degrees which is referred to as the modulus

The angles most popularly used are: for hexagons 60 degrees; octagons 45 degrees and 90 degrees; pentagons and decagons 36 degrees and 72 degrees; dodecagons 30 degrees, 60 degrees and 90 degrees; diamonds are always referred to by the smaller of the two supplementary angles they contain, for example a 60 degrees diamond is the same as a 120 degrees.

Any combination of angles may be used, providing they are compatible with each other. For example, 40 degrees and 50 degrees (i.e 90 degrees) could be substituted for 45 degrees diamonds and would produce an eight-sided symmetrical *irregular* polygon. Hexagons cannot be mixed with octagons as they are not compatible. Pentagons cannot be mixed with either. Squares can mix with both octagons and dodecagons because 90 degrees comprises both 30 degrees and 45° multiples.

Therefore, any odd angles, such as 27 degrees and 63 degrees can be combined to produce an *irregular polygon.*

Interchanging orders
A decagon, like the dodecagon, (but unlike the octagon) can be expanded to the next higher order; five diamonds can be exchanged for two pentagons and one diamond, without disturbing the pattern.

Ten pentagons side by side will enclose a decagon. Pentagons cannot be built up by using diamonds alone, but are formed with pentagons of a lower order. A pentagon is constructed from one and a half 72 degrees diamonds and half a 36 degrees diamond. By substituting pentagons in pairs, for the equivalent number of diamonds, the scope of design is greatly increased. (Fig.225.)

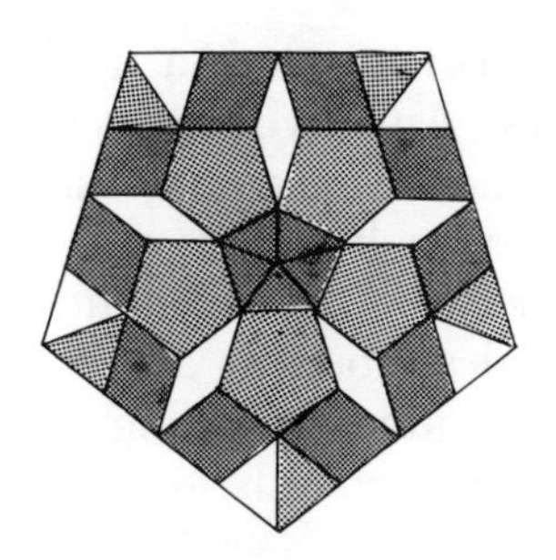

Fig. 225 A pentagon of the 4th order

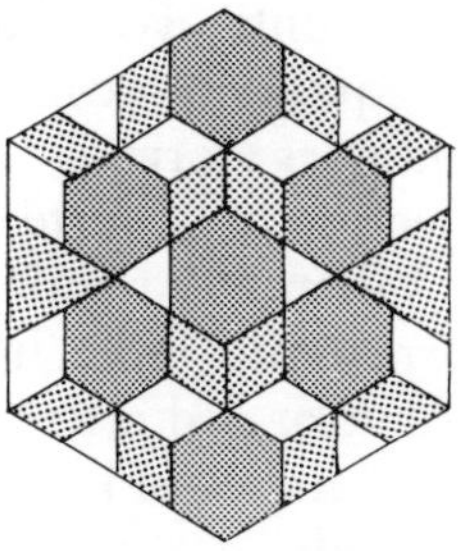

Fig. 226 A hexagon of the 4th order

Louis cube parquetry
Hexagons form the famous optical illusion of the 'reversing cube,' made popular in the Louis XV and XVI periods of marquetry furniture. Cube parquetry was made from tulipwood, rosewood, kingwood and amaranthe, into which exquisite floral marquetry would be cut, surrounded by intricate scrollwork, and a crossbanded border surrounds.

Cube parquetry is formed from hexagons, produced with a modulus of 60 degrees. When a 60 degrees diamond is cut in half, it remains both equilateral and equiangular; three such diamonds combine to form a hexagon, as in Fig. 227.

Draw a horizontal line, and divide it into any convenient number of parts to suit your project. Next, draw two series of parallel lines at 60 degrees and at 120 degrees, and where these intersect, draw more horizontal

Fig. 227 Louis cube parquetry

lines until you have constructed a grid of equilateral triangles. Any two adjacent triangles form a diamond, and any six meeting at a vertex form a hexagon.

When any regular polygon has diamonds forming its side, it is described as a "2nd order, or 3rd order" polygon, depending on the number of lengths of diamonds forming the side.

Symmetry

In parquetry, symmetry is the science of transformation geometry, and means that the pattern repeats itself in both directions at regular intervals.

Symmetry can be described as 'rotational', when the pattern matches in several places around a central pivot; 'radial symmetry' is where the pattern matches like the spokes of a wheel.

A 'Catherine wheel' pattern has rotational but not radial symmetry as the spiral curve meets at the vertex.

If the pattern can be moved in either the vertical or its horizontal direction, and the pattern co-incides at regular intervals it has bi-directional symmetry; if in only one direction, (as in the case of inlay bandings) it is in linear symmetry.

In a two-piece match, the centre line is the axis of symmetry if both halves are mirror images. In a four-piece match or an ellipse it has two axes of symmetry. Shapes such as pentagons have five axes, octagons eight, etc.

In parquetry, therefore, any pattern without rotational symmetry must have at least two axes of symmetry, and the veneers must have rotational symmetry in colour or figure.

Special cutting boards

Precision and accuracy are essential in cutting and assembling parquetry, as the smallest error in cutting has an accumulative effect and multiplies with every piece of the pattern.

Cutting boards are made, about 24 × 18 inches (600 × 450mm), with a fence stop protruding about ¼ inch (6mm) screwed to the top edge, with pairs of 'spacer-stops' cut from hardboard, as shown in Fig.228, which shows a pentagon cutting board, and Fig.229, a hexagon cutting board.

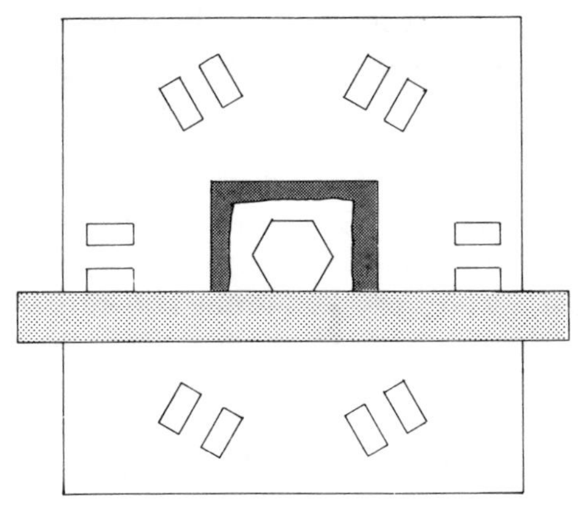

Fig. 229 Hexagon cutting board

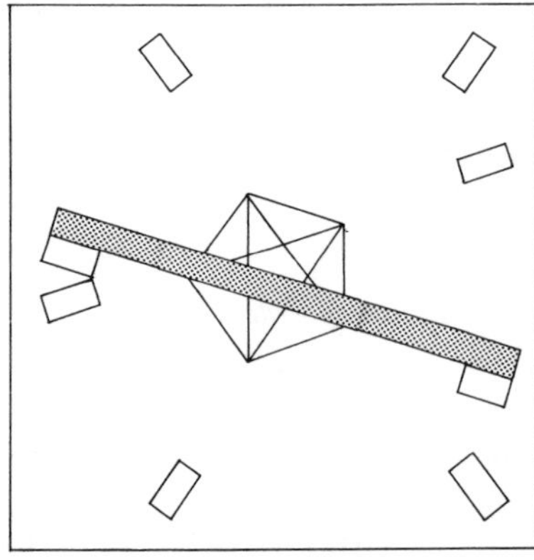

Fig. 228 Pentagon cutting board

A steel straightedge is lined up against the stops, for accurate cutting. A sheet of self-adhesive plastic sheet is also useful as the parquetry pieces can be assembled directly to it.

Line and dot parquetry

This is a trellis pattern of diamonds formed by diagonal crossing of inlay lines, carefully mitred at the intersections. A small black dot is inserted in each of the four 'V' angles of the intersections, and sometimes a smaller black diamond is inserted in the centre of a larger diamond, with two diagonal cross saw cuts separating this into four smaller diamonds. The larger diamond is assembled with black lines as before, mitred at the intersections.

Trellis parquetry

This does not rely upon geometric precision as does other forms of parquetry. Every individual cube or diamond shape is a picture in miniature. Each 'unit' would consist of a cube, oval or diamond, about 1½ inch (38mm) overall, with ornately curved or shaped scroll outlines about ⅛ inch (3mm) wide, encompassing a small floral motif such as a pimpernel.

The repeating pattern would be assembled to completely cover a surface, with an overall effect of trellis work entwined with flowers. The trellis was usually cut from boxwood or dyed black peartree, the parquetry from basswood, magnolia or plum, and the flowers from padauk and green oak.

Op-Art

William Rondholz, of Jersey City, N.J., U.S.A., developed and presented a process which he describes as 'Op-Art for marquetry' which dispenses with the use of a templet altogether.

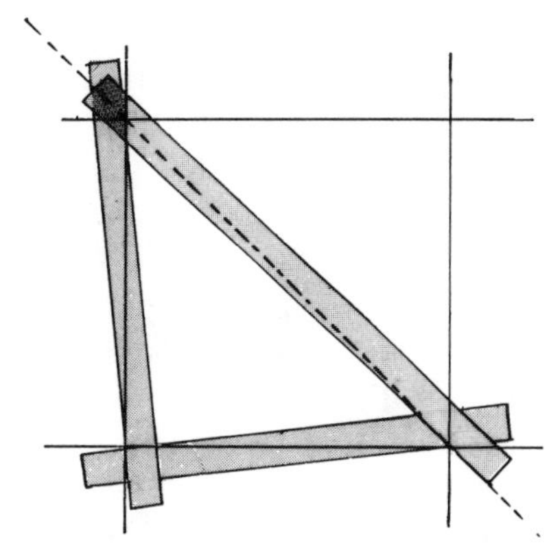

Fig. 230 Constructing the first 'Op-Art' triangle

It is constructed with veneer strips of uniform width and contrasting colours.

All the laws of transformation symmetry apply, as the pattern can be applied within the outline of any square, rectangle, or polygon; a larger shape can be broken down into smaller triangles or polygons, etc.

In this example the design is a 3 inch (76mm) square, divided into two equilateral triangles. (See Fig.230.)

Draw a 3 inch (76mm) square on the cutting board, extending all lines 1½ inch (38mm) beyond the borders. Divide the square across from top left corner to bottom right, with a diagonal line forming two triangles. Using two contrasting veneers of mahogany and maple, of 18 inch (450mm) lengths, cut into $\frac{3}{16}$ inch (5mm) strips.

The first mahogany strip is placed along the diagonal, so that its *centre* lies above the top left-hand corner of the triangle. Push the bottom right-hand edge of the strip upwards until the lower edge fits *exactly* into the bottom right corner and tape in position.

Now place the second mahogany strip along the left-hand side of the square and tuck it under the strip at the top left-hand corner, with the right-hand edge of strip 2 *at the point of contact with strip 1* (a little way down the left-hand line forming the square).

Position the bottom left-hand edge of strip 2 right into the bottom left-hand corner.

Lightly score, cut the joint and edge-glue the two veneers at the top left-hand corner, tape in position leaving a surplus of ½ inch (12mm) at the bottom.

Take mahogany strip 3 and place it across the bottom of the square, tucked under the ends of the first two strips, with the top edge of strip 3 exactly touching strip 2 where they meet *at the point of contact* on the bottom line, on the left, and the bottom edge into the corner at the right. Score and cut the bottom of strips 1 and 2 and edge-glue the third strip in position and secure to the board with tape.

These three strips will be trimmed to size later, when the design is more advanced. Next, using the maple veneer strips, cut and fit them inside the triangle following the same procedure as used for strips 2 and 3, positioning the lower edge of strip 4 at the point of contact of strips 1 and 3, and the upper edge of strip 4 into the point of contact of strips 1 and 2, i.e., *not into the corners*.

Use small pieces of Sellotape as temporary holds, until the triangle is completed. Continue the procedure with strips 5 and 6 of maple, and then 3 more alternating strips of mahogany and maple.

When the entire area is filled in, place a straightedge, from the point where strip 1 meets the top horizontal line of the square, (to the right of the top left corner) with the other end of the straightedge lined up into the bottom right-hand corner, and cut through strip 1. This has now provided strip 1 for the second triangle of the square.

The procedure continues by placing a new strip of mahogany under strip 1, across the top line of the square, with the left, lower edge touching *the point of contact* of strip 1 with the top horizontal line of the square, and the upper right-hand edge into the top right corner.

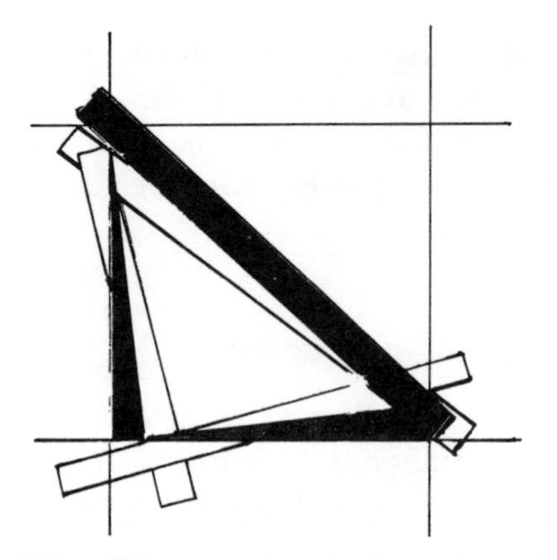

Fig. 231 The second triangle is formed

Fig. 232 One square completed

Complete this upper triangle working in a clockwise direction When both triangles are complete, trim off the surplus veneers to form the square.

If wider strips are used, the design loses the gracefulness of its curve and, conversely, the narrower the strips and the more used in the pattern, the more graceful the curve becomes.

By inserting strip 1 along the diagonal of the square, each half comprises identical triangles, but if the first strip is laid *on an outer edge*, each triangle would be a mirror image of the other.

Fig. 233 The completed panel

The Parquetry Orb

One of the most challenging and difficult pieces of parquetry was created by Ben Bedford, as is shown in the 'Gallery of Marquetry Prizewinners'.

The parquetry took the form of the basic cube design, formed into six 60 degree 'pear' shaped segments, inserted into a basket-weave patterned rim with looped ropes and a star on top to tie the design together. The inside of the jewel-box orb was lined in velvet. It is similar in appearance to Tunbridgeware.

Tunbridgeware

The techniques of making bandings and rosettes are also employed in the creation of this most painstaking form of 'English Mosaic' which was practised by the ancient Egyptians.

It was the discovery of chalybeate springs at Tunbridge Wells which made the town into a fashionable spa, and which brought the 'English Mosaic' firms to congregate at there in about 1720, at a time when inlays of shells and flowers, embellished with borders in ebony, green and white were produced for the decoration of tea caddies and workboxes, etc. (See the 'Hearts and Roses' box on page 164)

The craft reached its zenith of artistry in about 1850, when leading craftsmen were producing landscapes, perspective scenes of buildings, birds, butterflies and animals, which called for very tiny tesserae to be cut from about 150 different woods.

An interesting feature of Tunbridgeware is the use of green oak, a freak of nature caused by *Chlorosplenium aeruginosum*, an oak fungus.

The craftsman begins with a water colour painting of the picture. Next a working chart would be prepared on squared graph paper, with ten squares to the inch, (25mm).

To make a picture 10 × 8 inches, for example, in the scale of 32 to the inch, this would require, on graph paper of ten squares to the inch, 320 squares horizontally, by 256 squares vertically, a total of 81,920 squares. (Note: Similar examples using metric sizes and graphs could be used. The working method is the same for both systems of measurement.)

Therefore the original water colour would have to be 32 × 25.6 inches, each with ten squares per inch. In fact, the smaller the tesserae to be cut, the larger the original picture required for copying.

The next step is to cut strips of veneer from 12 to 18 inches long by 1 inch wide, in the thickness of the required tesserae, in this case $\frac{1}{32}$nd inch.

The chart is followed square by square, from the left-hand bottom square, vertically upwards, assembling together and gluing into a solid block, the strips of various woods to match the design.

When these are dry, the block is cut into veneer of $\frac{1}{32}$ inch thickness; about ten cuts would be made from the block, allowing for the expensive wastage lost in the sawcuts. Only one of these veneer strips is required for the picture, and the block would yield sufficient veneers (all of the first column of the design) for ten 'master assemblies'.

The process is repeated until all 320 such columns have been cut. These are now carefully glued together to form a master block, 256 veneers high by 320 columns wide. After gluing and allowing to dry, a total of ten master blocks would be prepared from the strips.

Finally, these blocks are sawn transversely, into the complete Tunbridgeware picture, exactly corresponding to the original painting. Up to 150 such pictures can be cut from one master block, and 1,500 pictures from the ten master blocks.

It is a very time consuming process, requiring a high degree of craftsmanship. Parquetry decoration is therefore a very accurate, precise mathematical skill with its own laws. Far greater freedom of expression can be enjoyed with veneer mosaic.

Veneer mosaic

The mosaic arts forming part of the Moslem culture, were originated in ancient Egypt, and later practised extensively by the Romans. This is an art form which is easy to create in veneers and most marquetry designs.

Unlike marquetry or parquetry, where the width of the visible glueline is virtually zero, and the cutting of the joints between parts is critically important, in mosaic the veneer pieces conform to no laws of symmetry or mathematics; the joints are open and visible and often emphasised to form an integral part of the overall design.

Each individual, irregular shaped piece of veneer mosaic (called *tesserae*) may be any shape to suit the pattern. For example, veneers may be cut into ¼ × 8 inches (6 × 200mm) long strips in various colours.

A design is prepared on graph paper with a grid of 1/4 inch (6mm) squares. A corresponding grid covers the baseboard. A little PVA glue is brushed on a small section of the groundwork, a square inch (25mm) at a time.

One end of a veneer strip is placed on a small square of the grid and a knife blade placed across the veneer about ¼ inch (6mm) from the tip and gentle pressure applied.

The veneer is severed leaving the *tessarae* in place. The art lies in cutting the *tesserae* in two different ways:

(a) The knife would snip off the *tesserae* to follow along the contour design outline of a tree foliage shape, for example, to emphasise the overall shape.

(b) The foliage within the outline would be in-filled with multi-shaped, different *tesserae*, which need not be squares, but can be cut into triangles, slivers, rectangles etc.

By turning the grain direction in various ways, laying the veneer either face and using different colours, the leaves in a tree can be given many autumnal tints.

Aerial perspective is achieved because tones can be gradated to the distance; sky and water effects can be given movement with waving contours and swirling backgrounds or crashing surf.

There are many ways of tackling pictorial subjects. The lines of the *tesserae* may be kept in straight rows in both directions, in which case light, plain veneers are used so as to allow the central motif or subject more prominence by contrast, in-filled with irregular shapes.

In contour backgrounds, the lines are given 'motion' and appear to flow outwards from the central subject in swirling wave patterns, following the contour of the motif.

An element of symbolism is also employed in the use of the actual *tesserae* to represent special features; slivers for grass, triangles for water, squares for sky, etc.

Another method allows the *tesserae* to be positioned with a gap between them, which is then filled with coloured PVA glue to emphasise the joins.

The mosaic idea can be extended, by cutting multi-shapes from thin 3-ply or hardboard, veneered in many different woods, (or by using solid woods bandsawn to about ⅛th inch (3mm) in thickness).

These thick *tesserae* may be assembled on a level surface and polished in the usual way, or the sheets may be polished before being cut into *tesserae*, and set at slightly different angles to the surface, (not perfectly level) by bedding them in a thick cement made of glue and sawdust. This provides a striking effect in different lighting conditions, due to reflected light, causing the mosaic to sparkle and the dramatic effect of shadows.

The joins between the *tesserae* may be closed by gluing together, or left open and filled with a stopping, to suit the design.

Oyster parquetry

This is a peculiarly English type of parquetry, made from saw-cut veneers from small stems and branches of trees with contrasting heart sapwood.

The limb is sawn at about 60 degree tangentially to the pith, producing an oval veneer with a sloping grain, which is less likely to lift when laid than a circular shape resulting from a 90 degree cut.

Oyster veneers are cut from green timber, or timber that has been steamed or boiled in a vat, as they are more easily controlled during the drying process than partially dried timber, due to their differential growth (both tangential and radial) in each oyster.

The green oysters are stacked in the same sequence as they were cut, so that they can be used to form matches, with small sticks between each veneer to allow a free circulation of air between, and to prevent any tendency to cockle. They should be kept weighted down until required for use. The sticks should be about ¼ inch (6mm) thick and carefully aligned above each other.

Put an oyster as a 'control' piece on top of each stack and if it shows signs of splitting, damp down the pile with a fine gardening spray, to slow down the drying rate.

After they are seasoned they are trimmed into elongated polygons, with paper glued to one side and the other side sealed with glue size, as they are almost end grain in texture and inclined to be brittle.

Oyster parquetry is used either as a border surround for a mirror, or as a centrepiece ornament in an otherwise plain panel, or used to completely cover a surface such as a door, table or box. Oysters should be laid with caul pressure.

Woods with a large ray figure such as oak, chestnut, beech, plane, mulberry, elm, etc., should be avoided. Ideal for oystering are blackthorn, kingwood, laburnum, lignum vitae, lilac, olivewood, pear, privet, robinia, rowan tree, walnut and whitebeam.

Before use, the sawteeth marks should be toothed from the surface or they may telegraph through to the finish.

The modern approach is to treat the 'green' oysters with polyethylene glycol 1000 (PEG), which stabilises the wood against future swelling, shrinkage or splitting.

Polyethylene Glycol 1000. (PEG)

The use of PEG is new to the marquetry world and, at the time of writing, no mention has been made of it in any marquetry publication.

The first experiments were carried out in America by Dr. A. J. Stamm in 1934. PEG resembles paraffin wax and is related to permanent anti-freeze. It is extensively used throughout the timber and veneer industry for the stabilization of wood to reduce swelling and shrinkage tendencies to at least half their potential movement, often less than the thermal movement of plastics.

When PEG is introduced to *completely green wood* it replaces the free water in the cell cavities and is then absorbed into the wood to replace the bound water in the cell walls, holding them relatively inert.

Dr.Stamm found that PEG in a molecular weight of 1000 was ideal and it is now extensively used around the world for the stabilization of rifle butts, turning and carving woods, and the treatment of veneers, plywood, blockboard, etc.

As far as oysters and veneers are concerned, it acts by 'bulking' the wood fibres, suppressing decay, without affecting the wood's physical properties, or reducing their gluing and finishing compabibility.

PEG dissolves in warm water, is non-toxic, non-corrosive and melts at 104°F (40°C) and it has a high flash point at 580°F (304°C). It is highly hygroscopic and actually attracts moisture, replacing the water in green timber when it is at its greatest dimension. When drying takes place, the PEG remains, eliminating about 80 per cent of the normal dimensional changes.

For optimum results, PEG 1000 should be diffused in amounts of 25 to 30 per cent of the dry weight of the wood, an approximate concentration of PEG being either a 30 or 50 per cent solution by weight. It would seem to be an ideal process for protecting oyster veneers for marquetry.

Use a fibreglass or plastic container fitted with a lid to inhibit evaporation. Immerse the veneers in a hot solution at room temperature and weight them down with wood or a bricks, stirring the mixture at frequent intervals. Top up with water and PEG as necessary to replace any loss of mixture due to evaporation. PEG will not spoil the natural colour of the veneer. Tools can be wiped clean of wax with warm water.

It is *not* suitable for use with white PVA adhesive, but works well with most adhesives if, after PEG treatment, the back of the veneer is properly prepared by de-greasing with a solvent such as white spirit, to cut the wax surface and raise the wood fibres. The most satisfactory adhesives, giving no problems at all after de-greasing, are the two-component resorcinols and epoxy resins, which are both heat and water proof.

Surface finishing with modified polyurethane gives excellent results, and moisture curing polyurethane varnish is highly recommended. Beeswax and carnuaba wax finishes are also ideal after the surface has been de-greased.

Note: The amenability of veneers to impregnation is given in *World Woods in Colour* (Stobart & Son Ltd). Also see *The Conversion and Seasoning of Wood* by William H. Brown (Stobart & Son Ltd) and *Working Green Wood with PEG* by Patrick Spielman (Sterling).

22
Groundwork

THE TYPE of baseboard or groundwork upon which to lay the marquetry assembly is not always a free choice. For example, the marquetry may be used to decorate furniture, or other considerations may have dictated the groundwork upon which the marquetry is to be laid.

Specifying Groundwork

A veneered panel will only be as good as the groundwork it is laid upon, so given a free choice, these are the points to be considered.

It is trade practice when ordering groundwork with veneered outer 'cases', such as plywood, blockboard, laminboard or veneered chipboard, to state first the dimension that is 'with the grain'.

A panel 18 × 24 inches (457 × 609mm) would have its surface veneer grain running in the 18 inch (457mm) direction, but a 24 × 18 inches panel has its grain in the 24 inch (609mm) direction.

In a marquetry assembly, the grain direction of the veneers runs in several directions, and the general rule that face veneers must always be laid *opposite* to the grain direction of the underlaying casing veneer of the plywood, blockboard, or veneered chipboard, must be broken in some part of the picture. Therefore, always specify a groundwork which has its veneered surface grain running opposite to the *predominating* grain direction of your marquetry assembly. In the case of *solid* groundwork such as hardwood or softwood, specify the dimension in the *same* direction as the marquetry veneers.

Here is a list of groundworks suitable for marquetry depending on the panel size.

Chipboard

Probably the best substrate universally used for the majority of marquetry pictures is dimensionally stable, medium density fibreboard (MDF).

Alternatively use furniture grade particleboard (in panel sizes 8ft 1 inch × 4ft 1 inch (2464 × 1245 mm) known in the trade as 'industrial grade' (not the building board grade which is sold in exactly 8ft × 4ft (2438 × 1219mm) panels). It is also free from all shrinkage and most other defects, and suitable for pictures up to about 4 sq. feet (0.037 sq. metres) in size.

Most marquetry pictures fall within this category. Some chipboard grades are made from two different grades of chips. Lay the face of the picture to the finest side and the backing veneer to the reverse. It is essential that chipboard is veneered on both sides to keep it balanced.

If the panel you have is an offcut of *veneered* chipboard, both sides must be 'keyed' and your veneers should be laid in the opposite grain direction.

Assume you have made a panoramic marquetry panel and for reasons of strength you need a panel 36 × 15 inches (914 ×

381 mm). But for veneering reasons you require the outer casing veneers to run in the 15 inch (381mm) direction, to enable your sea and sky veneers to run in the 36 inch (914mm) direction. The answer is to lay sub-veneers, sometimes called under-veneers or counter-veneers to *both* sides of the panel.

Counter-veneers

In some cases, where you have predominately vertical or horizontal features in the picture, it is necesssary to lay counter-veneers in the 45 degree angle diagonally across the panel and parallel to each other, on each side, using any cheap, soft veneer.

The reason why this is necessary is that in the rotary cutting of veneers for the outer casings of plywood or blockboard etc., the action of the veneer knife in shearing the veneer from the log, causes fine hair checks in the veneer, which run from the loose, open-pored under-side of the veneer, towards the closed-pored, upper-side, known as the 'true-face'.

Sometimes these outer-casing veneers are not laid true-face. The smooth face is laid in the glueline, leaving the coarse loose side on the outside which tends to dry out in the hot press during manufacture, resulting in further hairchecks.

Cheaper grades of plywood often have jointed veneer faces and these may telegraph through your marquetry assembly. By laying counter-veneers of sycamore, obeche or poplar, you will overcome this potential problem, but ensure that in your turn, they are laid true-face, ready to receive your marquetry.

To tell which is the face side of a veneer, either hold it to your cheek or run a fingertip along the cross grained edges and feel for the smooth side.

All counter veneers should be sized and flattened before being applied. The sizing helps to form a glue barrier and prevents glue sinkage into the groundwork caused by excessive pressure, which may starve the bond, or the penetration of glue drawn through the pores to the surface if heat is used to accelerate the bonding during pressing.

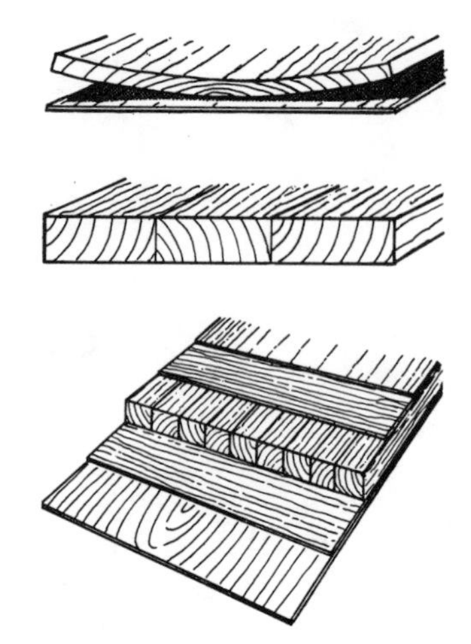

Fig. 234 Laminated board construction showing outer casing, crossbanding and strips laid 'head to tail'

For the majority of marquetry panels a groundwork of $\frac{5}{8}$ inch (16mm) dimensionally stable medium density fibreboard or furniture grade particleboard is ideal.

Laminboard

There is little doubt that laminboard is the strongest groundwork for larger panels for most types of pictorial and applied marquetry, but is rather expensive.

It is composed of a sandwich of core strips only $\frac{1}{8}$, $\frac{1}{4}$ or $\frac{5}{16}$ths of an inch (3, 6 or 8mm) wide, alternately arranged with their heart sides up and down to equalise any warping tendency. Across these core strips is laid a counter-veneer in the opposite direction and with stout outer casing veneers on both sides again, laid in the opposite direction and ready to receive your marquetry assembly. As shown at A in Fig.235.

You need to specify a panel *opposite* to the main grain direction of your marquetry, as explained above.

Blockboard

This material is second only to laminboard, because its core strips may be up to ½ inch (12mm) wide and, as a result, has a fractionally greater tendency to warp in very large sizes. Therefore, for panels from about 4 sq. feet up to about twelve sq. feet, (0.37 to 1.11 sq. metres) blockboard is suitable, and from 12 sq. feet to 32 sq. feet (1.11 to 2.97 sq. metres) a panel 8 feet × 4 feet (2438 × 1219mm) laminboard is preferred. (Fig.235,B).

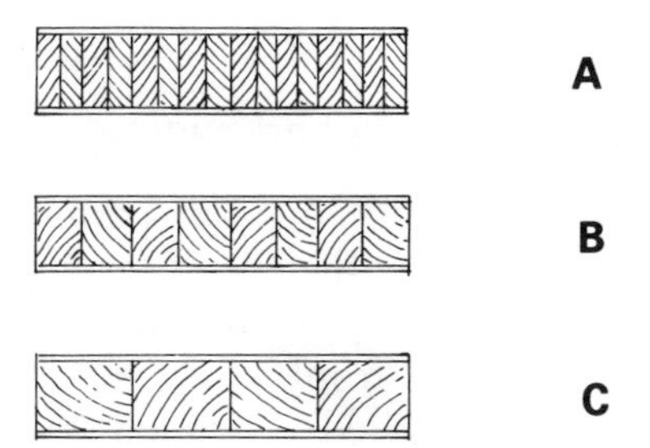

Fig. 235 (A) Laminboard (B) Blockboard (C) Battenboard

Battenboard

The same principle of construction is used but the core strips are up to 3 inch (76mm) wide (mostly used for partitioning, etc.), and although there is a greater tendency for it to warp in large panels, sizes up to 6 sq. feet (0.55 sq. metres) are satisfactory, as at C in Fig.235.

Plywood

This is a much abused material and contains many pitfalls for the unwary. Plywood is made from an odd number of laminations of constructional, rotary cut veneer, in 3-ply, 5-ply, 7-ply or 9-ply.

For all practical purposes, 3-ply would only be used as a core material to be built up into 5-ply for veneering.

For most small panels up to about 3 sq. feet, (0.27 sq. metres), 5-ply would be the minimum requirement. But for lids, tops, doors, and other hard wearing surfaces the minimum requirement would be 7-ply.

The act of veneeering a plywood panel unbalances it by exerting a pull which will warp the panel unless a compensating backing veneer is laid. The golden rule is, therefore, always veneer both sides of a plywood panel.

Where, for reasons of strength you decide to use a panel of plywood, blockboard or laminboard, with its outer casing veneers in the same direction as your marquetry face veneer, then an under-veneer must be laid on both sides of the panel, across the outer facing veneers, to enable your marquetry veneer and its compensating backing veneer to be laid in their correct directions, (i.e. parallel with the long grain direction of the panel).

If, for reasons of economy, you have cut up a large panel, or have a suitable offcut, and discover that these have the wrong grain direction (opposite to your marquetry) the same rule applies.

The best plywood for marquetry is 'marine plywood'. If this grade is not available, use any 'exterior grade' mahogany plywood with confidence. Alternatively, try to obtain plywood manufactured with medium-density or high-density impregnated paper overlays, (designated as M.D.O and H.D.O). It is specially made to receive painted surfaces for signwriting, etc.

Hardboard

Tempered exterior grade hardboard makes a suitable groundwork for very small pictures and miniatures.

The canvas side is best for veneering with its natural keyed surface, and the smooth side should be keyed for the backing veneer. Hardboard makes excellent corestock upon which to lay counter-veneers to build up suitable groundwork for marquetry. Normal grades are chiefly suitable for in-fillings, plinths, partition facings, etc.

Solid Hardwood
Contrary to popular belief, solid timber has proved to be inferior to man-made laminated and particleboards where marquetry is concerned. Shrinkage occurs along the growth rings, and boards tend to shrink across their width and to warp or wind away from the heart side. (The heart side is easily determined by looking at the end grain). However, you may need to lay a marquetry assembly on an existing panel, or have access to hardwood which you want to utilise.

Only use boards which have been radially cut, quarter sawn, in which the end grain shows almost vertical rings, so that any shrinkage will be in the thickness and this is practically eliminated in well seasoned wood.

Honduras mahogany, American whitewood, pine or obeche are suitable. Oak is unsuitable as the flat-sawn boards are prone to warp and quartered boards have strong ray figure which may telegraph through to the veneer.

To counteract the natural tendency to warp, solid timber must always be veneered on the heart side, and in the *same grain direction as the groundwork.*

Any knots, nail holes or other blemishes should be chopped out and replaced with pellets for small holes and plugs for larger ones and these must run in the same grain direction as the board. *Never use dowels to plug a hardwood board.*

The best way to use a solid board is to rip it into narrow widths, and glue them together with the heart side alternately up and down to equalize the warping tendency, in the blockboard construction method. (Fig.234)

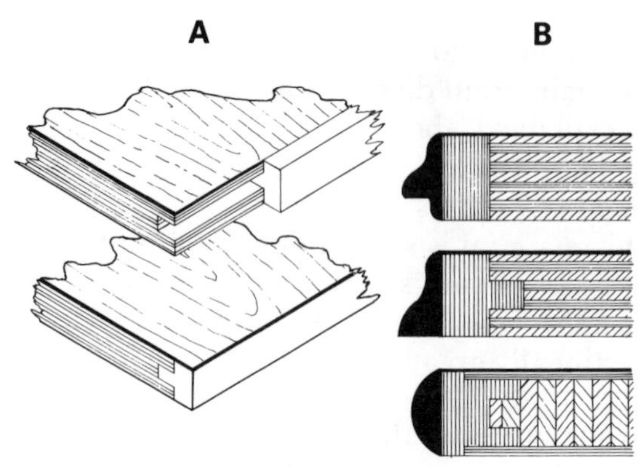

Fig. 236 (A) Lipping applied before or after veneering. (B) Profiled lippings with methods of fixing

Edge Lippings and Facings

Veneering the edges of panels is not very satisfactory as they tend to chip off in time, especially working edges which receive wear, such as the front edges of box lids, and items of applied marquetry such as trays and tables etc.

The usual practice is to protect the edge with a hardwood lipping or facing which are butt-jointed, tongued and grooved or pinned and glued.

This may be from a strip of the same species as the veneer used for the face, but it is universal practice to substitute a moderately priced hardwood for an expensive one, or a freely available one for one in short supply. Mahogany is used on rosewood panels for instance.

Edge lipping before veneering
The advantage of applying an edge lipping to the panel before veneering, is that the veneers may then completely cover the face of the panel, including the lipping, and an exact match can be obtained between panels.

The finished effect is that of a solid panel.

To each side of the panel glue a sub-veneer crossbanding of an easily worked, mild species such as Honduras mahogany or poplar. Veneer at right angles to the predominating grain direction of the picture assembly and, if possible, use the same veneer as the border veneer to cover the lipping, or the difference may show.

Any possibility of the lipping telegraphing through to the polished panel is eliminated. This happens either if the panel is not made perfectly flush before veneering, or if there is a differential in movement between the groundwork and the lipping due to moisture content variance.

Edge lipping after veneering
By applying the lipping after the surfaces have been veneered, special effects are possible. For example, picture frame moulding can be formed by the lipping. It may be shaped, rounded, bevelled, chamfered, reeded or fluted. The lipping should be wide enough to allow for the machining and should be tongued and grooved with the corners mitred.

The biggest advantage of all is that working surfaces will endure rougher handling without the risk of veneer damage.

The skill lies in making the lippings part of the decoration, either in contrast to, or in harmony with, the face veneers.

Note: Veneering circular edges, lacing edges, shaped and curved groundwork is dealt with more fully in the *Complete Manual of Wood Veneering*. (Stobart & Son Ltd)

Preparation of the Groundwork

Sub-veneering preparation.
1. Prepare a weak glue size of ten parts water to one part of glue. Brush on the glue to both surfaces of the panel and allow them to dry.
2. The panel is then worked over in both diagonal directions with a toothing plane, with its near vertical serrated edge finely adjusted. If you havn't a toothing plane, the fine teeth of a hacksaw blade would suffice. The teeth marks reveal any shallow hollows in the surface and remove any slight mounds.
3. If edge lippings have been applied they must be planed perfectly level with the surface.
4. A superficial, coarse grit sanding across the grain with a cork sanding block helps to form a keyed surface, which, in turn, prevents undue suction, the possible cause of blisters.
5. Test for a perfect level by sighting a straightedge in both directions.
6. Leave the panel (whether or not edge lippings have been fitted) a fraction oversize, in case the keying with the toothing plane has burred over the keen, sharp edges.
7. After laying the sub-veneers the panel is allowed to cure outside the press to restore its natural moisture content. To achieve this, ensure a free circulation of warm dry air to both sides of the panel.

Preparation for laying the assembly
The steps from 1 to 7 above are then repeated with the sub-veneered panel, in preparation for the final pressing of the marquetry and backing veneers. If high quality, dense surfaced chipboard is used, only steps 2 to 6 are necessary.

Counter-veneering only minimises the risk. The traditional way of curing this problem was to omit the counter-veneer stage and instead stretch fine silk or muslin over the keyed groundwork to eliminate all possibility of hairchecks or splits developing.

The modern counterpart is to buy a roll of 52 inch (1320 mm) wide impregnated paper overlay (H.D.O or M.D.O) such as "Yorkite", and use this as the sub-veneer crossbanding, on all veneer faced groundwork.

23
Preparation for Laying

The marquetry assembly

WHEN THE marquetry picture or parquetry assembly has been completed to your satisfaction, ready for trimming down to actual size and before the borders are fitted, it should be laid aside for a few days.

After working at a piece of marquetry for some time, one's approach to the work naturally becomes subjective, and like the artist in the cliché, now is the time to stand back from the easel to see the picture for an objective appraisal.

There are three points for you to consider before cleaning-up begins:
(a) the quality of the cutting,
(b) the artistic effects, and
(c) the levelling of the back.

The cutting

Examine the assembly critically for possible flaws, weaknesses in the veneer, bad cutting and open joints. Watch for tiny fragments which may have fallen out in handling, or damaged fine points and broken, cross grained detail.These parts should be removed and re-cut. Hold the assembly up to a strong light for a careful visual scrutiny.

The artistic effects

Errors in composition such as oblique and aerial perspective, the vanishing points of shadows and reflections, the insertion of highlights, etc. The effect of the transposition of veneers and whether the veneers are really achieving the desired special effects.

Many leading marquetarians have two different pictures in hand at the same time, even if one is a major work for an exhibition and the other is a simple 'pot-boiler'.

If one ever feels frustration at not having got the picture 'just right', it is best to leave it temporarily and turn to the other picture, rather than be tempted to 'let it go'!

Levelling the back

This is the most critical stage. Time spent on the work at this stage is time well spent. This is the point of no return.

I have repeatedly stressed that the face side of the picture should always be the smooth, tight, (compression side) of the veneer, and the coarser, loose (tension side) – the side with the knife checks – should be on the back of the assembly, to be laid in the glueline. The reason for this is clearly shown in Fig.237.

The diagramatic sketch represents a typical marquetry assembly of nine different veneers. Nos. 1 and 7, are Australian or American veneers of 0.9mm thickness. Nos. 2, 4, 6, and 9 are European veneers in 0.7mm thickness. No. 3 is a 0.65mm veneer, which is quite a common thickness these days. No. 5 may have been chosen for its special marquetry effect, but is only 0.5mm thickness. No.8 is another piece of this 0.5mm veneer which was turned over on its back to achieve a contrasting special effect.

This is typical of most marquetry assemblies. Many marquetarians would now use

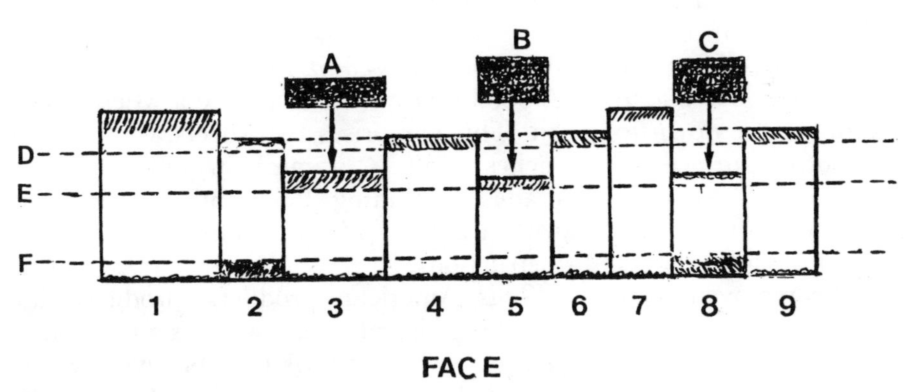

Fig. 237 Diagram of marquetry assembly. Veneers A, B and C require filling to D level

the scraper or wrap a piece of 4/0 garnet paper around a cork sanding block and proceed to level the back of the assembly.

As all knife-cut veneers have knife checks on their loose side – *sometimes to a depth of twenty per cent of the thickness* – in order to level the back, precious marquetry veneers would have to be reduced in thickness (on which such a labour of love have been expended), down to the line E, which is the thickness of the thinnest veneer.

A far better approach is to reduce the 0.9mm thick veneers 1 and 7, down to the level of the majority of the 0.7mm thick veneers, with a sharpened scraper, and bring the level down to line D. This will leave hollows above veneers 3, 5 and 8. Instead of attempting to lower the surface down to these thin veneers, they are *raised* to the general level at D.

Make up a 'wood stopping' of PVA mixed with veneer sawdust, (preferably from a similar veneer) and scrape it over the thinner veneers as shown at A,B and C. The short end of a scraper is ideal for this purpose. *This can only be attempted if all the joints in the assembly have been butt-joined with PVA.*

If the face of the assembly has been held together with gummed paper veneering tape, there would be a risk of the moisture in the filling causing the veneers to swell.

To avoid any possibility of this, after the filling has been mixed, compress it on a flat surface and let it stand to allow most of the moisture in the PVA to evaporate before spreading. Once the thin veneers have been filled, cover the assembly immediately with a polythene sheet and put it under pressure until dry.

A highly skilled marquetarian has overcome this problem by assembling his picture face side down on an oversized sheet of thin white card, embedded in rubber cement which is easily removed later. This is placed on a hard, smooth surface like melamine-faced chipboard.

He works over the back of the assembly with a cork block and a mallet to make sure that all face veneers are perfectly flat and level.Then he fills the back with a PVA and sawdust filler to the height of the thickest veneer, with no risk of the veneers swelling, and places the carded assembly in the press to dry out, before sanding the back level.

Finishing problems
The next problem is shown with veneers 2 and 8. These have not been let into the picture 'true-face', and have their coarse side on the face of the picture. After the panel is laid, this will result in having to scrape or sand the picture surface down to the level F to find a smoother surface for finishing.

Furthermore, the face side of the picture will have very minor compression checks which will also have to be removed after the panel has been laid.

The less work done to the face of the picture the better. Hence the critical importance of levelling the back of the picture.

If you have taken care to ensure that the majority of veneers used in the assembly are of the same thickness, and all true-face, there is no need to use the scraper on the back of the work. The back can easily be levelled with garnet paper grade 4/0 wrapped around a cork block. This will remove all traces of glue, grease spots, tapes, residue of Sellotape or masking tape, which might otherwise affect adhesion when the picture is laid.

Garnet paper
This is preferred by marquetarians for all papering purposes, including the finishing coats.It is available in grit grades from 180, 220, 280, 320 and 400, and has open coated aluminium oxide as the abrasive.

Silicon carbide paper
This flexible finishing paper has silicon carbide as the cutting agent and has a lubricant to minimise clogging when finishing polished surfaces. Available in grits 220, 280, 320, 400 and 600.

Wet and Dry
This waterproof carborundum paper is used for rubbing down the final top coats of the finish with water or oil, as described in Chapter 26, and is normally used in grits 400 and 600.

Micro-mesh Woodworker's Kit
A good investment would be a Micro-mesh kit. This comprises two sheets, each 6 × 3 inches (150 × 75mm) in nine different grades (including 1500 and 12,000) also with a 3 inch (75mm) foam block and full instructions.

This American product, (produced for polishing aircraft windows) has a cushioned backing, which allows the abrasive crystals to recede into a soft resilient latex background when in contact with the work surface, unlike the hard resin in conventional papers.

They are available in all abrasive types such as silicon carbide, aluminium oxide, garnet, etc.

When working with these papers, the crystals are allowed to rotate or recede when subjected to pressure and it is impossible to cut with a negative rake. All crystals cut with a positive rake with a planing action, unlike conventional papers where the crystals are mounted rigidly and unevenly, those crystals that are highest scratch the deepest. An extremely high gloss mirror finish is obtainable.

The flexible scraper

The beginner is advised to practice with a scraper on scrap veneers until the knack is acquired, before attempting to use the scaper on the back (or the face) of his picture.

Scraper blade preparation
A scraper blade is only a small rectangle of steel sheet which requires special preparation to make it into a tool. To do this, mount the scraper blade in a bench vice. File the edges straight, with a fine flat file,

but round the corners to prevent them from 'digging-in'.

Take care to ensure that the two long edges are at right angles to the sides of the blade. Pass the file diagonally across the surface of one of the edges. The blade is now held exactly upright, between two blocks of wood, and passed lightly over a medium grit dressing stone, and diagonally across it.

This is repeated across a fine oil stone, until both long edges are smooth and no scratches can be seen. It is best achieved by passing the blade over the oil stone first with its narrow top, then on its sides, and alternating these operations until an uninterrupted, straight, sharp scraper edge is achieved.

Forming the cutting edge

The freshly prepared blade is now well greased or oiled over all its edges and surfaces. Also the burnisher steel disc and the angle steel guide of the burnisher.

Clamp the blade in a vice again, and exerting *light* pressure only, the burnisher is passed only once forwards and backwards over the edge of the blade. If you want a stronger cutting edge, repeat the operation with slightly more pressure, but it is important to oil the scraper edge again.

Tilt the burnisher forward a little during the first pass over the disc, and bring it into the vertical position when subsequent passes are made with heavier pressure.

When the cutting edges have been formed on one long side of the blade, the blade is reversed and the other long edge worked upon. To protect the first pair of cutting edges, wrap them in a soft rag when clamping the blade in the vice.

The burnisher steel disc is set into the tool at the optimum angle for cutting efficiency when the blade is held correctly. The efficiency of the blade can be recognised by the fineness of the shavings it produces.

When the efficiency of the scraper blade diminishes as a result of wear, it is not necessary to start all over again with the preparation of the blade, it is sufficient just to restore the cutting edge. This is done by passing the slightly rounded point of the triangular *Ulmia* scraper blade sharpener No 1067, first under, and then over the cutting edge to restore it. This can be repeated until the entire cutting edge has worn off.

Never store a scraper blade with other tools or the edges will suffer. Store the blade in a slotted wooden block to protect the edge.

Method of use

Hold the scraper blade in both hands with the thumbs at the back, and flex it slightly in the middle with thumb pressure. Hold it at an angle to the work surface and use the burred cutting edge with a scything diagonal action, to prevent it from digging into the veneers. Veneers can stand a surprising amount of scraping. Always scrape *with* the grain. Interlocked grains need to be scraped from both ends towards the centre.

24
Laying without a Press

WE MET this method with the marquetry kit 'Evening on the Broads'. However, as my task was not to complicate or confuse, but to simplify, I'd like to re-examine the procedure and explain a little more about it.

The panel was off a production line and may not have been perfectly rectangular. It should be carefully measured across the hypoteneuse in both directions, and all corners tested with a T square. If necessary use a plane, or file or garnet paper to true the panel.

You were also invited to fit the fillets and borders of the kit *before* the picture was laid.

Let us pause to study three disadvantages with this method.

(1) If you did not check that the panel was true, the mass produced baseboard could have caused a problem with the mitres which would not align correctly at the corners. When laying the kit, we made two large basic assumptions. Firstly, that the groundwork was perfectly true and square. Secondly, when the panel was laid there was no risk of 'slippage' occurring. Faults in either case will mean that the mitres fail to meet exactly at the corners of the panel.

It is essential to ensure the groundwork is perfectly square to begin with and to apply the borders after the picture has been laid.

(2) Ideally, the pressure required for cold veneering is a minimum of 15 lbs p.s.i (1.054 kg per cm^2) in a vacuum press, and 30lbs p.s.i. (2.109 kg per cm^2) in a screw press. (Hot presses use much higher pressures from 60 lbs p.s.i. (4.218 kg per cm^2 upwards).

Translated into terms of a 10 × 8 inches (254 × 203 mm) panel, at the minimum pressure of 15 lbs p.s.i. (1.054 kg per cm^2) plus, it would require the pressure exerted by a weight of half a ton (508 kg) evenly distributed over every part of the panel.

Therefore, we use a warm iron to aid the rapid curing of the glueline. And we keep the panel on a flat surface and under the heaviest weight you can contrive for a few days, until it has thoroughly cured.

(3) When you are ready to progress to make larger pictures, the above method is unsuitable without a home-made press, as you will run the risk of blistering the picture, or suffering creepage, splits, etc.

However, there is another method you can use without the need of a press, which is successful and widely used, and that is by using impact adhesives.

Laying with impact adhesive

This method enables the complete assembly including border mounts to be laid simultaneously.

Fig. 238 Keying the groundwork with a toothing plane

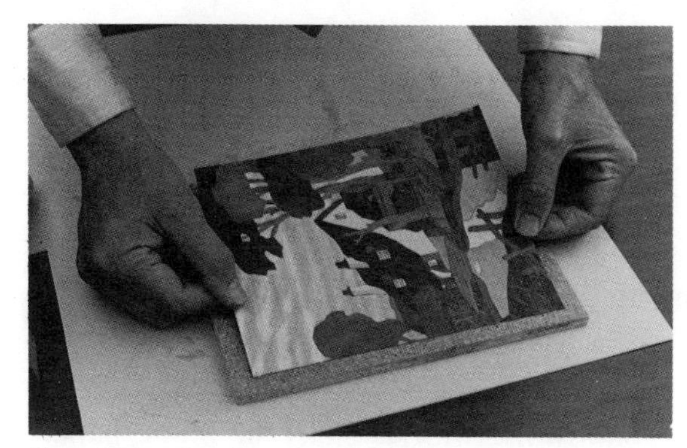

Fig. 239 Laying the picture without borders to be trued to the panel later

Impact adhesive relies on specific adhesion, in which both perfectly flat surfaces are coated, to allow the adhesive to stick to itself. Chipboard is ideal for this purpose.

Ensure the surface is flat by toothing in diagonal directions with the teeth of a backsaw, or toothing plane. A hacksaw blade slotted into a wooden handle also makes an ideal tool.

A simple jig

Lay the baseboard on a backing veneer which is 2 inch (50mm) oversize in each direction. Draw pencil lines around the board and remove it. Pin or tape four pieces of hardboard or thick veneer around the backing veneer up to the pencil lines. These form a frame for perfect alignment. The hardboard frame will not stick to the contact adhesive.

(1) Scrape on the impact adhesive and start by using the plastic comb supplied by the manufacturer for rapid distribution. As this comb is intended for plastic laminates, the resulting glueline is far too thick, therefore you should continue to work over the surface using the edge of a veneer to scrape the adhesive diagonally from corner to corner in both directions to ensure complete coverage. Cover the groundwork and allow to dry thoroughly for about an hour.

(2) Apply a second coat and allow this to dry too. Hold the panel against a strong light to check that every part of the surface is shiny and no part missed.

(3) Coat the backing veneer with two separate coats and allow them both to dry thoroughly. Hold the coated panel by the edges, and rest one end on the nearest hardboard edge and gently lower the panel above the coated backing veneer surface, and then drop it squarely into place. Lift out the panel, turn it over and roller the surface from the centre outwards.

Next apply contact adhesive to the two opposite ends of the panel, and then the two long edges. Each edge is finished in turn. Hold the panel above one oversized strip and lower it into contact, roller it, and trim to size. When all the edges are laid, repeat the process with the main picture assembly.

Impact adhesives rely on the rapid evaporation of the volatile and inflammable solvent into the atmosphere. It is therefore applied to the veneer without the risk of swelling, since no moisture is being introduced. During application it is advisable to wear an organic vapour mask. Do not use water-based contact adhesive as this will cause the veneer to swell.

In fact, never put water soluble adhesives of any kind on a marquetry assembly as it will swell and delaminate.

The slip sheet

An alternative method is to use a paper slip sheet. Cover the coated surface of the groundwork with a sheet of plain paper. The adhesive will not adhere to the paper. Carefully position the backing veneer on top of the paper, checking to see that the veneer overlaps all around the board.

Ease the paper sheet out at one end about an inch (25mm) and press the veneer down at the opposite end where the two coated surfaces are now exposed to each other, applying pressure with the fingers to help the adhesive grip.

Lift the other end of the veneer sheet with one hand to allow the air to escape from the bond. Gradually withdraw the paper sheet, using the boxwood roller to follow up and lay the veneer. Work quickly over the surface from the centre outwards to eliminate any air bubbles. Turn the panel over on the cutting board and trim off the surplus backing veneer.

Next apply the edge veneers one at a time in the same way. No paper separator is necessary; simply make sure the edge strips are oversize, position the strip at one end first and lower it on to the edge of the board.

Rub vigorously with a rounded tool or roller, making sure it is kept flat on the edge to avoid cracking the surplus veneer, or rounding the arris. Veneer the top and bottom edges first and then the two sides.

Hold the panel vertically, with the veneered edge on the cutting board and trim off the surplus with a veneer saw.

Fasten a couple of 4 inch (100mm) lengths of veneer tape to one end of the picture on the face side at each corner.

Lay the assembly face down on a flat surface and coat the back with two coats of adhesive, when dry cover the back of the picture with the paper slip sheet. Also give the panel two more coats and allow them to dry thoroughly.

Lower the panel and slide it carefully into position over the back of the picture checking that the mitres (slightly oversized borders) are aligned with the panel corners. Moisten and fasten the two tapes around the panel and turn the panel over, with the face of the picture uppermost.

Withdraw the slip sheet an inch (25mm) from under the border veneer at the end held fast by the two tapes, at the same time pressing the border into contact with the adhesive with the fingertips. Now withdraw the slip sheet completely, following the movement with a seam roller.

To ensure a good bond, cover the picture surface with the slip sheet and work over the surface with a warm domestic iron. Check for blisters and, if present, slit with a knife and inject more adhesive. Put a piece of polythene above the slit and cover with a wood block. Apply local pressure by clamp.

Oversize baseboard

Many marquetarians prefer to use a fractionally oversized baseboard, which can then be sawn and planed to size for perfect alignment of the mitres, just in case of any 'slippage' during the process.

It is a good tip to make a couple of 'dry-runs' until you are quite happy with the procedure. This method can be used on large areas such as coffee table tops and murals.

25
Laying with a Press

THE EQUIPMENT available will be the deciding factor in which adhesive to use, and this in turn will govern how the panel will be laid.

There are many types of marquetry assemblies where hand-laying techniques are not recommended. For example, when laying burrs, parts of curls, oysters, sawcut veneers, and those with end grain or open pores, etc.

Apart from small kit pictures, it is always best to lay all marquetry and parquetry in a simple home-made press.

CAUL VENEERING

Home-made veneering press

Obtain two pieces of $\frac{3}{4}$ inch (19mm) blockboard 18 × 15 inches (457 × 380mm). A press of this size should be large enough to cover most requirements of flatting veneers and laying marquetry pictures, but the dimensions can be increased or reduced to suit your own purpose. Check that these two panels are perfectly flat in each direction, as they are to become pressing cauls. (See Fig.240.)

You will also require six (or eight) crossbearers, about 18 × 2 × $1\frac{1}{2}$ inches (457mm × 50mm × 38mm) for the top bearers and $2\frac{1}{2}$ × 2 inches (63 × 50mm) for the bottom bearers to withstand the top pressure, cut from hardwood, and eight 7 inch (180mm) bolts, wing nuts and washers.

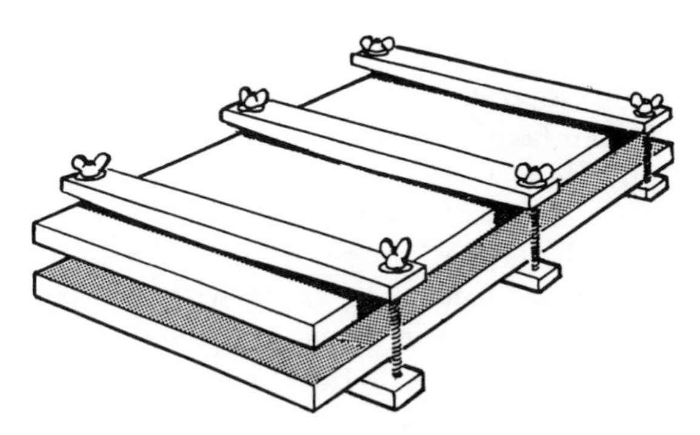

Fig. 240 Home-made veneering clamp press

Drill a $\frac{1}{2}$ inch (12mm) hole about $\frac{3}{4}$ inch (19mm) from the end of each bearer to take the bolts. Through four of the bearers, drill a hole about 3 inches (75mm) from each end and countersink them to take No.8 screws with countersunk heads.

Screw the four bottom bearers into position about 2 inches (50mm) from each end of the lower caul, with the other bearers spaced equidistant between them.

The top bearers now have to slightly convex shaped, tapering from their centres, out towards the ends, which should be reduced about $\frac{3}{16}$ths inch (5mm).

The bearers provide pressure across the *width* of the panel, but the actual pressure derives from the bolts or clamps at the *ends* of the bearers.

The gradual tapering on the underside of each bearer will ensure that when they are tightened, the pressure will commence at the centre of the panels, thus avoiding any slackening of the pressure at the centre of the panel.

Do not plane the bottoms of the bearers at each end, as this will have the effect, when tightened down, of *relieving* the pressure on the centre of the cauls as the bearers would arch in the middle. The tapering must be gradual along the whole length of the bearer from the centre towards the ends.

Test the top edge of caul with a straight-edge to see that it remains flat, and not convex, otherwise the end pressure will cause the cauls to bow in centre and the glue to migrate, giving a washboard effect.

When laying a narrow panel, put spacers each side of the panel being laid to prevent the cauls from bending.

The bolts and wing-nuts must be tightened in sequence, beginning with the two centre bearers, then the next pair and finally the outer ones, with the object of driving out any trapped air pockets – the cause of blisters.

Ideally, press screws should be tightened at each side simultaneously, and for large panels it is best to have a helper tightening the crossbearers on the opposite side of the press.

An alternative to bolts and wing nuts for applying the pressure, are quick action clamps. When tightening edge clamps, remember that the pressure radiates at 45 degrees to each side of the clamp head. Therefore position the crossbearers so that this pressure area overlaps. That means employing enough clamps, to ensure the pressure area overlaps all round. Do not over-tighten the clamp heads or this can cause glue starvation. Gradually increase the pressure to allow the glue squeeze-out to escape.

End pressure

The centre screw type of press, loses pressure around the edges. Small toggle clamps are fitted as standard on professional presses, but the amateur marquetarian can apply edge clamps after the central screw pressure has been applied. This applies only to presses with a central screw ram, especially when the groundwork protrudes beyond the top press caul at each end.

There are four problems met in laying a marquetry picture. The first two are caused by the baseboard not being accurately cut square (as discussed in Chapter 24.)

Most commercial kit baseboards are put through the saw in mass production and if measured carefully, may be found to be 'almost' true. Many marquetarians obtain a suitable panel locally, and may not have the facilities to saw the board perfectly true.

This may result in one of these errors:

Inaccurately trued baseboard

The resulting effects are exaggerated in the following illustrations to demonstrate the problem:

(a) If the picture is laid with *oversized* border mounts attached, even if great care is taken to position the board exactly on the pencilled registration marks, and the mitres are exactly aligned, when the picture is laid and the surplus border veneer trimmed off to the edge of the panel, result shown in Fig.241 can result.The picture is perfectly rectangular, but the borders are unequal, and tapering.

(b) If an *oversized* picture is laid without the borders, into the surrounding border margin, and the borders fitted after using a cutting gauge parallel to the baseboard edges, the borders will be uniform in width, but both the borders and the picture itself will be out of true. Fig.242.

Both of these problems are overcome by ensuring that the baseboard is perfectly true and square before it is used.

The third problem can occur even if the baseboard is accurate and true, and will aggravate, both (a) and (b).

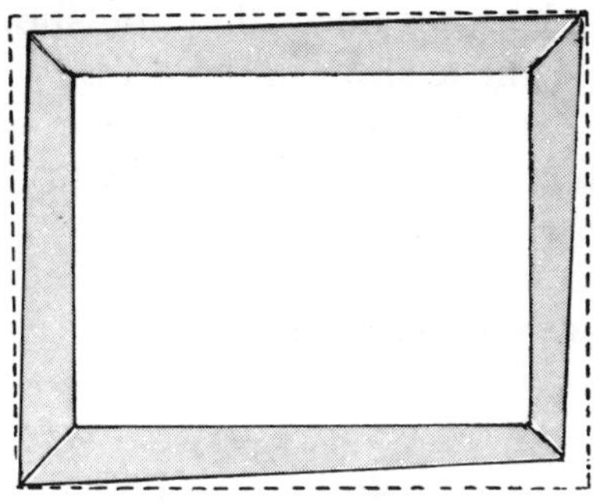

Fig. 241 (a) Can result when a complete assembly including oversized borders is laid on an untrued board

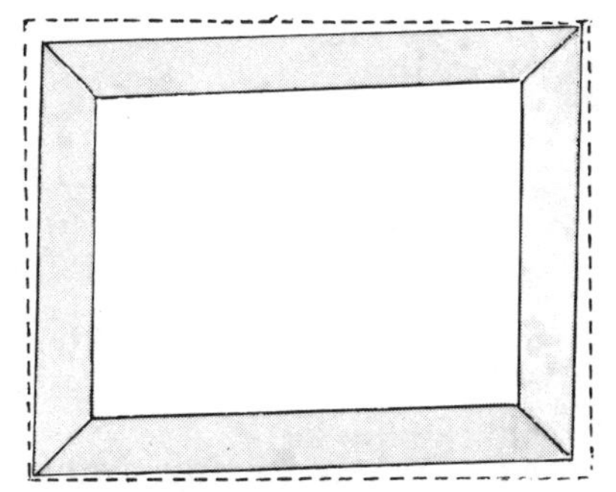

Fig. 242 (b) Result when an oversized picture, without borders, is squared to an untrue board

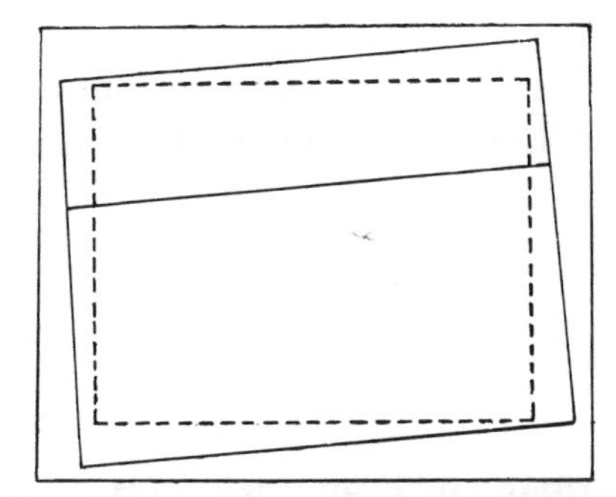

Fig. 243 (c) is the result of press slippage

(c) In central screw type presses, or where the top caul has any slight 'play' in it, before the press is closed the picture assembly can move a fraction. This is known as press slip.
(d) Especially disagreeable is when the horizon in a land or seascape is not perfectly horizontal. (Fig. 243.)

A tee square applied to the left-hand edge of the baseboard, to check the horizon is at right angles to it, will not cure the problem if the board is not perfectly true, as at (a) and (b) above, or if press slip results as at (c). Therefore, by whichever method the picture is laid there are three objectives;
(1) The panel must perfectly rectangular with true 90 degree corners.
(2) The mitres of the border mounts must align precisely at the apex of each corner.
(3) The bond resulting should be permanently enduring, and free from blisters or shrinkage.

To achieve objective (1) the obvious way is to ensure the panel is true before the veneer assembly is laid. But this is not necessarily the best way to achieve (2).

If the picture should move a fraction in handling during the laying process, (press slippage) the mitres will not align correctly.

The edges

There are other important considerations. The normal sequence of laying a panel is to lay the back first, then the edges, and finally the picture. This ensures that the glued joints are not visible when viewed from the front. The edges of the backing veneer are concealed by the edge veneers; the ends of the top and bottom edges are concealed by the two side strips, and all front edges are concealed by the border veneers.

For certain artistic effects, it is sometimes better to omit border veneers completely, and use either a contrasting edge veneer applied after the panel is laid. For example, a Chinese subject with a plain white sycamore background would be enhanced with a dark walnut edge veneer or lipping.

Solid edge lipping

There are two points to remember about lippings applied *before* veneering:
(a) when accurately *trued* groundwork is used, they form part of the overall dimension; (b) *oversized* groundwork includ-

ing lipping can be trued to size after laying. (See Chapter 22.)

Press loading requirements:

(1) Keep the veneers dry. Apply the adhesive to the groundwork only and never to the veneer assembly.
(2) Protect the face of the assembly by using a soft wad of white waste paper, or an absorbent yielding material such as baize or thin felt.

The purpose of the wad is to take up any unevenness in the veneer assembly, which is why the levelling the back is so important, and to equalise the pressure. Avoid putting magazines or newspapers *directly* against the veneers. They make an excellent wad, provided you avoid any folds, but the newsprint may offset on the veneers.

Impervious membranes
A polythene sheet may be used in the cold press between the panel and the wad of paper because adhesive will not adhere to polythene. It will prevent offset of the newsprint, and also any glue squeeze-out from sticking to the wad or cauls.

Many marquetarians use lino or vinyl tiles, or $\frac{1}{16}$th inch (1.5mm) rubber sheet, (like a tyre inner tube). But sometimes these impervious membranes may result in 'black spots' forming on the veneers. Refer to Chapter 6.

Black spot problems
The prime cause of spotting is caused by allowing the veneers in the press to become damp. Water based adhesives like white PVA rely upon evaporation of the moisture in the emulsion into the atmosphere. The impervious membrane prevents this and traps the excess water in the veneers. In wet conditions, many veneers are subject to black spot problems.

This does not mean that you should not use a polythene sheet in the press, but learn how to *prevent* black spots. It is a problem that can easily be avoided by the prevention of excessive dampness.

There are occasions when it is important that you *should* use polythene. For example, when applying cork or baize to a games board, if the glue was allowed to penetrate the baize or cork and only a paper wad was used, it would adhere to the cork or baize and be extremely difficult to remove.

Glue penetration

Another problem encountered with pressing is glue penetration, especially in burrs, oysters, short grain, end grain or soft open grain marquetry veneers. This and the black spot problem can both be avoided by using the correct technique:
(a) *The mix:* When mixing water based powdered adhesives, such as urea formaldehyde, do not exceed the recommended proportion of water/resin for ease of spreadability.
(b) *The glueline:* When using pre-mixed PVA white adhesives do not make the glueline too thick.
(c) *Tack:* It is essential that the adhesive is allowed to tack before the panel is placed on the glueline. This ensures the evaporation of the excess water into the atmosphere.
(d) *Heat:* In cold pressing with PVA or urea formaldehyde adhesives, pressure alone is sufficient to set the bond, but the introduction of gentle heat to disperse the solvent will rapidly reduce pressing time.

This type of low heat should not be confused with the high temperatures used in a hot press. A couple of thin sheets of aluminium heated over a hot-plate will retain their heat and are ideal for this purpose. But excessive heat can draw the

glue up through the fibres and result in glue penetration.
(e) *Pressure:* Adequate pressure to maintain contact is sufficient. Excess pressure causes glue penetration to the surface.
(f) *Time:* It is only necesssary to leave the panel in the press for the adhesive to set. Most modern adhesives such as PVA and UF will set in three to four hours.

The panel is then removed from the press for a general clean up of the glue squeeze-out excess which will still be liquid at the edges but set under the veneer.

The panel is then allowed to harden and cure outside the press in a free circulation of warm, dry air.
(g) *Flatting:* The value of the flatting process is now apparent. If the veneers have been treated, this will form a glue barrier and help to prevent penetration.

Prevention of press slippage

When the picture assembly without borders overlaps into the border margin, it has to be secured to prevent 'press slippage'. This may be achieved by:
(a) binding the two veneer 'lay-ons' with gummed veneer tape. If pulled tightly, this can crack the veneer overhang along the grain, or splinter it across the grain if the overhang is too wide.

This is overcome either by making the overhang only $\frac{1}{8}$ inch (3mm) wide, and laying four hardboard strips on edge, on the overhang, to prevent overhang damage. The hardboard strip would be cut fractionally less in width than the thickness of the groundwork panel.
(b) If you prefer to make the overhang wider, say $\frac{1}{4}$ inch (6mm), you need half a dozen small wooden glue-blocks of the same width to position immediately above the securing tapes.
(c) When a 'lay-on' has a surplus overhang on either an oversized baseboard, or on a correct sized baseboard fitted with glue blocks, or again on either sized baseboard when the picture is laid without borders, and allowed to overlap into the surrounding border margin, it is a simple matter to tap in a couple of veneer pins, and nip of their heads to prevent any possibility of movement in the press. These are removed the following day when the surplus is trimmed off.

Balanced construction

All panels will require veneering on both sides for balanced construction, but it is not always good policy to perform a simultaneous pressing. There are several reasons why single face pressing is more advantageous.
(1) The pressure is designed to squeeze out surplus adhesive from the bond, which will exude at the ends and edges and run down the thickness of the panel from the upper veneer and form into a thick globule on the lower veneer overhang.

If you have edge lipped the panel, this squeeze-out will have to be removed quickly, otherwise it will cure and harden and cause a clean-up problem later.
(2) The overhang surplus veneer will be difficult to trim off on the cutting board if hardened glue squeeze-out is present between the projecting veneers.
(3) Your marquetry picture or elaborate parquetry assembly requires your undivided attention. Therefore it is wiser to lay the backing veneer first as a single operation. Remove the panel for clean up and trim to size, and return the panel to the press for the face veneering sequence.
(4) When crossbanding borders are to be fitted, and the picture is to be laid undersize, the squeeze-out will occur on top of the panel as well as the sides, hence the need for the polythene sheet.

Dimension losses
During the pressing cycle the adhesive solvent disperses, resulting in overall dimensional losses, which continue during the curing cycle.It is therefore important in all manually operated screw presses (either centre screw or cross-bearer types), to retighten the press screws at regular intervals to take up his slackening of pressure.

If the centre screw type of book press is used, it is advisable to work over the surface with a seam roller or electric iron set at 'silk' to force out all air bubbles before placing the panel in the press, as this type of press gives uniform pressure simultaneously and can trap uneven gluelines or air pockets and cause blisters.

PRESS PROCEDURE

There are four stages to successfully laying your picture:
(a) select one of the options listed below from 1 to 10.
(b) check which of the press sequences (A to D) to be followed for the selected option.
(c) follow the press loading procedures listed below to suit the option and sequence you have chosen.
(d) complete the appropriate follow through procedures.

The Options

The first decision to take, therefore, is which of these options you prefer:
Accurately trued, correct sized panel
Option 1. Single pressing of oversize backing veneer.
Option 2. Single pressing of oversize picture assembly including borders.
Option 3. Single pressing of picture assembly without borders fitted. (overlapped into border margin.)
Option 4. Simultaneous pressing of two sides with oversized assemblies, including border veneers.
Option 5. Simultaneous pressing of two sides without border veneers. (Surplus overlapped into border margin.)
Oversized panel
Option 6. Single pressing of backing veneer.
Option 7. Single pressing of picture assembly including borders.
Option 8. Single pressing of picture assembly without borders fitted. (Overlapped into border margin.)
Option 9. Simultaneous pressing of two sides including border veneers.
Option 10. Simultaneous pressing of two sides without border veneers. (Surplus overlapped into border margin.)

For each of the above options, there is a special sequence of operations to be followed now listed in detail:

Accurately trued correct sized panel
Single pressing
Option 1.
Laying oversized backing veneer only. (Single pressing)
Note: The edge veneers should be fitted to the panel before proceeding further.

Sequence A:
1. Lay the veneer assembly in the press true face (smooth side) down against the polythene and paper wad.
2. Lay in the groundwork, coated and in tack condition, adhesive side down, against the untaped side of the backing veneer. Look across the surface against the light to make sure you havn't missed a spot. Check the pencil lines for perfect alignment.
Option 2.
Laying oversized picture assembly including borders (Single pressing)
Complete the edge veneering first, then follow above Sequence A.

Timescale.
When both sides of the panel are to be veneered in two separate operations following immediately one after the other,

the longer you leave the second operation, the greater the risk of the panel warping.

The veneers may have swelled when introduced to the adhesive (even though it was allowed to tack), and sufficient time has not elapsed to allow the bond to harden and the panel's equilibrium to be restored.

Therefore, if you first lay the back of the panel in sequence A, and remove it from the press after a few hours (perhaps to re-heat the metal plates for the second sequence), use the opportunity to remove the glue squeeze-out, and test the panel for blisters, which can be promptly corrected at this stage.

Immediately coat the groundwork and commence laying the picture face in Sequence A again, as soon as the surface is tacky.

When both sides have been pressed, remove the panel from the press after a further three hours for clean up and test for blisters, etc., and return to the press (without heat). The panel should be allowed to remain overnight to harden and for the panel's equilibrium to be restored. This timescale prevents any possibility of the glue squeeze-out from the backing veneer – now on top of the panel – from covering the newly veneered edges.

Option 3.

Laying undersized picture assembly without borders (overlapped into border margin area). Single pressing.

When crossbandings or borders are to be fitted to the picture, the assembly is kept undersize for trimming off after pressing. Use Sequence B.

Sequence B.

The panel would first be veneered with a backing veneer in a single pressing operation as at Sequence A.

The edge veneers are then fitted and trimmed to size. The loading of the groundwork and picture must be reversed for this second operation, to enable you to see the alignment of the corners of the picture in relation to the groundwork:

1. Load the coated groundwork, tacky side uppermost, to receive the undersized picture, taped side uppermost, and check the corner alignment with the pencilled lines of the groundwork.
2. Secure with tapes or pins through the surplus to prevent movement in the press.
3. After the glue has set, clean up glue squeeze-out and return to press overnight.
4. The following day, the cutting gauge is used to cut into the surplus picture veneers, and removed with a chisel or rounded blade knife. The borders are fitted exactly and parallel to the previously trued baseboard for accurate corner mitres.

Edge lippings can be applied before or after when consecutive single pressings are made using Sequence A

Accurately trued correct sized panel Simultaneous pressing

Option 4.

Simultaneous pressing of oversize backing and picture assembly (including borders)

When laying oversize veneers the glue squeeze-out may cover the edges. To avoid this problem use Sequence C.

Sequence C

This sequence is employed when:

(1) the edges are to be veneered afterwards or;

(2) edge lipping or picture frame mouldings are to be fitted after veneering or;

(3) where a fractionally oversize edge lipping has been fitted before laying to allow for a planing to size after veneering.

Preliminaries.

(a) Fasten three or four 4 inch (100mm) lengths of gummed veneering tape on each side and both ends of the backing veneer on its face side.

(b) In a 'dry run' lay the backing veneer on a flat surface and place the uncoated panel upon it, with the picture assembly on top.

(c) Carefully align the mitred corners with the true sized panel; moisten and fasten the tapes on one side to form a hinge, so that the two veneers can open like the covers of a book.

(d) Have four hardboard packing piece strips handy to take up the width of the $\frac{1}{8}$th inch (3mm) overhang at each side.

Proceed as follows:

1. Coat the groundwork both sides with adhesive and wait for it to tack.
2. Position the coated panel, over the backing veneer, with tapes protruding on all four sides.
3. Place the packing strips around the panel on the overhang.
4. Bring over the hinged picture assembly, and check that the border mitres coincide exactly with the groundwork corners.
5. Quickly fasten the veneer tapes all round to prevent movement.

Note: (i) (Optional) Instead of $\frac{1}{8}$th inch (3mm) hardboard packing pieces, the overhang could be wider, say $\frac{1}{4}$ inch (6mm), and a few glue blocks fitted.

(ii) Gummed veneering tapes, in short lengths of about 4 inches (100mm) are affixed to the picture veneer assembly in the same positions as the glue blocks. After loading the assembly, the gummed paper tapes are brought up and over the glue blocks and fastened to the veneers, to anchor them and prevent any possibility of press slippage.

(iii) Veneer pins could be tapped into the glue blocks and the heads nipped off.

(iv) The packing pieces protect the edges from squeeze-out when edge lippings have been fitted.

Option 5.

Simultaneous pressing of backing veneer and undersized picture assembly (without borders)

Sequence D

First follow the preliminaries of Sequence C (a) and (b).

1. Draw pencil registration marks on the groundwork in the position of the required mitres, from the true corners of the picture to the corners of the baseboard.
2. Moisten and fasten the tapes on one side to form a hinge so that the two veneers can open like the covers of a book.
3. Have four hardboard packing piece strips handy to take up the width of the $\frac{1}{8}$th inch (3mm) overhang at each side.
4. Coat the groundwork both sides with adhesive and wait for it to tack.
5. Position the coated panel over the backing veneer, with tapes protruding on all four sides.
6. Bring over the hinged picture assembly and check that the pencilled registration lines are aligned.
7. Quickly fasten the veneer tapes all round to prevent movement, or drive in a few veneer pins and nip off their heads in the picture surplus.

The edges should be veneered before the borders are fitted. Follow through procedure 1. (Pictures laid without borders on a true sized panel. Page 214.)

Oversized panels. (Veneered edges.)
Single pressing

Note: With oversized panels all edge treatments must be applied after the front and back are veneered.

Option 6.

Single pressing of backing veneer
Use Sequence A.

Option 7.

Single pressing of picture assembly including borders.
Use Sequence B.

Note: As there is no veneer overhang, no packing strips or glue blocks are required. The picture assembly can be taped or pinned around the surplus panel edge. Follow through procedure 2. (Pictures laid with borders on an oversized panel. Page 214.)

Option 8.

Single pressing of picture assembly without borders fitted (overlapped into border margin).

Use Sequence B, steps 1 to 3.

Edge veneers cannot be fitted as the panel is oversize. This method is suitable when edge lipping is to be applied after the panel has been trued to size. The loading of the groundwork and picture must be reversed if this is a second operation, with the picture on top, to enable you to see the alignment of the corners of the picture in relation to the groundwork. Follow through procedure 3. (Pictures laid without borders on an oversized panel. Page 214.)

Simultaneous pressing both sides

Option 9.

Including border veneers

Use Sequence C. Preliminaries (i) and (ii) steps 1, 2, 4 and 5. (Also see note (iii). Follow through procedure 2. (Pictures laid with borders on an oversized panel.)

Option 10.

Without border veneers (surplus overlapped into border margin).

Use Sequence D. Steps 1, 2, 4, 5, 6 and 7. Follow through procedure 3. (Pictures laid without borders on an oversized panel.)

Loading the press

In addition to the option and sequence you have selected for your project, which is carried out at item No 5 below, to avoid repetition, the remaining procedures apply to all press operations.

Some features such as the use of polythene sheet and heated cauls are optional.

1. Brush dust from and load lower wooden caul on bottom crossbearers.
2. (Optional) Load heated aluminium caul, brushed clean, into the press.
3. Insert the wad.
4. (Optional). Cover with polythene sheet to prevent sticking.
5. Then carry out your chosen option and laying sequence.
6. (Optional). Cover the panel with the second sheet of polythene (in case there are any glue traces on the upper caul from a previous laying).
7. The upper wad is placed in position.
8. (Optional heated metal plate)
9. The wood caul is placed on top.
10. The crossbearers are placed on top and tightened down in sequence.

Follow through procedures

After about 3–4 hours (depending on the type of adhesive and the workroom temperature) the glue will have set sufficiently to avoid press slippage. Before it has hardened, the panel is removed from the press for cleaning off the glue squeeze-out and checking for blisters. No attempt should be made to remove the veneer tapes, or to do any other work on the panel, such as applying the border mounts. The panel is returned to the press (without the metal plates or polythene protection if used) and left overnight to harden.

Trimming off the overhang

The next day, the panel is removed from the press. Check that the cutting board is brushed free from dust, grit or splinters. The panel is placed on the cutting board where the tapes and the glue blocks or veneer pins (if used) are removed.

The panel should then be stood in a room with a free circulation of warm dry air while the curing process continues and allowed time to restore itself to the moisture content of the workroom environment.

Upon inspection, the panel may reveal patches of glue penetration on the surface. It will hamper the finishing process unless it is wiped off immediately with a lightly dampened cloth and the panel allowed to dry out again.

When the panel is dry and the glueline has cured, the overhang is trimmed from the back of the panel first. As an aid to crossgrain trimming at the ends of the panel use a strip of location paper tape where the cut will come, and cut through the veneer and tape, which will ensure a clean cut. Any tiny fragment that does break away will be retained by the tape and can be glued back.

Make a light score-cut before severing the overhang to prevent the knife wandering in the strong grained edge of the border or backing veneers.

Many marquetarians use a veneer saw for trimming across the grain. The saw should be kept sharp by using a triangular file on the teeth, but also sharpen the sides of the saw blade like a knife, by honing the edges and rotating it against a stone.

When trimming the overhang, always remember to cut from the corners of the panel in towards the middle of the panel's edge.

Fitting the borders

1. Pictures laid without borders on a true sized panel:

The picture surplus is overlapped into the surrounding border margin. Cut through the veneer surplus with a cutting gauge (or mark it with a marking gauge) and remove the surplus with a chisel or rounded knife blade.

The border margin is thoroughly cleaned of all traces of glue squeeze-out. The fillet and border mounts – or crossbandings – are then carefully measured and laid with contact adhesive. It is also important to check with a tee square that the horizon is exactly horizontal and no press slippage has occurred.

Alternatively, the borders can be fitted and taped in position and the panel returned to the press using PVA or other adhesive as a second operation.

2. Pictures laid with borders on an oversized panel:

The border surround is carefully measured with ruler and try-square and the panel is sawn to size and planed smooth, ensuring perfect alignment of the panel corners with the border mitres. Remember to check with a tee square that the horizon is exactly horizontal.

3. Pictures laid without borders on an oversized panel:

Adopt the same procedure as No. 1 above, except that the panel is then sawn true and planed smooth to ensure perfect alignment of the panel corners and border mitres.

Using contact adhesive

For fitting the edges and borders.

It is best to coat the veneer intended for use as edging, fillet and border veneers, with two coats of contact adhesive, allowing time for each coat to thoroughly dry.

Then cut the veneers into the narrow fillet strips, edging, or consecutive border mounts.

Next scrape the adhesive on to the panel with the edge of a veneer scrap and allow to dry. Give that a second coat too.

The edges may be placed directly on the panel and rubbed with a rounded tool. The fillets and borders require special handling, because the 'triangular offcut', created by the mitres, has to be released from the lower veneer strips.

This is simply accomplished with the use of four 'corner slip sheets', about 3 × 2 inches (75 × 50mm), cut from kraft wrapping paper, or preferably from a siliconised backing sheet from a 'Fablon' plastic sheet.

The corner slips are placed at each corner, and the two longest fillets and borders are laid, by rubbing with a rounded tool like the pene of a hammer.

Next the two shorter fillets and border are laid, and the mitres accurately cut with

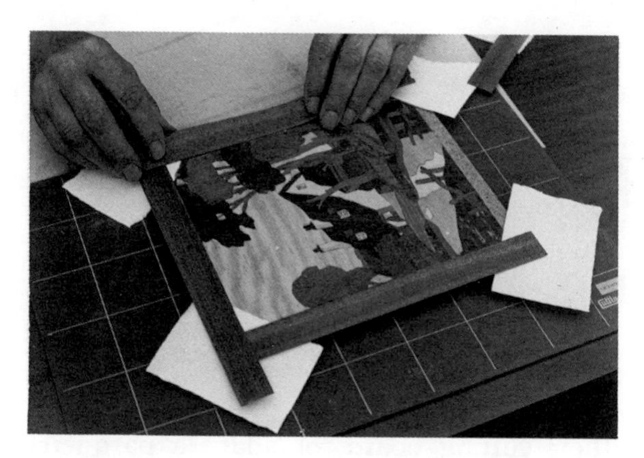

Fig. 244 Place corner slip sheets beneath overlapped borders

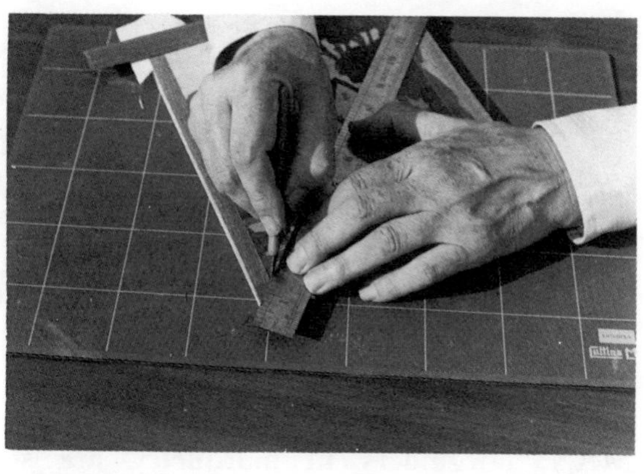

Fig. 245 Mitre the borders before removing the corner slip sheet

straightedge and knife. The corner slips enable the trapped triangular pieces to be easily removed and they are discarded.

Blisters

When examining the surface for blisters, tap the surface with the fingertips or the end of a lightly held pencil. Blisters are indicated by a hollow 'pappy' sound.

The blister should be slit with a knife point along the grain and fresh glue inserted. The blister is covered with paper or polythene and returned to the press.

Note: Shaped veneering is dealt with fully in *The Complete Manual of Wood Veneering* (Stobart & Son Ltd).

26
The Finishing Process

MANY beginners in marquetry are so anxious to see the results of their work that they hurry the finishing phase and spoil the project. A mirror-like finish can only be achieved by hand, sometimes over a period of weeks, using many careful 'deep-build' coats and the use of progressively finer abrasives.

No doubt as time goes by, modern materials and techniques will enable the process to be speeded up.

It is important to accept right at the outset, that a marquetry picture may require as many coats of finish as your car – and many cars have a build-up of up to thirty coats applied! Which is why many marquetarians begin work on a second picture while they are finishing the first. Your work will be judged by its finish. A poor finish can mar the appearance of an otherwise first class marquetry picture or project. It can be one of the most rewarding aspects of creating a marquetry project.

Finishing a marquetry picture is different from polishing a normal veneering project – such as a piece of furniture – because it comprises all types of veneers of different thicknesses and textures which all absorb polish and reflect light in various ways. Normal finishing instructions do not apply.

Sanding and Polishing jig

Equip yourself with a jig to hold the panel firm and secure. Some marquetarians use their cutting board, or adapt a parquetry jig.

A suitable sanding board can be made from chipboard, plywood or blockboard about 2 inches (50mm) larger all around than the panel, with battens along two edges about $\frac{3}{8}$ inch (9mm) thick, but less than the thickness of the panel.

Make couple of slots in the base to enable G clamps to hold it securely to the work table. These grooves should be deeper than thickness of the metal cramp so that the panel lies flat.

The picture is secured either with wedges or a simple cam made from plywood, about 2 inches (50mm) in diameter with a screw offset about $\frac{1}{4}$ inch (6mm) from its centre.

Illustrated in Fig.246, is a revolving 'Lazy Susan' type of polishing board, with rubber strips laid in the base to prevent the panel from slipping. It can be revolved for successive coats, and the panel turned against a strong light to see the surface clearly.

Curing period

Before the picture was laid in the press, the back of the picture assembly was filled, scraped or papered flat and level and the groundwork correctly toothed and levelled. There should now be very little work required to smooth the face side of the picture.

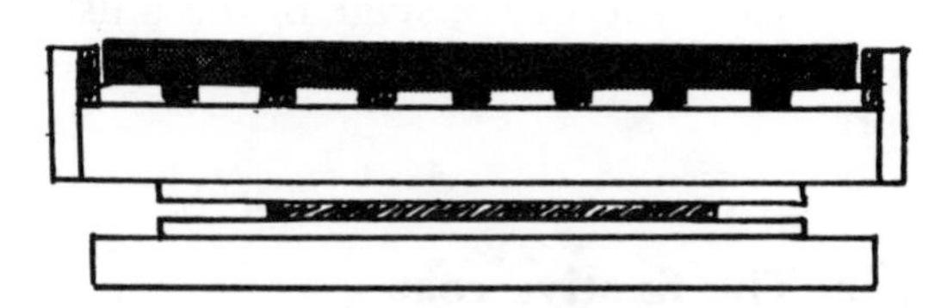

Fig. 246 'Lazy Susan' revolving jig

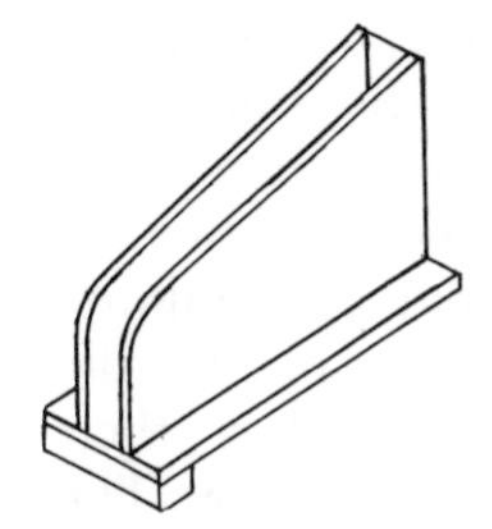

Fig. 247 Vertical jig for edge finishing

But however flat and level the surface appears when taken from the press, after a period of time has elapsed it will reveal a patchy appearance due to unequal veneer shrinkage.

You should allow from a month to six weeks for the glueline to fully cure and shrink, prior to beginning the finishing process. For a perfect finish, we now have to remember that the face of the picture was given a coating of glue size during the flatting procedure, which has served to prevent penetration during the laying stage but now has to be removed to avoid it affecting the finish.

Step 1. Cleaning up.

The first step is to clean the picture and render the surface smooth, flat and level again and free from surface dirt. Very lightly and gently scrape off any trace of adhesive. The surface will require cleaning of all traces of the white paper wad used in the press, gummed paper tape, glue spots, carbon paper and pencil marks, fingermarks, or any very slight difference in veneer thickness caused by unequal shrinkage and tiny knife checks from veneer segments laid loose face up.

Pay close attention to this phase. When the carbon paper or pencil marks disappear *stop scraping*. If Sellotape, or masking tape residue, or contact glue traces remain, remove with cellulose thinners or lighter fuel, and while the surface is wet, quickly scrape off the 'gunge'. *Never* do this if contact adhesives have been used to lay the marquetry as the solvent will cause blisters as the bond delaminates. After scraping, use a soft brush or vacuum cleaner on the surface to remove all traces of dust or minute shavings from the pores of the wood.

Do not attempt to use abrasive papers on the surface until it is sealed.

There are several reasons for this:

(a) The natural beauty of the veneers is only 'skin-deep', and after scraping and sanding the back, the remaining picture veneers may be only 0.5mm thin.

(b) The minute compression knife checks on the face side of the picture are easily removed with a light scraping, but the knife checks of the thinner veneers on the tension side now laid in the glue, may reach within about 0.3mm below the surface.

It is not desirable for this thin layer of veneer to be subjected to any abrasion until a barrier of the finish has been applied.

(c) The action of papering would cause powdered dust to be ground and massaged into the open pores of other veneers and cause discolouration.

(d) Many natural woods such as padauk, rosa peroba, rosewood, violet-wood, etc., contain a natural pigment which would stain sycamore, horse chestnut and open grain woods like oak and obeche. The

first coat of polish would cause staining immediately. This is especially important when inlay motifs using dyed black are included, or any dyed veneers are used.
(e) The abrasive action would cause minute scratches and 'fuzziness of grain' on the surface of the veneers, which blurr their vividness and are difficult to remove. The scraper, on the other hand, removes tiny shavings which are too big to clog the pores of open grained woods. Also, the larger fibres of the more grainy veneers which will have been flattened in the press, are easily cleaned off with the scraper.

If, however, you are not skilled in the use of a scraper, and have to resort to papering the surface flat and smooth, be extremely careful and use a cork block with 180 grit garnet finishing paper and use this only for a superficial clean up.
Consider these factors:
(1) Marquetry veneers are absorbent, easily stained and must be given only 'water-clear' transparent finishes, to retain their hue and tonal values.
(2) The adhesive below the thin veneer layer must not be affected by the finishing treatment which must be compatible.
(3) Subsequent top coats of finish should not dissolve the underlying base coat and ideally the sealer should not contain the solvent of the finishing material.
(4) This will not apply to 'wet-backing' techniques for certain types of finish, such as oil, polyurethane, melamine and similar finishes in which the finish, diluted with solvent, is used for the sealing and base coats.
(5) The picture may contain veneers which are resinous, oily, gummy, pigmented, open pored, soft grained etc.
Never use grainfillers on a marquetry assembly. All grainfillers (even 'transparent' types such as cellulose decorator's paste) will show up as tiny white specs in the grain of the darker woods.

Resting Periods
The panel requires several rest periods in between each successive stage of the finishing process. Now is the time to start another picture!

Step 2. The fixative coat

This is, perhaps, the most critical step in the whole sequence of finishing the panel and has to be carried out very carefully. The objectives are to partially fill the open pored woods to protect them from staining, and to completely fill the pigmented woods to prevent discolouration. It is also to raise and stiffen the grain of the veneers to facilitate the subsequent block-sanding of the surface without clogging the open pored woods.

For the fixative coat, you can use either the finishing material diluted with solvent, or sanding sealer.

There are various types of sanding sealer available, with either a shellac, cellulose or vinyl base, and the correct one will be supplied by the finish manufacturer to suit the chosen finish.
(a) Cellulose sanding sealer for use under shellac, cellulose and wax finishes. This is highly volatile and should be used in a well ventilated room, garage, or in the open air away from any source of heat.
(b) Shellac based sealer for use under french polish or wax. Not as inflammable as cellulose and not such a good sealer either.
(c) Special purpose modified nitro-cellulose sealers are available which can be used under french polish, cellulose, pre-catalysed lacquers, acid-catalysed lacquers and certain types of polyurethane.

These special sealers also have an ultra violet light absorber to protect the natural wood tones.
(d) Polyurethane and melamine finishes are ideal for applied marquetry, but tend to

create a yellow tinge over the white veneers in marquetry pictures. These types of finish are not compatible with sanding sealer. For these finishes, do not use a sanding sealer but dilute some of the finish 5 to 1 with solvent.

Also widely used by leading marquetarians, and recommended for marquetry is the two part catalytic cold cure lacquer like Rustins Plastic Coating, which can be burnished to a very high gloss and can be used over a cellulose or special purpose modified nitro-cellulose sealer. The finish is available in matt, semi-matt and high gloss.

For the fixative coat use the sealer supplied for your chosen finish, (or the finish itself) diluted with a little of the solvent.

It is important that the fixative coat and the following base coats of sanding sealer dry invisibly and prevent the penetration of subsequent coats and the suction caused by the finishing coats of polish.

This also acts to cut down on the number of finishing coats as it fills the pores with a tough film which will permit the minimum of grain sinkage.

The fixative coat is not 'flowed-on' like a wash-coat, but carefully applied with a fine camel hair or squirrel hair mop brush. Many marquetarians prefer to rub it into the pores with a finger tip protected with a disposable vinyl glove making sure that any open grained veneers are treated first. (The sealer solvent can be injurious to health if in contact with the skin).

This is always an exciting moment. When the full rich beauty of the veneer hues appear, and you can get some idea of the finished appearance.

Pick out the whitest woods first such as sycamore, horse chestnut, obeche, etc., to seal them. Then work over the highly coloured woods painting each of them within their outline.

Do not paper after this coat.

Allow half hour for the panel to dry, and examine the panel against a strong light to see if the grain is completely sealed, or whether there are patches of veneer which are still open.

Have a small quantity of solvent in a jar handy, to dip the brush in between coating each veneer, to keep it clean, and wipe the brush on a piece of kitchen roll each time.

Do not go back over parts already treated while the sealer is wet. When the complete surface of the panel and all edges have been protected with this fixative coat, allow the surface to dry for an hour or two, even though it may feel surface dry to the touch in a few minutes. This first fixative coat will stiffen and raise the grain.

Do not use abrasive papers on the surface at this stage.

Step 3. The Base coat

Apply three or four coats of full strength sanding sealer in rapid succession. Use a vinyl gloved finger, or a 'fad' made from a folded paper towel wrapped inside a muslin cloth. Don't get the fad too wet.

Try dabbing it on a sheet of plain paper until it leaves a damp – not wet – mark, before using the fad.

Work in circular, spiral and figure-of-eight movements over a small area at time. Concentrate on filling any low places. Apply coats to the front and the four edges in one session. As soon as they are touch-dry, turn the panel over and work on the back of the panel and the edges again in the next session, until both sides have received three or four coats of sealer, at about half hour intervals *without* sanding between coats.

The easiest way to tackle this is by placing the picture on a felt covered block while one side and the edges are coated and allowed to dry, then the panel is turned over and the process repeated. The edges receive twice as many coats as the back and front, as they are vertical surfaces.

Alternatively, you can use the 'lazy susan' type of rotating stand, smaller than the picture size, mentioned earler.

Now the panel should be left propped against a wall in a warm, dry, dust free atmosphere for a week or more, to allow for thorough drying out and grain sinkage.

The surface will present a dry, rough,patchy appearance, where some of the veneers have soaked up the sealer, and some will not appear to have been sealed at all.The sealer shrinks as it dries, and the more coats applied, the greater the shrinkage. The number of coats you will need to apply will depend on the types and porosity of the veneers used and the thickness of the sealing coat.

Papering

Now the papering process can begin! Wrap a half sheet of 220 grit finishing garnet paper around a cork block. It is very important at this stage, not to paper too hard. As there are only a few coats of sealer on the surface it is very easy to rub through and expose veneers which had been fixed and sealed.

Be particularly careful when rubbing the edges to keep three quarters of the block on the surface. Also keep the block flat on the edge and let your fingers protrude down each side of the panel to keep the cork block perfectly flat and avoid rounding the arris. Rub along the main grain direction of the panel, (in four directions around border veneers) and in the predominating grain direction of the picture.

Keep the surface free from dust. Use a tack rag, or a soft brush or small vacuum cleaner.

Check the panel against a strong light, and you will see a blotchy appearance indicating parts which require further sealing, and perhaps a few shiney low spots.

If you have used a shellac sealer, (as opposed to a cellulose one) you will find it tends to clog the garnet paper, so use a little white spirit (turps substitute) on the paper to prevent it from clogging on this first papering operation, and it will also clean the surface from any oiliness or residue on the surface. Discard this paper after an initial light rubbing and do not use any more lubricant.

Using a camel or squirrel haired brush, (or a plastic foam brush which will not leave brushmarks), brush on three or four more coats of full strength sealer in rapid succession, as each is touch-dry.

Stand the panel with a free circulation of warm, dry air around it for another week for further sinkage to take place. The panel will now have received about six to eight base coats of sealer and we can now change tactics.

From now on you can block sand the surfaces using progressively finer abrasive papers, using 220, 280 and 320 grit between each further coat of sealer and apply at least another four coats, allowing each to dry thoroughly before papering and applying the next coat.

If you want to use an orbital sander, do not use it until you have reached this base coat stage. If you have not kept all the picture veneers tight-faced and some parts of the picture have loose-faced segments, it is not unusual to apply twelve or more coats of sanding sealer in this way, with rubbing down between them, until the surface is totally filled, completely flat and perfectly smooth. No brushmarks should be visible on the surface. Most of these twelve coats are papered off again, leaving only one thin coating on the surface and up to twelve coats or more in the hollows, thereby forming a deep build to a level surface, ready to receive the top coats of finish. Experience shows it is best to paper the finishing coats by hand.

By the time you have applied twelve coats of sealer you can progress to using 600 grit Lubrisil paper or 1200 grit wet and dry silicon carbide paper on any subsequent coats.

You will have already decided on the the type of finish (before you could decide which sealer to use) but you now have three further options in choosing the type of finish.

From here on, you choose any suitable finish obtainable from your supplier.

Types of Finish

There are three main types of finish for a marquetry picture.

Matt, semi-matt or high gloss, and they are attainable in that order.

(a) *The matt finish* This is the simplest to obtain. It will not reflect room lighting and will give a natural wood appearance to the picture. After two full strength coats of sanding sealer at half hour intervals, the surfaces are then rubbed with grade 0000 wirewool, in straight strokes across the grain. Complete the treatment by finishing off with a soft duster. Alternatively, use catalyst cold cure matt finish, applied with a fad, and burnished with a duster.

(b) *Semi-matt finish*

This is perhaps one of the most popular finishes for marquetry as it does not reveal all the imperfections. The simplest way is to impregnate 0000 wirewool with siliconised white wax polish and burnish with the soft cloth.

(c) *High gloss finish*

This provides a mirror-like surface, revealing every detail (and cutting imperfection!). It also depends on your level of skill. Many marquetarians adhere to the traditional techniques of french polishing using white or transparent polish. More modern methods employ cold cure catalyst lacquers which involve 'bodying-up' with several coats of finish, then 'flatting-down' with abrasive paste or rubbing compounds from the car paint stockists, followed by metal cleaning polish such as 'Duraglit' or 'Brasso' and finish off with good quality furniture cream. Readers who wish to pursue the subject further are recommended to read *The Complete Manual of Wood Finishing* by Frederick Oughton (Stobart & Son Ltd).

27
Framing and Hanging

A PICTURE frame can greatly enhance the appeal of a picture and concentrate the attention of the viewer if selected with great care. It is best to 'test' the picture against several possible frame sections in order to determine the best for the purpose. Choosing the frame requires just as much thought as selecting the border mount, and these decisions are mutually dependent.

As a general guide, the framing should be fairly plain and simple, subtly flattering the picture by contrast.

Parts of a moulding

A. Outside edge	G. Lip of rabbet
B. Profile	H. Fluting
C. Height	I. Beading
D. Width	J. Ridge
E. Rabbet	K. Moulding face
F. Inside edge	

The four considerations are colour, texture, depth and weight. Avoid heavy, multi-coloured, richly textured, elaborately reeded, or excessively ornate mouldings which incorporate carving or gilding, which will compete with the picture for attention and detract the eye from it.

A neat brass trimmed frame can contrast equally well with a rosewood or sycamore border, and an ebonised frame can enhance

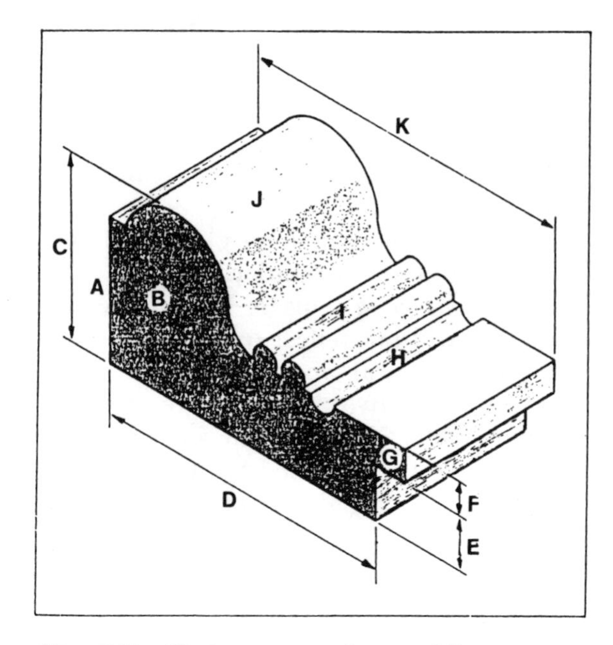

Fig. 248 Various parts of a moulding

most natural veneer borders. Many frames are finished in natural wood, while others incorporate in-fillings of hessian or leather.

A strong frame will protect the picture if accidentally dropped. It will also safeguard against the possibility of the panel warping, cupping or bowing due to climatic conditions, especially if the groundwork was not thick enough for the size of the panel.

It is best to fit flush hangers on the back, especially if you want to send the picture

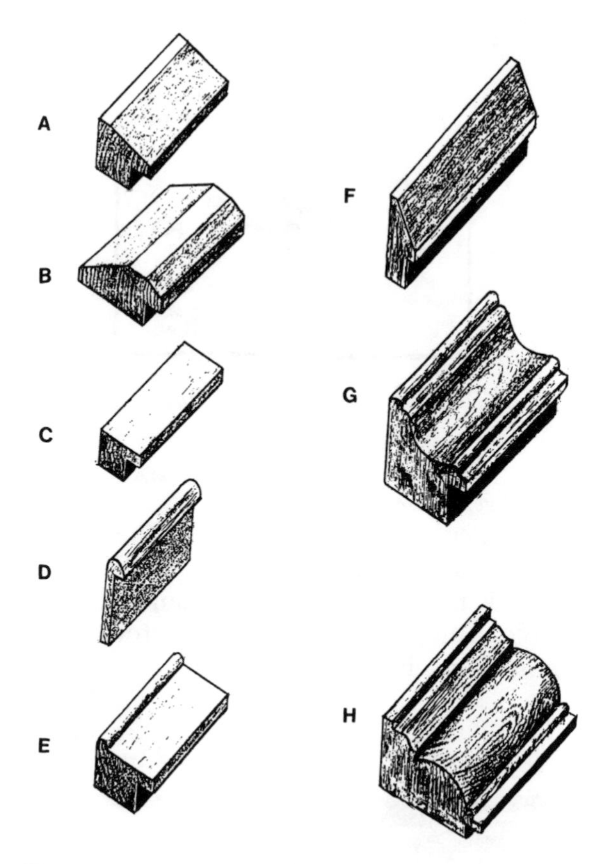

Fig. 249 Moulding styles: A. Box, B. Reverse, C. Flat, D. Half-round (Hockey stick), E. Raised bead and flat. F. Box, G. Spoon, H. Composite.

to an exhibition. Projecting hangers cause havoc to your own and to other people's pictures, however carefully they are handled.

Strengthen the mitred joints of the framing on the back with staples. The rabbet should be the depth of the panel,but when making the frame allow a $\frac{1}{16}$th inch (1.5mm) clearance on all four sides of the panel between the picture and the frame. Tape over the open join. It acts as a dust barrier.

Another important point to remember is to keep the back of the panel from coming into contact with the wall. The external walls of a house are usually colder than interior partition walls, and condensation, temperature or humidity changes can affect the panel unless a free circulation of air of allowed behind it.

To achieve this, fasten a small triangular piece of $\frac{1}{4}$ inch (6mm) plywood at each corner to act as a pad. This keeps the panel away from the wall and allows the picture to 'breathe' and equalise to atmospheric conditions and humidity changes.

It will need a fitting for hanging purposes and it is a good idea to fit escutcheon plates into the triangular corner pieces as shown in Fig. 250.
A = reverse moulding, B = the picture, C = triangular corner pad, D = tapes over gap, E = brass escutcheon, F = hole for screwhead.

Unframed pictures

Many marquetarians prefer not to fit picture frame mouldings to their pictures. It is still best to fit hangers which fit flush to the back.

In either case, use a 1 inch (25mm) diameter Forstner bit with a flat bottom to countersink brass keyway escutcheons into the back of the frame, and then a $\frac{5}{8}$ inch

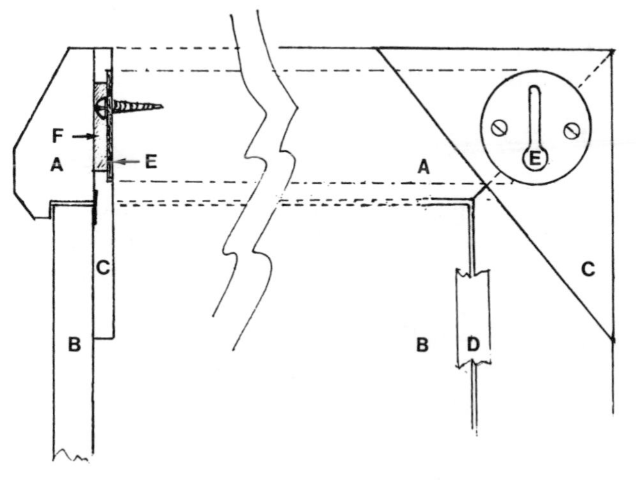

Fig. 250 Flush fitting brass escutcheon plates

(16mm) hole in the centre to allow for screw head clearance.

Correct location of hangers

In Fig.251 'A' represents one eighth of the width of the panel, and 'B' one quarter. 'C' is one sixth of the depth and 'D' is one third. This is a useful guide and a panel hung from this position will hang correctly, allowing air to circulate behind the panel.

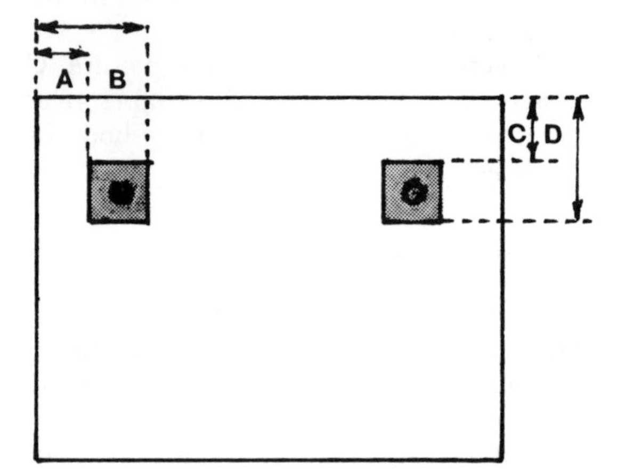

Fig. 251 Where to locate picture hangers

Although screw eyes, and screw eye with split ring types, are the most simple to fit, they are not recommended as they force the fibres of the panel apart and this can telegraph through to the picture.

1. Insert Wire

This is the most popular flush type hanger. The hole is drilled and the back of the panel is grooved before the backing veneer is laid. Use 12 to 14 s.w.g piano wire, extending $1\frac{1}{2}$ inches (38mm) on each side of the hole. When the backing is laid, locate the holes and knife-cut away the veneer to clear the hole diameter and scrape out the glue. Some dedicated people veneer the inside of the hole!

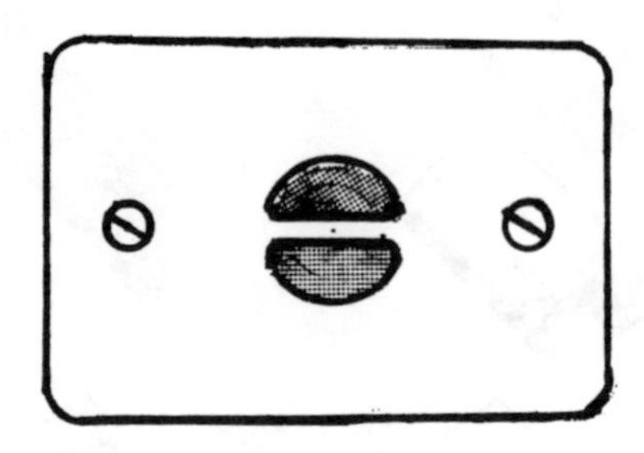

Fig. 252 Brass hanger plate fitting

2. Hanger plate

Another favourite fitting is the brass hanger plate (as illustrated in Fig.252) which is inlayed flush with the surface, over a hole, using small brass fixing screws with countersunk heads.

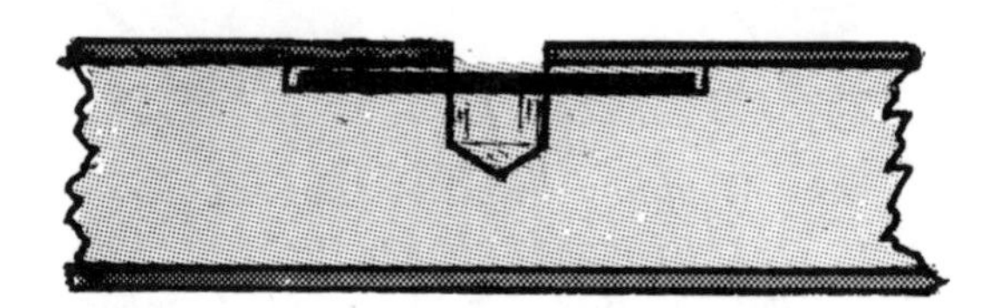

Fig. 253 Tube wire insert fitting

3. Tube-wire insert

A wire is soldered across a short piece of brass or copper tubing and fixed with 'Super-glue' or 'Araldite', into a hole drilled to receive it. Use woven picture cord if obtainable locally, or strong nylon cord. Wrap a short piece of fuse wire around the end of the cord, to enable you to thread it around the hanger and feed the cord through. It is safest to avoid using wire, except for the heaviest of panels, which are best fitted over escutcheons direct to plugged walls.

28
Designs for Marquetry

AFTER YOU have made up a few marquetry kits, you will want to progress to the pleasures of finding your own subjects.

The public library is the obvious source for book illustrations of a wide range of suitable subjects: beauty spots, landscapes, seascapes, urban architecture, interiors, figure studies, still life, wildlife, animals and birds, gardening, natural history, pottery, industrial design, traditional and modern art, and photography.

Your local bookshop or stationer will have full colour views in calendars, and Christmas cards, many of which have excellent scenes for adapatation.

Art galleries sell inexpensive prints of famous paintings, and lavishly illustrated books of their exhibits. Photography magazines are also an excellent source of ideas. Magazine and newspaper advertisements and chocolate boxes are other useful possibilities.

Flowers or plant subjects may be adapted from garden centre and nurserymen's catalogues.

But bear in mind that very often these pictures have been cropped to suit the space in the book, calendar or card, rather than to make an aesthetically pleasing picture, and may need further adaptation.

Silhouettes

A simple silhouette makes an excellent practice piece. Familiar places such as the Statue of Liberty, the Eiffel Tower, or some local familiar beauty spot etc., make good subjects, or try a tracing from a photograph of a loved one or of a pet.

Fig. 254 Edwardian silhouettes
John Secker

Two-tone contrasts

Better still is the even wider range of 'two wood' colour contrasting subjects to be found in every travel brochure you pick up.

They are packed with exotic scenes featuring beautiful sunrise or sunset skies, usually with a very dark foreground objects silhouetted against them.

Also by using two tonal contrasting woods, there are great possibilities in creating subjects such as the Taj Mahal by moonlight; moonlight on the Nile, or bird subjects such as the night owl.

It is a good idea to compile a portfolio of possible design subjects. Very often there is a cross pollination of ideas, and you may be able to superimpose one part of a scene (such as a house or bridge) over another scene, to create a composite.

Also, with a bit of practice you may discover more than one focal point in a picture, which will divide and make two or more pictures from one scene.

It's also possible to crop a large picture down to make a more dramatic picture. For instance, a scene of a tiger stalking through jungle foliage may look more dramatic if only the head was used from a stylised dark background.

Your choice of subject is really governed by three factors. Firstly, your aesthetic taste. There's no point in making a subject that hasn't got a strong emotional appeal.

Secondly, in the early days of your venture into marquetry, the deciding factor may well be whether the subject is within the your present capabilities. Stretch your talent by all means but be sure to aim at attainable targets at first, and don't tackle subjects which are too ambitious. Wait until you have gained some experience in cutting pictures, or you may lose heart.

Developing cutting technique is something that evolves with time and experience.

This is especially true if you select a subject which will require the use of very hard, brittle or thick gauge woods which demand a fretsaw to cut them and would be virtually impossible or too difficult to cut with a knife. Until you are also proficient with both knife cutting and the various fretsaw techniques, some subjects may be out of reach or deter you at first sight by what appears to be the sheer volume of cutting required for the intricate detail.

With experience, you will find that a picture which looked difficult last year will be quite easy for you to tackle today; subjects which appear impossible today, may still be rather difficult next week but you will take them in your stride next year.

Thirdly, if the picture is coloured, can available veneers match those colours? This problem will become clearer after you have studied the next chapter.

Enlarging or reducing the print

The first step after selecting a possible subject is to decide the 'optimum' size, that is, the best size to suit the subject. A charming picture in postcard size will often lose its charm when enlarged. A poster sized print may be greatly improved by reduction.

Quite apart from these aesthetic considerations, there are four other factors which may determine the final size of the picture. (a) The size of your available veneers, (b) the size of your workspace, (c) the equipment available for laying the panel, which may decide (d) the adhesive to be used. These factors are considered in other chapters.

When you have found a subject that appeals to you, there are several ways of getting the print enlarged or reduced.

1. Photocopying

The easiest method of all is to take it along to your local stationer or 'instant-print' shop and have a photocopy made which will provide an enlargement or reduction to suit your requirements.

Most machines will take a colour print and reproduce it in black and white. Enlargements can be made up to A3 paper size. Some enlarge in set increments such as A5 to A4, and A4 to A3 etc., but others have an infinitely variable zoom lens. The most common seems to be the type which will increase in fixed percentages up to 315% or reduce down to 65% of the original.

By paying a separate fee each time, it is possible to keep returning the new print to the machine for further enlargements or reductions.

2. Squared graph

A popular method is to make an India ink grid of ½ inch (12mm) squares, on a sheet of transparent plastic film, through which you can see the original print or photograph.

If you want your enlargement to be four times the original proportion, draw 1 inch (25mm) squares on a sheet of cartridge paper and copy the outline in map fashion where every line on the original crosses the grid.

A reduction is made by reversing the process. This is suitable only for fairly simple subjects but not portraits, where the variation of the line itself can alter expression.

3. Pantograph

The pantograph has largely been superceded by modern photocopying processes, but is still used for enlarging or reducing simple outlines and proportions.

Avoid cheap plastic types as the arms flex and distort the subject. Some have fixed gradations of enlargement and reduction but the best type have an infinitely variable range. Check the maximum size of original subject that the pantograph can cope with. They require a table top or worktable to work on.

4. Epidiascope

A good investment is an epidiascope, which enables you to project books, prints, brochures, cards etc., on to a wall or screen, rather than risk defacing them by making a direct tracing.

It will accept originals up to about 4½ inches (115mm) square. Tape tracing paper to a sheet of glass or the back of a flushdoor and project the image on to it in a darkened room. As these were intended for lecture room use, check that the projection will remain in sharp focus down to about 6 or 7 feet (2 metres) for use at home.

5. Slide projector

Using a close-up lens, photograph the original subject direct from the book or magazine on to colour reversal film. Make sure the camera is exactly square to the original when taking the shot and the projector is square to the wall or flat surface when projecting the resulting slide to avoid distortion.

Project coloured transparencies on to white paper 'Blue-tacked' to a wall. The home projector screen is not suitable as this may cause distortion.

The best way is to use a frosted glass screen on which the white paper is fixed on the reverse, and you can stand behind it to make the drawing. By moving the projector forwards or backwards from the screen the picture can be made larger or smaller.

One advantage is to trace the background ignoring some focal point, and then move the projector's position to make the focal point smaller or larger, or to move its position with the frame. Another advantage is when reverse drawings are required for some cutting processes, the slide is simply reversed in the projector.

6. Overhead angled mirror

Another method is to project the transparency or the epidiascope image to a mirror set up at 45 degrees above a table, and reflect down on to paper of the required size.

7. Photographic enlarger

Copy the original as a coloured slide or black and white negative into a transparency and project the image using a photographic enlarger, on to white paper taped to the enlarger baseboard. Raise or lower the enlarger head to produce the image to the required size and trace around the design with a pencil.

Two prints of the picture can be made at the same time. It may be necessary to tape two or more sheets of photographic paper together to get the picture area large enough. Separate them after exposure and develop them in normal developing dishes.

8. Vivitar Instant Slide Printer

With this machine, just insert a colour slide (it may be cropped in size to suit your requirements) into the slot and press a button. It will deliver a $3\frac{1}{4} \times 4\frac{1}{4}$ inch (83mm × 108mm) colour print in 70 seconds, or a black and white print or negative in only 35 seconds, and even an overhead transparency in 4 minutes.

9. Line drawings from a print

If you have an enlarged black and white photograph on matt paper and wish to make a line drawing from it, (a glossy print should be dusted with French chalk), copy the required outline with waterproof India ink and allow to dry thoroughly.

Prepare a solution of loz of fixing solution to the strength of 4oz. of hypo or fixer to 1 pint of water. When you are ready to use it, add 20 gr. potassium ferricyanide until the solution becomes straw-coloured and it rapidly loses its power. Swill the enlargement around in this solution for three minutes before rinsing the picture in fresh water.

The photograph will have disappeared and the line drawing will remain. Take care during the process not to handle the print as the drawing may rub off. When it is dry the line drawing will be indelible.

An alternative formula is to make up a 5 per cent solution of potassium iodine, say loz in 19 ozs water, to which is added as many iodine crystals as the solution will dissolve. When immersed, the print will leave a brown stain.

Rinse under running water and lay in another solution of 4ozs hypo or fixer, to 1 pint of water to remove the brown stain. After further rinsing under a cold tap, the print may be dried ready for handling.

10. Commercial Printer

If you have a good black India ink drawing of the original, the local printer will make a proof bromide from it. You can specify the percentage enlargement required up to 315 per cent. The camera will not register a blue ink drawing, it has to be black.

11. Video Camera – Personal Computer

Many people now have both a video camera and a personal home computer. By taking suitable scenes with a video camera, these can be screened on the video display linked to the computer. The video is 'freeze-framed' at a scene which may make into a good marquetry subject.

With suitable interface modem, the digitised image can be printed out on the matrix dot or laser printer.

12. Optical scanner

Another recent computer advance, uses an optical scanning interface, which is attached to the printer, and with software such as 'Masterscan', the image fed to the printer can be brought to the screen and incorporated with graphics from other Desk Top Publishing software.

This can be used to produce drawings which can be altered, amended, reduced or enlarged up to six times magnification; can incorporate 'on screen' freehand drawings, and a host of pre-programmed graphics for geometric marquetry or parquetry.

The Working Line Drawing

Having got the original print to the required size the next step is to produce a working line drawing, featuring only the simplified outline.

This is best done on good quality tracing paper obtainable from your local commercial artist's shop, or on transparent plastic film using black waterproof India ink, or graphic designer pens such as Rotring Rapidograph or similar.

Every line you draw on paper has to be cut with a knife or saw. The more irregular and jagged the lines, the more difficult the cutting phase of the work will become. Aim at simple, flowing lines and try to simplify the outline as much as possible.

Keep the original as a reference to the minor details which can be added to the working drawing as work proceeds. What is required at this stage are the major parts only of the picture background.

Simplification and omission

It is often possible to simplify the subject by the omission of a great deal of detail without spoiling the picture. (See Fig.255 and Fig.256.)

For example white puff-ball clouds or wafting chimney smoke do not translate easily into veneers and may result looking more like balloons. Discard unwanted items like the crane on the horizon or the intrusive road sign, street light or delivery van. Tiny branches and twigs of trees in winter, may entail cutting minute pieces beyond your present ability. However, before omitting any detail, keep an eye on your reference copy in case you are able to add the detail later. *Keep the line flowing and simple.*

Although simplication and the elimination of detail is a negative but necessary aspect of preparing a line drawing, on the more positive side the composition can be improved by the addition of some elements and the repositioning of others.

Fig. 255 How to adapt a scene by addition of elements, omission and simplification

Fig. 256

Addition of elements

To give the picture perspective realism, it is sometimes necesssary to add detail, such as a winding road or river, a fence or stone wall in the foreground, or to frame the subject with a silhouetted tree or archway.

The addition of 'signs of life' in the picture such as people in the distance, or a passing bird or domestic pet, can bring life to the subject.

To keep figures in true perspective, contrive to have a fence or wall -which we know is about waist height – or put the figure near a cottage where you know the front door will be about 6ft. 6in (2 metres) tall and the figures smaller, to provide a reference scale.

Repositioning and transposing

It is possible to transpose figures or cottages from other drawings, suitably scaled up or down to size, by trying them in various positions.

If a rock in a stream is drawn in a fixed position, its location can be repositioned later if the natural flow of grain in the veneer selected for water could be made to appear to swirl around it; and if details can be found occurring naturally in veneer during cutting, the veneer would be allowed to do the work instead of cutting in the detail.

29
The Colours of Veneer

AN ARTIST can mix his paints to capture reality from the whole colour spectrum, using colour and tonal contrasts, harmonious blends and subtle hues, tinted and shaded to achieve his purpose.

The marquetarian is much more strictly controlled. He has to find inspiration in his veneers and let the veneers suggest the subject of his picture and do the work of creating the illusion of the third dimension. His palette of colours is far lower in the chromatic scale of the colour spectrum than either film or paint.

Although there is a wide variety of natural wood tones, they cannot always meet the needs of the marquetarian. This often leads to the temptation to use dyed or chemically treated woods in an attempt to imitate the original colour.

For a better understanding of the use of the colours of veneers for marquetry let us first look at the 'Colour Wheel'.

THE COLOUR WHEEL

An elementary colour wheel will be a useful aid to the marquetarian, in conjunction with a tonal values scale and selection grids. (See Fig. 257.)
1 red, 2 yellow, 3 blue, 4 orange, 5 green, 6 violet, 7 orange-yellow, 8 orange-red, 9 purple, 10 indigo, 11 blue-green, 12 yellow-green, 13 citron, 14 olive-green, 15 russet brown, 16 brown.

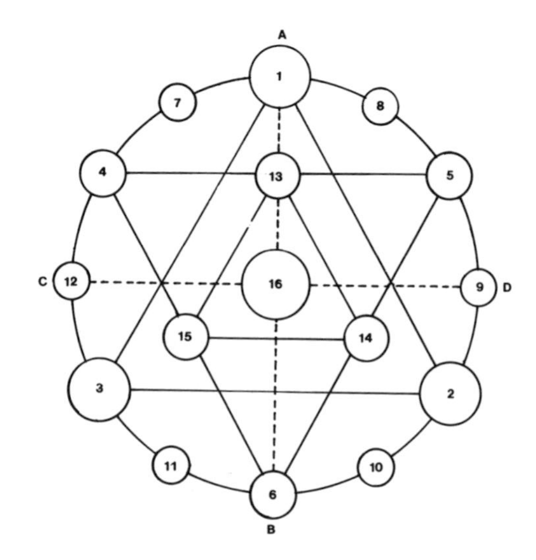

Fig. 257 The colour wheel

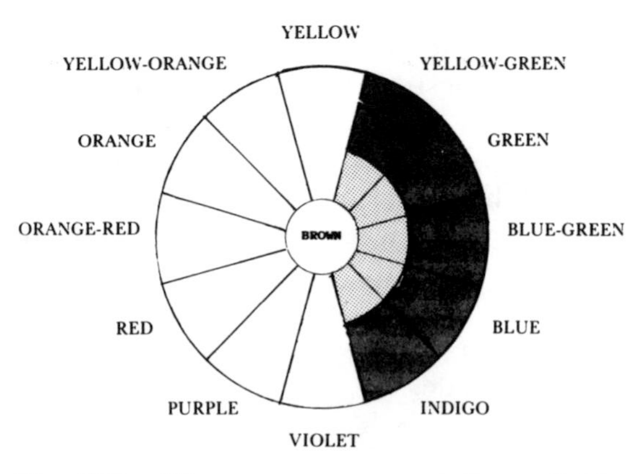

Fig. 258 There are no commercially available veneers in the shaded area

Spectrum palette

In a true colour spectrum, prismatic colours are those into which pure white light is resolved when transmitted through a prism, and are red, orange, yellow, green, blue, indigo and violet.

The Impressionists confined their work to this 'spectrum palette' (with the addition of white). Of these, the three *primary* colours are red (1), yellow (2), and blue (3). In theory, all other colours can be mixed from these three, but in practice the pigments are not pure enough.

The three *secondary* colours are made by mixing together any two of the primary colours. ie.,red and yellow make orange (4), yellow and blue make green (5), while blue and red form violet (6).

Intermediate colours are mixtures of adjacent sections of primary and secondary colours and are placed in circles 7 to 12, such as red and violet to make purple (9), etc.

Tertiary colours are mixtures of primary and or secondary colours, and are chromatic variations of greys and browns lower down in the chromatic scale towards the centre, shown as citron (13), olive green (14), and russet (15). The centre circle is brown.

Complementary colours, are those which together, in prismatic form, make up white light. The complementary of any of the primary colours is formed by a mixture of the other two, so that any of the three primary colours is complementary to the other two.

To find the complementary colour of red for example, which is green, you will see that it appears immediately opposite on the other side of the colour wheel. Green is a secondary colour formed by the mixture of the two primaries, blue and yellow.

Orange is the complement of blue and violet to yellow. The juxtaposition in a picture of any two complementary colours gives the greatest contrast – a favourite technique of impressionist artists.

Harmonious blends are achieved by placing colours together which are adjacent aound the colour wheel. All colours above the line C-D are light colours and all those below are dark. Colours to the left of the line A-B are said to be 'warm' colours and those to the right are 'cool'.

There is an important difference between the true spectrum of prismatic colours and the colour wheel used by painters and marquetarians.

In a prismatic colour wheel (created by joining both ends of a 'rainbow' spectrum to form a circle) when the primary or the complementary colours are mixed they form white light, shown as a white centre circle. But when paints are mixed together they form dark brown, (not black, as that is not a colour; there can be no colour without light). Therefore, in the painter's colour wheel, the centre circle is brown, obtained by a mixture of any two complementary colours.

Restricted palette

But what of the marquetarian's colour wheel? We cannot mix colours together to form complementaries and tertiaries. Our colours are provided by natural woods.

When we make a comparison of the colour wheel and the colours available to us in veneers, we discover that *more than a third of our palette of colours is missing!* (Fig.258.)

The marquetarian has to learn to work with a restricted palette of colour hues and tones. Many famous artists work in only one or two hues. There have been many paintings using burnt umber alone.

The only limitation for the marquetarian lies in the choice and suitability of the subject. Nature does not provide true green primary colours in wood, and few, if any, violet. Therefore, we cannot contrast red with either of the other two primaries.

When we examine the secondary, intermediate and tertiary colours directly opposite to each other around the wheel, which are complementary to each other for colour contrasts, we find there are no veneers available in the green, green-blue, blue, or blue-violet segments. Which also means we cannot use them as complementaries for the abundant red, orange-red, orange, yellow-orange, or yellow woods. It is a fact that there are very few, if any, complementary colours for most of the woods that are available in great profusion.

The absence of true greens and blues, poses a problem and a challenge for the marquetarian. Should he resort to faking the colours nature cannot provide in natural woods by dyeing them?

The 'purists' will declare that the moment we resort to using arificial dyes to colour our woods, we might as well take up painting or photography! They claim that using dyed woods defeats the whole essence of marquetry, i.e., making pictures from natural woods.

But many artist-craftsmen argue that by dyeing veneers to complete the spectrum, it enables a far greater variety of yellow-red-brown woods to be utilised.

The skill in dyeing veneers would be to keep strictly to tertiary (third order) colours nearer to the brown centre of the wheel, such as greenish-browns, bluish-browns, etc., avoiding true saturated colour for the sole purpose of finding complementary colours as a foil to natural woods.

Generally, marquetarians should strive to use the woods nature provides in abundance, and their artistic skill in subject selection.

Why the emphasis on complementary colours? They are vitally important in pictures. If you stare at a red coloured veneer long and hard for a minute or two, and then look at a sheet of white paper, a patch of green light should appear as an illusion or 'after image'.

Orange will produce a blue after-image and yellow will appear as violet. The reason is, that as the eye grows tired of the primary colour, the brain registers its complementary instead. A piece of grey next to red, may often appear tinged with green. The same grey next to purple-violet may appear yellowish. For this reason, the shadow of an object should contain a tone of its complementary colour.

As an example, the shadow under the eaves of a yellow-orange thatch should be violet-indigo and not black. Yellow-green foliage would throw a purple shadow.

With about a third of the complementary colours missing from our palette of woods, how can we create colour contrasts so vital for marquetry pictures? Many subjects are not possible, without resorting to dyed woods.

There are plenty of red woods, but we cannot find suitable complementary colours in green. Therefore, high noon landscapes of countryside with fields of grass, bushes and trees are not possible in green woods, and neither are brilliant blue seas and skies.

Increasing your palette

The first practical step is to try to obtain as many 'fringe-colour' woods as possible as every step around the colour wheel towards green, blue and violet segments, enables more of the red and orange and yellow woods to be used.

Look for veneers lower down the tonal range towards brown. Yellowish-green woods like American whitewood or magnolia complement purpleheart. Greenish-brown woods such as green cypress burr complement the mahoganies. Bluish-browns like mansonia complement the orange woods.

Consider the value of bandsawing solid 'wood collectors samples' into veneers such as violet wood and kingwood for the indigo and violet segments to take advantage of all the orange and yellow veneers.

How to use the colour wheel
Select veneers in matched pairs. First select the main veneer for the principal element of the picture, and then test to find if there is a complementary colour from opposite sides of the wheel to pair with it.

If that is not possible, move clockwise or anti-clockwise around the colour wheel to find a 'matching pair' that complement each other.

Remember that complementary colours in the lower order (towards the brown centre) are also to be found near the centre on the opposite side of the wheel.

Colours can be found which are higher or lower in intensity. Red becomes orange-red or orange if a brighter colour is required; or reddish-purple if a duller colour would suit.

If this proves unsuccessful and suitable complementaries cannot be found to provide the correct contrast, consider changing the time of day in your picture from noon to dawn or dusk.

For summer skies, as we have no true blue woods to complement the wide range of orange woods available, convert the scene using darker tones, into a sunset or sunrise. Orange-red tones and brown shadows can be used and the need for blues and greens is avoided.

Or change the picture's season of the year, using the paler creams and pink woods to suggest springtime, or the delicate hues of autumn – golden and russet browns and reds, from which exquisite harmonies of tone can be created.

Scenes with a mass of foliage may with advantage be adapted to a winter snowscene. In fact, a cool, retarding scene can be enlivened by a small detail in red, yellow or orange which immediately catches the eye and these colours are widely available to us. A small section in a vivid colour can be used to contrast strongly with the prevailing tones of a picture and can be a vital compositional element, or even the focal point of interest.

A small piece of yellow in a purple background would not be 'lost' but would have greater intensity and stand out. It is the orange-violet and yellow-purple sectors which offer the best opportunities to find complementaries.

Although magnificient pictures can be created by using strong colour contrasts, it is advisable to limit the number of colours used and avoid their dispersal in a disorderly fashion, as this can be confusing to the eye. A limited range of colour is usually far more effective.

Another plan is to select light colours from above the central horizontal axis of the wheel, and contrast them with dark colours from below the line. Or contrast 'warm' colours from the left of the vertical axis of the wheel, with 'cool' colours on the right.

Generally, we use adjacent colours from the colour wheel to form blends and harmonies, and complementaries for contrasts, and it is vitally important for the marquetarian to understand the principles of making up the deficiency of colour in the normal colour range. Once understood, the advantages can be fully exploited and craftsmen will be less likely to choose unsuitable subjects.

Chromatic colours
All colours in the colour wheel are chromatic colours. Black, white and greys are known as achromatic colours and are concerned with tone.

Colour Contrasts
We have eight different ways of obtaining colour contrasts in marquetry:
(1) Primary colours contrasted with each other (if you can find any blue wood).

(2) Primary colours.
(3) Secondary colours.
(4) Intermediate colours and
(5) Tertiary colours. ((2) to (5) each contrasted with their complementaries).
(6) Any of these colours (2 to 5) contrasted with neutral brown.
(7) Contrasting warm and cold colours from above or below the center line.
(8) Contrasting light and dark colours from left and right of the vertical line.

Characteristics

Let us look at some of the other characteristics which veneers share with paint:
(a) *Hue*, which is the colour type;
(b) *Chroma*, which is the hue and saturation of a colour – the degree of vividness – and is the distinguishing element between chromatic and the achromatic colours of black, white and grey.
(c) *Tonal value* is a broad term used variously to describe the degree of brightness in a colour; its saturation (either a deep or pale tone), or its value (a light or dark tone).
(d) *Brilliance* is its intensity of colour tone, and/or its light reflection potential when polished.
(e) *Transparency or opaqueness*. This is an illusionary quality in veneers, which are all opaque of course, but some veneers are considered in comparison to others to be less opaque and have a quality of transparency due to the surface figure.
(f) *Temperature*. This is concerned with its chroma and suggests that the chromatic colours possess qualities of 'warmth' and 'coolness'. For example, red woods are 'advancing' and warm; bluish-brown woods have a 'cool' retarding quality suggesting distance, and are therefore used to portray aerial perspective.

This is not due entirely to mental association but colours possess some form of interpretive basis.

These characteristics also possess emotional qualities, giving impressions of warmth with red woods, coldness with bluish woods, heaviness with dark brown, cheerfulness or lightness with yellow and restfulness with the greenish woods.

The Tonal Values scale

The need to set off the colour of one wood with one of a contrasting colour, is only one part of the equation. A full understanding of the use of *tonal contrasts* is equally important before we can put the colour-wheel to practical use in the selection of *colour contrasts* in marquetry.

Draw a tonal values scale of ten 1 inch (25mm) squares on a sheet of white cartridge paper as shown in Fig.259.

Achromatic colours are white, black and grey. I made this scale by using graduated tones of Letraset but it can be made with charcoal or pencil hatching. Begin with white at one end, black at the other and neutral grey (harewood) in the centre. Although the centre of a colour wheel is *brown* which is a mixture of all the colours and the centre of the spectrum is white, the centre section of an achromatic tonal scale is neutral *grey*, which is midway between black and white.

We will use this as a handy reference 'scale-ruler' in conjunction with the veneer selection grid. You will see it all begin to come together now.

Veneer selection grids

Draw a grid of 1 inch (25 mm) squares on a piece of card, as shown in Fig.260, to match the tonal scale, by three rows down. The number of squares in each grid will depend on the number of veneers you have in your veneer bank.

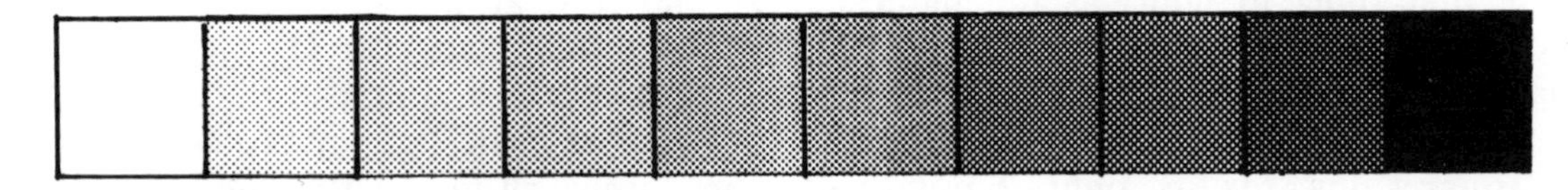

Fig. 259 Achromatic tonal values scale

The *achromatic* (black-grey-white) 'Tonal values scale' fits neatly across the top of the grid.

Obtain a stock of veneers from your supplier (a range of veneer packets, including a harewood pack of dyed greys) or a veneer collector's set.

Select the whitest veneer you have in your stock (holly, horse chestnut or sycamore), and glue this over the white square. Place the blackest veneer you can find, such as Macassar ebony, over the black square.

Now take a selection of greys, such as silver grey harewood, slate grey and charcoal grey, and position these matching the tones to the chart as closely as possible, as at A, in Fig.260. Now we need to make a *chromatic* tonal values scale, (shown at F), this time featuring some of the brown woods, such as agba, African walnut, afrormosia, Australian blackwood, brown oak, Indian laurel, Macassar ebony, opepe, teak and wenge. These two scales are used in the creation of veneer selection grids.

Position the black and white scale at the top of the grid to aid comparison when selecting the other colours, and the brown scale across the bottom to ensure that the row of squares above are a tone lighter.

The next thing to do is to make a chromatic veneer selection grid for each colour of the wheel, in a range from darkest to lightest in any one colour hue. One row of squares on the grid for each colour.

As you compile the chromatic grid, compare the tonal values, and try to match them to correspond with the black-grey-white squares above and compare the tones with the brown scale below.

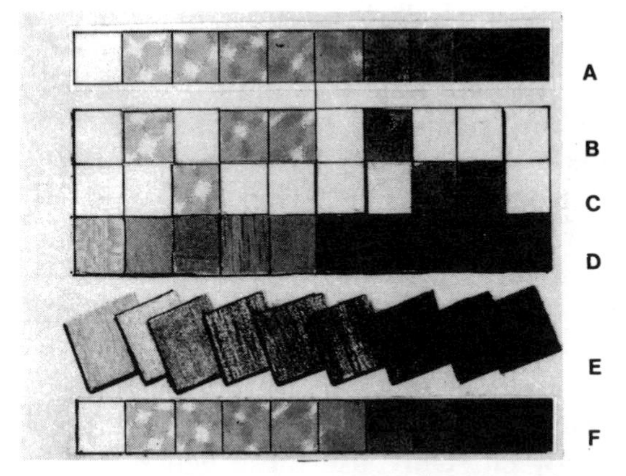

Fig. 260 Chromatic veneer selection grid

For the purpose of this exercisê, we will now complete a row representing the yellow segment of the colour wheel.

Assemble all the yellowish veneers you have available, and arrange them with the palest or lightest yellow towards the left of the grid on the top line and the deepest or darkest yellow towards the right hand side. Do not include any 'yellow-orange' or 'yellow-greenish' veneers.

It helps considerably when arranging veneers in tonal order, to wear sunglasses. A more effective but more costly way is to take the grid to an instant print shop with the veneer squares temporarily affixed and identified, and make a photocopy. The black and white reproduction will clearly show the tonal differences and enable you to position them corrrectly.

The first thing to notice is the lightest yellow does not correspond with the white square of the achromatic scale – which is several tones lighter – but lies about one or two squares towards its right. Similarly, none of the yellows approaches the darkness of the black square. Do not worry that you cannot fill up all the squares to match the tonal scales.

The truest yellow colour is to the left of centre. This demonstrates that you are only using a small portion of the ten squares to show any significant tonal gradation.

Let's suppose you have afara, antiaris, ash, avodire, ayan, birch, boxwood, capomo, horse chestnut, iroko, lime, maple, obeche, olon, white peroba, satinwood, Swedish pine, poplar, prima vera, sycamore, and willow, but they do not marry up with the white-to-black tones shown on the scale.

Select the lightest and darkest and a few in between. Only use those which match the tones, even if you only position five or six on the grid.

What you have now, is the colour yellow, looked at across the two extremes of its tonal range, as at B.

Tints and shades

If the colours were paints, you would add white to a primary colour to obtain a 'tint', and black to obtain a 'shade'. In marquetry, you use the tonal scale to select the nearest equivalent of 'shades' and 'tints' of a colour.

As you gather more veneers you can add to the grid as you find lighter or darker veneers. Keep a separate reference chart as a key for identification purposes, by lettering or numbering the veneer squares.

Now assemble together all your 'yellow-brown' veneers such as as afara, ayan, eucalyptus, hornbeam, idigbo, iroko, peroba white, satinwood, etc., and complete the second row, at C. Complete the third row of the tertiary range at D.

Now continue across to the other side of the colour wheel from 'brown' through the 'brownish-to-violet' veneers, such as American walnut, and mansonia, to the 'Violet' colours of Indian rosewood and kingwood. You will find there is no true violet.

To reduce the number of grids, instead of making up twelve charts, one for each colour of the wheel, make a chart which displays a complete tangential segment across the colour wheel. For example, from the primary yellow, through neutral brown to yellow's complementary colour violet, in which case the brown scale goes in the centre, and you'll need six charts to cover the entire colour wheel.

The method of use of the colour wheel and veneer selection grid charts, is to look first at the wheel and decide on the colour segment required for your picture *and its complementary* on the opposite side of the wheel for colour contrast. Then check to see which tonal contrasts are available.

Tonal contrasts

The great advantage of this type of grid, is that it provides six ways for you to select tonal contrasts:

(1) Selection of one colour contrasted with a shade from the dark end of the tonal scale.
(2) Selection of one colour contrasted with a tint from the light end of the scale.
(3) Contrast of the colour with neutral grey harewood.
(4) Contrast using a black veneer.
(5) Contrast using a white veneer.
(6) Contrasts using sand shading techniques.

Black can be used to emphasise the brightness of the colours, or grey, which has similar effect due to its neutral tone and white which makes colours look more intense, by its brightness.

When you have completed making up these selection grids, you will see there are indeed very few squares filled on the green, blue-green, blue indigo and violet segments, although, opposite these, the red, orange-red, orange, and yellow-orange and yellow are in plentiful supply.

It is vitally important for the marquetarian to understand this deficiency in the veneer palette – a third doesn't exist! Unless this fact is understood, and the advantages fully exploited, craftsmen may choose unsuitable subjects.

There is an almost universal desire among marquetarians to capture photographic realism from prints and coloured slides coupled with accurate colour matching of the original. Many of the subjects which are ideal for the cameraman in colour are unsuitable for marquetry. The best subjects are often found in black and white prints.

Copying subjects which originate in other media such as painting or photography may bring problems which wood cannot solve. That is the wrong way to approach marquetry.

What the marquetry artist has to do is to gain an understanding of the limitations imposed by the colours of wood veneers, and the effect of this on the designs he attempts. Then allow the available veneers to suggest suitable subjects and exploit their natural beauty of colour, their rare and exotic wood grains, beautiful figures, natural stains, peculiar markings, surface textures and patterns full of interest and their infinite range of tonal variations.

The art of marquetry is to let the wood tell its own story. A carefully chosen freak wood will transform an ordinary subject into something extraordinary. Many prizewinners have to thank a spectacular veneer choice for their success. This doesn't mean we have to work in monochrome shades and tints of black and white – the tonal grid shows we don't have many woods which are actually black or white.

The Italian masters gave us the word 'chiaroscuro' which refers in pictures to the balance between light and shadows, in different tones of the same colour hue. This is precisely what the modern marquetarian has to introduce into his pictures for maximum effect. Before we can fully understand how to apply chiaroscuro techniques to marquetry, we have to understand the value to us of monochrome, before we can fully master colour contrasts.

Monochrome

When the camera first came into its own, most exhibition prizewinning photographs were in sephia. A dramatic monochrome scene, which the practised photographer captures through his lens, can be extremely effective for aesthetic marquetry pictures, and especially evocative when a mood or atmosphere needs to be portrayed.

A coloured photograph is one part of a selection process, being an arrangement of coloured shapes on paper in two dimensions. It is merely representative of the original three dimensional scene. Not so much discarding has taken place as in black and white, where the colours are represented as varying shades of grey from black to white.

Monochrome is always a distortion of reality because it lacks the vital ingredient – natural colour. But monochrome provides more scope for personal interpretation of reality and permits a greater degree of abstraction from reality.

Many creative photographers prefer to work in black and white for aesthetic reasons. It is interesting to note that although the brilliantly coloured marquetry of David Roentgen (1743–1807) has now

Fig. 261 'Desert Moon' by Solomon Banks

faded, his pictures reproduce beautifully in black and white. This is because they were originally conceived as line and tone compositions, with a carefully studied balance between line and mass, tonal harmony, and contrast in line and form, rather than in colour. They were conceived as monochrome pictures, their beauty of design took precedence over colour.

Mr. Solomon Banks of the Redbridge Group of the Marquetry Society, created a prizewinning picture *Desert Moon* from one leaf of American red gum (satin walnut) *Liquidambar styraciflua.*

What is remarkable about this picture is that it was created entirely from one leaf of wood. The two pieces of the moon, the camel and rider, and the sand dunes on the horizon, were all from various parts of one multi-coloured leaf. The sky and desert at the horizon, were one unjointed piece. Even more laudable, the dark stringers and the border veneers were all from the same leaf. This picture symbolises marquetry. It comes close to the very essence – the pure distillation – of pictorial marquetry.

Subjectively, whether this picture appeals or not, it demonstrates objectively – better than any words of mine – that marquetry is all about wood. The artist's role was to conceive a subject by sensory insight and creative visualisation, to display that leaf of veneer to its best advantage.

The actual cutting, laying and finishing of the picture were elements of his craftsmanship – a means to an end – which enabled us to share his imaginative conception.

There is more scope for personal interpretation of reality, the greater the degree of abstraction from it.

In a black and white photograph, everything in the viewfinder is recorded by the impartial camera, including all the superfluous elements in the picture to disturb the composition.

Unlike the camera lens, the image seen by the human eye is capable of being interpreted very selectively. This can be converted into an asset for marquetry purposes.

The marquetry artist can delete all extraneous elements and exploit the highlights and harsh shadows and reflections which lend drama to the image, especially if darker tones prevail, to transform otherwise mundane subjects. With the right subject, a predominance of light tones and attenuated contrasts can be used to create images of softness and serenity.

There is another factor to be taken into consideration in the selection of colours. The effect of time.

Effects of time and light

The process of cutting veneers requires the log to be steamed. This destroys wood insects, and draws out various chemicals, and eventually changes the natural colour of the original log. The resulting veneer does not match exactly the solid woods from the same log, a fact which architects have to take into account when specifying veneers to match solid hardwoods from the same species.

Veneers are subject to a change in colourtone when exposed to the ultra-violet rays present in both natural and artificial light. Upon exposure to light, some woods darken and other will fade. In the case of purpleheart for example, strong light will fade the veneer and moderate light will darken it. Bleached woods become yellow in time, and chemically treated woods such as silver harewood, will lose their original brilliance and turn slightly greenish.

The white veneers, such as sycamore, maple, willow, horse chestnut and holly will gradually 'weather' and turn yellow, biscuit or tan coloured, depending on their exposure to light.

The results of exposure to partial light are very disagreeable, as for example, when a shadow from a window falls across a piece of work resulting in a discolouring stripe which is virtually impossible to eradicate.

Therefore, the most artistic marquetry pictures rely upon the skilful juxtaposition of tonal and textural contrasts which will endure, rather than brilliant colour contrasts which will fade in time. Any slight fading, should uniformly affect the veneers, giving the picture a mature patina of age.

A picture should not contain odd pieces which stand out in stark contrast. The museums of the world contain many examples of inlaid work, where this has happened, when ivory or mother of pearl were used and these 'foreign' materials now predominate the work.

Veneer album

Comprehensive veneer collections of specimens are available in various forms, complete with labels giving the standard, trade and botanical name, and country of origin.

Mini-wood collections of 45 veneer samples of 3 × 1 inches (75 × 25mm) – 15 to a card – are useful for creating the colour wheel and veneer tonal grid charts. It is a good idea to seal and polish one half of each sample, in order to compare the veneer in its natural and polished state.

Collector's sets comprising 50 veneers size 4 × 3 inches (100 × 75mm) are available. Parts of these samples can be used for the colour wheel and veneer grids and the remainder can be held in veneer album form.

Cigarette card albums are available with clear plastic pockets which will hold either eight veneer samples, 3 × 2 inches (75 × 50mm) or four samples, 4 × 3 inches (100 × 75mm) per page. The album leaves can be purchased individually as your collection grows.

Stobart & Son Ltd., the publishers of this book, also sell folding wallets containing 40 wood veneer samples approximately 3 × 1 inches (75 × 25mm). These are the species covered in their publication *What Wood is That?* by H.L.Edlin, from which the wallet is taken.

30
Perspective and Composition

VERY FEW people have received a formal art training, and if you have not enjoyed this pleasureable experience this chapter will outline some of the fundamentals of perspective and composition to help you create a marquetry picture.

I strongly recommend you to expose your mind to art, perhaps at your local art gallery, or better still, to enrol at an art class and receive first hand tuition which may bring out your latent talent.

Perfect proportion

Since Egyptian times, mathematics have played an important part in the compositional theories of art. Euclid, the ancient Greek geometrician, laid down in his *Optics* in 300 B.C., the geometric theory and principles of linear perspective (which were not fully understood until the 14th century).

Vitruvius in the 1st century B.C., calculated the Euclidean theory in his book '*De Architectura*' that the ideal proportion is found by dividing a line such that the smaller part is to the larger, in the same ratio as the larger part is to the whole for 'mystical perfection'.

Luca Pacioli's work '*De Divina Proportione*' in 1509, which was illustrated by Leonardo da Vinci, defines it as the 'divine proportion'.

Euclid evolved the Golden Section, which divided the picture plane into perfect proportions of balance and symmetry.

The Golden Section

The classic principles of perfect proportion can be used to produce a 'Golden Section'. This can be calculated geometrically, or may be found by using the '618' formula.

This is a very special number which works 'magic' for us in determining perfect proportion for our pictures! I'm not suggesting that we have to work with mathematical accuracy in creating pictures, but this 'magic' number will tell us:

(a) The perfect width for a picture, of any given depth.
(b) The ideal depth of a picture, for a given width.
(c) The best position for a low horizon.
(d) The ideal location for a high horizon.
(e) The location of the best 'focal points of interest'.

Here's how it works. You choose any measurement for one side of your picture. Multiply that number by .618 for a smaller dimension or by 1.618 for a larger dimension. In practice, we do not use all the decimal places. You can work to the nearest $\frac{1}{4}$ or $\frac{1}{8}$ inch (6mm or 3mm).

For the purposes of illustration only, here is an example using an extended number .61805.

We want to create an upright portrait type picture with a depth of 18 inches and we require the width to be smaller. Therefore multiply 18 by .61805 and the ideal width is 11.1249 or $11\frac{1}{8}$ inches. To prove this multiply the newly discovered width of 11.1249 by 1.61805 to get back to 18 inches.

This works in metric sizes in exactly the same way. In practice we only use the reduced .618.

Upright pictures

Horizon positions are simply determined by positioning the horizon at the same distance as the picture width from either the top or bottom of the picture.

Focal points

These four positions are determined by multiplying the width by .618 again and measuring this dimension in from either side.

(Example: in a 12 inch (305mm) wide picture the focal points are found by multiplying by .618 or 7.416 inches (188mm) from either side, on both the low and high horizon positions.

Landscape pictures

Horizon positions are found by multiplying the depth by .618 and position the horizon this distance from either the top or bottom of the picture.

Focal points

These positions are drawn where the two horizon lines are intersected by vertical lines drawn at .618 of the width from either side.

The proportion also applies to ovals, of course, created within the rectangle.

For all practical purposes, we do not reach for our pocket calculators, but use the simple proportion of 5:8 (or .625) which is as near to the 'magic' .618 as necessary for our use.

We can also construct a 'golden section' *geometrically* with the same result. Drop a vertical line A-B from the centre diagonal of a square at A, and put the compass point at B. The line B-C is the radius of an arc as shown in Fig.262.

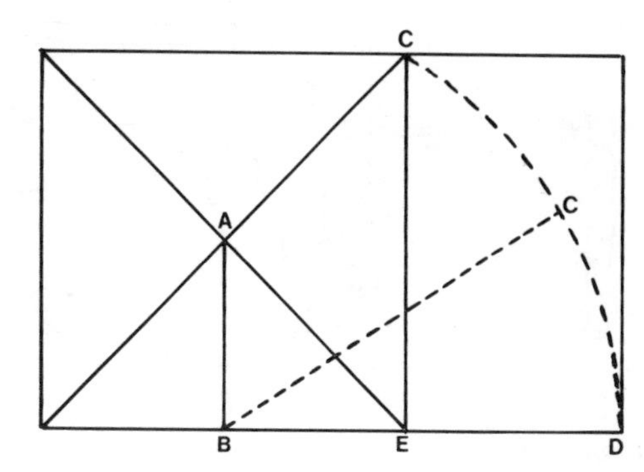

Fig. 262 How to construct the 'Golden Section'

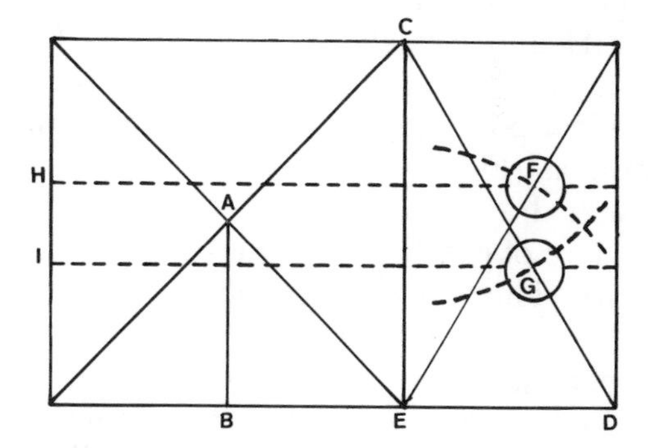

Fig. 263 Determining the high and low horizons

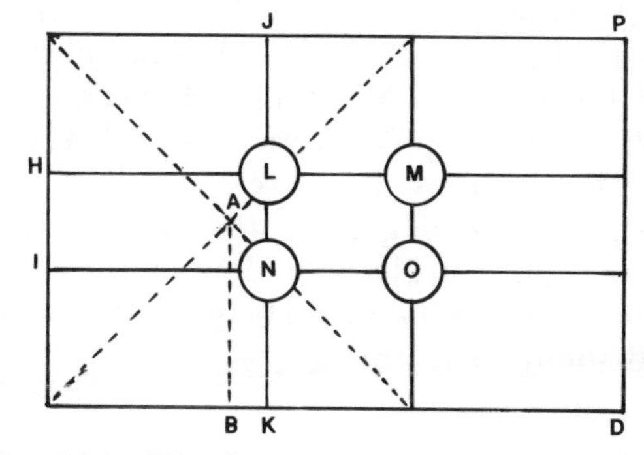

Fig. 264 The four focal points of interest

Draw an arc C-D. Draw a vertical from D and complete the perfectly proportioned rectangle.

Draw diagonal lines in the extension to the square. Using the line A-E as a radius, draw line F and pinpoint the intersection. Draw the same radius (A-E) from C to

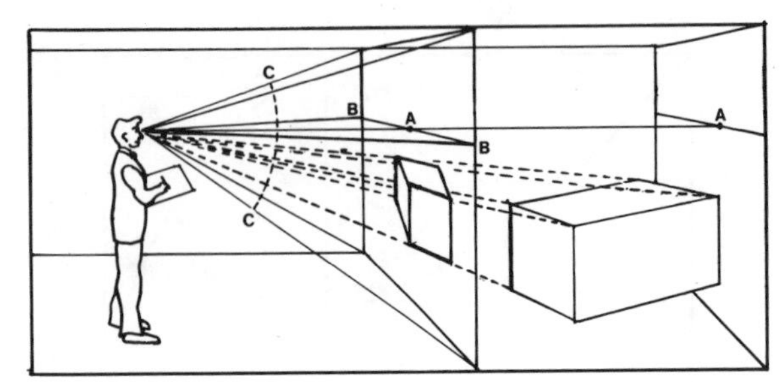

Fig. 265 The picture plane. The centre, angle and cone of vision

pinpoint position G. Draw two horizontal lines H and I as shown, from F and G.

The horizontal lines H and I represent the ideal positions for high and low horizon pictures. (Fig.263).

Next draw a vertical line at J-K to form a square of exactly the same size as the first square. The four intersections L, M, N and O are considered to be the the ideal positions for placing picture elements which are the focal points of interest within a frame. The line J-K does not coincide with the line A-B. (Fig.264).

Throughout history, the masters have applied this 'Golden Section'. The Florentine master Brunelleschi used the same rules, as did Leonardo da Vinci and Michelangelo.

In practice, just position your horizons and focal points in a five-as-to-eight proportion. Having got the theory of perfect proportion clear, let's get down to basics to understand the difference between the *horizon* and the *centre of vision.*

The ground plane

The ground where you stand is known as the 'ground plane' and your eye level will depend on its relation to the ground, ie, whether you are standing or sitting or on top of a ladder; whether you are on a mountain top or lying on a beach, the horizon travels with you and is always at your eye level.

The picture plane

Your perspective of the scene before you – the picture plane – will depend on its relationship to your eye level, and whether you are looking at the subject from below, above or level with it, and upon the angle the subject is from you. Our eye can follow across our field of vision from side to side *without moving the head.* The horizon appears to move with us.

In Fig.265, A is the *centre of vision* at eye level. B-B is the *angle of vision* on the picture plane. C is the *cone of vision.*

The centre of vision

An imaginary line drawn perpendicularly from our position to the horizon, meeting it at right angles, is known as the *centre of vision.* In every picture the horizon line is important, and is present even in subjects such as portraits and interiors, even when it can't be seen.

The angle of vision

This is at horizon level, at the centre of vision.

The cone of vision

Although the horizon can extend about 180 degrees, by moving the head slightly to left or right, our eye can actually see a narrow area known as the *cone of vision* of from 30 to 60 degrees and this dictates what you can include in your picture. If you move your head, you change the perspective.

This cone of vision produces two effects. The first is an accurate mental image of the scene; the second is our interpretation of the scene, edited by the brain to emphasise some features and to disregard others. It is this second feature which enables the artist to rearrange the elements in the frame, for which purpose we need to make a viewfinder.

Making a viewfinder

First of all you will need a correctly proportioned viewfinder. A viewfinder may be either a rectangular hole cut in a postcard, about 2 × 1 inches (50 × 25mm) or in the same proportion as the picture you propose to create. Or make it from two right angle pieces of cardboard which you can move to form varying rectangles. (Fig.266)

Another idea is to use two pieces of card, one with a rectangular hole and the other with a square one and you can test various options by moving them across each other as in Fig.267.

Through this small aperture, shapes and tones are accentuated when separated from the major scene. A good tip is to make the viewfinder from a card which is neutral grey on one side. By a quick comparison, from the aperture to the card, the tonal value of the elements in the frame can be gauged more accurately.

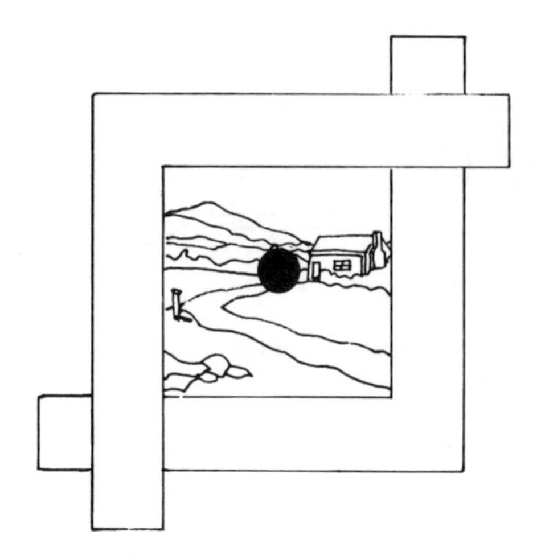

Fig. 266 A square viewfinder made from two pieces of card

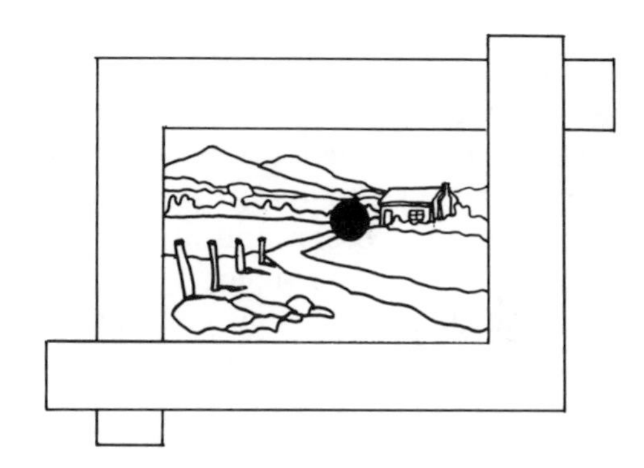

Fig. 267 The foreground is detailed in a high horizon subject

Composition

Framing the subject

Having made your preferred type of viewfinder, frame the subject by deciding where you want the horizon (low or high), arranging the various picture elements in their respective golden sections and contrive a focal point of interest – usually whatever interested you about the scene in the first place.

Remember to close one eye when assessing the scene. As your viewpoint changes, the perspective changes too. It is important to understand the difference between the angle of vision, and the frame *determined* by the angle of vision. The angle of vision remains

Fig. 268 The sky is the main feature in a low horizon subject

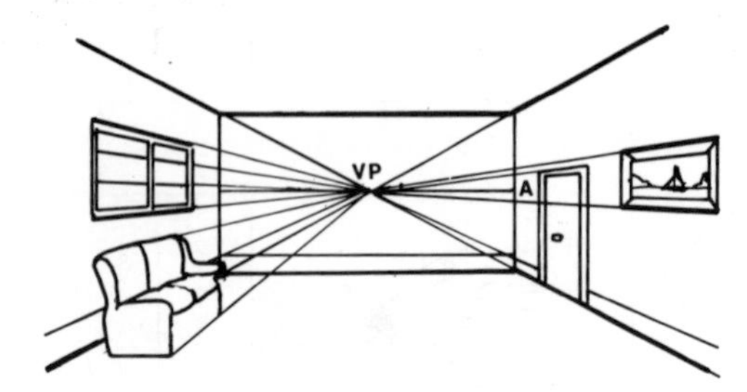

Fig. 269 Parallel perspective with only one vanishing point

the same but the frame can move. In Fig. 266 the dot is on the *centre of vision.*

If you keep your head still and close one eye, you can move the viewfinder and the frame of your picture, so that the centre of vision is no longer in the centre of the frame, but it is still in the centre of your angle of vision, which remains unchanged in the middle of the horizon. (Fig.267).

The centre of vision remains unchanged when the frame is moved, if the head is held still. Note that Fig. 267 has a high horizon, which makes the foreground detail more important. The same subject with a low horizon, Fig.268, puts the emphasis on spectacular sky effects and buildings appear taller.

PERSPECTIVE

The very thought of perspective drawing, may deter the average person from trying their hand at creating their own pictures. Wrestling with rulers, set squares and angles is such a deterrent in itself. For those who haven't yet mastered this essential aspect of design, I hope the following text and illustrations will make clear some of the seemingly daunting aspects.

Simply being aware of what to look for is half the battle!

Parallel perspective

All parallel lines converge on one vanishing point at the centre of vision. Normally, we look at a scene from an oblique angle rather than head-on and 'one vanishing point' would only be found in a situation such as standing in the centre of a road or in a middle of a room. The centre of vision coincides with the vanishing point (VP) *only in parallel perspective.* (Fig.269).
A is at eye level on the horizon with one VP in parallel perspective.

Oblique perspective

Objects which have three or more planes will have two vanishing points, to which the lines converge on the horizon, sometimes outside the area of the picture frame. (Fig.270).

When drawing a circle in oblique perspective it becomes an ellipse. Remember, it is always an ellipse even when foreshortened, and the ends are always round, never pointed.
Note: The correct way to find the centre of a square at line A-B is by connecting the corner diagonals. In oblique perspective make sure the angle of the square nearest to you, as at C, in Fig.271, is greater than 90 degrees.

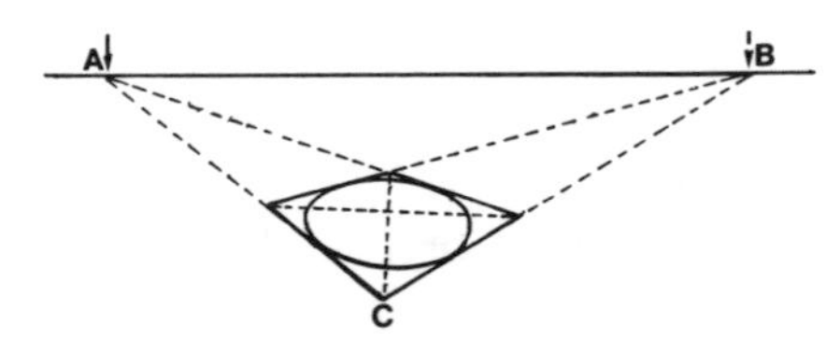

Fig. 270 Oblique perspective with two vanishing points

Aerial perspective

This is somtimes known as *atmospheric perspective.* If we look down upon, or up to an object, a third vanishing point is required. Therefore, the horizon line is vitally important, as without it we cannot correctly position these vanishing points. There may be two vanishing points on the horizon and

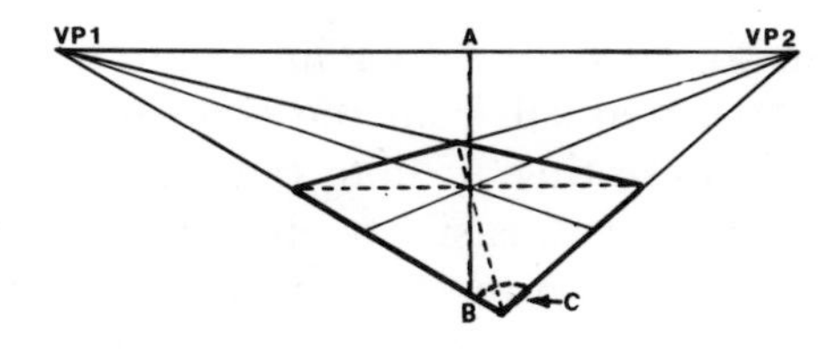

Fig. 271 How to find the centre of a square in oblique perspective

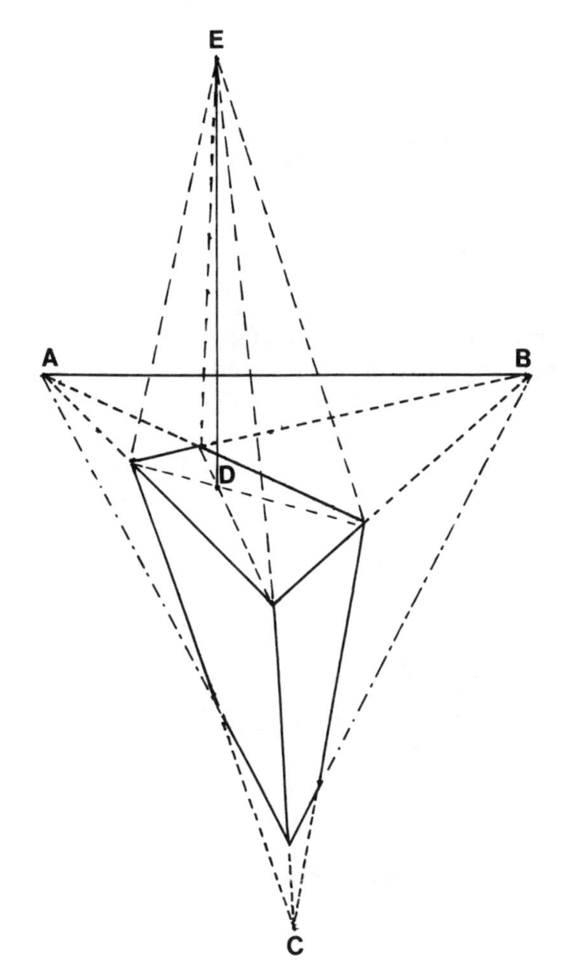

Fig. 272 How to draw a steeple in aerial perspective

one either above or below the horizon to which the verticals converge.

Picture elements such as buildings, which may be at different oblique angles to the picture plane, will have different vanishing points, and there may be several in one picture.

Mastery of oblique perspective drawing is necessary before aerial perspective can be fully understood. The line A-B is the horizon at eye level. The rectangle converges on the VP's at A and B. The downward lines converge at the VP C. (Fig.272).

If this was a church building viewed from above, which required a steeple to be accurately positioned, draw diagonals in the roof rectangle to find the centre point D and extend this to the top of the spire, which becomes the vanishing point E. Since church steeples are often featured in marquetry incorrectly, this is a point worth remembering.

We can now have a closer look at another problem: the difference between the division of *depth* and the division of *space.*

Division of Depth

When tackling street scenes, the lamp posts, trees and telegraph poles must also be in perspective and maintain equal distances apart while appearing to become closer together as they recede. This is achieved by using a new VP called a diagonal vanishing point, (DVP).

In a horizontal plane, this is located on the horizon line. Diagonals in a vertical plane have their vanishing point on a line vertically below or above the normal VP on the horizon.

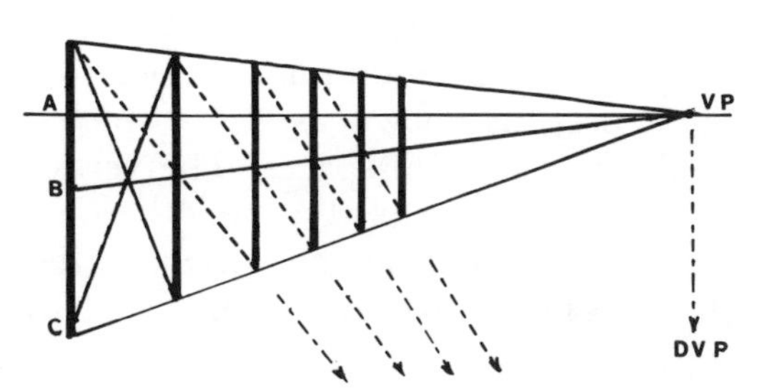

Fig. 273 The division of depth using a diagonal vanishing point

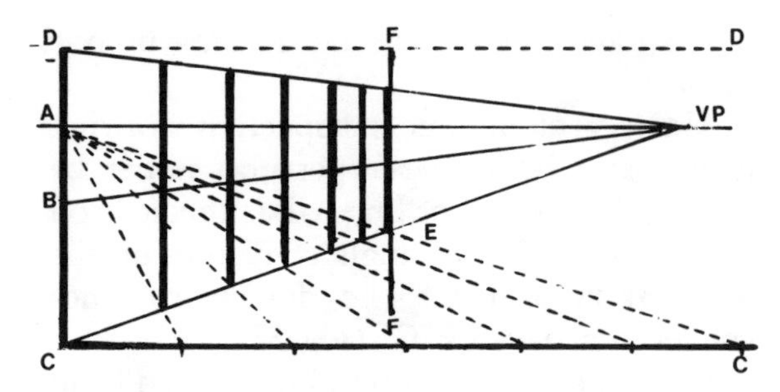

Fig. 274 Dividing a given space into equal parts in oblique perspective

Diagonal Vanishing Points. (DVP)

A is the eye level horizon, with the normal VP. Draw in the first two vertical posts, with lines converging to the VP. Draw diagonals in the first section to find the centre, and draw a line from the 'measuring point' B, extended to the VP.

When a line is drawn from the top of the first post, through the second where it meets the line from B, and is extended to the line from C, this marks the position of the third post.

If the dotted lines were extended, they would converge to a new DVP perpendicular to and immediately below the normal VP. (See Fig.273).

Dividing a space into equal parts

Sometimes it is necessary to arrange columns, poles, doors or windows in receding perspective but in a *fixed* space, unlike in the preceding example where we were not concerned with a given space. (Fig.274).

First we need a 'ground line' drawn from the first post, as shown as C-C, which is divided into six equal spaces. The vertical line F-F indicates the fixed space. A becomes the measuring point on the horizon at eye level, and is joined to C at the vortex E. Now all the posts can be drawn in perspective, by verticals extended from the baseline.

It is interesting to note that the ground line could just as easily be drawn above the first vertical with the same result. Also note the different location of the measuring point B in Fig. 273 which required six posts to be drawn in perspective, but not in a fixed space; and the measuring point A in Fig. 274 which required seven posts in a shorter, given space.

When you wish to get a building's features or windows in correct aerial perspective, the same methods are used.

Dividing equal spaces in aerial perspective

First locate the measuring point A on the horizon between VP's 1 and 2, in line with the nearest line drawn in perspective down to VP 3. Insert the ground line B-C and divide this into the required number of equal spaces, converging on the measuring point A.
The lines D and E, are then divided into equal spaces as in Fig.275.

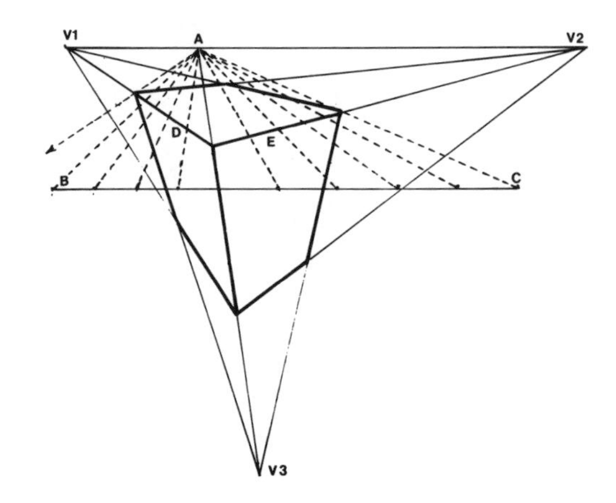

Fig. 275 Dividing equal spaces in aerial perspective

31
Shadows and Reflections

ONE OF the most common mistakes made by marquetarians is their failure to make the shadows in their pictures fall correctly in perspective. Highlights and shadows bring all pictures to life and give them the illusion of roundness and solidity. Most are content to let the shadows fall away from the source of light. Very simple, but quite wrong.

Different laws apply to artificial light and to natural sunlight and moonlight. Let's deal with artificial light first.

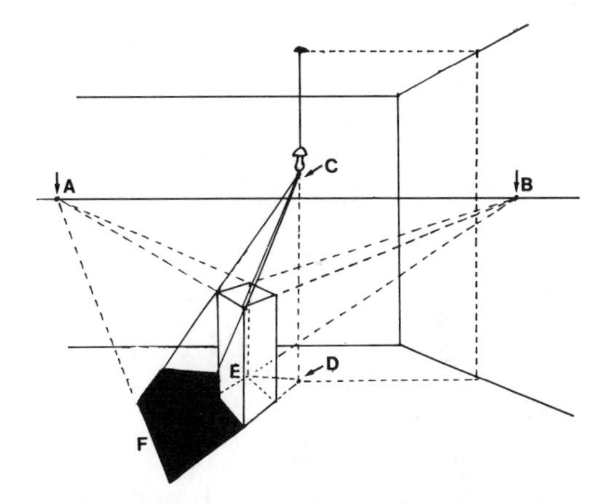

Fig. 276 The VP of light and the VP of shadow

Artificial Light

We are going to meet up with two new vanishing points. The first is called the vanishing point of light (VPL) and the second is the vanishing point of shadow (VPS).

A and B are the normal oblique perspective vanishing points at eye level to which the box's lines converge. C is the VPL and D is the VPS. C determines the limits of the shadow's length; D provides the direction and shape. Side F (the top of the box) converges back to A.

Lines extended from the object which casts the shadow converge on the normal vanishing points on the horizon.

But the light bulb itself (or other artificial light source such as candle, lantern, oil lamp, etc.,) becomes the VPL to which the beams forming the shadow's shape converge. This is known as the *angle of illumination.*

In addition, the VPS is always at a point vertically below the VPL on the ground. (Fig.276).

In order to fully understand the way each of these VP's control shadows, draw 'crystal' boxes so that you can see right through them to the angles at the rear which may affect the line from the VPS, as in Fig.277.

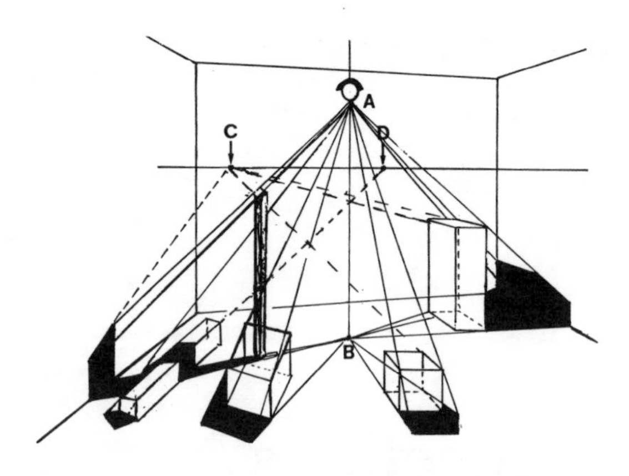

Fig. 277 The shapes of shadows conform to both oblique VP's as well as VPS and VPL

Objects conform to oblique perspective at VP's C and D. A is the VPL and B is the VPS on the ground vertically below the VPL. Notice how the shadows rise vertically up a wall, and climb over obstructions. Also how the extreme shape of the shadow returns to the normal VP's.

The same principles apply to exterior artificial lighting. The VPS is at the base of the lamp-post and the shadows radiate outwards as in Fig. 278.

When light is received from an artificial light source outside the frame of your picture, the same laws apply. Project the VPS from a point immediately below the VPL at ground level, and the beams to the VPL.

Fig. 278 The length and shape of shadows decided by the VPS and VPL from a street light

Front lit subjects
The light source comes from *behind* and casts shadows *away* from you. In artificial light when the light source is outside the picture frame, the VPS (A) is projected from a point on the ground vertically below the VPL (B) as in Fig. 279.

Back lit subjects
The light source comes from in *front* and casts shadows *towards* you. The VPS (B) is projected to a point on the ground vertically below the VPL shown by the two converging lines at (A) as in Fig. 280.

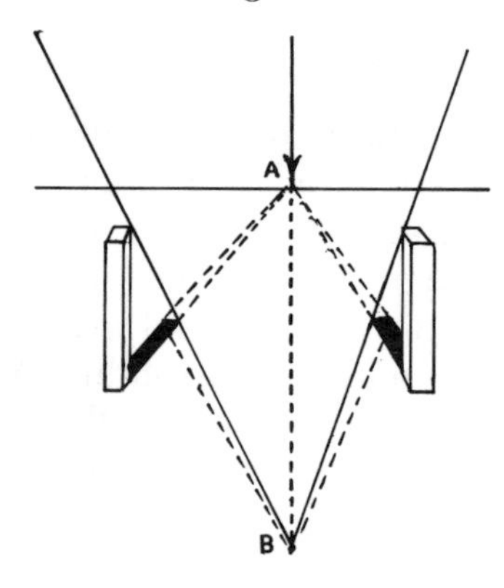

Fig. 279 Front lit subject in artificial light

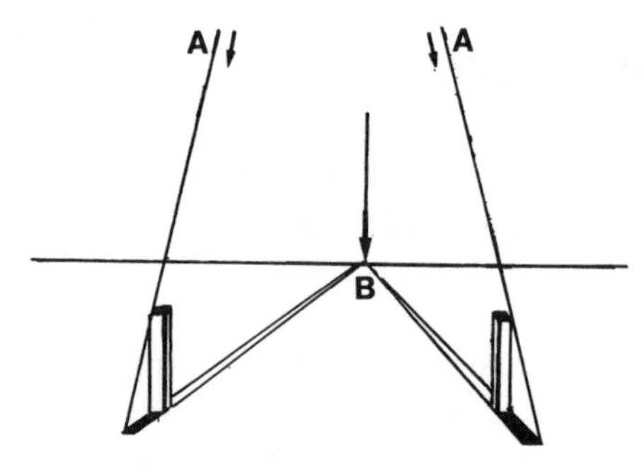

Fig. 280 Back lit subject in artificial light.

Natural Daylight

Here we have to differentiate between what happens in aerial perspective and with both parallel and oblique perspective.

Because the sun's rays arrive on earth almost parallel – for our purpose anyway – the shadows in aerial perspective have practically no perspective because the sunbeams fall straight down.

Here's a 'Golden Rule' which will apply to parallel and oblique perspective and sometimes to aerial perspective.

The VPS of sunlight, is always on the horizon at a point vertically below the sun.

Parallel perspective

The VPS at A is on the horizon vertically below the sun. The sun's rays are parallel, but mark the extremes of the shadow's shape. The shadows converge back to the normal VP on the horizon at B. (Fig.281).

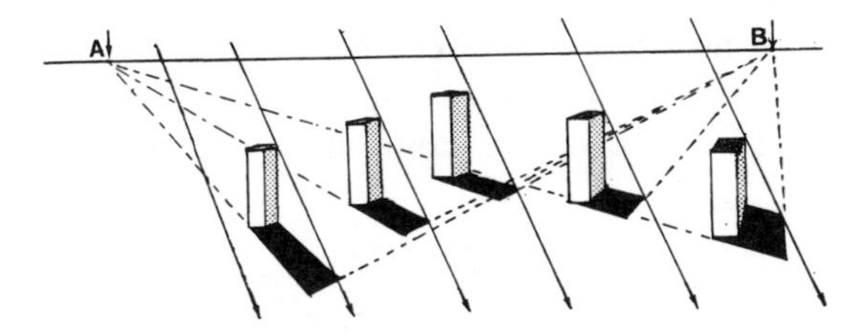

Fig. 281 The VPS of sunlight is on the horizon immediately below the sun

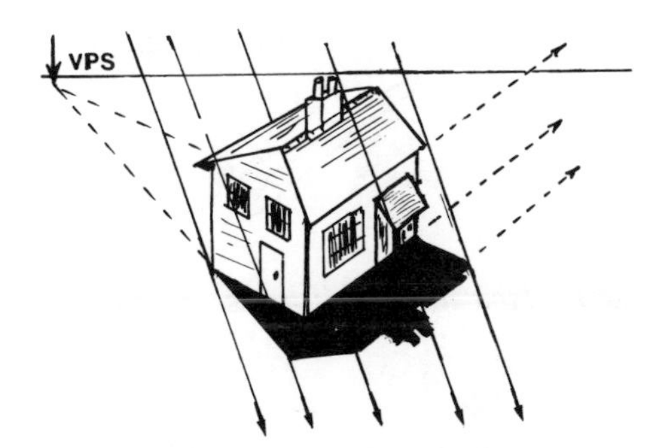

Fig. 282 Shadows in aerial perspective with the VPS on the horizon below the sun

Again, the same rules apply with the VPS on the horizon below the sun. The house and shadow converging to the normal VP's, on the horizon in oblique perspective or above or below the horizon in aerial perspective as shown in Fig.282.

It is well worth repeating this to clear up any confusion. Shadows are governed by *three* vanishing points. The VP of light; the VP of shadow and the normal VP's on, above or below the horizon.

REFLECTIONS

Marquetarians who experience difficulty with shadows in perspective usually have even more difficulty in getting their reflections in water and reflected light correctly drawn in.

Both of these are often incorrectly depicted in pictures, and as trees, boats and bridges reflected in water make appealing subjects, the laws about reflections need to be clarified.

Here are the golden rules.

1. Reflections always have the same vanishing points as the objects they reflect. For this reason reflections in a river are rarely mirror inversions of the objects lining its banks. They are not the same shape when projected to meet the same VP's.
2. Reflections always advance towards the viewer and *do not* obey the same laws as shadows. In fact, the reflection of a tree in a pond will come towards you, while its shadow may fall across the grass in the opposite direction away from you if the sun was behind you.

In Fig.283, A is the *angle of incidence*, B is the *angle of reflection* and both are always exactly the same. The height C is always identical to its reflection D.

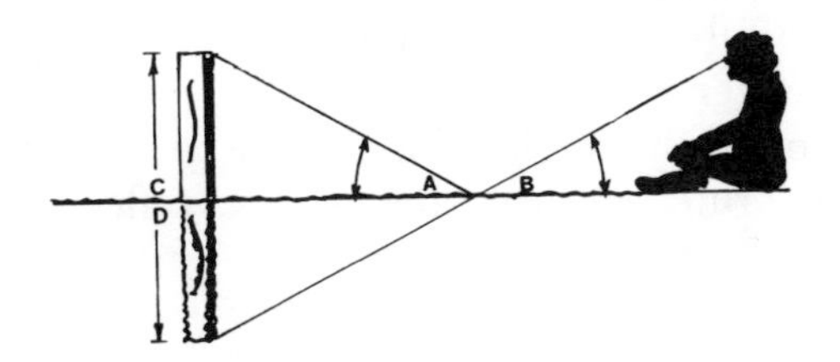

Fig. 283 The angle of incidence and angle of reflection are identical

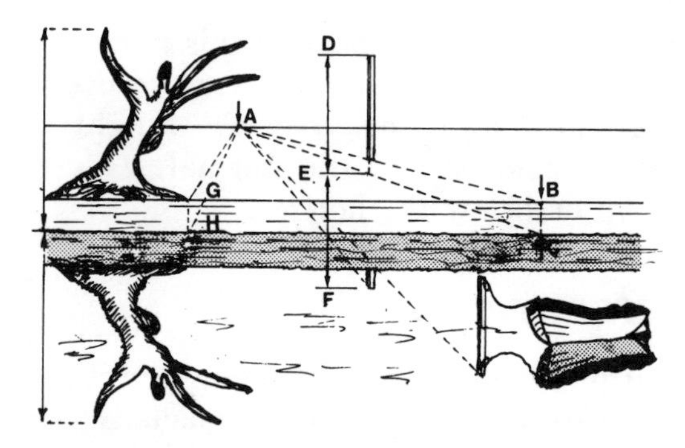

Fig. 284 How to establish the ground line for reflections in parallel perspective

3. When the object reflected is set back from the water's edge, it will be only partially reflected. But the reflection will be in the same direction and at the same angle as the object reflected.
4. Shadows falling across water are always *lighter* than reflections in the water. A wall in shade is always lighter than the shadow of the wall on the ground.

Reflections conform to normal laws of parallel, oblique or aerial perspective, but require a 'ground line' measuring point. It is this ground line that causes some confusion.

Parallel perspective
Project a line from the VP on the horizon at A, to the top of the river bank at B, touching the base of the post. Drop a vertical line from B to the water's edge at C and take this back to the VP at A. Extend the post to touch line C-A at E as in Fig. 284.

This gives us our *ground line* A-C. The height from E to D, is identical to the depth E-F. Only the top of the post is reflected in the water.

Notice the angle of incidence at G. The same rule governs the tree's reflection. Because the tree's base is on the edge of the river bank, the ground line is at H at the water's edge.

Oblique perspective
Project a line from the vanishing point A on the horizon, along the base of the house to G on the river bank. Drop a vertical line to the water's edge at H, and project this back to A. *The line A-H is the ground line*, as shown in Fig.285. Extend the vertical wall of the house down to touch the line A-H. A horizontal line from this point at I, determines the height C, which is identical to the depth D.

In this case, that end of the wall of the house does not reach the reflection in the water. Similarly, the wall at the other end of the house is extended to the ground line at J and projected to the other VP at B. The height E is the same as the depth F.

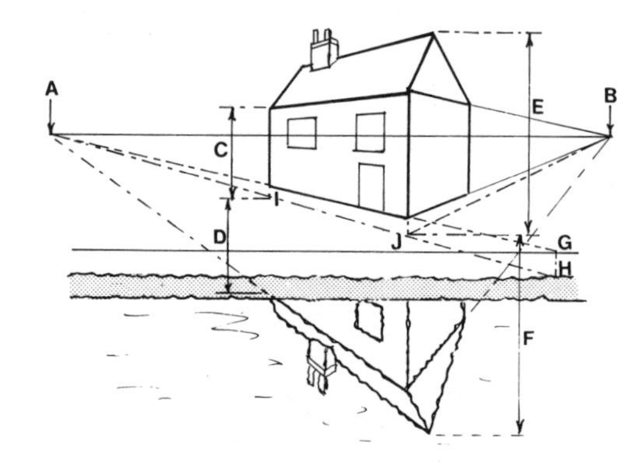

Fig. 285 How to establish the ground line in aerial perspective

The reflection itself is projected to the same VP's as the house, and may appear distorted and not a perfect mirror image. Also remember, the movement in the water may cause some distortion.

32
Creating Original Designs

IF THIS is your first attempt at sketching an original drawing, try a still life. Some of the best subjects to practice on are the everyday objects and inanimate life which are to be found around us.

By beginning with these you will be able to rapidly assess your creative ability and perhaps reveal a hidden talent.

Fig. 286 'Fruit 'N Fibre' (3rd Advanced miniatures) *Alan Townsend*

Still Life

Pots and pans, jars, indoor plants, bowls of fruit and vases of flowers for example. Books on shelves, open cupboards, knick-knacks on window sills or a log basket in the fireplace. Barrels, bottles, flasks or decanters, with all types of drinking vessels make good subjects, also with hung game or musical instruments.

Begin with three or four objects that interest you. Aim at choosing objects which contrast with each other in colour and shape, (curved or straight); size (large or small), and vertical or horizontal, or perhaps something patterned or textured set beside something smooth.

Arrange them on a suitable plain background cloth. Avoid placing the objects an equal distance apart or in a straight line. Stagger them so that they overlap each other and put the tallest at the back, one behind the other to create depth, one set an an angle to another with various shapes arranged into an aesthetically satisfying group.

It is the ability to visualise objects separately from their surroundings that is essential in the creation of attractive still-life subjects.

Sketch or rough out an overall 'block' composition, into which you impose your assessment of the correct tonal values. The basic problems to overcome are volume, proportion, light and shade, including highlights and reflected lights, and the correct perspective of the total composition.

Having got the outline established, the next step is to make a black and white soft charcoal sketch on white cartridge paper, filled in with six to eight gradated tonal changes.

Sketch in the dark tonal masses first, before adding the medium and lighter tones. Tackle the project with bold strokes, getting the masses right.

If you obtain a sheet of *tinted* paper (grey or brown) representing the middle value of the tonal scale, you can use soft charcoal sticks for the black tones and bring the sketch to life by using white and coloured chalks for the highlights and reflected lights.

Study the subtle colour differences in various textures like china and glass; the effects that complementary colours have on each other. Also how to blend the secondary and tertiary colours in harmony.

Experiment with the arrangement and the way the subject is lit. Ideally you need one constant source of light, from one side; but experiment by moving the source of artificial light and see the different effects obtained between the deep shadows, highlights and reflected light.

Compare natural daylight from a window, with artificial light from various positions which you can move and control, including candlelight or oil lamp.

Not all the light will strike directly. Some will pass by to strike other planes and bounce off them, reflecting the light back on to the darker side of the subect, especially with spheres and cylinders.

Front lighting minimises relief and gives a lack of plasticity. Side lighting gives strong shadows for dramatic effects and increases with the degree of contast between light and dark areas.

Back lighting is fascinating and very effective. Notice the way that shadows falling, for instance, across a light pot can be darker than a beam of light reflecting on a black pot. If the group is set against a wall on a tabletop, ensure that this 'artificial horizon' is at eye level, and conforms to the *golden section* rules of ideal proportion and is not in the centre of the picture.

See what happens to the tone of shadows formed by a the projected shapes of other lighted objects and the difference between dark tones and shadows, and the hue of colours and their complementaries in reflected light.

Self-portrait

Another excellent way to learn original drawing is with a self-portrait. Begin by

Fig. 287 'Self-portrait Gabriel Fuchs (Ecole Boulle, Paris)

projecting a transparency, either on to a white card or angled through a mirror rigged up at 45 degrees so that work can proceed comfortably at the worktable. Move the projector to adjust the image to the required size and adjust the focus.

What is required is more than photographic realism. Some extra insight into personality. Use the gridding method, by establishing horizontal and vertical reference points on graph paper.

Start with eyes, and sketch in the triangle formed by the corners of the eyes down to the corners of the mouth. Trace with an HB pencil, the outlines around the highlights and shadows.

Next, using a charcoal stick and soft pencils, sketch in the the shadows and tonal variations. Mark between the shaded areas with a zig-zag line to blur the shading and improve the uniformity of the finished portrait.

Another tip is to project the image on to tinted neutral grey paper, instead of white, and use coloured chalks to enter the highlights and reflected lights, as suggested for still life sketching.

Now use the veneer selection grid to arrange all the fleshy toned veneers you have available, from the darkest to lightest. Your veneer selection will be relative to these two extremes even if the darkest veneer you have is not as dark as either the tone in the picture, or the black in your tonal values scale.

If the projection, sketch and final ink line drawing are made in reverse, the veneer assembly can be held up to a mirror to check as work proceeds.

The actual work of cutting will begin with the eyes, which are the most important features for achieving a likeness. To do this, study the exact number and shape of the highlights and get them in the right places, including tiny white dots, rhomboids or half moons.

Eyes tip up or down according to mood and are usually 'one eye' apart, with the space of an eye between the eye and eyebrow.

Slightly exaggerate any predominant feature such as a large nose or prominent teeth or protruding ears. All the best portraits contain a very slight suggestion of caricature. Next work around the perimeter of the portrait, starting with the hair, forehead, eyebrows, neck and chin.

Arrange the light from a single source, as the shadows falling across the various planes of the face are vitally important.

Discover the 'best side' of the face and turn the head slightly, as a full-faced portrait looks artificially posed.

The choice of background veneer will help to 'make' the picture. If the right-hand side of the head is in deep shadow, the right-hand side of the veneer background should be a tone lighter in order to show up the outline of the head, unless the back of the head is required to be lost in shadow.

The shadows on an indoor portrait are always in 'warm' toned woods and the highlights in 'cool' tones. The reverse is true of shadows on outdoor portraits.

Portraits

A successful portrait should include the characteristic clothing of the person, their attitude and stance, and other personality attributes.

For example, there is an instantly recognisable portrait of Sir Winston Churchill's silhouette, featuring a cigar, a spotted bowtie, Churchillian attitude of neck thrust forward, heavy jowled. These hallmarks formed a 'logo' even before details of facial expression are filled.

It is good practice for the beginner to select someone who is instantly recognisable as a household name, or go to the other extreme and find a completely unknown person with a 'strong' face filled with pronounced features of character and personality. Elderly people usually have more character in their faces.

It is important to get the features correct, including the shape of the head which differs with age and ancestry. Children's heads are much rounder than adults and flatter on top. Note the bone structure of the face, and general outline.

As in the self-portrait, take great care in selecting a 'one-piece' suitable background veneer avoiding any joins. Arrange for soft diffused lighting, and avoid harshness by positioning a white sheet or reflector on the opposite side from the main lighting source, to throw reflected light from the other side to soften the shadows.

A useful tip is to search for prizewinning portraits in black and white photography,

Fig. 288 'Sir Winston Churchill' (Three veneers class H.C.) *H. A. Pedder*

Fig. 289 'February Morn' *Gary Wright, U.S.A.* *(Artistic Merit award and M.S.A. winner)*

where lighting plays a big part. The dramatic effects of candlelight held below an upturned face makes excellent material for a portrait artist.

Perhaps the most difficult subject to portray would be a beautiful young woman's face, because her complexion would be too smooth for fleshy toned woods. If this is attempted, full use should be made of the hair, clothing, jewellery, shadows and highlights.

Light refraction

Because veneers display a changing tone due to light refraction, an amazing likeness in a portrait, for instance, when viewed from one position, can vanish when the viewer moves. The effect is lost; where the picture sparkled, it now appears lifeless and dull.

In an ideal world, the viewing angle and constant source of light in the workroom and the viewing room should be identical if a marquetry picture is to be appreciated as its creator designed it. This is obviously impractical, since all marquetry work is carried out on a horizontal workbench!

Many marquetarians are disappointed when they see their work hung at an exhibition, as the picture fails to have the visual impact it had while work was in progress. For this reason it is a good tip to prop up your picture on a stand in the workroom and make your veneer selection accordingly.

Landscape

When tackling an original landscape subject, do not try for a total panorama, with foreground trees, foliage and elaborate sky effects. Limit what you frame in the viewfinder. Be very selective. Avoid crowding all the interest in the foreground. You will see several changes take place in the appearance of picture elements through the viewfinder.

Check the composition by moving the frame. If there is too much detail on one side the picture may be out of balance.

You will find the viewfinder is invaluable. Remember that rules are made to be broken if you have something important to state.

Balance the compositon from foreground to background. Decide on your focal point of interest, position it in the *golden section* and try to contrive that a road or river or line of posts or trees leads the eye to the focal point.

In a low horizon picture the sky is the most important feature. A leaden grey sky will enable features to stand out starkly. Try to avoid a cloud-filled, bright clear sky which will demand the foreground to be green in the strong sun light, which veneers cannot provide.

You will require a wide suitably figured veneer, with plenty of natural markings or mineral stains to create the right effect of aerial perspective.

Several changes take place in the appearance of objects when seen in perspective at a distance: they appear smaller; their colour contast is lowered; the colours lose their intensity, as they gradually lose their hue; their tonal value is reduced, and they become more indistinct as their textures become blurred.

High horizon scenes are popular in marquetry because it is easier to find a wide range of suitable foreground veneer types, whereas suitable veneers for cloudy skies are much more difficult to find.

Since perspective applies equally to colour, shape, and texture as well as to tone and line, the foreground detail should be kept bold and clearly defined, with small, sharply defined detail, and with large shapes and textures, pronounced ray figures, and strong colours such as reds and browns, and dark tones.

To aid the balance of composition, contrive for a few branches or foliage to enter the top of the frame to aid perspective.

Aerial perspective is achieved with contrasting tones. This is the opportunity to use the tonal values grid and colour wheel to provide brilliant woods for the foreground, with their complementaries in the distance.

In the middle distance use medium shapes and cooler woods, several tones weaker in hue, and in the far distance, make the shapes of the landscape less sharply defined, with only large detail discernable, and of a slightly 'bluish' tinge which will appear to retreat into the distance.

This is caused by the scattering of light. The longer the distance the bluer the tone and the more indistinct. The clouds, too, are not so pronounced.

Water effects

If you use aspen, avodire, red gum, or olive ash for skies, never use them in conjunction with harewood for water.

Whether the water in the picture is a stream, or lake, or the sea, it reflects a mirror image of the the sky. Therefore it should be similar in grain, figure and markings, except for three important differ-

Fig. 290 'Cool Waters' *W. A. Spinks*

ences. (a) The sky should be slightly darker at the top of the picture, getting progressively lighter towards the horizon; (b) the water should be a tone darker than the sky. Or (c) reduce visibility and 'lose' the horizon if you would prefer to use one whole leaf for the background.

If you want to use harewood, which is excellent for depicting water effects, use silver grey for the sky and slate grey or harewood blue for the water.

The weather also modifies the scene. In clear, cool air and good weather the visibility is perfect to the horizon. In hot weather, a heat haze can obscure the horizon. In bad weather, atmospheric perspective produces a grey mist or fog with rapidly diminishing visibility, hues with little colour or tonal contrast.

Try to create an atmosphere in which the distant hills or mountains are very close in hue and tone to the sky at the horizon, where the pale tones should merge into the chosen colour of the sky veneer, but just one tone darker.

A scene through a silhouetted arch or gateway will also help to create the illusion of distance.

Another way of introducing atmosphere is for the immediate foreground to include interesting features such as dry stone walls, tree stumps, five bar gates, rock formations, shrubs, pathways, streams, and shadows falling across cobbled streets,etc.

When choosing veneers to depict paths or roads, select large ray figured woods such as lacewood or elm, and try to increase perspective by using that part of the leaf where the lace figure gradates from large to small, or where the longitudinal rings and grain markings vary from wide to narrow.

If the subject lends itself, try to arrange a few similar objects such as cottages, trees or posts, to be placed at different distances to aid perspective.

Although straight vertical lines of buildings will tend to dominate the frame, never use a ruler to draw a straight line as this will ruin the natural appearance of the picture. Keep the horizon straight and remember,verticals are always vertical.

Autumn skies just after sunset make excellent low horizon pictures. Clouds do not translate easily in veneer form. Those puff-ball cumulus clouds, tend to appear like balloons, even if the joints around them are invisible.

Clouds should be drawn in aerial perspective with their lines converging towards a vanishing point on the horizon. They should be lighter on top than at their base, except at sunset and sunrise, when the light comes from below.

Mottled avodire or fiddleback maple or sycamore veneer are unsuitable, as the regular mottle will destroy the illusion of aerial perspective. A 'freak' veneer, with a streaky or stripey figure or a slightly sappy edge is ideal, such as olive ash, American red gum, or rosa peroba.

The sky at sunset can be very dramatic as many features are thrown into silhouette against a rose-pink or orange-red sky.

Aim to depict familiar landscape with a new insight. Try to analyse what it was that appealed to you most about the scene and focus upon it. Do not copy exactly what you see. Set down the broad skyline, sweep of hills and the shape of trees. Make adjustments in scale of relative parts or tones to suit your aim of three dimensional illusion.

At this stage, do not try to draw a house, boat or tree, but simply draw a 'box' or a series of 'boxes'. When you have the perspective and overall balanced composition correct, begin to fit your house, boat or tree etc., into the pencilled 'boxes' which are then erased. After a little practice, you will be able to dispense with the preliminary 'box guide' to perspective line drawing.

The geometrical flow of a picture

Paul Cezanne's famous formula was to reduce everything to a series of cubes, cylinders and spheres, from which Picasso's cubism was born and later, his 'triangular phase' emerged as in the *Portrait of Ambroise Vollard.*

It was Piero della Francesca (1410–92) who first found that various shaped triangles and rectangles had pleasing or displeasing properties. The composition of classical paintings are often given a 'triangular' shape. Not rigidly drawn, but wide at the base and the eye was conducted upwards into the picture to the focal point of interest. The tradition persists to this day.

The idea is to arrange a natural 'flow' for the eye to follow, leading the viewer gently towards the focal point.

Horizontal lines suggest a calm equilibrium. Be careful when using diagonals which animate and give dynamism but which can upset the balance of the picture, unless counterbalanced.

On the other hand curved lines can create a rhythm and harmony, tying the subject together, and leading the eye into the picture to follow the natural flow of the various components of the picture towards the focal point.

A basic country scene, for instance, as in Fig. 291, can be improved in various ways.

Aerial perspective can be achieved by closing up the field boundaries; the addition of a distant church spire; fences, and a dark stone wall in the foreground, as in Fig.292.

Or a winding road could lead the eye into the picture; receding trees are added, and foliage silhouetted in the foreground all accentuate aerial perspective.

Break up the landscape with patches of bare earth, arable fields of corn, yellows, browns, purples, and the limited range of brown-greens available to you.

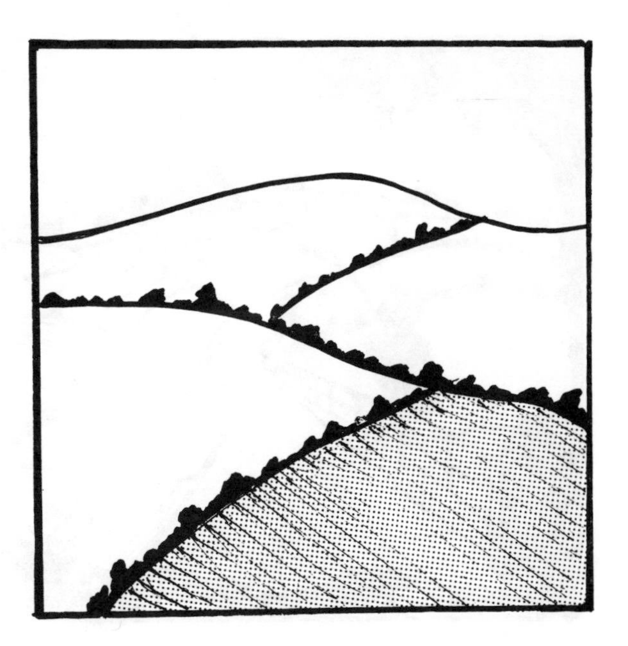

Fig. 291 A very basic country scene can be improved in many ways

Fig. 292 Field boundaries closed up and additional elements added to bring the scene to life

Fig. 293 A winding road, fencing and trees accentuate aerial perspective

Fig. 294 A bridge over a winding river creates an alternative treatment

To animate the picture remember the effect of wind on the landscape, causing trees and crops to bend and water to ripple. All parallel surfaces, lakes, rivers, fields tend to be light.

Disturbed water does not show reflections. Objects against the sky such as trees, buildings, tend to be silhouetted unless in sunlight.

Landscape can also be successful in monochrome, where bulky, massive parts and large scale distance is concerned. Archeological 'digs' with large stones, deep ditches, with dramatic shadows are a good example, and it is best to work from black and white photographs.

By adopting a suitable viewpoint, the lines formed by shadows can give depth and emphasise perspective. Exploit the dramatic quality of shadows. Make sure the source of light sends shadows the way you want them and increases the range of tones available to you.

The light at dawn is thin and hazy, by mid-day the light may be harsh with deep shadows, and in the warm evening glow the reflected light of sunset may provide you with a wide range of suitable hues.

The delicate colours of spring are cool in tone as the sun lacks strength; the warm tones of autumn offer a wide range of reds, gold, orange and tawny browns.

The winter scene calls for greys, dark browns, and purples. Snow scenes offer the stark contrasts of whites and dark greys and browns. Make the sky darker than the ground in a snowscene.

Dawn skies of yellow to gold can utilise violet complementaries. Moonlit night skies, enable the tonal scale to be used for dramatic effects.

Landscapes are improved by the addition of a cluster of old farm buildings. It is important that all sloping roof tops, doorways, windows, converge to the correct vanishing points. And remember about those shadows!

Personalise the picture

Introduce some form of life into the picture. Possibly a bird on the wing or a man walking his dog, or even a cat sunning itself on a window ledge. But avoid 'cutting-in' smoke from chimneys as this does not translate well in veneer. These little touches personalise a picture and bring it to life.

Fig. 295 'The Pantiles'
(Advanced class highly commended)
B. Bedford

Architectural scenes

Some of the most attractive scenes are created from 'olde-world' subjects like the 'Curiosity Shop,' the 'Shambles' of York and the 'Mermaid Inn' of Rye. Tudor houses, urban alleys and back streets, may be equally as appealing as rose covered country cottages, Georgian houses, farmhouses, old millhouses, windmills and churches. Try to frame these subjects by looking at them over a wall, or through railings, archway or gate.

Inclined planes in perspective

There are many instances in these subjects when you meet with inclined surfaces, such as the camber of a road or a road winding over a hill. To draw them accurately you need to introduce more vanishing points.

In Fig.297 the roof of the cottage converges to VP's A ,B and C, the road in the foreground to VP 1, before it plunges downhill to VP2, then climbs steeply to the left to VP 3, and finally recedes to the horizon to VP 4.

When houses are built on an upward sloping hill, the uphill road, pavement, lamp posts, trees and vehicles on the hill outside the house will have their vanishing points above the horizon. If houses are on a road going steeply downhill, the VP's of those objects will converge below the horizon. But the houses, will have their VPs on the horizon, because they are built on level foundations as shown in Fig 298.

Houses around a bend present another problem as every building is set at an angle to its neighbour and requires a different vanishing point as in Fig.296.

In architectural subjects try to avoid converging verticals. In reality, the brain compensates for parallax automatically but not in a drawing, which has to be in aerial perspective.

Very often, in aerial or oblique perspective scenes of buildings, the vanishing points are outside the frame of your picture.The way to overcome this problem is to draw in the nearest vertical of the building at B-C, and also the ground and roof lines to the edge of the frame.Now insert vertical lines D-E and F-G. These may be positioned anywhere to suit your purpose (move them to left or right) to enable them to be divided easily into an equal number of parts. Project the roof line B and ground line C to the lines D-E, and F-G. The main elements of the building can now be drawn in perspective, as in Fig.299.

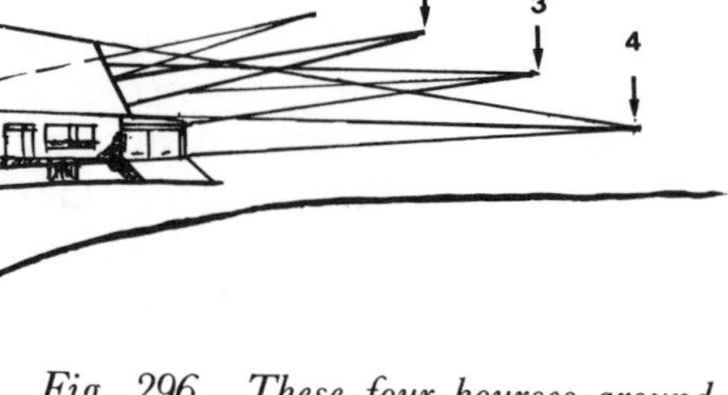

Fig. 296 These four hourses around a bend on a sloping hill have four different VPs

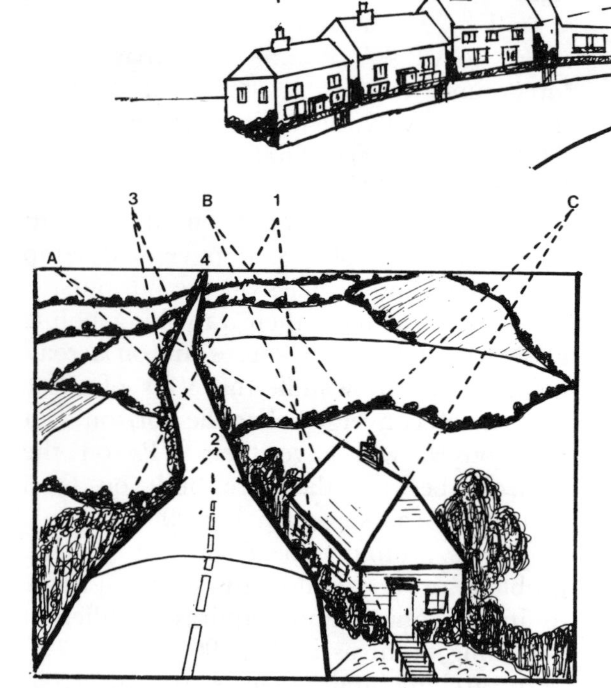

Fig. 297 The cottage roof converges on VP's at A. B and C. The climbing road leads up to VP's, 1, and 3 above the horizon and downhill to VP 2 below the horizon

Fig. 298 The VP of a steep hill may be above the horizon, but the houses remain horizontal as they are built on level foundations

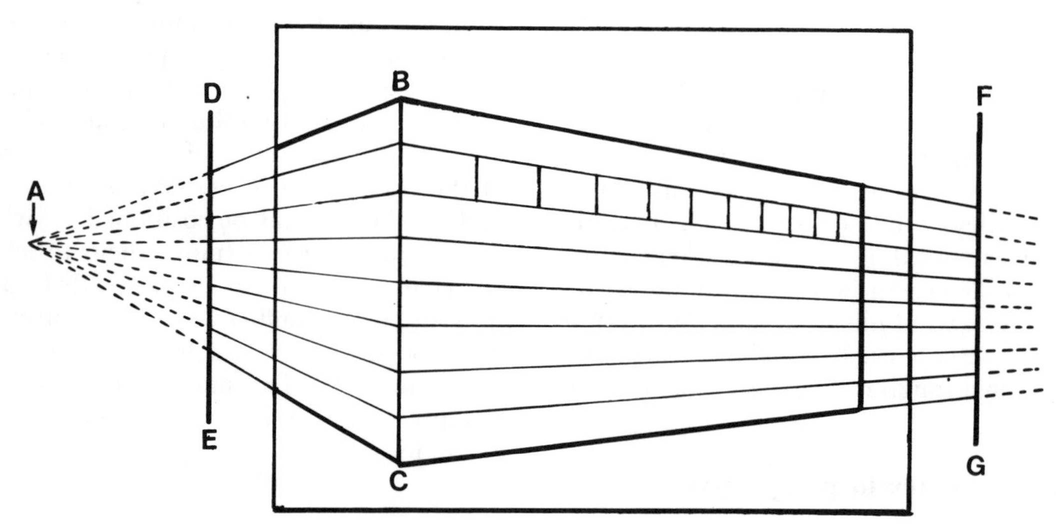

Fig. 299 How to divide a building into equal parts in aerial perspective

Interiors

For centuries, interior scenes have proved to be very popular, especially the *trompe l'oeil* form of illusion, where open cupboard doors reveal their contents (as exemplified by the work of Silas Kopf).

Grand staircases with balustrading, doorways, archways, fireplaces and inglenooks, windows,ledges and panelling make excellent subjects.

Not all interior subjects are in parallel perspective with one vanishing point. When furniture is set at different oblique angles to the 'picture plane' they may have different vanishing points, which will be at eye level, as shown in Fig.301.

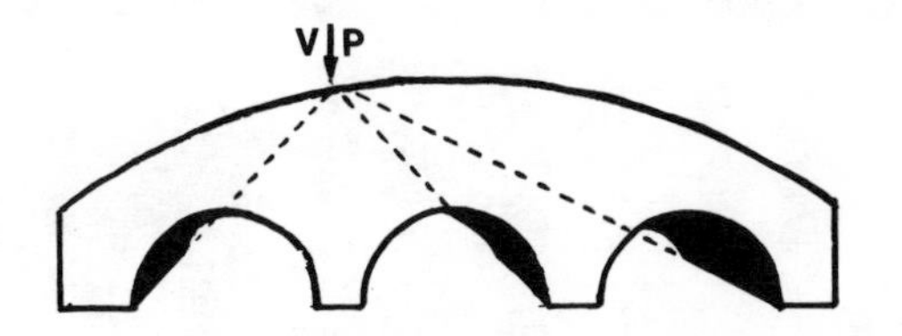

Fig. 300 Notice how the shadows under the arches of bridges change in perspective as they converge on their vanishing points.

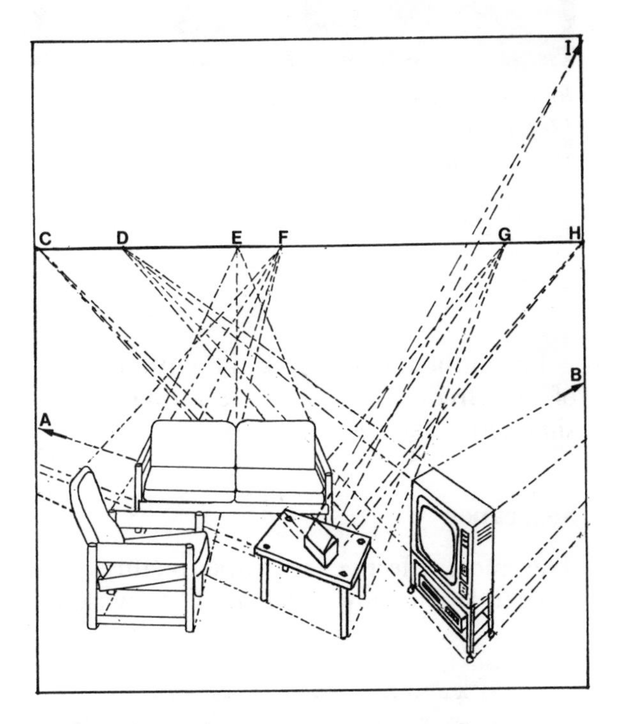

Fig. 301 This interior shows 8 vanishing points within the picture frame. Note: It is more usual for the vanishing points to be outside the frame of the picture in oblique perspective interiors. (See Chapter 30).

Trees

All wooden objects make good marquetry subjects, especially trees. Trees in spring blossom, or hung with summer lanterns; cloaked in their multi-coloured autumn leaves of red and gold; or with their lacework of twigs and branches patterned against the snow in a winter scene. Particular care should be taken with foliage.

Remember every line you draw has to be cut, and intricate leaf patterns and branches are very difficult to produce. The best way is to cut several small pieces of burr veneer, gradated in tone, to form tree foliage – rather than a 'one-piece silhouette' – with the lighter burrs to one side and the top, to suggest light reflection and shadows.

Pieces of the sky should show between the foliage. It is best to depict trees in the middle and far distance when covered in foliage and strive for an accumulative effect by depicting their silhouette outline shapes.

The weeping willow and spreading cedar, or tall poplar, and sculptured yew are all favourite trees for marquetry. The gnarled trunk of the olive tree; the patchy trunk of the planetree; the silver of the birch, or even an old tree stump, make attractive elements for the foreground of a picture when used to frame the subject.

Fig. 302 'Good Companions'
(3rd Premier class)
P. J. Levins

For authenticity, check the outline shape of the trees as they are all different in silhouette.

Seascapes

The most effective seascape pictures are created looking towards land. Otherwise we would be faced with the task of finding a 'freak' veneer to represent the sky down to the horizon, and another to use for the sea effect which is a tone darker. If you want to make a picture looking towards the horizon, try to find a veneer with unusual figure which suggests both sea and sky in one leaf, with the darkest part of the veneer at the bottom of the picture.

This would have the great advantage of providing a blurring of the horizon and at the same time increase the perspective, but the time of day would have to be adjusted.

Some of the most spectacular pictures are those which use red and orange sunset skies reflected in the sea.

Avoid selecting a veneer with a cross-mottle or fiddleback figure because the figure will run at right angles to the grain direction and appear in a vertical direction. This will destroy the illusion of perspective, as the mottle should also be in perspective.

A diagonal cross-mottled or block mottled veneer such as avodire or quilted maple can be positioned so that the diagonal mottle runs towards one of two vanishing points in aerial perspective if outside the picture frame. The same applies to the veneer chosen to represent the sea or water effects. The only time you can justifiably use one wood to achieve this effect is if the horizon is lost in a heat haze or blurred by mist.

The best subjects for seascape pictures are wooden boats afloat or beached, barges, and yachts or fisherman's wharves, harbours, piers. moorings, quays, marinas and lighthouses.

The foreshore is full of interest with cliffs and rock formations, breakwaters, groins, capstans, bollards, pools, lobster pots, nets, seaweed, shells and shingle. Also the texture and pattern of seawalls and clapboarded fishermen's houses and harbour inns.

Use these features to lead the eye into the picture, or include a few silhouetted boats in perspective at varying distances to draw the eye to the focal point of interest.

Fig. 303 'Low Tide'
(Premier HC and Artistic award winner)
A. Reindorp

Contrast some prominent vertical lines with the predominately horizonal lines of the sea and sky.
And always try to include the ever present seagulls!

Nature and Wild Life

There are a wide variety of very attractive subjects to be found in nature and marine life. Exotic fish, sea shells and sponges, fossils from the beach, frogs on a lilly pond, for example.

Perhaps the most popular of all are bird subjects from golden eagles, ospreys and falcons to owls, parrots and the pet budgerigar. Kingfishers and humming-birds, storks and flamingoes are all good subjects, but be very careful of the kingfisher which has bright blue plumage because you will have to use a dyed veneer in a high noon subject. If you change the time of day to sunset in order to use a purpleheart veneer the bird will not be recognised as a kingfisher.

Also along the riversides and hedgerows can be found beavers and otters, stoats, hedgehogs and the field mouse.

There are many excellent books featuring animals. The safari parks and zoos can provide wonderful subjects from pandas to elephants, giraffe or playful lion cubs, cuddly polar bears to tigers, leopards and jaguars, and from the impala or the gentle gazelle to the striped zebra.

Try to capture movement and the form of the creature, for example the alertness and stealth of the leopard. Select a veneer that will create the special effect of imitating the skin, fur or feathers of your chosen subject.

Fig. 304 'Red Squirrel'
(Beginner's class winner)
I. Beer

Fig. 305 'Feline Splendour'
(Premier Class, highly commended)
G. J. Baker

We can learn from the graphic and poster artist, who strives to encapsulate the mood or essence of the subject by reducing it to a striking symbol for maximum dramatic effect. Try to simplify and eliminate all fussy detail.

Domestic pets

Other favourite subjects are domestic pets, including cats, dogs, birds, hamsters and tropical fish.

Sporting subjects

A favourite source for subjects is the field of sport. Show jumping, horse and greyhound

Fig. 306 'The Cat at Bay'
(Advanced class winner)
P. J. Levins

racing, foxhunting, sheep dog trials, skiing and tobogganing, aquasport, and mountaineering.

Floral subjects

All kinds of plant life make attractive subjects but perhaps the most popular of all are floral arrangements.

Select blooms of different sizes, and create an arrangement at different levels; include foliage, buds and seedheads. Choose flowers of definite form such as roses, and not species which will require extremely difficult cutting technique, such as chrysanthemums.

Try to show the life cycle of the flower, with its stem, a tight bud, a full bloom and a mature flower beginning to shed its petals. The choice of container, pot or vase can heighten interest, with reflected light and shadows.

Figure studies

Human figures have always been the main subjects of all forms of art. Religious figures, family groups, portraits, figures in landscape and interiors.

To succeed in this field a thorough understanding of human anatomy is essential. The clothed figure cannot be drawn properly until the anatomy and muscle structure of the nude figure is fully understood.

This experience is only gained by practice at an art class or with a sitter. Classical nude studies, such as *David*, make excellent marquetry subjects when sand-shaded.

It is unnecessary to get involved with the minute cutting of human figures for the inclusion of human interest in a landscape or seascape, where only a basic outline in proportion is required. However, the attitude of the figure should generally suggest movement.

Leonardo da Vinci's *Study of Human Proportions* describes the navel as the centre of the body; from this centre a circle touches the outstretched fingers and toes of a man lying on his back. The distance between the finger tips is the same as that from the crown of his head to the soles of his feet. He claimed that a human body was 'eight

Fig. 307 'Spring Bouquet'
(Advanced class winner)
Doris Beecher

heads tall'. Richter however, made his human figures seven and a half heads tall.

Today, it is generally accepted that the human body divides into eight sections, but the body is between six and a half to seven heads tall. The distance from the crown of the head to the chin is one eighth of the whole body, and the navel about five eighths. A hand should be slightly less than the size of a face.

Generally, a female torso is like a triangle, with narrow shoulders and wide hips, and a male torso is similar to an inverted triangle with broad shoulders and narrow hips.

Costume and drapery

Marquetry can reproduce excellent drapery, and some delightful effects can be obtained by exploiting the range of attractive grains, freak figures, peculiar markings and patterned textures of veneers.

The best results are not obtained by clever cutting techniques, but by the selection of unusual figures which can provide the desired effect.

For example, fiddleback, bees-wing, mottled, and moiré figured woods and the swirl figure found on curls, and around knots and butts are suitable. Burr figure, bird's eye, and lace figure are also suitable, as well as vascular ray markings found on quartered woods.

Notice the way in which the folds forming in light materials like silks and satins, are angular in appearance, while the folds are oval in shape in heavier materials such as brocades or heavy tweeds.

Fig. 308 'Time to Chat' (after Sutcliffe) Eddie Stevens

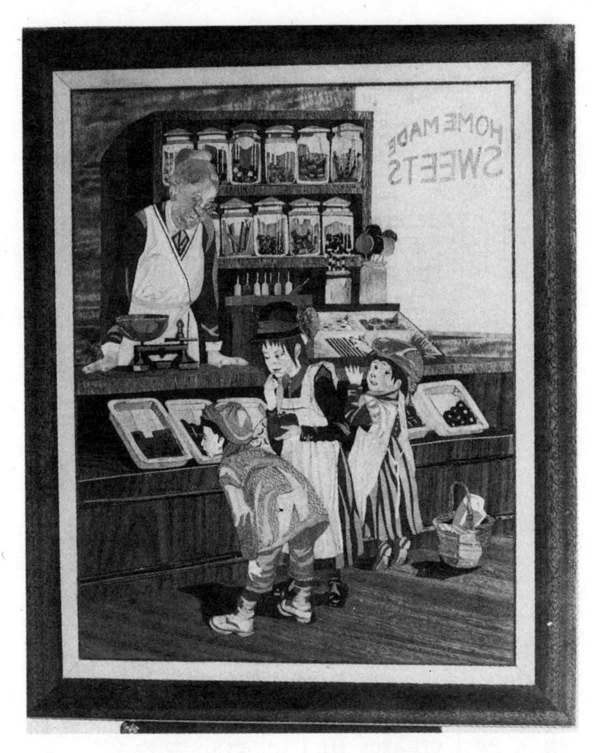

Fig. 309 'Sweetshop' (After Embleton) Eddie Stevens

Fig. 310 'Stop! Thief!'
(3rd Intermediate class)
Joan Meadows

Fig. 311 'GWR Auto-tank'
(3rd Secondary class)
D. J. Hazelden

Fig. 312 'The Waterhole'
Roy Lambert

Fig. 313 'Brass Rubbing'
(Secondary class H.C)
K. C. Mortimer

Also try to capture the way in which clothes are worn; the way a coat hangs, the folds of a skirt, a crumpled sleeve or worn shoe and creases in trousers.

If the subject is a period piece, it is vital that you have researched the authenticity of the clothes worn in that period or the veneer selection and cutting will be in vain.

Success lies in close attention to detailed authenticity on one hand, but applying it selectively in the picture.

A table cloth or curtain makes an ideal background for a still life subject. To practice sketching, dip a handkerchief or table napkin into a mixture of plaster, let it fall into natural folds when wet and allow it to set.

Caricature

The essence of caricature is to tease without malice. Distort and emphasise by exaggeration, any prominent facial feature and stance. Make fun of the hairline, brow, chin, Adam's apple, and prominent teeth.

Children's nursery subjects

There are scores of suitable subjects suitable for children's rooms, from the range of Disney characters, Coco the clown, Rupert Bear, through the whole gamut of nursery rhyme characters to the latest extra-terrestial space monsters!

Leaded glass abstracts

Thin black lines are used around each segment of the design to produce a stained glass window effect.

Modern abstract art

This art form has various guises. The subject is concerned with design, rhythm and

Fig. 314 The Jubilee Mural which celebrates the Silver Jubilee of H.M. The Queen. Created under the direction of Charles Good by Members of the former London Group of The Marquetry Society.

balance, and the juxtaposition of different shapes,colours, and textures.

One popular form for marquetry creates the illusion of gently curving lines from an arrangement of straight lines cut in geometric angles, to form pleasing geometric patterns as in 'Op-Art' (see Chapter 21)

Murals

The creation of a large wall mural is tempting for the marquetarian. But it has many attendant problems. I once produced a marquetry mural at Olympia in London, which measured 40 feet by 5ft, called 'Language of the Stars'.

The first problem is, how is the panel going to be pressed? Next comes the problem of avoiding a vertical join in the sky or foreground veneer, if the length of veneer required is too long. Another problem is encountered with low horizon subjects where the width of the sky veneer may have to be exceptional.

Putting a vertical or diagonal join in the sky or sea will destroy the illusion unless a vertical building or pole or other element is contrived to break the picture at that point.

For a first attempt at a mural panel, avoid panoramic scenes which require large sky or foreground effects, and try a montage.

Montage

The first thing to decide is a theme to link all the many components together. For example 'Merrie England' or 'The age of Steam" or 'London's famous landmarks', 'The Armada', etc.

The various picture elements are then superimposed or juxtapositioned, and arranged into a composition.

Miniatures

The miniature represents the biggest single challenge to the marquetarian's skill as a craftsman. It has led to a vogue for ever smaller miniatures being made for exhibition purposes. Miniatures of postcard size were ousted by others of playing card size and these in their turn by others of matchbox size. And the number of pieces cut into these miniatures increases year by year.

It is only a matter of time before some enthusiast will create a picture of postage stamp size!

Fig. 315 'The Quiet Backwater'
(Advanced Miniature winner) Richard Shellard

Fig. 316 'Dibden Farm'
(Advanced Miniature winner) Cliff Daniells

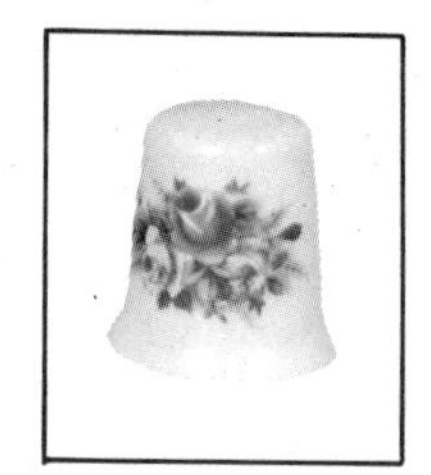

For size comparison only

Fig. 318 'Old Time Travel'
(Advanced Miniature winner)
Ron Gibbons

Fig. 317 'Castle Combe'
(Advanced Miniature winner)
Richard Shellard

Although miniatures demonstrate brilliant virtuosity of technique, they have little to do with the beauty of natural wood. Any picture in which the veneers are mutilated into splinters or powdered into micro-dust completely defeats the aesthetic aspirations of marquetry. Every fragment in a picture is a step away from art towards craft. Technique has taken marquetry too far down the wrong road. Time to cry halt! Time to begin again with a new conception of marquetry.

Marquetry has had to test and probe the frontiers of its own world to discover its boundaries. I salute the pioneers at the forefront of research and technical experiment and many of their brilliant works are featured in this book as a tribute to their consummate craftsmanship. But now the time has come for marquetry to raise its head to search for new horizons. To welcome a new generation of marquetarians with a thorough art training, who will accept the challenge and the opportunities offered by working with this medium. It is to these 'artists in wood' to whom this book is dedicated.

Marquetry Society Exhibition Classes

(For members only)

Class 1.	Beginners.	One or more of the member's first four pictures.
Class 2.	Secondary.	A picture by a member who has not won an award in any class but is not eligible for Class 1.
Class 3.	Intermediate.	Pictures by a member who has won an award in any class except classes 3, 4 or 5.
Class 4.	Advanced.	Pictures by a member who has won an award in Class 3, but not in 4 or 5.
Class 5.	Premier.	Pictures by a member who has won an award in Class 4, or who have previously won the Rosebowl.
Class 6A. (Advanced).	Miniatures	Pictures having an overall dimension not exceeding 12 square inches (77.41 sq cms) including the frame.
Class 6B. (Beginners).	Miniatures	Open only to members who are eligible to enter Classes 1, 2 and 3 and not having previously won an award in the Miniature class.
Class 7A. (Advanced).	Applied	Any work of decorative veneering or parquetry applied to a suitable article, e.g., table, cabinet, tray, box, clock, gameboard etc.
Class 7B. (Beginners).	Applied	Open to members eligible for Classes 1, 2 or 3 and not having previously won an award in the Applied class.
Class 8.	Three veneers.	A picture from any member, cut from three leaves or part leaves, including the borders and edges.
Class 9.	Exhibition only.	A picture or article not entered for competition.

Awards

The Rosebowl.	For the entry adjudged best in the competition.
Artistic Merit award.	The entry showing the greatest artistic merit.
Walter Dolley Salver.	The best entry from a non-group member.
Jack Byrne cup.	For the best geometric marquetry or parquetry.
Richard Shellard Challenge Cup.	For the best Advanced miniature.
Petty & Byron Challenge Cup.	For the best beginner's miniature.
Marquetry for the Millions Award.	For the entry most admired by an independent non-marquetarian member of the public.

Further Reading

Artist's Guide to Composition Ralph Fabri (Watson-Guptil, New York)
Artist's Sketchbook (series) (Wm Collins)
Bloomsbury Art Class (series) Ed. K. Howard (Bloomsbury)
Conversion & Seasoning of Wood W. H. Brown (Stobart)
The Complete Manual of Wood Veneering W. A. Lincoln (Stobart & Macmillan)
Draw (series of 14 titles) (A. & C. Black)
Drawing Workbooks (series) (Macdonald)
Handbook of Art Techniques Roy Sparkes (Batsford)
How to draw (series) José Parramon (Fountain Press)
Landscape Drawing John O'Connor (Batsford)
Painting the Portrait John Devane (Phaidon)
Techniques of Drawing Howard Simon (Oak Tree Press)
What Wood Is That? Herbert J. Edlin (Stobart)
Working Green Wood with PEG Patrick Spielman (Sterling)
World Woods in Colour W. A. Lincoln (Stobart & Macmillan)

Suppliers Guide

(U.K.)

R. Aaronson (Veneers) Ltd
45, Redchurch St.
London E2.

Abbey Marquetry,
Unit 14,
Fiddlebridge Industrial Est. Lemsford
Rd. Hatfield AL10 0DE.

Art Veneers Co Ltd
Industrial Estate, Mildenhall
W. Suffolk IP28 7AY

John Boddy Timber Ltd
Riverside Sawmills
Boroughbridge
N. Yorks YO5 9LJ

J. Crispin & Sons
92–96 Curtain Road, London EC2

C. B. Veneers Ltd
River Pinn Works
Yiewsley High St, West Drayton
Middlesex UB7 7TA

Elliott Bros
26 Meadowgrove Rd.
Sheffield S17 4FF

Canada and U.S.A.

Albert Constantine & Son Inc
2050 Eastchester Road, N.Y. 10461

Craftsman Wood Service Co Inc
1735 West Courtland C.T.
Addison, Illinois 60101

Henegan's Woodshed
7760 Southern Boulevard
West Palm Beach, Florida 33411

Unicorn Universal Woods Ltd
4190 Steeles Ave W.
Unit 4,
Woodbridge, Ontario

The Woodworker's Store
21801 Industrial Boulevard
Rogers, Minnesota 55374

Woodcraft Supply Corp
313 Montvale Avenue, Woburn
Massachusetts 01801

Wood Shed
1807 Elmwood Avenue, Buffalo,
NY 14207

Organisations

The Marquetry Society
The Hon. General Secretary
Mrs Pat Austin
The Barn House, Llanon,
Nr. Aberystwyth, Dyfed SY23 5LZ
(27 groups in the U.K.)

The Marquetry Society of Australia
Lionel Pavey, 17 Barton Street,
Kyneton, Victoria 3444, Australia

Marquetry Society of America
P. O. Box 224, Lindenhurst
NY 11757, U.S.A.

Marquetry Society of Ontario
J. R. Colter
36 McIntyre Crescent,
Georgetown, Ontario, Canada L7G
1N3

International Wood Collector's Society,
Bruce T. Forness
PO Box 1102, Chautauqua
NY 14722–1102

Index